Feb 04
To Jeannie Doremus
from Linda Lynch
970.923.2045

Praise for *Smoke and Mirrors*!

"*Smoke and Mirrors* is a passionate exposé of the living nightmare caused by false allegations of sexual abuse. When interviewers, or therapists, use misguided techniques in the name of finding out the 'truth,' the outcome can be disastrous. It can happen anywhere, to anyone, at anytime. Campbell's insights will, I hope, make a big difference."

—**Elizabeth Loftus, Ph.D.,** Professor of Psychology, University of Washington, Seattle, Washington; President, American Psychological Society; Co-author, *The Myth of Repressed Memory*

"*Smoke and Mirrors* is a must read! At last, here is a book that exposes the faulty beliefs and assumptions about child abuse. How can false allegations of sexual abuse seem so credible? Can we trust childhood memories? Does trauma cause memory loss? The author explores these questions, and points to fundamental changes necessary for psychotherapy."

—**Ralph Slovenko, J.D., Ph.D.,** Professor of Law and Psychiatry, Wayne State University School of Law, Detroit, Michigan

"Through compelling and disturbing case studies, Campbell introduces the reader to the Alice-in-Wonderland world of false accusations of sexual abuse. . . . An indispensable guide for those involved in or merely appalled at a modern witch hunt."

—**Mark Pendergrast,** Author, *Victims of Memory*

"*Smoke and Mirrors* uses the tragedy of sexual abuse and allegations of abuse to show that what is sold as healing destroys families and rends the social fabric of our nation. Nobody can read this book without becoming infuriated at the hoax being imposed on us all."

—**Hollida Wakefield,** Editor, *Issues in Child Abuse Accusations*

"Provocative and interesting. Inevitably controversial, the book addresses two of the hottest current topics in psychology, therapy, criminal, and personal injury law—determination of the truth or falsity of child sexual abuse allegations and 'repressed-memory' claims. Campbell offers always thoughtful, research-based (but disputed) insights about both topics. The book concludes with an intriguing critique of and recommendations for improvements in the practice of clinical therapy."

—**Robert J. Levy, J.D.,** William L. Prosser Professor of Law, University of Minnesota Law School, Minneapolis, Minnesota

"A comprehensive and fully informed review of the pitfalls attending allegations of sexual abuse based on rumor, leading questions, and recovered memory. Judges, prosecutors, attorneys, and police would be especially well advised to keep this book handy and to follow its eminently sane advice."

—**Frederick Crews,** Author, *The Memory Wars*; Editor, *Unauthorized Freud*

"[This book] provides an important overview of the tragic consequences of false accusations at both the child and adult level. The author's firsthand clinical and forensic experiences bring the stories he tells to life and leave no ambiguity as to the message."

—**Pamela Freyd, Ph.D.,** Executive Director, FMS (False Memory Syndrome) Foundation, Philadelphia, Pennsylvania

"Campbell blends his extensive clinical and forensic psychological experiences with research to document how some well-trained therapists egregiously harm the people they are paid to help. Readers will experience the devastation of those falsely accused of sexual abuse and the gross injustices created by therapists who replace science with their biases and prejudices to treat patients."

—**Allen Feld, LCSW,** Retired Associate Professor, Social Work, Marywood University, Scranton, Pennsylvania; Continuing Education Director, FMS Foundation

SMOKE AND MIRRORS

The Devastating Effect of False Sexual Abuse Claims

SMOKE AND MIRRORS

The Devastating Effect of False Sexual Abuse Claims

TERENCE W. CAMPBELL, Ph.D.

✸ INSIGHT BOOKS

PLENUM PRESS • NEW YORK AND LONDON

Library of Congress Cataloging-in-Publication Data

Campbell, Terence W.
    Smoke and mirrors : the devastating effect of false sexual abuse
claims / Terence W. Campbell.
        p.   cm.
    Includes bibliographical references and index.
    ISBN 0-306-45984-1
    1. False memory syndrome. 2. Child sexual abuse--Investigation.
3. False testimony.   I. Title.
RC455.2.F35C35   1998
616.85'836--dc21   98-12417
                                                                    CIP

ISBN 0-306-45984-1

©1998 Terence W. Campbell
Insight Books is a Division of Plenum Publishing Corporation
233 Spring Street, New York, N.Y. 10013

http://www.plenum.com

An Insight Book

10 9 8 7 6 5 4 3 2 1

Printed in the United States of America

For Sharon Kay

A gentle critic, persistently encouraging, and always a source of inspiration and determination.

Contents

12. PARENTS SUING RECOVERED MEMORY THERAPY   239

13. MYOPIC GUILDS AND FLAWED EVIDENCE:
    PROFESSIONAL ORGANIZATIONS DEFENDING THEIR REPUTATIONS   259

14. CHANGING PSYCHOTHERAPY   281

    NOTES   301

    INDEX   333

Preface

False allegations of sexual abuse are dramatically compelling stories attracting persistent media attention. The familiarity of otherwise unknown hamlets—such as Edenton, North Carolina, and Wenatchee, Washington—demonstrates the level of awareness created by these cases. TV documentaries aired by *Dateline, 20/20, Prime Time Live,* and *48 Hours* have detailed the heart-wrenching tragedies of false allegations. *Time, Newsweek, The Wall Street Journal,* and countless local newspapers periodically cover the outrageous injustices endured by the falsely accused.

Smoke and Mirrors is written for readers who want to know more about false allegations of sexual abuse. This book is an in-depth examination of how false allegations originate, gather momentum, and too often culminate by ripping apart the lives of innocent people. More often than not, false allegations develop from a convoluted combination of half-truths, misinformation, conjecture, and wild speculation. The typical case amounts to a dense fog of innuendo obscuring a rolling sea of rumor. You can hardly see it, and what little you can discern is forever shifting and changing, blown by unpredictable winds. Allowing this kind of evidence into courts of law inevitably results in horrible miscarriages of justice.

This book is divided into two parts. Part I (Chapters 1–7) examines false allegations of child sexual abuse. The typical scenario in these cases originates with the vague, ill-defined statements of a young child. Well-intended but horribly misinformed adults misinterpret these ambiguous statements, and conclude that the child has been sexually abused.

In response to adult misinterpretations of what young children say, the children undergo numerous interviews. The sheer number of these interviews—and the biased expectations of the interviewers—leads children into describing events that never occurred. In particular, children can report the most heinous sounding versions of sexual abuse; but without realizing it, they have contaminated what they think they remember with what they imagine. These children then find themselves in therapy, and tragically enough, their therapists manage to further contaminate what they think they remember. The combined effects of these outcomes can result in innocent people facing criminal charges, and/or loving parents losing their children.

Part II, Chapters 8–14, examines what is known as "recovered memory therapy." These kinds of cases originate when an adult ventures into therapy seeking assistance with problems such as anxiety or depression. Too many therapists, however, persuade these adults that their problems originated when they were sexually abused as children. In response to the typical client reaction of wide-eyed disbelief, their therapists convince them that they repressed their memories of the horrific abuse they supposedly endured as young children. More often than not, therapists identify the abuser(s) as members of the clients' own families. The preferred targets of these allegations are the clients' fathers.

In response to the therapists' influence, clients begin imagining abuse scenarios. Though resorting to their imaginations, the clients think they are recalling previously repressed memories. Unfortunately, ill-informed therapists enthusiastically applaud the imaginary memories of their clients. Seeking more approval from their therapist, clients proceed to recall abuse memories with increasing frequency.

Convinced that all of their problems originated with the sexual abuse they presumably endured as children, the clients then develop symptoms consistent with the expectations of their therapists. These can be very debilitating symptoms because—and only because—the therapists expect that repressed memories of supposed childhood sexual abuse lead to especially serious psychological problems.

False memories of childhood sexual abuse acquired in therapy often rip families apart. Falsely accused parents may face criminal charges and/or civil suits. Ill-informed therapists also find themselves sued with increasing frequency. The practices of ill-informed "recovered memory" therapists ultimately threaten to discredit all psychotherapy.

The case examples reviewed in Chapter 1 are "high-profile" cases covered by the mass media. As a result of my past position as a consulting psychologist with the Macomb County (Michigan) Circuit Court, I had firsthand contact with "Jennifer's" case discussed in Chapter 2. All of the names in this case have been changed to preserve the anonymity of those involved. I encountered "Jane's" case, detailed in Chapter 4, as a result of the defense attorney seeking my assistance. All of the names in this case have also been changed. In the case of *Kentucky v. Noble*, also reviewed in Chapter 4, I assisted the public defender—Carolyn Clark—representing Mr. Noble. Except for Mr. Noble and Ms. Clark, all of the names in this case have been changed.

In the case of *Ohio v. Johnson*, considered in Chapter 5, I assisted the public defender—Rolf Baumgartel—appointed to represent Mr. Johnson. Except for Mr. Johnson, Mr. Baumgartel, Judge Lane, and the prosecutor, all of the names in this case have been changed. In the case of *Ohio v. Carlson*, discussed in Chapter 6, the names of all involved have been changed. In the Bielaska–Orley case, also reviewed in Chapter 6, only the names of the two minor children involved have been changed. For the case of "Rachel," detailed in Chapter 7, the names of all who were involved have been changed.

For the case of "Jim Bauer," reviewed in Chapter 10, I changed the names of all parties involved, as I did for that of "Sandra Green" discussed in Chapter 11 and the "Thomas" case detailed in Chapter 12.

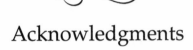

Acknowledgments

The encouragement, feedback, and helpful suggestions of Edwin Arnfield and Constance Arnfield-O'Connell in reading preliminary versions of this manuscript are gratefully acknowledged. Special gratitude is reserved for my father—Dr. J. Frank Campbell, professor emeritus of educational and clinical psychology at Wayne State University—who read and reread numerous versions of this manuscript. His comments and suggestions were particularly helpful. The support of my editor, Frank K. Darmstadt, and his confidence in the importance of this book is also deeply appreciated.

My affiliation with the Professional and Scientific Advisory Board of the False Memory Syndrome Foundation has also been invaluable in writing this book. Pamela Freyd, executive director of the FMS Foundation, regularly sends me reprints of articles and other documents related to false allegations of sexual abuse. A great deal of this information would otherwise have been unavailable to me. Serving on the FMS Advisory Board has afforded me the opportunity to share ideas with such distinguished colleagues as Rob Dawes, Elizabeth Loftus, August Piper, Ralph Slovenko, and Holly Wakefield.

Permission of the following journals to reprint portions of my previously published articles in this book is also gratefully acknowledged.

American Journal of Forensic Psychology

False allegations of sexual abuse and their apparent credibility, 1992, 10 (4), 21–35.

Allegations of sexual abuse II: Case of a criminal defense, 1992, 10 (4), 37–48.

Indicators of child sexual abuse and their unreliability, 1997, 15 (1), 5–18.

American Journal of Forensic Psychiatry

Repressed memories and statutes of limitations: Examining the data and weighing the consequences, 1995, 16 (2), 25–51.

Issues in Child Abuse Accusations

Promoting play therapy: Marketing dream or empirical nightmare? 1992, 4, 111–117.

False allegations of sexual abuse and the persuasiveness of play therapy, 1992, 4, 118–124.

The reliability and validity of Gardner's indicators of pedophilia, 1993, 5, 170–182.

Reliable classification vs. idiosyncratic opinion: A reply to Gardner, 1993, 5, 192–199.

Creating repressed memories: A case example, 1995, 7, 164–174.

Good news and bad news: The burden is ours, 1995, 7, 209–214.

Journal of Systemic Therapies

Systemic therapies and basic research, 1996, 15 (3), 15–39.

Psychotherapy

Therapeutic relationships and iatrogenic outcomes: The blame-and-change maneuver in psychotherapy, 1992, 29, 474–480.

Psychotherapy with children of divorce: The pitfalls of triangulated relationships, 1992, 29, 646–652.

I

False Allegations of Child Sexual Abuse

1

An Overview of False Allegations

Anyone and Anywhere

A worried, anxious mother files a report with a child protection agency complaining that her 5-year-old daughter has been sexually abused. The agency undertakes a preliminary investigation of the mother's complaints and concludes the alleged abuse likely occurred. The child is then referred to a mental health professional for further evaluation of her psychological status.

The child convincingly states that she was abused and identifies the alleged perpetrator. She claims that "a bad man touched me down there." As a result, the protection agency and the mental health professional forward their evidence to law enforcement officials. Police arrest the suspect, and TV news coverage shows a handcuffed man looking bewildered while led into court for a preliminary arraignment.

Simultaneously, the child begins treatment addressing the traumas she apparently suffered. The therapist reports preliminary progress despite the many problems supposedly burdening the child. The police investigation, however, discovers evidence that appears to exonerate the alleged perpetrator. The accused appears not to have been alone with the child when the apparent abuse occurred. Inconsistencies also begin to undermine the veracity of the mother's allegations. Her recall of what she asked her daughter, and how the child replied, significantly shifts and changes over time. The police department then abandons its investigation when the accused passes a polygraph examination.

ALLEGATIONS OF CHILD SEXUAL ABUSE AS HOAXES

Scenarios such as the previous one—too often resulting in even greater damage to an accused but innocent person—are occurring with distressing regularity. For example, the longest and most expensive criminal trial in U.S. history ensued as a result of false allegations of child sexual abuse.

In 1983, seven defendants working at the McMartin Preschool facility in Manhattan Beach, California, were charged with sexually abusing children in their care. The legal proceedings that evolved took over 6 years, and cost the state of California more than $15 million.[1] Five of the defendants were found not guilty. After a jury could not reach a unanimous decision in the trials of the remaining two, the prosecutor himself characterized the charges as "patently absurd,"[2] and declined to seek another trial.[3]

Above and beyond the blatant waste of public funds and resources, the human tragedy of this case—and so many others like it—is chilling. The director of the McMartin facility, Peggy Ann Buckey, spent almost 24 months in jail. Ms. Buckey's daughter was confined in excess of 2 years before her acquittal. Ms. Buckey's son endured more than 5 years behind bars until allowed to post a property bond of $3 million.[4] Thus, three innocent people spent a combined total of more than 9 years in jail for alleged offenses never proven in a court of law. Though the Buckeys eventually regained their freedom, this ordeal tore their lives asunder, stripping them of practically everything they had worked so hard to accomplish.

Parents as Targets of False Allegations

Cruel and unjust as the McMartin hoax was, perhaps even more shocking is the specter of parents falsely accused of sexually abusing their own children. In the small town of Jordan, Minnesota, in 1984, James Rud—who eked out a meager living as a trash collector and occasional baby-sitter—was arrested for sexually abusing two children.[5] Responding to the prosecution's offer of a reduced sentence for his cooperation, Rud claimed to have participated in a "child-sex ring" involving other Jordan parents. He further demonstrated his eagerness to assist the prosecutor by identifying numerous parents who had allegedly betrayed their children in this hideous manner.

Rather than thoroughly investigate Rud's story, the police reacted by arresting 24 parents, and placing their children in the custody of the local child welfare agency. In addition to undergoing intrusive physical examinations, these children also endured grilling questions related to Rud's allegations. Investigators suggested that if they told the "truth" about their supposedly abusive parents, their families might be reunited. Stunned and overwhelmed by the abrupt separation from their parents, many of the children promptly began reporting what the investigators expected to hear.

Except for statements coerced from the children, the subsequent investigation failed to uncover any other evidence. Physical examinations of the children were totally inconsistent with their reported disclosures. None of them exhibited any evidence of physical abuse, and genital examinations all yielded normal findings. In the process of vouching for the good reputations of those who had been arrested, other Jordan citizens protested the prosecutor's arbitrary tactics. The prosecutor responded to these challenges by obtaining arrest warrants against some of the protestors, and placing their children in custody.[6]

Desperately determined to save face and obtain at least a few convictions, the prosecutor offered plea bargains to some of the accused parents. One of them, a police officer, was offered a new identity, relocation to another locale, no prison time, and money if he would testify against the other parents. Tempting as this offer may have been, the officer steadfastly refused it, instead demanding his day in court.

In September 1984, a jury returned a not guilty verdict in the first trial of two of the parents. Then, during a radio interview in November, Rud admitted that he had lied. He had fabricated the "sex ring" story in an attempt to avoid a long prison sentence. Many of the children also began recanting the statements overzealous investigators previously extorted from them. The prosecutor, however, stubbornly refused to recognize the significance of these developments. She continued to contend that the parents were guilty, while also insisting they would never get their children back.

As a result of investigations undertaken by the FBI and the Attorney General of Minnesota, the prosecutor—Kathleen Morris—was censured for prosecutorial misconduct. Soon after, intensive media coverage publicly exposed this case as a colossal hoax. James Rud was the only person involved in the Jordan fiasco convicted of child sexual abuse. The accused parents and their children were reunited, and in what amounted to at least a small concession to justice, voters threw Ms. Morris out of office.

Professionals as Sources of False Allegations

Not only can unscrupulous prosecutors promote false allegations of child sexual abuse, ill-informed health care professionals can also do the same. In the small English town of Cleveland, during the summer of 1986, two British physicians began finding physical evidence of what seemed an epidemic of child sexual abuse. Physical evidence of sexual abuse understandably appears more reliable, and thus more compelling, than the tentative statements of a child. These latter expressions often seem so ambiguous that they confuse more than clarify. Nevertheless, this assumption amounts to another example of how deceptive appearances can be.

Drs. Higgs and Wyatt, who practiced in Cleveland, attended a seminar presented by Drs. Hobbs and Wynne. Hobbs and Wynne had published an article in the British medical journal, *Lancet,* outlining their impressions regarding the physical characteristics of sexually abused children.[7] They reported that "dilatation and/or reflex dilatation of the anal canal" was not found in normal children. As a result, they concluded that these physical characteristics were indicative of sodomy. Hobbs and Wynne cited "clinical experience" to support their position regarding what they also called "anal twitchiness."

While relying on their "experience," Hobbs and Wynne neglected to test what was merely a theory. They failed to compare the physical characteristics of sexually abused children with those of nonabused children, to determine whether their theory was accurate. Rather than obtain evidence that would confirm or disconfirm their theory-driven thinking, they inappropriately relied on impressions gathered from their clinical practice. Their grossly mistaken judgment in this regard resulted in a tragic fiasco.

In the countryside town of Cleveland, Drs. Higgs and Wyatt enthusiastically embraced the unsubstantiated impressions of Hobbs and Wynne.[8] In one of her first cases of suspected child sexual abuse, Dr. Higgs discovered what she considered evidence of anal twitchiness. This finding led her to conclude that the child had suffered anal abuse, and within a very short period of time, Drs. Higgs and Wyatt identified numerous other children who had supposedly been sodomized.

Drs. Higgs and Wyatt felt eminently confident in the diagnostic procedures they had learned from Hobbs and Wynne. They remained unperturbed even when finding the reappearance of anal twitchiness *after* a child had been removed from his or her home. In situations such as these, they concluded that the child had been sodomized again by someone else other than the original perpetrator. In the case of one child, for example, by the time anal twitchiness had been found for the fourth time, the child's father, grandfather, and foster parents had all been accused of sexual abuse. Over a period of 5 months, Drs. Higgs and Wyatt "diagnosed" sexual abuse in 121 children from 57 different families.

The many outraged families and parents in Cleveland eventually demanded a formal inquiry into the practices of Drs. Higgs and Wyatt. Second opinions were sought from well-respected British pediatricians. The vast majority of these examinations led to findings quite inconsistent with those of Higgs and Wyatt. The British courts gradually realized that most of the children had not been abused, and 98 of them were finally returned to their families. In response to this tragic hoax, the massive investigation undertaken by the government eventually amounted to a cost of some 4 million British pounds.[9]

JUSTICE GONE AWRY

Not only do innocent adults find their lives ripped apart by false allegations of sexual abuse; equally innocent children also endure these living nightmares. In the late morning of August 28, 1989, 14-year-old Bobby Fijne (pronounced FAIN-ya) relaxed at home in Miami, Florida, before leaving for his job at a local Burger King. Dressed in his work uniform while sitting at the computer in his room, Bobby looked like the proverbial boy next door. The arrival of four police officers at the Fijne house, however, rapidly disrupted this all-American scene. The officers informed Bobby's father that they wanted to question his son and search his room. This event marked the beginning of a 20-month-long ordeal that almost completely shattered the lives of Bobby and his family.[10]

From the Big Bad Wolf to Ritualistic Cults

What would later develop into an unbelievable chronology of injustice in Bobby's case actually originated in early 1989. At that time, the mother of 3-year-old Jane Smith (a pseudonym) felt increasingly worried by recent changes in her daughter's behavior. Nightmares about the "big bad wolf" frequently terrifed Jane; in addition, she seemed frightened of being touched, and she wanted nothing to do with Bobby Fijne. Bobby served as a volunteer baby-sitter at the church attended by both his family and Jane's. As a result of her determination to avoid Bobby, Jane refused to attend Sunday school.

In response to the recommendation of her minister, Jane's mother obtained the services of Suzanne Keeley, a psychologist who also belonged to the church. Though Ms. Keeley's limited experience included only one previous case of possible sexual abuse, she quickly concluded that Jane had been abused. This was an altogether curious conclusion because Jane never mentioned anyone abusing her when initially questioned by Ms. Keeley. Under Florida law, however, merely suspecting that a child has been sexually abused requires a formal report to the Florida Department of Health and Rehabilitative Services. Consequently, Ms. Keeley eagerly complied with the relevant law and reported her suspicions.

As a result of Ms. Keeley's report, caseworker Sylvia Santos evaluated Jane and found no basis for substantiating the allegations of sexual abuse. Ms. Santos concluded that a videotape of "Little Red Riding Hood," played for Jane at home by her parents, had likely provoked her fears of the "big bad wolf." A trained interviewer from the Dade County Prosecuting Attorneys Office also uncovered nothing to even suggest that Jane had been sexually abused. Nevertheless, Ms. Keeley clung tenaciously to her suspicions, convinced in particular that Bobby Fijne had sexually abused Jane.

Ms. Keeley persuaded Jane's mother that her daughter needed therapy to contend with the traumatic experiences she had supposedly suffered. Over the course of numerous counseling sessions, Ms. Keeley persistently encouraged Jane to disclose what terrible things she had endured—and, most of all, to identify who did them. After 8 weeks of indoctrination in the guise of therapy, Jane eventually responded to Ms. Keeley's influence and said Bobby had touched her.

Jane's apparent disclosures rapidly became known to other families affiliated with the church. In response to the many rumors that ensued, parents whose children attended the same Sunday school began questioning them. In turn, additional allegations developed like wild fire, many of them bizarre enough to defy imagination. There were claims that Bobby had urinated in a child's mouth, and forced her to eat feces. A 5-year-old boy insisted that Bobby had taken him to New Zealand by airplane where he sexually abused him. A 6-year-old said that after he and his brother observed the birth of a baby in the church, Bobby forced him to eat the newborn's arm.

Additional therapists became involved, and some of them obtained more incredible tales from the children they interviewed. Psychologist Deborah Day, for instance, reported a 5-year-old describing "events where adults were costumed and doing things like killing babies, chopping up the babies, killing animals."[11] These reports convinced Ms. Day that she had discovered the clandestine activities of a ritualistic cult.

Interrogation by Inquisition via Coercion

Because of the apparently compelling information coming from the therapists, Dade County prosecutors believed the search of the Fijne home would uncover more incriminating evidence. Despite this confidence, however, the police officers never found the pornographic pictures they expected to discover, nor any other evidence even hinting that Bobby could have committed these unthinkable atrocities. After the officers completed their search of the home, they escorted Bobby to their office and began interrogating him. Bobby's father was present for the first 40 minutes of questioning, but left after the officers requested that they speak to Bobby by themselves.

Once Mr. Fijne exited the interrogation, the pace and intensity of the questioning rapidly increased. The officers repeatedly suggested that it would be better for everyone—the kids, their parents, his parents, and even Bobby himself—if he confessed to what he allegedly did. As a juvenile diabetic, Bobby soon began to wilt in response to the hammering questions directed at him. Without the two daily shots of insulin necessitated by his diabetes, Bobby's blood sugar level dropped precipitously. His ensuing hypoglycemia left him confused almost to the point of disorientation, and while in this state of mind, he admitted his supposed guilt. Pressed to further clarify his admission, Bobby could only say, "It just happened" and ask, "Now can I go home?"[12]

Standard operating procedure for the vast majority of police departments requires audio- or videotaping confessions, or at the very least, the suspect signs a written statement. In Bobby's case, however, the officers failed to document his supposed confession. As of August 1989, the Metro-Dade Police Department had not developed a specifically defined policy for documenting confessions. Consequently, the interviewing officers avoided censure for their oversights.

The officer in charge of interviewing Bobby—Mark Martinez—also destroyed his notes shortly after obtaining Bobby's "confession." In the aftermath of this case following the trial's conclusion, former Miami Police Chief Ken Harms labeled Martinez's performance as "inept, incompetent." Harms further emphasized, "These are things you absolutely do not do in these cases."[13] At the very least, Harms's blunt comments lent credibility to Bobby's explanation for his own confession. He told his parents, "I didn't do it, but they made me say I did."[14]

Question: Why Does the Lady of Justice Wear a Blindfold? Answer: Too Often She Can't Bear to Look

Despite the numerous errors of omission and commission undermining the veracity of Bobby's confession, the juvenile court booked him on charges of child sexual abuse. The court furthermore confined him in a detention facility. The Dade County Prosecutors Office then petitioned the court to try Bobby as an adult. The court concurred with the petition, and denied the request for Bobby's pretrial release on bond. In June 1990, another bond hearing was held before Judge Gerstein who later presided at Bobby's trial. Bobby's uncle, a retired justice of the Connecticut Supreme Court, offered to supervise him if he were released on bond. The prosecutor, Abbe Rifkin, vehemently objected to this proposal. In opposing bail, Ms. Rifkin characterized Bobby as "a danger to children." Judge Gerstein denied the request for Bobby's pretrial release.

Mel Black, Bobby's attorney, undertook a massive investigation, reviewing an incredible amount of information related to the charges Bobby faced. By the summer of 1990, Black and his colleagues had interviewed 600 church members, and carefully examined the physical characteristics of the church building. They also developed a list of 700 people in the vicinity of the alleged incidents when they supposedly occurred.

Black's investigation revealed that the church was a rather busy place with people regularly coming and going. Windows allowed a clear view from the crib room into the nursery where Bobby had worked as a volunteer. Of the hundreds of people who could have observed signs of inappropriate activity between Bobby and a child, not one reported seeing anything suspicious. Encouraging as this development was, Black and his cocounsel Peter Miller realized they faced an uphill battle on Bobby's behalf. Though the law demands that the prosecution bear the burden of proof in all criminal trials, Black and Miller knew they would have to prove Bobby's innocence. Maintaining reasonable doubts related to the question of Bobby's guilt would not suffice.

Because juries assume that children do not lie in cases such as these, they frequently overlook how suggestibility and imagination can influence a child's testimony. As a result, jurors place more confidence in the testimony of a child than it deserves. They disregard how children can sincerely believe they are telling the truth, but report events contaminated by their own fantasy and adult influence.

The Scales Hang—and Then Tip

On January 30, 1991, trial in the matter of Florida v. Fijne began. Just prior to the start of the trial, the prosecutor reduced the charges against Bobby to six counts of sexual battery and one count of lewd and lascivious assault. The prosecutor chose to drop additional charges involving another girl who claimed she saw—among other unlikely events—a woman turn into a witch and fly. Persuasive as such claims were in Massachusetts in the 1690s, the prosecutor apparently doubted their credibility in Florida in the 1990s. Perhaps this one concession to logic and rationality cleared Ms. Rifkin's conscience. Otherwise, her case would have resorted to the same kind of evidence that sent "witches" to the gallows more than 300 years ago.

Over a period of 48 days, the State of Florida presented its case against Bobby. The jury saw videotapes of the children's therapy sessions. Ms. Keeley and other therapists explained what they regarded as the significance of their work. Officer Martinez outlined and summarized his investigation, and different physicians described physical signs of sexual abuse. On March 19, 1991, the prosecution rested.

In preparation for cross-examining Ms. Keeley, Mel Black spent many hours reviewing the transcripts of her counseling sessions with Jane. Black found a very predictable pattern. Whenever Jane cited some event that could not have occurred—such as a woman turning into a witch—Keeley would pointedly ask her, "Is that real or make believe?"[15] In response to Black's questioning, Keeley insisted she responded to Jane in an entirely neutral manner. Black inquired if she knew how many times she had asked Jane, "Is that real or make believe?" Keeley replied she had no idea, and Black rhetorically replied, "Would you be surprised to know it was in excess of 50 times?"[16]

As a result of Black's well-prepared and perceptive cross-examination, the jury began to understand how Keeley had influenced Jane. She subtly but persistently demanded that Jane abandon fanciful tales defying imagination and adopt more logical narratives. These issues became even more clear and evident for the jury when Dr. Steven Ceci, a professor of psychology at Cornell University, testified. He explained how adults can influence children to think they remember events that never actually occurred. Ceci further clarified that children become more confident in the reality of these fictitious memories over time, even adding new details that seem quite persuasive.

Dr. Richard Gardner, a psychiatrist on the faculty of Columbia University, also testified on Bobby's behalf. He emphasized that worried parents can inadvertently influence the thinking and memory of their children. Gardner moreover explained, "Emotions have an infectious quality, and children are suggestible. If a parent is frightened of something, the child will pick up the message." Also asked about Keeley's therapy with Jane, Dr. Gardner exclaimed, "This is not therapy. This is a brainwashing process from the word go."[17]

Although pleased by the impact of Drs. Ceci and Gardner on the jury, Black knew he also had to contend with the medical evidence previously offered by the prosecutor. None of the physicians who appeared for the prosecution specialized in pediatric gynecology. Consequently, Black obtained the assistance of a pediatric gynecologist, Dr. David Muram. Prior to this trial, Dr. Muram had testified in courts exclusively as a prosecution expert. In Bobby's trial, however, his review of the photographs and examination records of the two girls led him to conclude there was "no physical evidence of sexual abuse."

In its unrelenting pursuit of justice, or more likely in response to its case rapidly sinking into disrepute, the prosecution resorted to the legal equivalent of "Let's Make a Deal"—a plea bargain. If Bobby confessed to the charges, he would serve his time in a treatment center for sexual offenders rather than prison. Moreover, the treatment center could release him much earlier than the prison system. Bobby briefly considered the offer, sighed heavily, and then emphatically replied, "No—I'm not guilty."

When he testified on his own behalf, Bobby denied abusing any child in any manner whatsoever. Asked about his confession, Bobby replied, "I was scared." He continued to explain, "My father wasn't there. I wasn't feeling too well. I was worried if he [Officer Martinez] was going to let me out."[18] The next witness established that Bobby's description of himself when he "confessed"—"I wasn't feeling too well"—amounted to a major understatement. Dr. Michael Novogroder, an expert on juvenile diabetes, testified that Bobby's blood sugar was so low when he supposedly confessed it likely impaired his thinking.

At this point, both prosecution and defense rested, and on May 3, 1991, the jurors began deliberating Bobby's fate. The next morning, the jury notified the court that it had reached a verdict. In response to each and every charge against Bobby, the jurors unanimously agreed—"Not guilty." After more than 20 months, this gut-wrenching ordeal for Bobby and his family had finally come to an end. Hardworking defense attorneys, well-informed experts, and an open-minded jury had served the goals of justice. In other cases, however, the pursuit of justice does not always proceed in such a direct manner.

JUSTICE DELAYED

Only a few credits shy of her degree in theater arts, Kelly Michaels headed east from her hometown of Pittsburgh setting her sights on Broadway. Considerations of food and shelter, however, necessitated a slight detour to Maplewood, New Jersey, a bedroom community about 1 hour outside of Manhattan. There, Kelly took a job with the Wee-Care Nursery School in September 1984 to support herself until she could find work as an actress.

When interviewed by Wee-Care personnel, Kelly acknowledged having no teaching experience. She explained, however, that she had grown up in a large family, enjoyed little children, and would like to try teaching. The Wee-Care staff felt favorably impressed by Kelly's background. Her musical talents, especially her piano playing ability, impressed the Wee-Care director. Kelly was hired as a teacher's aide for a probationary period, and 3 weeks later, she assumed the responsibilities of a teacher for the 3-year-old class.

On April 15, 1985, Kelly submitted her letter of resignation to the Wee-Care director. During the 8 months she spent there, the school never received any complaints about her. The children in her class seemed quite comfortable with Kelly. None of her co-workers noticed anything even suggesting she responded inappropriately to the preschoolers in her care. In late April 1985, however, events began rapidly unfolding that would eventually hurl the ugliest of allegations at Kelly Michaels.[19, 20]

The Volatility of Petroleum Jelly

On April 30, 1985, 4-year-old Matthew Parks (a pseudonym) appeared ill, and his mother took him to his pediatrician. As a nurse took Matthew's rectal temperature, she reassuringly rubbed his back. He reportedly commented that his teacher (Kelly Michaels) did the same thing to him. No one ever clarified whether Matthew was referring to the nurse taking his temperature rectally, or rubbing his back reassuringly. Nevertheless, Matt's mother and the nurse promptly concluded that Kelly had sodomized him. Later, in response to further questioning, Matthew apparently indicated that he did not like "nap time." At nap time, Kelly allegedly put "gasoline" (vaseline) on a thermometer and inserted it in his rectum.

According to Matthew, Kelly said nothing despite his protests as she put the thermometer in his "bum." Matthew also indicated he saw Kelly remove the pants of two other children and take their temperatures. Both of those children, however, denied anyone ever taking their temperature at school. Matthew's mother reported her impressions to the New Jersey Division of Youth and Family Services (DYFS), which undertook an investigation. From the very outset of the investigation, Kelly denied ever doing anything improper to the children enrolled at the school. On May 6, 1985, she submitted to a polygraph examination, and the examiner concluded she was telling the truth.

Despite the accumulating evidence clearly exonerating Kelly of any wrongdoing, DYFS expanded its investigation. Investigators interviewed practically every child at Wee-Care with whom Kelly might have had contact. The stories they obtained from some of them were shocking to say the least. The children disclosed numerous experiences of sexual abuse supposedly perpetrated by Kelly. These alleged acts ranged from minor touching to acts so heinous and bizarre they defied imagination.

Can You Top This?

Both boys and girls claimed that Kelly inserted knives, forks, and spoons into their "butts," penises, or vaginas. A girl said that Kelly put a light bulb in her vaginal orifice, and a boy reported that Kelly inserted "Legos" in his "tushie." The children described games where both they and Kelly removed all of their clothing, smeared themselves with peanut butter and jelly, and then licked each other. Other children alleged that Kelly forced them into intercourse with her during her menstrual period. Various boys claimed that she subjected them to fellatio.

Kelly also supposedly played "Jingle Bells" on the piano while sexually abusing her students. These many acts reportedly transpired in the music room, the lunchroom, the nap room, the bathroom, and the gym. Various children claimed that Kelly "pooped and peed" on the piano bench, then made a "cake of poop," and forced them to taste it with wooden spoons. Interestingly enough, however, subsequent testing of the piano bench and the wooden spoons at the FBI laboratory found nothing to corroborate these outrageous accusations.

Several children said they told their parents about Kelly's alleged abusiveness while it was happening. Other children claimed that various Wee-

Care personnel were present during these activities, or at least knew of them. Some children insisted other adults had witnessed Kelly remove her clothes in the lunchroom. Nevertheless, none of these accounts of what parents and teachers reportedly knew or saw were substantiated by any adult.

Pressure Cooker Interviews

During numerous interviews, the children encountered enormous pressure to disclose information consistent with the investigators' expectations. Interviewers persuaded them that Kelly was "bad" because she had done "bad things" to the children at Wee-Care. They met the police officer who had arrested Kelly, and saw the handcuffs he used. These children eagerly cooperated when interviewers encouraged them to "help us bust this case wide open"; in turn, they received mock police badges for their cooperation. The children were moreover reassured that by cooperating, Kelly would remain in jail, and therefore, they and their families could be safe.

Despite the persuasive tactics to which they were subjected, many children initially insisted Kelly had not abused them. Other children who resisted participating in the interviews endured persistent pressure to cooperate. One child learned she had to talk with the interviewers in order to help her friends. Interviewers told this child they had already spoken to five other children, and all of them revealed terrible things Kelly had supposedly done. Still other children heard specific details of what their friends had previously disclosed. Investigators also suggested to "uncooperative" children that their friends would be disappointed in them for not helping.

Understandably, almost all of the children eventually succumbed to the influences of the investigators, which ranged from mildly suggestive to exceedingly coercive. For example, the investigator who interviewed most of the children profoundly influenced them via his own thinking. He assumed, "The interview process is in essence the beginning of the healing process."[21] Convinced that Kelly Michaels had sexually abused these children, this investigator demanded they discuss their experiences in graphic detail. He assumed only the most explicit disclosures would allow the children to recover from the ordeals they apparently endured. As a result, he and other interviewers solicited explicitly sexual language from the children, and practically applauded when they complied.

During the late spring and early summer of 1985, mental health professionals held group meetings with Wee-Care parents. The professionals recited laundry lists of symptoms supposedly indicative of children who had been sexually abused. Many worried and anxious parents then proceeded to closely observe their children, looking for any evidence of the critical symptoms the professionals had described. These parents also questioned their children repeatedly, attempting to determine if anything had happened to them.

Unfortunately, the mental health professionals did not realize how severely flawed their symptom lists were. Though these lists can sometimes identify a sexually abused child, they also mistakenly classify many nonabused children as abused. While relying on the misinformation related to these symptom lists, numerous parents concluded that their children had been sexually abused.

By the summer of 1985, 11 of the 20 children considered victims of Kelly's abuse were involved in psychotherapy. Having spoken with the investigators before they even started treatment, the therapists also believed the children had been sexually abused. Consequently, all of the counseling experiences for these children regarded their supposed sexual abuse as an established fact. By this time, then, the children found themselves surrounded by a network of adults—including DYFS personnel, police officers, prosecutors, therapists, and their parents—all assuming that Kelly Michaels was a child molester. Not surprisingly, this formidable network of adult influence motivated the children to conform their thinking with its assumptions.

The Gears of Justice Begin to Grind

More than 2 years after the original investigation started, trial in the matter of *New Jersey v. Michaels* began on June 22, 1987. Kelly faced 131 counts related to various criminal charges including aggravated sexual assault, sexual assault, endangering the welfare of children, and making terroristic threats.

Though she was an unlicensed psychologist with only a master's degree, Eileen Treacy emerged as the prosecution's star witness. The judge qualified Ms. Treacy as an expert witness on the basis of her therapy experience with child victims of sexual abuse. Treacy's testimony relied on what she considered 32 behavioral indicators of sexually abused children, and related theories outlining the different phases of sexual abuse.

In particular, Treacy specified five different phases related to a cycle of child sexual abuse: (1) *engagement phase*—the offender engages the child into a relationship; (2) *sexual interaction phase*—the offender initiates sexual activity with the child; (3) *secrecy phase*—the offender attempts to commit the child to silence via bribes, tricks, or threats; (4) *disclosure phase*—the child discloses sexual abuse creating a crisis for him- or herself and his or her family; and (5) *suppression phase*—the child attempts to cope with the abuse by denying that it happened, avoiding talking about it, and/or minimizing its significance. Treacy also identified common behaviors exhibited by sexually abused children as including eating disorders, sleep problems, regression, sexual symptomatology, and the development of various fears.

Treacy initially testified before the jury in July 1987. At that time, she confined her testimony to considerations of children's memory, their ability to discriminate between fantasy and reality, and their stages of sexual development. Then in December, Treacy returned to spend more than 5 days testifying. She confidently expressed her opinions regarding whether the behaviors of the Wee-Care children were consistent with cases of known sexual abuse. Ms. Treacy ultimately concluded that all of the children she interviewed had been sexually abused, except for one child. In that one case, she indicated that she could not reach a firm conclusion.

Expert Misinformation

Persuasive as Ms. Treacy's testimony appeared to the jury, it was in fact severely flawed. She resorted to the phases theory of child sexual abuse to support her position that the Wee-Care children had been abused. Nevertheless, her thinking in this regard was seriously mistaken. The phases of child sexual abuse were never intended to diagnose abuse; instead, this theory assumes that the child has been abused, and confines itself to explaining the child's reactions to the abuse. Addressing this very issue, an article published in the *Nebraska Law Review* after Kelly's trial emphasized:

> Widespread misunderstanding of child sexual abuse accommodation syndrome [the phases theory] had unfortunate consequences. Expert testimony based in whole or part on the syndrome led some courts to believe the accommodation syndrome was designed to diagnose child sexual abuse. So viewed, the syndrome is doomed to fail because it simply does not diagnose.[22]

Similarly, relying on behavioral indicators to conclude that a child has been sexually abused is ill-advised. Too many children who have never been sexually abused also exhibit behavioral characteristics supposedly indicative of abuse. Various traumas in a child's life such as family conflicts, acute illness, or enduring the harsh spotlight of a sexual abuse investigation can provoke the indicators Treacy emphasized so frequently for the jury. In fact, Dr. Suzanne Sgroi—whose work Treacy cited extensively—has emphasized: "Behavioral indicators of child sexual abuse may be helpful [in assessment work], but are rarely conclusive."[23]

Expert witnesses appearing on behalf of Kelly criticized the wholesale unreliability of the techniques used by Treacy. Dr. Ralph Underwager—whose many publications and professional presentations related to child sexual abuse have earned him international respect—pointed out there was no available evidence supporting Ms. Treacy's assumptions. He further explained that none of Treacy's 32 behavioral indicators could be attributed exclusively to the effects of sexual abuse. Underwager also clarified how the phases of sexual abuse amounted to no more than a theory, and in particular, a theory without any evidence to verify it.

Impressive as Dr. Underwager's testimony was, the testimony of the children left the defense backed against a wall. Responding to the effects of unrelenting adult influence over a 2-year period of time, 19 children described various degrading experiences to which Kelly had supposedly subjected them. As the children testified on closed-circuit TV, their statements appeared quite compelling. Of course, this was to be expected as the prosecution team carefully prepared the children just before testifying.

Because of his own colossally poor judgment, the judge increased the credibility of the children's testimony far beyond what it deserved. As the jury watched the closed-circuit TV, the judge played games with the children and held them on his lap. He also whispered to them while suggesting they reciprocate, and both encouraged and praised their testimony. Kelly's attorneys found it almost impossible to question the children effectively. The judge typically took charge of the questioning himself, relying on leading and suggestive inquiries that accomplished little more than revealing his own biases. Basically, the judge all but enthusiastically applauded anything and everything the children said. The subsequent impact on the jury was profound to say the least.

On April 3, 1988, nine months after Kelly's trial began, the case went to the jury. The jury deliberated for 12 days before reaching guilty verdicts on 115 counts of the various charges against Kelly. The judge sentenced Kelly to a total of 47 years in prison, further specifying her ineligibility for parole until she had served at least 14 years. Kelly and the defense team reacted with shock and disbelief. She was sent to the women's correctional facility in the State of New Jersey, and the defense team undertook a lengthy appeals process.

The Wheels of Justice Begin to Turn—Ever So Slowly

On February 1, 1993, the Appellate Division of the Superior Court of New Jersey presided over Kelly's appeal. On March 26, 1993, the appeals court announced its decision reversing Kelly's conviction, and she walked out of prison after almost 5 years of confinement.

The appeals court reversed the conviction in response to two exceedingly important issues. First, it ruled that Treacy's testimony was so grossly ill-informed that the judge never should have allowed the jury to hear it. In criticizing the unreliable methods to which Treacy resorted, the court specifically deplored how "she was permitted to lead the jury to believe that the process [she used] was rooted in science and thus was a reliable means of determining sexual abuse."[24]

The appeals court also reversed Kelly's conviction as a result of the judge's conduct during the trial. Commenting on how the judge responded to the children during their testimony, the court emphasized:

> For all appearances, the State's witnesses [the children] became the judge's witnesses. The atmosphere became such, after this manner of presentation of testimony from 19 children, that a jury considering a verdict in favor of the defendant might feel that it was personally offending the judge. The required atmosphere of the bench's impartiality was lost in this trial.[25]

Apparently unpersuaded by the emphatic position of the appeals court, the Essex County Prosecutor's office attempted to try Kelly a second time. This decision was appealed to the New Jersey Supreme Court. This court indicated that it was obligated to determine whether:

> the interview techniques used by the State in this case were so coercive or suggestive that they had a capacity to substantially distort the children's recollections of actual events and thus compromise the reliability of the children's statements and testimony based on their recollections.[26]

The New Jersey Supreme Court pointed out how the initial investigation produced little, if any, incriminating evidence against Kelly. The court specifically noted that practically none of the children volunteered any information indicating that Kelly had abused them. The court was moreover disturbed because the earliest interviews of the children were not electronically recorded, and in some cases, the original notes were destroyed.

More than any other issue, however, the court vehemently criticized the manner in which the children had been interviewed. It noted: "The record is replete with instances in which children were asked blatantly leading questions that furnished information the children themselves had not mentioned."[27] For example, the court's analysis of the children's testimony revealed that all but 5 of 34 children encountered leading questions assuming Kelly had sexually abused them. Seventeen children heard questions suggesting their firsthand experiences with oral–genital sexual contact, and consuming human waste. Interviewers asked questions of 23 children presuming their experiences of nudity at Wee-Care. The interviewers also responded to the children with praise and approval when they said anything that could incriminate Kelly. They responded disapprovingly, however, when the children said something that might exonerate her.

On June 23, 1994, the New Jersey Supreme Court upheld the previous appeals court ruling overturning Kelly's conviction. This court all but foreclosed the possibility of Kelly being tried again. It emphasized that the children were interviewed so improperly that any evidence obtained from them should be considered inherently unreliable. The court's opinion also referred to the "egregious prosecutorial abuses" evident prior to and throughout the previous trial. As a result, the court indicated it was unlikely that testimony of the children would be allowed at any future trial. After more than 9 years, the unthinkable injustices endured by Kelly Michaels and her family had finally come to an end.

OVERVIEW

Nursery school teachers, parents, grandparents, church volunteers, and young or old—in California, Minnesota, Europe, Florida, and New Jersey—the events chronicled in this chapter dramatically demonstrate how false allegations of child sexual abuse can occur anywhere to anyone. Directing attention to false allegations of child sexual abuse should not be interpreted as denying or minimizing the traumas of actual sexual abuse. The effects of child sexual abuse can be tragic and long-lasting; consequently, actual victims deserve our understanding and support. At the same time, victims of false allegations also struggle with their own living nightmares that demand vindication and justice.

Surprising as it may seem, the frequency of false allegations of child sexual abuse likely exceeds that of reports of actual abuse. For example, John Eckenrode and his colleagues at Cornell University found that 61% of all allegations of child sexual abuse reported during 1985 in the State of

New York could not be substantiated.[28] More recently, 57% of the allegations of child sexual abuse reported during 1992 in the State of Kentucky were unsubstantiated.[29] Other estimates indicate that the rate of unfounded reports of sexual abuse may be as high as 65%.[30] These data also correspond to a nationwide trend observed during the past decade. While the number of abuse and neglect reports have soared, the substantiation rate has declined. At the very least, these data suggest that any randomly selected allegation of child sexual abuse is more likely false than not.

Considerations such as these obviously lead to the question of how can false allegations of sexual abuse seem so credible. What transpires in these situations that can lead so many professionals into such erroneous conclusions? We turn to the next chapter for answers to these questions and related issues.

2

The Origins of False Allegations

Rumors Running Out of Control

At 5 years of age, Jennifer's parents had been divorced for more than a year. Jennifer resided in her mother's custody, and every other weekend she spent with her father. Jennifer's mother regarded her former husband as a tyrannical, callous man who regularly resorted to intimidation as his preferred method for dealing with people. As a result, Jennifer's visits with her father aroused considerable anxiety for her mother.

The ensuing visitation dispute between Jennifer's mother and father eventually brought this case to my attention. The many events preceding my involvement in this matter demonstrate how false allegations originate, gather momentum, and threaten the welfare of all involved. Therefore, we will focus on those critically important events in order to explain them.

When Jennifer returned home after her weekend visitations, her mother would cross-examine her about her every activity. Convinced that her former husband had somehow betrayed Jennifer's welfare, mother's voice would quiver and her body sometimes trembled while conducting these interrogations. The number of questions she posed, and the rapid rate at which she asked them reduced Jennifer to feeling confused and bewildered.

Unable to understand all of her mother's questions, Jennifer evaded them and responded more to mom's obvious distress. Seeing her mother in such turmoil left Jenny upset, worried, and frequently in tears. In response to Jennifer's distress, her mother became increasingly convinced that her ex-husband had subjected their daughter to some kind of trauma. Nevertheless, Jennifer did not identify her father doing anything to have affected her so adversely.

The frequency with which Jennifer's mother had encountered anecdotes of child sexual abuse, via TV talk shows and tabloid newspapers, led her to wonder if such a fate had befallen her daughter. She began to examine Jenny surreptitiously, looking for any physical evidence of sexual abuse, but she found nothing. She also questioned Jennifer about whether anyone had touched her "private places," and whether she had been coerced into touching someone else's "private places." Jennifer responded negatively to her mother's questions, but rather than reassure her, her negative replies further aroused her mother's anxiety.

When parents suspect that their child has been sexually abused, they struggle with a very difficult situation. As long as the child denies any abuse, worried parents must contend with a gnawing, unrelenting sense of anxious uncertainty. Just as any negative premise can never be conclusively proven, anxious parents can never know for sure that nothing traumatic happened to their child. Any parent in these circumstances wonders: Are the child's denials born out of some perpetrator's intimidation, is the child too embarrassed or traumatized to tell the truth, or has the parent overlooked some telltale signs of abuse? The related research evidence indicates that these kinds of uncertain situations motivate people to seek out and rely on the opinions of others.[1,2]

RUMOR FORMATION

While seeking the opinions of others under conditions of uncertainty or ambiguity, anxious people can influence how those others respond to their questions. For example, an individual who contends with an ambiguous situation might explain: "I think [some event such as sexual abuse] happened, what do you think?" Any response of "Don't worry, it's probably all in your imagination" can seem very callous and uncaring. At the very least, people who encounter these concerns feel obligated to ask, "Why do you think this happened?" In turn, anxious parents who worry about the possible sexual abuse of their children are rarely at a loss for answers.

Self-Indoctrination

As anxious parents outline the reasons for their anxiety, they cite one detail after another appearing to verify their assumptions of sexual abuse. The "evidence" they present can progressively persuade themselves, and others, as to the legitimacy of the concerns. Related research, for example, demonstrates that attempting to explain why some event *might* have occurred progressively persuades people that the event *did* occur.[3] Seeking explanations for something that might have happened distracts people from considering an alternative hypothesis—the event did not occur.

To the degree that another person endorses the thinking of an anxious parent, they will interact more frequently because of the views they share.[4] These endorsements also encourage the development of loyal alliances between anxious parents and concerned others. Loyalty prevails within these alliances because any two people who endorse the same attitudes are more inclined to regard each other positively.[5]

In fact, Jennifer's mother felt compelled to disclose her distressing concerns to her own mother. She described how upset and traumatized Jennifer seemed after returning from visits with her father. Mother additionally reported that Jenny appeared hesitant and wary just prior to her visits. As she expressed her many worries and concerns, mother never considered how her own anxiety influenced Jennifer's reactions more than anything else. Instead, she took a deep breath before ominously whispering her ultimate worry—maybe her former husband had sexually abused Jenny.

After listening attentively to her daughter's dramatic narration, grandmother expressed her own alarming observation. She revealed long suspecting that Jennifer's father might do something "fishy" to Jenny. She further suggested that her daughter's former husband had always struck her as an "odd kind of duck." Despite the mixed metaphor, grandmother's observation began to alleviate many of the doubts with which mother was struggling. As a result, they both agreed that mother should continue questioning Jenny about what her father had apparently done to her.

Exchanging Rumors and Creating Facts

When anxious parents and concerned others gravitate into loyal alliances, as mother and grandmother did, the anxiety of the parents is no longer confined within each of them. Instead, a situation develops where two or more people share the same anxiety of struggling with ambiguous circumstances limiting the information available to them. People obviously need information to make rational decisions, and without such information, they feel increasingly frustrated and anxious. This is the kind of situation that readily encourages rumor formation and rumor dissemination.[6]

In the McMartin case described in Chapter 1, for example, wildly speculative rumors began spiraling out of control in response to decisions made by the police department.[7] Perplexed by the vague allegations originally initiated by one parent, the Manhattan Beach Police sent a letter of inquiry to 450 parents throughout the community. The letter asked the parents to question their children about possible sexual abuse at the McMartin preschool. Though seeking information, this letter alarmed practically everyone who received it, creating an exceedingly ambiguous situation provoking wholesale dissemination of unsubstantiated rumors.

The intense needs of people to obtain information under ambiguous circumstances motivates them to exchange imaginative speculations with each other.[8] In turn, these speculative exchanges create fertile ground for a bountiful harvest of rumors.[9] For anxious parents who worry that their child has been sexually abused, some information—no matter how unreliable it may be—is preferable to no information at all.

Suspecting sexual abuse, anxious parents start asking their children more and more questions. Young children, however, often respond to these questions in a vague, open-ended manner that invites considerable interpretation. For example, in a case I evaluated, I asked a 5-year-old where she visited with her father. She replied, "I visit with Daddy where we live." Initially, I found this to be a curious response. I knew that her visits with her father were supervised at the offices of the Department of Social Services. On further consideration, however, it became evident that this child was—in a sense—correct. She resided in Big Rapids (MI), her father visited her in Big Rapids, therefore her father visited her "where we live." Nevertheless, this child's response could have easily led an interviewer to wrongly conclude that her father visited her at her residence.

Ambiguity and Biased Interpretations

The relevant research demonstrates that when confronted with ambiguous statements, anxious people interpret them in a biased manner. In response to the following sentence, "The doctor examined little Emma's growth," anxious people interpreted "growth" to mean tumor rather than height.[10] Related data also demonstrate that anxious people skew their interpretations of ambiguous homophones (words that sound the same but have different meanings). For instance, when hearing the homophone *morning–mourning*, anxious people more frequently interpret it as an emotional reaction provoked by death.[11]

Children often express themselves in a very ambiguous manner (e.g., "He touched me"). Consequently, the anxiety level of worried parents can rapidly lead them into a biased interpretation of what their child says. In other words, these parents expect to discover the worst-case scenario, and consequently, that is what they eventually think they have discovered.

In response to the media coverage of the McMartin case, for example, more and more rumors circulated throughout southern California. As a result, various police departments found themselves inundated by phone calls. Callers reported suspicious behaviors involving neighbors, teachers, school-bus drivers, and others. Overwhelmed by the number of baseless reports, police personnel commented, "Everyone was researching their memories and all these little incidents suddenly seemed like abuse." Overreactions were quite common, such as the mother of a 4-year-old boy informing police that her son's erection alerted her to him having been sexually abused. Diplomatically as possible, an officer explained to her, "Lady, it's perfectly normal for a 4-year-old boy to have an erection."

Motivated to reduce the uncertainty of the ambiguous situations confronting them, anxious parents and concerned others speculate about various issues related to the alleged abuse. They can discuss where it could have occurred, when it likely transpired, and how it might have been concealed. Because ominous situations surely demand more than speculation, speculative exchanges can also lead to heightened frustration. Nevertheless, frustration reduction is available by conferring the status of fact on what was originally speculation.

In a small village in the Netherlands, for example, two small boys suffered slight anal injuries as a result of their sex-play with each other. Discovery of these injuries led to the repeated interrogations of practically every pre-schoolchild in the village. Over a period of several months, rumors developed suggesting a massive conspiracy involving sadomasochism, manufacture of child pornography, bizarre rites related to drug abuse, and the sacrificial torture and murder of infants. Other than the slight anal injuries found on the two boys, no additional evidence was ever discovered to substantiate any of these rumors. The police eventually dismissed the entire episode as an outburst of mass hysteria. Nevertheless, some residents of this Dutch village still remain convinced of the legitimacy of the rumors.[12]

Shared Theories

The speculative exchanges of anxious parents and concerned others frequently converge into commonly shared theories. They rapidly reach a consensus via processes of "leveling" and "sharpening."[13] In their dialogues, they "sharpen"—or emphasize—impressions consistent with their preexisting expectations. Simultaneously, they "level"—or deemphasize— any information inconsistent with their *a priori* thinking. In response to the effects of leveling and sharpening, any significant differences in their thinking disappear as their attitudes about the alleged abuse become increasingly similar. In turn, the similarities of their thinking convince them they have discovered important facts—"We agree, therefore we must be right!" Thus, two or more people can verify for each other that some imaginary event actually occurred—and what originated as a worrisome rumor (sexual abuse) acquires the unwarranted status of an indisputable fact.[14]

As the allegations in the Kelly Michaels case gathered momentum, the prosecutor's expert—Eileen Treacy—met with parents whose children attended the Wee-Care school. These meetings encouraged the parents to resort to processes of sharpening and leveling. Treacy distributed her checklist of 32 symptoms, claiming it could be used to identify sexually abused children. Though the parents observed nothing unusual in their children's behavior before the DYFS investigation, the checklist altered their memories.

Without intending to or realizing it, the parents "sharpened" instances of their children's behavior even remotely similar to any of Treacy's 32 symptoms. They also "leveled" other behavioral examples inconsistent with the checklist. Over time, these processes of sharpening and leveling left many of the parents convinced they had uncovered important evidence. They thought they could remember episodes of their children's sleep disturbances, eating problems, accident proneness, and baby talk. Simultaneously, the parents remained unaware of how they actually responded to their own heightened suggestibility aroused by Treacy and her checklist.

REDUCING AMBIGUITY

A child's continued denials of sexual abuse, in the face of a parent's growing convictions to the contrary, reduce the parent to frustration and exasperation. Without the child's acknowledgment, the parent's thinking remains less than credible. Thus, suspicious parents increase the frequency with which they question their child about issues of sexual abuse. These questions are also frequently designed to reassure children. They hear they have nothing to be ashamed of, nothing bad will happen if they tell the "truth," and no one will be able to hurt them again.

Demanding Questions

One evening while drying Jennifer off after her nighttime bath, mother vigorously rubbed her daughter's vaginal area with a towel. Simultaneously she asked, "Is that one of the things Daddy does to you?" Mother's intensity provoked a startled silence from Jennifer before she nodded her head affirmatively. In response to Jennifer's nonverbal response, mother nodded her own head as she suggestively asked, "And he did other things to you, didn't he?" Jennifer again responded positively— this time with a tentatively whispered "yes"—prompting her mother to further suggest, "Like touch your private place with his private place?" Jennifer's still hesitant but affirmative response to this question moved mother to embrace her while exclaiming, "Oh thank you for telling me the truth, Jenny. I won't let Daddy hurt you again."

As this parent–child dialogue transpired, mother assumed that Jennifer responded to her questions as requests for information. Jennifer, however, considered her mother's questions as demands for compliance. Unsure as to exactly how she should comply, Jennifer confined her responses to replies of "Yes." She knew from past experience that affirmative responses more often led to mother's acceptance—and cessation of questioning—than responses of "No."

Mother's questions also gave Jennifer information that would influence how she answered future queries about her father. Jennifer specifically learned that her father had supposedly rubbed her vaginal area, and touched her "private place" with his "private place." Most importantly, mother did not set out with any premeditated malice deliberately intending to distort Jenny's thinking and memory. Instead, her elevated anxiety level influenced Jennifer in ways she never realized.

Repeated Questions

Over the course of their development, children learn that parental questions asked repeatedly often mean they have responded incorrectly.[15]

For example, consider a situation where a 2-year-old receives a stuffed toy as a gift, and the following dialogue ensues:

PARENT   What is this?
CHILD   A teddy bear.
PARENT   *What* is this?
CHILD   A doggy.
PARENT   *Now what* is this?
CHILD   A kitty cat.
PARENT   That's right!

Also consider the following interaction between a parent and a 5-year-old as they examine the alphabet together.

PARENT   Where is the "b"?
CHILD   Points to a "p"
PARENT   *Where* is the "b"?
CHILD   Points to a "d"
PARENT   *Now where* is the "b"?
CHILD   [points to the correct letter]
PARENT   That's right!

As the previous examples illustrate, prior learning experiences motivate children to change what they say in response to questions asked repeatedly by their parents. Children test out various possibilities attempting to identify the reply that brings parental approval. Parental questions also provoke vivid imagery for children—"What did the pebble in your shoe feel like when you were walking?"—or alternatively—"What did it feel like when he touched you?" Once the critical imagery is planted via suggestive questions, it can provide children the alternative responses they are seeking.

Consequently, children may initially deny any experience of sexual abuse at one point in time, but acknowledge themselves as victims at a later point because of repeated parental questioning. In turn, a child's acknowledgment of alleged sexual abuse confers an impressive appearance of credibility on what was once a mere rumor.

CREDIBILITY EXPANSION

When children finally respond to questions regarding alleged sexual abuse by indicating, "Yes, he did it"—or any other response that could possibly be interpreted as affirmative—parents experience a surprising sense of relief. The parents at least think they know what happened, and as a result, they can more confidently initiate various courses of action to help their child. Thus, in this circumstance, parents no longer contend with the agonizing paralysis of doubting uncertainty. Instead, they can express warmth and understanding in the service of reassurance. Obviously, then, the child disclosing apparent sexual abuse results in parental approval.

Expanding Adult Influences

Jennifer's apparent disclosure convinced her mother to contact the county child protection agency. Mother then explained to Jennifer how a "nice lady" would be coming to their home to talk with her. The lady would want to know about "Daddy hurting your private place with his private place." To further help her daughter, mother also reminded her where her "private place" was.

When the child protection investigator asked Jennifer, "What did your Daddy do to you?" she dutifully replied, "He hurt my private place with his private place." Though Jennifer was disinclined to elaborate any further, the investigator regarded her report as substantive evidence. The investigator advised mother that Jenny should be further evaluated at a local mental health clinic. She reassuringly explained how the clinic was staffed by "experts" in sexual abuse. The investigator also added that the therapist assigned to Jenny's case would use anatomically detailed dolls. Mother felt relieved when told these dolls would help Jennifer cope with what she had endured.

As Jennifer and her mother drove to their first appointment with the therapist, grandmother also accompanied them. While in the car, both mother and grandmother took turns reassuring Jennifer that the therapist was another "very nice lady." They moreover explained how the therapist would give Jenny a "boy doll" and a "girl doll" with "private parts"; then, she could show the therapist how "Daddy hurt you."

Remembering What Others Think

When called from the clinic's waiting room, Jennifer marched confidently into the therapist's office. There, she lifted her skirt while pointing to her vaginal area, and announced with a conviction that would have made her mother and grandmother proud, "My Daddy hurt me here." Given this apparently compelling evidence, the therapist thought she knew how to best assist Jennifer. She encouraged her to assertively tell an adult male doll, "This is *my* private place and you can't touch it." The therapist felt quite confident that this opportunity to express her feelings would help Jenny enormously. Unfortunately, the therapist neglected to consider that rather than enhancing the accuracy of Jennifer's memory, she was contaminating it via suggestibility.

More than 90 years of accumulated research clearly demonstrates that memory does not necessarily diminish with the passage of time; instead it grows and expands.[16] What fades from memory over time is the actual experience of an event. Consequently, each time people recall some event they must reconstruct it. They ask themselves, "What happened and how did it transpire?" and with each reconstruction, the memory can change.

Therefore, memory recall—or the reconstruction of some event—responds primarily to an individual's sense of what is plausible. In other words, people recall events so that they seem to make sense, but what seems sensible—the "sounds good" effect—can be horribly mistaken. In particular, the influences of adult authority figures can profoundly distort a child's memory via biased definitions of plausibility.[17]

VALIDATING NETWORKS

Jennifer's mother, grandmother, and the therapist gravitated closer together drawn by their mutual concerns for Jenny's welfare. In talking with mother and grandmother, the therapist effusively referred to herself as "Suzzy." She felt confident that this demonstration of affable openness reassured clients of her genuine authenticity.

Suzzy explained to mother and grandmother how Jenny remained tight-lipped regarding the details of some "secrets" shared with her father. Nonetheless, Suzzy also reassured them that Jennifer was "getting her feelings out" via increasing assertiveness in play therapy. Mother and grandmother felt duly impressed by this information. As a result, they reported to Suzzy that Jenny seemed more comfortable and spontaneous since her treatment began. This feedback satisfied Suzzy that she had indeed assessed Jennifer's ordeal accurately.

The Influence of Supportive Groups

In response to Suzzy's urging, mother and grandmother joined a group for parents of sexually abused children. This group met at the same facility where Jennifer was in treatment. They felt shocked and dismayed in response to the many accounts of sexual abuse reported by other members of their group. The more they thought about the anecdotes they encountered, the more they found reasons persuading themselves that Jennifer's father was a seriously disturbed man.

While excavating their memories for evidence of the father's supposed disturbances, mother and grandmother never considered how unreliable long-term memory is.[18] Surprising as it may seem, today's attitudes and expectations influence our memories of the past more than anything else. When asked what time of the year John Kennedy was assassinated, for example, many residents of Great Britain reported it was summer.[19] Remembering JFK riding in an open car on a warm and sunny day, and unfamiliar with the mild Dallas weather in November, they mistakenly recalled the assassination as occurring during the summer months. In other words, people frequently reinvent the past in accordance with their present-day thinking and assumptions.[20]

Mother and grandmother felt particularly warmed by their own empathy when they concluded that Jennifer's father had been sexually abused himself as a child. They insisted that his distant relationships with his own family confirmed their suspicions. In arriving at this conclusion, mother conveniently overlooked how her ex-husband had complied with her demands. She previously insisted they spend holidays with her family while married to each other. When mother and grandmother summarized their reasoning for the parents group, the other members commended their thinking as remarkably insightful and open-minded. Suzzy, however, cautioned mother and grandmother against getting carried away by their own compassion.

Characteristically leaping at any opportunity to sound authoritative, Suzzy insisted that excessive compassion for father would encourage him to deny his serious maladjustments. Suzzy had never met Jennifer's father, and she most certainly did not intend to. Nonetheless, she described him as a cruel and predatory man indulging his own sick needs while disregarding the trauma he inflicted on others. Unlike mother and grandmother, Suzzy had never seen Jennifer laughing with delight as she ran with outstretched arms to her father. Relying exclusively on second- and thirdhand impressions allowed Suzzy to view Jennifer's father in more extreme terms.[21] In response to Suzzy's influence, mother and grandmother further revised their memories of Jennifer's father and soon found themselves in agreement with her.

Mother's and grandmother's participation in the parents group also prompted them to talk with each other more often than before. As a result of their increasingly frequent dialogues, they no longer disagreed about how to deal with Jennifer as they previously did. Comforted by the growing alliance between her mother and grandmother, Jennifer's past episodes of defiant disobedience rapidly disappeared. This development additionally verified for mother and grandmother how seriously distressed Jenny had been—as a result of her father's supposed abuse—before treatment began to help her. They never considered how Jennifer's previous disobedience reflected the inconsistencies between mother's more easygoing parental style and grandmother's greater strictness.

During one of their many discussions, mother, grandmother, and Suzzy all agreed it was imperative to legally terminate the father's visitation rights via court order. Until then, mother had blocked visitation by telling her ex-husband that Jennifer was ill, or involved in other activities that precluded visits. Nevertheless, Jennifer's father was rapidly losing patience with these excuses and becoming more demanding about seeing his daughter.

Supportive Groups and the Need for Boundaries

Jennifer's mother made an appointment with the attorney who had handled her divorce. When she met with him, however, he shocked her by suggesting that the allegations directed at her ex-husband could be unfounded. Mother cited what Jennifer had told her, emphasized how the child protection agency had verified her concerns, explained Jennifer's treatment, and summarized all she had learned in the parents group. The attorney, though, advised caution while advocating that psychologists known for their objectivity and experience in these matters evaluate Jennifer.

Mother departed the attorney's office less than satisfied and promptly drove to grandmother's residence. As she walked into the house, grandmother was on the phone with another member of the parents group. An impromptu conference call ensued, and they all concluded that Suzzy would know how to deal with this situation created by the attorney's insensitivity.

Suzzy empathized both warmly and genuinely with mother and grandmother, and moreover, she directed them to Mr. Lester. She reassured them he was an attorney who would properly understand their ordeal. When mother and grandmother met with Mr. Lester, he listened sympathetically and nodded agreeably in response to their recitations detailing Jennifer's alleged trauma. He explained how he would petition the court to immediately terminate the visitation rights for Jennifer's father. As a result, mother and grandmother knew that Mr. Lester was a wise and perceptive man whom they could trust completely.

Though they may be totally unfounded, accusations of sexual abuse can create a social network that emphatically endorses the allegations. These networks encourage conformity with their definitions of reality by surrounding themselves with a kind of semipermeable membrane. Any input, ranging from accurate anecdote to unbridled conjecture, is allowed into the network as long as it assumes that sexual abuse has occurred. In contrast, input that challenges the veracity of these allegations marks the individual who expresses it as a deviant, and such input is rejected by the network as undeserving of any consideration.

INVALIDATING INFORMATION

In response to documented complaints from the child protection agency and Jennifer's treatment facility, a police department undertook an investigation of the father. He initially responded to the police interview with bewildered disbelief, followed by outraged protests, and ending with his decision to terminate the interview and obtain the services of an attorney.

The father's attorney, Ms. Martin, arranged for a private polygraph examination, which he passed with flying colors. When Ms. Martin forwarded this evidence to the police department, they requested that the father take a polygraph examination given by their examiner. After conferring with Ms. Martin, Jennifer's father took the second polygraph, which he passed as decisively as the first. At this point, the police investigation came to a grinding halt.

Subsequent psychological evaluation by a court clinic revealed that the father had been living with his fiancée for approximately 1 year. He worried that the court might terminate visitation for a noncustodial parent residing with "an unrelated member of the opposite sex." As a result, he concealed his living arrangement from most people except Jennifer. In fact, his fiancée was the "secret" that Jenny would not discuss.

As the falsity of the allegations in this case became more evident, the father's relationship with Jennifer was partially restored via supervised visitation. Nonetheless, their father–daughter bond still suffers from the false accusations of sexual abuse. Supervised visitation was ordered in this situation to both protect the father from future unfounded allegations and reduce the opposition of mother, grandmother, and the therapist to any visitation contact between Jennifer and her father.

Overview

False allegations of sexual abuse both influence and are influenced by the situational settings in which they occur. Overwhelmed by unrelenting worry about their children's welfare, anxious parents convince themselves that their child has been sexually abused. Child protection agencies and treatment facilities respond to the genuine convictions of these parents, endorsing the apparent legitimacy of their concerns. The parents conform to the expectations of these agencies and facilities, while also expressing gratitude for the "help" they and their children receive. Thus, individuals such as anxious parents and concerned others—and social institutions such as child protection agencies and treatment facilities—alternate back and forth both influencing and being influenced by each other. They take turns constructing rumors that appear to verify false allegations of sexual abuse.

It is mistaken to assume that false allegations of sexual abuse originate exclusively as a result of the personality characteristics of those who promote them. Admittedly, some personality types appear more inclined to embrace premature conclusions regarding sexual abuse. Nonetheless, false allegations of sexual abuse typically involve powerful situational considerations.

Ambiguous situations arouse so much anxiety, for example, that they motivate persistent attempts at clarifying them. If we cannot clearly define a situation, we do not know how to deal with it. When attempting to contend with the ambiguity of suspected child sexual abuse, people often confuse clarification with rumor formation. Ultimately, then, false allegations of sexual abuse thrive in response to rumors, but they originate as a result of ambiguity.

It is therefore imperative to point out the differences between a *false* allegation of sexual abuse and a *fabricated* allegation. False allegations typically do not involve situations where someone sets out with premeditated malice to create a groundless accusation of sexual abuse. Instead, false allegations characteristically involve situations where people prematurely leap to mistaken conclusions—but do so genuinely and sincerely. Cases of fabricated allegations—wherein someone sets out with deliberate intent to concoct an allegation of sexual abuse—do happen, but they occur much less frequently than cases of false allegations.

For example, I was involved in a case in which a mother directed allegations of sexual abuse at her former husband. She claimed he had sexually abused their 5-year-old daughter. In response to these allegations, the father took a private polygraph examination and passed it. He then underwent a police polygraph, which he also passed. In turn, the mother also passed both private and police polygraph exams. These developments left the attorneys and the judge bewildered. Convinced that either mother or father was lying, they could not reconcile the results of the polygraphs. In fact, however, both mother and father were telling the truth. Father had not responded in any sexually inappropriate manner to his daughter, and mother had not premeditatedly led the child into fabricating the allegations.

Circumstances such as these underscore a difficult dilemma for professionals contending with allegations of sexual abuse; namely, parents and children alike can report false allegations of sexual abuse without consciously fabricating them. Consequently, assessing allegations of sexual abuse requires that evaluators determine: (1) Who first suspected that the child had been sexually abused—who was the original complainant? (2) How much time elapsed from initial suspicion until apparent "confirmation" of sexual abuse? (3) Between initial suspicion and apparent confirmation, with whom did the original complainant share his or her concerns, what was discussed, and how did those dialogues influence the child's reports? These questions allow interviewers to identify the characteristics of the social networks that develop in response to allegations of sexual abuse, and to assess the capacity of those networks for transforming worrisome rumors into unwarranted facts.

The considerations outlined above obviously raise questions related to how effectively do mental health professionals assess allegations of sexual abuse. Can mental health professionals obtain reliable evidence about these allegations for police agencies and courts? And what kinds of standards should be established for evaluating these cases? We turn to Chapter 3 to examine these issues and others.

3

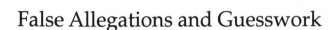

False Allegations and Guesswork

In 1962, the *Journal of the American Medical Association* published one of its best-known and most influential articles, "The Battered-child Syndrome."[1] This article specified well-defined indicators for identifying children who have been physically battered. In particular, the article explained that children under 4 years old who exhibit multiple injuries, in different stages of healing, are likely suffering the effects of physical abuse. Though children will experience sprains, fractures, bruises, and abrasions in the normal course of their everyday activities, multiple injuries in different stages of healing are more uncommon than not. As a result, medical personnel who encounter young children exhibiting numerous injuries in various stages of healing must consider the possibility that they are dealing with a battered child.

ACCOMMODATION SYNDROME

In 1983, child psychiatrist Roland Summit outlined what he termed the "Child Sexual Abuse Accommodation Syndrome."[2] In a manner similar to the "battered-child syndrome," Summit described five characteristics he claimed were commonly observed in sexually abused children:

1. *Secrecy*—The child has been programmed by a perpetrator of sexual abuse to keep the abuse a secret.
2. *Helplessness*—The child is overwhelmed with feelings of helplessness in contending with the abuse.
3. *Entrapment and accommodation*—Feeling overwhelmed with helplessness, the child "accommodates"—or complies with—the perpetrator's expectations.
4. *Delayed, conflicted, and unconvincing disclosure*—Feelings of helplessness, and the related history of accommodation, leave the child very ambivalent about disclosing abuse. As a result, the child's disclosure is delayed, conflicted, and/or unconvincing.
5. *Retraction*—Having disclosed past sexual abuse, children will then retract their disclosure in response to pressure from the perpetrator and other adults attempting to protect the perpetrator.

The accommodation syndrome cannot be used as a diagnostic procedure equivalent to the battered-child syndrome.[3] Rather than detect sexual abuse, the accommodation syndrome *assumes* that abuse has occurred and explains the child's reactions to it. In cases of battered child syndrome, one proceeds from the characteristics of the injury to conclusions regarding the cause of the injury. Therefore, battered child syndrome can be indicative of physical abuse. With the accommodation syndrome, however, one reasons from the *assumption* of sexual abuse, to explaining the child's reactions to this assumed event. Thus, the accommodation syndrome is not a sexual abuse version of the battered child syndrome.

Misuse of the Accommodation Syndrome

Unfortunately, mental health professionals frequently misuse the accommodation syndrome. In particular, they often rely on this syndrome to support their opinions concluding that a child has been sexually abused. Reviewing the five defining characteristics of the syndrome, however, leads to the conclusion that they are vague and ill-defined. Consequently, they invite a wide range of subjective opinion resulting in an unacceptable number of mistaken classifications.

Secrecy.   Attempts at applying this characteristic in practice raise questions such as what behaviors qualify as secrecy. All families have family secrets—Mom sometimes swears when she's angry, and Dad really does not like Uncle Elmer for always eating both drumsticks at Thanksgiving. Therefore, at what point does a child's secretive behavior reflect the programming suggested by the accommodation syndrome? There is no available evidence indicating that mental health professionals can agree on this issue.

Helplessness. By definition, all children are helpless compared with their adult caretakers. Therefore, at what point does the relative helplessness of a child become overwhelming as the accommodation syndrome implies, and can mental health professionals agree on this issue?

Entrapment and Accommodation. To belabor the obvious, psychologically well-adjusted children comply with the behavioral expectations of their parents. Therefore, at what point does the compliance of well-adjusted children amount to "entrapment and accommodation," and can mental health professionals agree in response to this question?

Delayed, Conflicted, and Unconvincing Disclosure. Children who mistakenly report false allegations of sexual abuse—as a result of contaminating memory with imagination—will also express delayed disclosures that are conflicted and unconvincing. In other words, both false disclosures of sexual abuse and legitimate disclosures can be delayed, conflicted, and unconvincing. These considerations then raise the following question: How accurately can mental health professionals discriminate between the delayed, conflicted, and unconvincing disclosures related to false allegations, and those same kinds of disclosures when associated with legitimate allegations?

Retraction. This characteristic is "double-headed," and as such it is grossly unreliable. If a child does not retract a previous disclosure of sexual abuse, mental health professionals can assume the disclosure is legitimate. On the other hand, if a child does retract a previous disclosure, these professionals can still assume sexual abuse. Quite obviously, then, this characteristic can never reliably discriminate between children who have been sexually abused and those who have not.

OTHER INDICATOR LISTS

Despite the many shortcomings undermining the accommodation syndrome, similar lists attempting to identify sexually abused children continue to proliferate. For example, consider the following list published by the American Medical Association in 1985.[4] This list also claims to identify children who have been sexually abused by specifying their behavioral characteristics.

- Become withdrawn and daydream excessively
- Evidence poor peer relationships
- Experience poor self-esteem
- Seem frightened or phobic, especially of adults
- Experience deterioration of body image
- Express general feelings of shame or guilt
- Exhibit a sudden deterioration in academic performance
- Show pseudomature personality development
- Attempt suicide
- Display a positive relationship toward the offender
- Display regressive behavior
- Display enuresis and/or encopresis
- Engage in excessive masturbation
- Engage in highly sexualized play
- Become sexually promiscuous

Another list claims that the following behavioral characteristics can be used to identify sexually abused children.[5]

- Overly compliant behavior
- Acting-out aggressive behavior
- Pseudomature behavior
- Hints about sexual activity
- Persistent and inappropriate sexual play with peers or toys or with themselves
- Sexually aggressive behavior with others
- Detailed and age-inappropriate understanding of sexual behavior
- Arriving early at school or leaving late with few, if any, absences
- Poor peer relationships or inability to make friends
- Lack of trust, particularly with significant others
- Nonparticipation in school and school activities
- Inability to concentrate in school
- Sudden drop in school performance

- Extraordinary fear of males, of strangers, or of being left alone
- Complaints of fatigue or physical illness, which could mask depression
- Low self-esteem

Questions of Diagnostic Sensitivity and Specificity

Ultimately, all indicator lists of sexual abuse fail because they neglect considerations of both "diagnostic sensitivity" and "diagnostic specificity."[6] Diagnostic sensitivity refers to how accurately an indicator identifies a population exhibiting some characteristic such as sexual abuse. Diagnostic specificity refers to how accurately an indicator identifies the population that does *not* exhibit that characteristic. Applied to allegations of sexual abuse, diagnostic sensitivity asks, can this indicator *rule in* sexual abuse? Diagnostic specificity asks, can this indicator *rule out* sexual abuse?

Interestingly enough, the diagnostic sensitivity of an indicator might be quite good, but its specificity can be very poor. For example, consider the following classification rule based on age and gender: Diagnose all males over 50 years of age as having prostate cancer. In fact, these are very sensitive indicators of prostate cancer. More than 99% of the population suffering from prostate cancer are males over 50 years of age. Thus, this decision making rule will miss less than 1% of the population with prostate cancer.

The obvious flaws of this classification rule only become evident when we consider that portion of the population that does not have prostate cancer. In fact, only about 10% of the male population over 50 years of age ever develops prostate cancer. Therefore, this classification rule will be mistaken approximately 90% of the time. Nevertheless, this 90% rate of error does not reveal itself until we address considerations of diagnostic specificity—or ruling out a condition.

Indicator lists of sexual abuse, however, preoccupy themselves excessively with considerations of diagnostic sensitivity, and they naively overlook considerations of diagnostic specificity. In other words, the ill-informed professionals who rely on these indicator lists are so determined to rule in sexual abuse, they overlook evidence ruling out abuse.

Because children who have not been sexually abused frequently exhibit the behaviors specified by various indicator lists, relying on them leads to an unacceptable number of misclassifications. In particular, indicator lists result in many more false-positive classifications (concluding a child has been sexually abused, when in fact no abuse occurred) than false-negative classifications (concluding a child has not been sexually abused, when in fact the abuse did occur).

Affirming the Consequent

Attempting to invoke "behavorial indicators" as evidence of prior sexual abuse also commits the logical error of "affirming the consequent." This error can be outlined in the following manner:

1. Given that condition A prevails, we can then assume condition B.
2. Therefore, if condition B is present, we can also assume condition A.

For example, if I am told that a person unknown to me is pregnant (condition A), I can accurately assume that this person is female (condition B). However, if I know that some person is female (condition B), I cannot necessarily assume that she is pregnant (condition A).

Inferring that someone has been sexually abused as a result of exhibiting various behavioral indicators amounts to a mistaken attempt at "affirming the consequent." For instance, mental health professionals frequently infer a history of sexual abuse on the basis of a child's "sexualized play." Nevertheless, exploration of genitals (e.g., playing doctor) and other sexually related acts (e.g., kissing games) are also characteristic of children who have not been sexually abused.[7] In particular, 85% of a sample of nonabused college women reported having participated in sexual games during childhood.[8]

Misuse of Indicator Lists

Despite the many problems undermining the reliability of indicator lists of sexual abuse, they are frequently used by professionals to support their testimony in courts of law. In the Kelly Michaels case, for example, the prosecution's horribly ill-informed expert—Eileen Treacy—repeatedly cited her own indicator list. Treacy relied on her version of Summit's accommodation syndrome, calling it the "child sexual abuse syndrome."

In addition to her "child sexual abuse syndrome," Treacy also relied on a list of 32 behaviors. She described these behaviors as reliable indicators for identifying sexually abused children. Items on her checklist were: (1) eating problems (over/under), (2) sleep problems, (3) needs to sleep with light on, (4) won't sleep alone, (5) comes into others' beds at night, (6) nightmares, (7) cries out in sleep, (8) accident prone, (9) sucks thumb, (10) baby talk, (11) toilet accidents (day or night), (12) clinging behavior, (13) separation problems, (14) won't dress self, (15) won't feed self, (16) excessive bathing/fear of bathing, (17) won't toilet by self, (18) seems to be in a fog, (19) serious temper tantrum, (20) daydreams, (21) aggressive to smaller children/animals, (22) stares blankly, (23) talks about sex a lot, (24) touches self excessively in private spots, (25) postures body sexually, (26) sexually acts out with toys or children/animals, (27) crying spells, (28) hyperactive, (29) withdrawn, (30) change in school behavior, (31) overcompliant behavior, and (32) fear of men.

Unreliability of Indicator Lists

To belabor the obvious, many of Treacy's 32 indicators are so ill-defined that they cannot be used consistently by two or more professionals evaluating the same child. For example, at what point do the normal mishaps characteristic of 3- to 6-year-olds amount to being "accident prone"? Children of this age also frequently respond to new and unfamiliar situations by maintaining physical closeness with a trusted caregiver. At what point does this normal behavior qualify as "separation problems"? And when does the brief, unthinking aggressiveness of a child amount to "aggressive to smaller children/animals"? In other words, these indicators lead mental health professionals into ill-conceived opinions premised on intuitive impressions.

Even more alarming is the extent to which Treacy's indicators cite behaviors commonly seen in well-adjusted children without any history of sexual abuse. For example, what child has not periodically frustrated his or her parents by not eating? Furthermore, how many perfectly normal children prefer to sleep with a night light? Additionally, show me a 3- to 6-year old who never appears "lost in a fog" because of "daydreaming," and I will show you a child who is not developing normally. Finally, children between the ages of 3 and 5 typically exhibit a heightened interest in sexual matters.

In the Kelly Michaels trial, Treacy told the jury that the presence of 5 to 15 of her indicators confirmed sexual abuse. Consequently, Treacy was much more committed to concluding that a child had suffered abuse than identifying children who had not been abused. If it takes only 5 of Treacy's indicators to substantiate sexual abuse, then practically any and all children can be classified in this manner.

The prosecutor in the Kelly Michaels case eagerly cheered Treacy's testimony, describing her as "an encyclopedia of sexual abuse." The judge recognized her as an "expert in the field of psychology, including child psychology and child sexual abuse treatment." In fact, however, Treacy had never earned a doctoral degree, nor was she licensed to practice psychology in New Jersey or any other state. She moreover admitted that her credentials as a sex abuse expert were essentially self-proclaimed. Nonetheless, these sobering considerations never dissuaded the prosecutor and the judge from portraying Ms. Treacy as some kind of oracle.

Cross-Examining Indicator Lists

If the judge in the Kelly Michaels case had not been so determined to protect Ms. Treacy, well-prepared cross-examination could have effectively discredited her indicator list. In particular, any professional who resorts to indicator lists when testifying should be prepared to answer the following questions:

1. Is it your opinion that the behavioral indicators you relied on in arriving at your opinion in this matter are, in fact, *reliable indicators* of sexually abused children?

Ms. Treacy, or any other professional who relies on indicator lists, would most assuredly answer "Yes" to this question. Otherwise, why would they premise their opinions on these lists? An affirmative response then leads to the next question.

2. If these indicators are reliable indicators of sexually abused children, then can we expect that two or more mental health professionals—independently evaluating the same child—would reach the same conclusions using these indicators?

In response to this question, many mental health professionals reply that they and their colleagues agree regarding the supposed significance of these indicators. Taking this position also allows them to confidently claim that these indicators are "generally recognized and accepted" by their particular profession. With the next question, however, their confidence begins to erode.

3. If two or more mental health professionals independently evaluate the same child and reach the same conclusion, does that demonstrate interrater reliability?

Interrater reliability refers to statistical procedures for assessing the extent of agreement between two or more people making the same kinds of judgments. Applied to indicators of sexual abuse, questions of interrater reliability ask: If two or more mental health professionals rely on the same indicator list, will they agree in their findings for the same case? If mental health professional A finds evidence of a child exhibiting characteristics of secrecy or helplessness, for example, will mental health professional B reach the same conclusions regarding the same child?

To further explain, assume that a new procedure has been developed for diagnosing skin cancer. Assume also that ten dermatologists examine the same sample of skin using this new diagnostic procedure. If these dermatologists arrive at different opinions regarding the presence or absence of cancer, this diagnostic procedure is unreliable. For example, if five dermatologists conclude that cancer was present, but the other five conclude the opposite, then 50% of the opinions are wrong—underscoring the unreliability of this procedure. The next question addresses just such a problem.

4. In your opinion this list of behavioral indicators is reliable, but can you cite any empirical evidence published in a legitimate, peer-reviewed journal demonstrating their interrater reliability?

There has never been any evidence published in a legitimate journal demonstrating an acceptable level of interrater reliability for indicators of child sexual abuse. Therefore, a self-proclaimed expert may insist that these indicators are reliable, but such claims merely amount to unsubstantiated opinion. There is no factual evidence available to support those claims. The next question emphasizes the extent to which the expert's opinion is inherently unreliable.

5. In other words, this court can only rely on your unsubstantiated opinions regarding the reliability of these indicators. Correct?

At this point, ill-informed experts can be expected to begin losing their composure. In replying to the above question, any expert who has relied on an indicator list can only answer "Yes." The expert's affirmative response also suggests that he or she practices in a grossly unreliable manner.

If the mental health professional who has relied on an indicator list is a psychologist, then he or she is also contending with difficult ethical considerations. Principle 1.06 of the relevant ethical code for psychologists states: "Psychologists rely on scientifically and professionally derived knowledge when making scientific or professional judgments or when engaging in scholarly or professional endeavors."[9] Quite simply, there is no scientifically or professionally derived knowledge available to support the use of indicator lists.

Moreover, Principle 7.04 (b) of this ethical code, regarding the legally related endeavors of psychologists, states: "Whenever necessary to avoid misleading, psychologists acknowledge the limits of their data or conclusions."[10] Consequently, psychologists are ethically obligated to respond accordingly. They must acknowledge that the unavailability of interrater reliability data for indicator lists profoundly limits any conclusions premised on them.

6.   Would you please explain to the court what the difference is between diagnostic sensitivity and diagnostic specificity?

The previous five questions typically leave self-proclaimed experts so shaken, they often find it difficult to answer this question. Many professionals who rely on indicator lists are so ill-informed, they fail to comprehend the differences between diagnostic sensitivity and diagnostic specificity. Consequently, it is often necessary to ask the next question for clarification purposes.

7.   Would you agree that applied to this case, (a) diagnostic sensitivity refers to how accurately an indicator identifies children who have been sexually abused? (b) Diagnostic specificity refers to how accurately an indicator identifies children who have not been sexually abused?

The answers to these two questions are so self-evident that even a moderately informed expert is obligated to answer "Yes." Some experts, however, may try evading this question by claiming they do not recognize the distinctions between diagnostic sensitivity and diagnostic specificity.

Experts who respond in this manner are merely demonstrating how woefully ill-informed they are.

8. In arriving at your opinions in this matter, I assume you were very concerned with considerations of diagnostic sensitivity. Do these indicators accurately identify children who have been sexually abused?

Indicator lists have been designed for the express purpose of ruling in allegations of sexual abuse. The lists do not allow a mental health professional to rule out such allegations. Therefore, any expert who has relied on an indicator list is obligated to answer "Yes" to this question.

9. In arriving at your opinions in this matter, did you even think about considerations of diagnostic specificity, that is, do these indicators accurately identify children who have *not* been sexually abused?

This question identifies the biases often undermining the professionals who assess allegations of sexual abuse. Too often, they disregard the possibility of false allegations. In fact, some of these professionals describe their assessments of sexual abuse allegations as "validation" procedures, while also designating themselves as "validators."[11] In their determination to "validate" or confirm allegations, they overlook another compelling hypothesis, namely, that the allegations amount to rumors masquerading as facts.

In a pretrial deposition, for example, a particularly ill-informed expert was asked: "What evidence could you have found to persuade you that Mr. Smith did not sexually abuse his daughter?" The expert replied, "Only if he could have proven he was in China when the alleged abuse occurred." In other words, the only outcome that could have disconfirmed the allegation for this expert was an exceedingly unlikely event. Admittedly, this expert's response may have been motivated by her glibness more than anything else. Nonetheless, her inability to specify any other evidence that might have ruled out the allegations indicates a persistent bias in her thinking.

10. Can you cite any empirical evidence published in a legitimate, peer-reviewed journal reporting the diagnostic sensitivity and diagnostic specificity of these indicators?

As previously indicated, this evidence does not exist. Consequently, this question alerts a court to how ill-advised it is for any mental health professional to rely on indicator lists when testifying in a legal proceeding.

11.   Once again, then, this court can only rely on your unsubstantiated opinions regarding the diagnostic sensitivity and diagnostic specificity of these indicators. Correct?

This question establishes that experts who resort to indicator lists cannot claim their position is generally accepted by the relevant scientific or professional community. General acceptance of some classification procedure necessitates that those using it consistently reach the same conclusions. In other words, professionals cannot claim general acceptance of a procedure without agreeing on the results obtained from it.

12.   If your thinking in this case responded more to considerations of diagnostic sensitivity than diagnostic specificity, could that be indicative of a systematic and persistent bias on your part?

This final question forces ill-informed experts to acknowledge the likelihood of their own biases. The combined impact of these 12 questions typically leaves the undeserved confidence of biased experts severely shaken. An attorney who used these 12 questions quite effectively in a criminal case wanted to conclude her cross-examination with one more: "Dr. Jones, would you now like to limp off the stand and go lick your many wounds?" Tempted as she was, however, this attorney decided against such a coup de grace.

SEXUAL ABUSE LEGITIMACY SCALE

In the midst of the growing hysteria related to allegations of child sexual abuse, Dr. Richard Gardner stands out as a courageous figure. He has wisely advised careful deliberation in situations that too often provoke reckless abandon. His numerous articles and books have resulted in him acquiring the status of nationally recognized expert. Gardner's 1987 book *The Parental Alienation Syndrome* perceptively identified allegations of child sexual abuse as minefields that mental health professionals should navigate with skeptical caution. In particular, *Alienation Syndrome* prompted considerable attention for Gardner's "Sexual Abuse Legitimacy Scale" (SAL scale).

His 1992 book *True and False Accusations of Child Sex Abuse* further outlined developments and refinements related to the SAL scale. Unfortunately, however, Gardner's commendable sense of social responsibility motivated the development of a seriously flawed evaluative procedure.[12] Despite his well-deserved reputation as a paragon of reason confronting powerful but frequently irrational forces, Gardner's SAL scale creates many more problems than it solves.

Gardner emphasizes that his SAL scale should be used only after: (1) interviewing the child, (2) interviewing the accuser, and (3) interviewing the alleged perpetrator. Typically, however, it is rare that an expert retained by the defense in a criminal matter will be allowed to interview the child. Moreover, it is equally rare that an expert retained by the prosecution will be allowed to interview and evaluate the alleged perpetrator. Nevertheless, mental health professionals too often disregard these procedural recommendations, instead focusing their attention on that portion of the SAL scale for "the child who alleges sex abuse."

The Child Who Alleges Sex Abuse

In assessing allegations of child sexual abuse, Gardner relies on the following criteria for differentiating between legitimate and false allegations. The criteria listed below constitute only a portion of Gardner's SAL scale; nevertheless, examining only these criteria suffices for identifying its many shortcomings. Gardner regards these criteria as "very valuable," compared with other criteria he considers only "moderately valuable," and still other criteria he describes as "low but potentially higher value."

- Is the child very hesitant to divulge the alleged sexual abuse?
- Does the child fear retaliation by the accused?
- Does the child exhibit guilt over the consequences to the accused of the divulgences?
- Does the child experience guilt over participation in the alleged sexual acts?
- Does the child provide specific details of the alleged abuse?
- Is the child's description of the alleged abuse credible?
- Does the child's description of the alleged abuse vary over repeated interviews, or is it consistent?
- Has the child exhibited frequent episodes of sexual excitation, apart from the alleged abuse?

- Does the child consider his or her genitals to have been damaged?
- Has the child engaged in sexualized play at home or during the interview?
- Has the child been threatened or bribed by the accused to discourage disclosing the alleged abuse?
- Did the allegation originate in the context of a child custody dispute?

Shortcomings of Gardner's SAL Scale

Though Gardner prefers to speak of the "criteria" on which the SAL scale relies, his scale merely amounts to another indicator list. Therefore, it is necessary to apply the all-important question of interrater agreement to Gardner's SAL scale: If two or more mental health professionals assess the same child using Gardner's SAL scale, to what extent will they agree in their assessments? There has never been any evidence published in a peer-reviewed journal demonstrating that professionals use the SAL scale in a consistent and reliable manner.

In reviewing the various SAL scale criteria, it also becomes evident that they are vague and ill-defined; as a result, they also invite a wide range of subjective opinion. For example, what is the difference between a child who is reluctant to divulge sexual abuse and a child who is *very* reluctant to divulge? Moreover, can those differences be reliably assessed by two or more mental health professionals? How do two or more professionals differentiate between children experiencing genuine guilt subsequent to participating in sexual acts, and children who feel guilty because of events suggested to them? And how do two or more professionals reliably assess whether a child has engaged in sexualized play at home?

Given the questions posed above, Gardner's SAL scale is as vulnerable to challenge as any other "indicator list." In particular, it would not withstand the previous cross-examination procedure any better than the lists of Summit or Treacy. A careful review of the SAL scale clearly demonstrates that Gardner's "criteria" cannot support expert testimony in legal proceedings. Given the legal tests for determining the admissibility of expert testimomy, Gardner's SAL scale repeatedly falls short of relevant legal standards. Without demonstrated interrater agreement, the SAL scale cannot claim general acceptance by the relevant scientific or professional community.

PROJECTIVE DRAWINGS

Other mental health professionals have sought to identify sexually abused children by examining their drawings. Asking individuals to draw a picture of a house, tree, or person has long been used as a psychological test for assessing personality characteristics. Those requested to make such drawings contend with an ambiguous situation: Where on the paper do they place the drawing? What kind of house? What kind of tree? Draw a male or a female?

This very ambiguity supposedly leads people into projecting facets of their personalities onto their drawings. As a result, these drawings are but one example of the many assessment procedures called "projective techniques." Unfortunately, however, appealing as the assumptions underlying projective techniques may be in theory, there is practically no evidence to support them.

Shortcomings of Projective Drawings

In the fifth edition of her definitive text *Psychological Testing,* Dr. Anne Anastasi perceptively summarized the major problems undermining all projective tests including projective drawings:

> the final interpretation of the projective test responses may reveal more about the theoretical orientation, favorite hypotheses, and personality idiosyncracies of the examiner than it does about the examinee's personality dynamics.[13]

In other words, Anastasi emphasizes how the interpretation of tests such as projective drawings can reveal more about the interpreting psychologist than the person who drew them.

Sharply critical reviews of projective drawings were published as far back as 1957.[14] The 1957 review summarized the results of more than 80 studies related to projective drawings. It concluded: (1) Assumptions regarding the diagnostic utility of projective drawings were not supported by objective evidence. (2) Because of a limited number of cases in which they yielded dramatic results, psychologists continued to rely on them. (3) Some evidence suggested that projective drawings could be used as a rough screening device, serving as a "gross indicator" of overall adjustment. (4) The accumulated evidence available in 1957 more often contradicted—instead of supporting—the assumptions underlying projective drawings.

A 1969 study obtained projective drawings from different groups of subjects including normals and schizophrenics.[15] Twenty well-recognized "experts" were asked to identify the diagnostic group corresponding to each drawing. Although the experts identified the drawings of mentally retarded individuals with considerable accuracy, their accuracy in identifiying other diagnostic groups—including normal and schizophrenic subjects—did not exceed what would be expected from random guessing.

Despite the accumulated data clearly demonstrating the many shortcomings of projective drawings, psychologists continue to use them while indulging in unbridled conjecture. For example, a 1995 study revealed experienced psychologists making the following kinds of ill-advised interpretations based on projective drawings.[16]

> Well it's a rather big man with a lot of anxiety. Short hands that are stiffly held down, I would say an inadequate, anxiously depressed person with identity problems.
>
> There are indications of dependency, lots of buttons and buckles.
>
> Looks [like] a bit of transparency there. Belt with a buckle, button: dependency. There seems to be some sexual problems, certainly that's what the manual would say.
>
> Large, big shoulders; somebody who stands firm. But [he] has his head [inclined] like maybe a child or somebody who is not social.
>
> His eyes are strange and overemphasized. I think he may have problems with men, with some paranoid suspiciousness. . . . The belt buckle would tend to fit in with my suspicions that he's not comfortable in his role as a man.

This 1995 study concluded by emphasizing: "It would seem that therapists tend to find in the projectives that they use whatever they are already disposed to find."[17] In other words, interpretations of projective drawings are substantially influenced by the preexisting expectations of the psychologists who interpret them.

Children's Drawings

Despite the notorious legacy of conjecture and subjectivity undermining the use of projective drawings, another psychologist claims they can be used for identifying children who have been sexually abused. In his 1995 book *The Custody Evaluation Handbook*, Dr. Barry Bricklin outlines his methods for assessing allegations of sexual abuse by analyzing the drawings of children.

Bricklin confidently proclaims:

Some have argued that drawings cannot validly detect sexual abuse. This is misleading. What is true is that psychological tests cannot detect abuse directly; what they *can* detect are the *psychological consequences* of abuse.[18]

Bricklin appears undeterred by 40 years of accumulated data demonstrating that interpreting drawings is tantamount to reading tea leaves. While blithely disregarding this compelling evidence, Bricklin developed criteria for assessing the drawings of children to determine whether they have been sexually abused.

Bricklin specializes in child custody evaluations, also assessing allegations of child sexual abuse in divorce proceedings. As a result, he routinely asks children to draw: (1) a picture of themselves and their mother and (2) a picture of themselves and their father. The drawing characteristics he considers indicative of sexual abuse are the following:

- Lines that are wavy or severely broken in children's drawings of themselves, or in the children's drawings of the accused parent, are seen in the critical body area (hips, genital area, thighs, breasts).
- Compared with the distance between the children's drawings of themselves and the nonaccused parent, there is a dramatic increase in distance between the children's drawings of themselves and the accused parent.
- Children's drawings of themselves, or their drawings of the accused parent, exhibit severe slanting (more than 45 degrees).
- Abused children position a protective boundary around their drawings of themselves (most common) or around their drawings of the accused parent (less common). Bricklin further contends, "If asked about this 'boundary' representation, the child will make light of what she or he has drawn ('Oh, that's nothing,' or 'It's his little bed,' or 'That's really a swing'). Do not be put off by how a child reacts after-the-fact to any aspect of a drawing. What is drawn is always more important than how a child reacts later to what is drawn or how a child verbally describes what has been drawn."
- When children's drawings of their parents' hand or finger size are dramatically different for each parent, Bricklin suspects something negative a parent has done with an enlarged hand or finger. Bricklin further suggests that this indicator is relevant to allegations of abuse only if the enlargement involves one hand, or the fingers of one hand. He contends that enlargements of

both hands correspond to the child enjoying an especially positive relationship with that parent.

• Explicit genitalia are found only rarely in children's drawings
and therefore always amount to a "red-flag" indicator.

• Drawings that involve idiosyncratic or graphic positioning of the
child relative to the accused parent; in particular, for example,
drawings wherein the child's genital area is directly over the face
of a parent.[19]

Evaluating Children's Drawings as Indicators of Sexual Abuse

Carefully reviewing Bricklin's seven criteria indicates that they amount
to another indicator list. His indicators are unique only as a result of relying
on children's drawings. Consequently, our cross-examination outline challenging indicator lists is altogether relevant when evaluating the interpretation of children's drawings.

For example, Bricklin claims that wavy or severely broken lines are
particularly significant in the drawings of children. This claim raises the
question of whether two or more psychologists evaluating the drawings
of the same children would agree regarding the presence of wavy or broken lines. Exactly what constitutes a wavy or broken line can become a
matter of subjective impression. In turn, this subjectivity can result in a
wide range of opinions between two or more psychologists. Similarly, at
what point does the distance between children's drawings of themselves
and the accused parent become significant? Moreover, can two or more
psychologists evaluating the drawings of the same children concur regarding this indicator?

Relatedly, it is necessary to ask if two or more psychologists could
agree whether: (1) a drawing involves severe slanting of 45 degrees or
more, (2) objects seen in a child's drawing qualify as a boundary, (3) there
is an appreciable difference in the hand or finger size between the drawings of each parent, (4) a particular drawing reveals genitalia, or rather the
drawing simply invites overinterpretation of careless scribbling, and (5) a
drawing depicts suggestive positioning of child and parent relative to
each other, versus this merely being a matter of primitive drawing skills.

There are no data available indicating that two or more psychologists
can consistently agree regarding the above questions. As a result, these
questions underscore how using children's drawings to assess allegations
of sexual abuse is colossally ill-advised. Psychologists who attempt to interpret these drawings indulge in totally irresponsible conjecture.

In cases of alleged sexual abuse, psychologists who premise their opinions on projective drawings also risk censure for ethical misconduct. Principle 2.02 (a) of the previously quoted ethical code for psychologists states:

> Psychologists who develop, administer, score, interpret or use psychological assessment techniques, interviews, tests, or instruments do so in a manner and for purposes that are appropriate in light of the research on or evidence of the usefulness and proper application of the techniques.[20]

There are no research data, or any other evidence, even suggesting that projective drawings can accurately identify sexually abused children. Consequently, resorting to projective drawings for this purpose violates Principle 2.02 (a) of the ethical code for psychologists. Such practices neglect to consider the research and relevant evidence regarding the "usefulness and proper application" of projective drawings.

Additionally, Principle 2.04 (a) of this ethical code states:

> Psychologists who perform interventions or administer, score, interpret, or use assessment techniques are familiar with the reliability, validation, and related standardization or outcome studies of, and proper applications and uses of, the techniques they use.[21]

Therefore, even a limited familiarity with the relevant research accumulated since 1957 prohibits responsible psychologists from using projective drawings when assessing allegations of child sexual abuse. Psychologists who ignore these considerations have practically pinned a sign to their backs proclaiming in large, bold letters, "Sue me."

ANATOMICALLY DETAILED DOLLS

Sexually abused children sometimes contend with feelings of embarrassment and humiliation inhibiting their willingness to disclose their abuse. The limited verbal abilities of younger children also make assessments of alleged sexual abuse a difficult endeavor. Throughout the 1980s, various professionals increasingly used anatomically detailed (AD) dolls. They assumed the dolls would facilitate disclosures from abused children. These dolls are typically found in adult and child versions, as well as male and female. The dolls are anatomically correct, possessing detailed male or female genitalia.

When interviewing children in cases of alleged sexual abuse, AD dolls are used encouraging them to demonstrate what they experienced. Many professionals assume that giving children AD dolls reduces the problems related to their limited verbal abilities. Such assumptions led numerous professionals to describe AD dolls as "the magic instrument to entice a child to disclose abuse incidents."[22] Others insisted the dolls are "the most helpful means of interviewing children about sexual abuse."[23] As a result of such claims, still others described the dolls as "common, if not standard, practice in the assessment of sexual victimization in young children."[24] Claims enthusiastically endorsing AD dolls necessitate inquiring as to what evidence is available to support them.

Research Related to AD Dolls

Because AD dolls are sold by different manufacturers, the various dolls are not always comparable. Some of the dolls have oral, anal, and vaginal openings, whereas others do not. There is also no generally recognized and accepted method for using AD dolls when interviewing children. Some professionals videotape children's interactions with the dolls, but others do not. How children respond to the dolls can be as influenced by the particular doll used, or how the child is interviewed, as by whether or not the child has been abused. Not surprisingly, then, two or more professionals can reach different conclusions relying on AD dolls when interviewing the same child.[25]

A 1989 study systematically recorded how 91 nonabused children, aged 2–6, responded to AD dolls.[26] With little to no encouragement, 74% of these children spontaneously undressed the dolls. Trained observers concluded that 64% of the children exhibited emotional reactions to the dolls while undressing them; 71% of the children touched the doll's penis, 13% touched the anus, and 4% touched the vaginal opening.

Many professionals contend that spontaneously undressing an AD doll identifies a child as sexually abused. Other professionals conclude that children who exhibit an emotional reaction to the dolls have been sexually abused. These professionals also consider it quite likely that children have been abused if they touch the dolls' genitalia. Using AD dolls as these professionals recommend could result in numerous misclassifications. These recommendations could mistakenly confirm as many as 74% of nonabused children as sexually abused. To say the least, this is a rather shocking rate of error.

Another study examined how 35 children between the ages of 2 and 6, referred for evaluation of possible sexual abuse, interacted with AD dolls.[27] This study compared the responses of these children with another

35 age-matched children who had not been sexually abused. Of the children referred for possible sexual abuse, 30 of them touched the AD dolls' genitalia at least once during the interview, but 25 of the nonreferred children did the same. Nine of the referred children engaged in sexually explicit play with the dolls, and five of the nonreferred children also did so. In other words, this study found no evidence even suggesting that AD dolls can accurately identify sexually abused children.

Current Status of AD Dolls

In view of the evidence cited above, it is not surprising that AD dolls have fallen into disrepute. Relying on AD dolls can lead professionals into two kinds of errors: (1) mistakenly classifying children who have been sexually abused as not abused and (2) mistakenly classifying children who have not been sexually abused as abused. The frequency with which AD dolls can lead to these kinds of errors resulted in one reviewer emphasizing: "AD dolls are not useful, and should not be used, for determining whether or not sexual abuse has occurred."[28]

Various professionals continue to defend the use of AD dolls despite the issues and evidence cited above. These professionals insist that AD doll interviews are only one component of a more comprehensive evaluation. Their reasoning suggests that even though AD dolls result in many mistakes, using them with other evaluation procedures is somehow justifiable.

Such thinking is tantamount to claiming that when combined with sophisticated procedures such as CAT scans, phrenology can assist neurologists in their diagnostic work. Phrenology is a totally discredited procedure for measuring the bumps and curvatures of the head. Nevertheless, if Dr. A relies on a CAT scan only for diagnostic work, but Dr. B uses a CAT scan and phrenology, we can apparently place greater faith in the opinions of Dr. B. While emphatically rejecting this kind of nonsensical argument, other reviewers have also deplored the use of AD dolls: "We are left with the conclusion that there is simply no scientific evidence available that would justify clinical or forensic diagnosis of abuse on the basis of doll play."[29]

OVERVIEW

For various methods and procedures including Summit's accommodation syndrome, numerous indicator lists of abuse, Treacy's sexual abuse syndrome, Gardner's SAL scale, projective drawings, and AD dolls, the verdict is clear and evident: They do not work. Nevertheless, the failures of these procedures teach us an important lesson. Appealing as some procedure may be in theory when assessing allegations of child sexual abuse, theoretical appeal is never an acceptable substitute for hard evidence. Many elegant theories have been slain by ugly facts, and the issues and evidence reviewed in this chapter further confirm that observation.

The failed methods and procedures for assessing allegations of child sexual abuse reviewed in this chapter all involve inferential approaches. The assumptions underlying these methods assume that professionals can indirectly infer sexual abuse on the basis of other considerations related to the child's behavior. In other words, attempts are made to infer sexual abuse on the basis of a child's symptoms or behavioral indicators, on the basis of drawings, or on the basis of how a child interacts with AD dolls. Because these indirect inferences result in a chilling rate of error, most investigations of alleged sexual abuse focus more on information obtained directly from children by interviewing them.

In Chapter 4, then, we closely examine how children are interviewed, and how much confidence those interviews deserve. Again, it is imperative to remember that the extent to which interview procedures appear effective does not guarantee their effectiveness.

4

Interviewing Children
or Indoctrinating Them?

Effectively interviewing children in cases of alleged sexual abuse necessitates obtaining critical background information before beginning the interview. As pointed out in Chapter 2, assessing these allegations demands that interviewers first determine: (1) Who originally suspected that the child had been sexually abused—who was the first complainant? (2) How much time elapsed from original suspicion until apparent "confirmation" of sexual abuse? (3) Between original suspicion and apparent confirmation, with whom did the initial complainant share his or her concerns, what was discussed, and how did those dialogues influence the child's reports?

Too often, however, professionals assessing allegations of sexual abuse neglect to obtain this crucially important background information. Rather than carefully identify the circumstances surrounding how an allegation developed, they immediately proceed with interviewing the child premised on what they think they know. Approaching interviews in this manner leads professionals into committing one blunder after another, and quite frequently, these blunders so severely contaminate the entire investigation that they cannot be corrected.

Rumor Formation and Dissemination

At 10 years of age and enrolled in the fifth grade, Jane enjoyed school. She especially liked presenting oral reports to her classmates, and she felt quite pleased with the report she had just given about sexually abused children. Immediately after Jane finished her report, she and the rest of her class went to lunch and then to recess. While on the playground with two of her friends, Jane noticed that one of them—Mary Thompson— seemed unusually quiet and preoccupied. In response to Jane's expressions of concern, Mary told her about being in her Uncle Jerry's hot tub. She thought she remembered Uncle Jerry yelling and pushing her on her behind. Nevertheless, it was difficult for Mary to recall exactly what had happened because it occurred more than 3 months ago.

Sensitized by her earlier report, Jane promptly concluded that Mary's uncle had sexually abused her. Jane shared her opinions with Patti, the other friend on the playground, and the two persuaded Mary that they should inform their teacher, Mrs. Burns, about the abuse she had suffered. Jane eagerly assumed the role of spokesperson as she gathered with Patti and Mary in Mrs. Burns's classroom. In fact, Mary never spoke directly to Mrs. Burns, deferring instead to Jane. Still feeling unsure about what happened in the hot tub, Mary felt content allowing Jane to speak for her. As Mary listened carefully to Jane's dramatic narration of her alleged ordeal, she thought she understood more about what Uncle Jerry did in the hot tub. Mrs. Burns further reassured Mary, telling her she was doing "the right thing by telling the truth."

Mrs. Burns asked the girls to briefly wait by themselves in the classroom while she spoke with another teacher, Mrs. Knight. In response to the concerns Mrs. Burns outlined, Mrs. Knight concluded that Mary's situation was a serious one. Though Jane had not specified exactly what Mary's uncle had done to her, both Mrs. Knight and Mrs. Burns decided the school principal, Sister Agnes Mary, should know about Mary's abuse. The two proceeded to Sr. Agnes Mary's office where they recited the allegations as they understood them. In response to what she heard, Sr. Agnes Mary telephoned Mary's parents. She informed them of Mary's supposed disclosure of her Uncle Jerry molesting her.

Mary did not speak with her worried parents until later that day. By that time, she felt more confident in what she thought she remembered about Uncle Jerry and the hot tub. Jane had helped by explaining what happened to her, listening to what Jane told Mrs. Burns further convinced

Mary of her abuse, and Mrs. Burns moreover told her she had done "the right thing" to tell Jane. When Mary arrived home from school, her mother assumed she already knew what had happened after speaking with Sr. Agnes Mary. In mother's thinking, if you could not trust a nun, then whom could you trust? As a result of presuming what she thought she knew, Mary's mother did not question her daughter. She preferred to avoid further upsetting Mary by pressing for the details of what had occurred. Instead, she contacted the county mental health agency seeking counseling services for Mary.

The mental health agency assigned Mary's case to Mrs. Kneller, a "therapist" who claimed to "specialize" in treating sexually abused children. Subsequent to interviewing Mary's parents for less than 20 minutes, and before interviewing Mary, Mrs. Kneller documented her diagnostic conclusions. She noted that Mary had been "molested by a family member." While rushing to her premature conclusion, Mrs. Kneller remained oblivious to how the allegations in this case originated via a chain of rumors.

In particular, consider the rapid sequence of events in Mary's case: (1) Jane obtains secondhand information from Mary regarding Uncle Jerry's alleged abuse. (2) Jane then conveys thirdhand information to Mrs. Burns (recall that Mrs. Burns never spoke directly to Mary). (3) Mrs. Burns next conveys fourthhand information to Mrs. Knight (Mrs. Knight did not speak with either Jane or Mary). (4) Mrs. Knight and Mrs. Burns transmit fifthhand information to Sr. Agnes Mary. (5) Sr. Agnes Mary then directs her sixthhand impressions to Mary's parents. In other words, by the time Mary's mother learned about these allegations, she was laboring under information removed six times from its original source.

The extent to which rumors and misinformation prevailed over accurate facts in Mary's case became more evident on further investigation. Three months earlier, Uncle Jerry had become irritated with Mary's continual splashing about in his hot tub. He preferred a more tranquil atmosphere for relaxing after a hard day's work. After repeatedly warning Mary that his patience was wearing thin, he finally put his hand beneath her bottom and ejected her from the tub as he had threatened to do. Three months later, this episode was colossally misinterpreted via rumors that progressively spiraled out of control.

When the prosecutor learned how the charges in this case had originated, he offered Jerry a plea bargain. If he pled guilty to a misdemeanor, he would be placed on probation. The charges would also be expunged, and he would have no criminal record, if there were no more "problems" over the next 5 years. Overwhelmed with exorbitant costs related to his legal defense, Jerry accepted the plea.

INTERVIEWER EFFECTIVENESS

It might seem reasonable to assume that the education, training, and accumulated experience of mental health professionals afford them expertise when interviewing children in cases of alleged sexual abuse. In fact, however, this assumption is more often mistaken than not.[1] Additionally, professional identity is unrelated to interviewer effectiveness. The interviews of psychiatrists, psychologists, and social workers are all equally unreliable because they commit the same kinds of errors. To briefly belabor the obvious, the patients mental health professionals see in treatment exhibit problems more frequently than effective adjustment. This skewed exposure to maladjustment results in psychiatrists, psychologists, and social workers developing an exaggerated sensitivity to emotional and behavioral difficulties.

Biased Interviews

In cases of alleged sexual abuse, professionals typically evaluate children by judging whether their symptoms correspond to the kinds of indicator lists outlined in Chapter 3. As previously emphasized, however, these symptoms also frequently occur in normal populations. Unfortunately, mental health professionals commonly ignore this consideration. As a result, they can find evidence of abuse anywhere and everywhere—even when interviewing normal children.[2] They often see evidence of sexual abuse not because it really exists, but merely because they expect to discover it.[3]

For example, consider the following question-and-answer exchange with a child interviewed during the Kelly Michaels case. Notice how the interviewer—Eileen Treacy in this instance—persistently assumed the child had been abused, and proceeded to focus on details consistent with her assumption. Simultaneously, Ms. Treacy disregarded the child's responses indicating that Kelly Michaels had never abused her. In particular, note how the child claims that Kelly's genital area looked the same as hers.

INTERVIEWER   Did Kelly have [pubic] hair?

CHILD   Nah, I know cause it's grown ups . . . I know about that.

INTERVIEWER   So I guess that means you saw her private parts huh? Did Kelly ask the kids to look at her private parts, or to kiss her private part or . . .

CHILD   I didn't really do that . . . I didn't even do it.

INTERVIEWER   But she made you.

CHILD   She made me. She made me . . . But I couldn't do it . . . So I didn't really do it. I didn't do it.

INTERVIEWER   Did it smell good?

CHILD   Shhh.

INTERVIEWER   Her private parts?

CHILD   I don't know.

INTERVIEWER   Did it taste good? Did it taste like chocolate?

CHILD   Ha, ha. No, I didn't even do it.

INTERVIEWER   You *Wee Care* kids seem so scared of her?

CHILD   I wasn't. I'm not even.

INTERVIEWER   But while you were there, were you real scared?

CHILD   I don't know.

INTERVIEWER   What was so frightening about her, what was so scary about her?

CHILD   I don't know. Why don't you ask her?

INTERVIEWER   Did she drink the pee-pee?

CHILD   Please that sounds just crazy. I don't remember about that. Really don't.[4]

Disregarding Incredible Information

The following interview, also from the Kelly Michaels case, demonstrates how an interviewer can remain oblivious to a child's statements that are incredible enough to defy imagination.

INTERVIEWER   Your mommy told me that you had a picture of yourself in your room and there was blood on your penis. Who hurt you?

CHILD   Kelly.

INTERVIEWER   So, your penis was bleeding, oh. Your penis was bleeding. Tell me something else; was your hiney bleeding, too?

CHILD   No.

It is important to remember that the child did not tell the interviewer his penis was bleeding. Instead, the interviewer assumed the child's bleeding penis as an established fact, and then proceeded to mislead the child as a result of this mistaken assumption.

INTERVIEWER   Did Kelly bleed too?

CHILD   No.

INTERVIEWER   Are you sure she didn't bleed?

CHILD   Yes . . . I saw her penis, too.

INTERVIEWER   Show me on [anatomical] doll . . . you saw that? Oh.

CHILD   She doodied on me . . . She peed on us.

INTERVIEWER   And did you have to pee on her at all?

CHILD   Yeah.

INTERVIEWER   You did? And who peed on her, you and who else?

CHILD   [Child names a friend]

INTERVIEWER   Didn't his penis bleed?

CHILD   Yes.

INTERVIEWER   It did? What made it bleed? What was she doing?

CHILD   She was bleeding.

INTERVIEWER   She was bleeding in her penis? Did you have to put your penis in her penis? Yes or no?

CHILD   Yeah . . . and I peed in her penis.

INTERVIEWER   What was that like? What did it feel like?

CHILD   Like a shot.

INTERVIEWER   Did [child's friend] have to put his penis in her penis too?

CHILD   Yes, at the same time.

INTERVIEWER   At the same time? How did you do that?

CHILD   We chopped our penises off.

INTERVIEWER   So, she was bleeding in her penis and you had your penis and your friend's inside her penis?

CHILD   At the same time.[5]

Using Peer-Group Pressure

In the Kelly Michaels case, the interviewers also pressured children into complying with their expectations by telling them what their friends had supposedly said.

INTERVIEWER   All the other friends I talked to told me everything that happened. Johnny told me. Jimmy told me. And now it's your turn to tell. You don't want to be left out, do you?

INTERVIEWER   Boy, I'd hate having to tell your friends that you didn't want to help them.

INTERVIEWER   Oh, come on, we talked to a few more of your buddies. We talked to everybody now. And everyone told me about the nap room, and the bathroom stuff and the music room stuff and the choir room stuff and the peanut butter stuff and everything. Nothing surprises me anymore.

INTERVIEWER   All your friends that I mentioned before were telling us that Kelly, the teacher that we are talking about, was doing something they didn't like very much. She was bothering them in kind of a private way and they were all pretty brave and they told us everything, and we were wondering if you could help us out too, doing the same thing?[6]

As long ago as 1900, a study demonstrated how children change their statements to conform with their peer group—even when the altered reports are mistaken.[7] Peer influences also profoundly influenced children's recollections of a sniper attack on a school in 1984. Some of the children interviewed about this incident were not at the school during the shooting. They were either already on their way home after school, or absent the day of the shooting. Nevertheless, even these nonwitnesses reported memories of the shooting:

One girl initially said that she was at the school gate nearest the sniper when the shootings began. In truth, she was not only out of the line of fire, she was half a block away. A boy who had been away on vacation said that he had been on his way to the school, had seen someone lying on the ground, had heard the shots, and then turned back. In actuality, a police barricade prevented anyone from approaching the block around the school.[8]

Wanting to define themselves as part of the "in-group" that experienced this attack, these children subsequently revised their reports of what they witnessed. Otherwise, they would have felt reduced to "out-group" status. Not surprisingly, many of the children in the Kelly Michaels case responded similarly to avoid feeling excluded from their peer group. This was especially true in response to the encouragement of biased interviewers.

Coercive Interviews

Though the ill-advised interview methods reviewed up to now influence children in subtle and indirect ways, this is not always the case. Consider, for example, the blatantly coercive manner in which the following child was interviewed.

INTERVIEWER   Well, we can get out of here real quick if you just tell me what you told me last time.

CHILD   I forgot.

INTERVIEWER   No you didn't, I know you didn't.

CHILD   I did. I did.

INTERVIEWER   No, come on.

CHILD   I forgot.

INTERVIEWER   I thought we were friends last time.

CHILD   I'm not your friend anymore.

INTERVIEWER   How come?

CHILD   Because I hate you.

INTERVIEWER   Is it because we are talking about stuff you don't want to talk about? What are you a monster now? Huh?

CHILD   I hate you.

INTERVIEWER   No you don't . . . You just don't like talking about this, but you don't hate me.

CHILD   Yes I do hate you.

INTERVIEWER   We can finish this real fast if you just show me real fast what you showed me last time.

CHILD   No.

INTERVIEWER   I will let you play my tape recorder . . . Come on, do you want to help us out? Do you want to help us keep her in jail, huh? . . . Tell me what happened to [three other children]. Tell me what happened to them. Come on . . . I need your help again, buddy. Come on.

CHILD   No.[9]

Though this child withstood the coercive tactics used by this interviewer, most children find it quite difficult to resist such heavy-handed influences. Girls in particular respond to the still prevailing cultural influences calling for their compliance and deference in response to adults. This becomes an especially sobering consideration when we realize that false allegations of sexual abuse involve girls much more frequently than boys.

EFFECTS OF BIASED INTERVIEWS

In cases of alleged child sexual abuse, there is a considerable range of ill-informed interview tactics undermining the reliability of children's statements. Interviewers can persistently indulge their biased assumptions, disregard incredible claims that stagger the imagination, create feelings of peer pressure via suggestibility, and coerce children to the point of intimidating them. As a result, we now shift our attention to examining the effects of these tactics on the children who encounter them.

The case of the *Commonwealth of Kentucky v. Andy Noble* graphically illustrates how children respond to biased interview tactics. This case also demonstrates that despite various objections to the contrary,[10, 11] high-profile cases such as those reviewed in Chapter 1 are not that unusual. As we are about to see, the kinds of errors committed in these relatively well-known cases are often found in comparatively unknown cases. Except for the name of the defendant in the following case—Andy Noble—the names of the other figures have been changed to preserve their anonymity.

Ill-Defined Background and History

Ms. Louise Warren, a social worker employed by Kentucky Child Protective Services, completed documents indicating that allegations of sexual abuse directed at Andy Noble were reported on March 7, 1995. The 62-year-old man was specifically accused of sexually abusing two sisters: Beth, then 5 years old, and Colleen, 6. These allegations originated when Beth supposedly disclosed to her step-grandmother (Emily Larson) that Andy Noble had been fondling her.

In particular, the CPS report of Ms. Warren stated:

> Mr. Larson (the girls' paternal grandfather) stated girls often go to a cousin's house, Belinda, to play and Mr. Noble resides next door to the cousin. Last Thursday, 3-2-95, Beth told his wife Emily that Andy runs his fingers up her butt. Mr. Larson was upset and said his son Jimmy had gone to Mr. Noble's house and confronted him and warned him not to be touching his girls.

In fact, however, Mr. Larson was reporting thirdhand information obtained from his wife. Whatever Beth and Colleen told Ms. Larson about Mr. Noble amounted to secondhand information. Ms. Warren, though, never seemed to recognize how unreliable this information could have been.

In undertaking the investigation of these allegations, Ms. Warren was joined by Detective Brown of the Kentucky State Police. In their preliminary investigation of this case, Ms. Warren and Det. Brown neglected to adequately assess the origins of these allegations. We do not know what supposedly prompted Beth's disclosure, and we do not know if Ms. Larson suspected sexual abuse even before Beth said anything. Moreover, we do not know the extent to which Ms. Larson may have questioned Beth in a leading and suggestive manner. These oversights corresponded to the persistent biases of Ms. Warren and Det. Brown exhibited throughout their investigation. They limited their efforts to finding evidence of Mr. Noble sexually abusing Beth and Colleen. They did not seek evidence indicating that the allegations directed against Mr. Noble could have been false.

On March 9, 1995, Ms. Warren and Det. Brown interviewed Beth, and then Colleen, regarding the allegations of sexual abuse. During the interview, Ms. Warren asked Beth where she was when Mr. Noble allegedly abused her.

> Ms. W   Now where are you when he [Mr. Noble] plays with your putty cat?
>
> BETH   At Theresa's [Belinda's daughter].

Beth's report, indicating she was at Theresa's when Mr. Noble allegedly abused her, is totally inconsistent with subsequent statements Colleen made in her interview. This interview then continued with Ms. Warren asking:

> Ms. W   At Theresa's. And where is Belinda when he's doing this thing? Huh? Who is, who has seen Andy play with your putty cat?
>
> BETH   I don't know.

The above question-and-answer exchange is an example of serious problems related to Ms. Warren's interview technique. She frequently directed multiple questions at Beth; as a result, Beth's responses were often open to interpretation. When Beth said "I don't know," for example, was she responding to (1) Where is Belinda when he's doing this thing? or (2) Who has seen Andy play with your putty cat? or (3) Was she responding to both questions? Ms. Warren then proceeded to direct numerous leading questions at Beth. The following exchange is an example.

Leading and Suggestive Questions

> Ms. W   And what does he do with your butt?
>
> BETH   He sticks his finger up in our hole.
>
> Ms. W   Does he say anything to you when he does this?
>
> BETH   Uh, huh uh [a negative reply].
>
> Ms. W   Does he tell you not to tell?
>
> BETH   He tells me not to tell but I do.

Beth replied negatively when Ms. Warren asked her "Does he say anything to you . . . ?" Ms. Warren then suggested to Beth that Mr. Noble told her not to say anything. Beth, in turn, answered in a manner that complied with the expectation suggested by Ms. Warren. This kind of suggestiveness profoundly undermines the reliability of an interview. Nevertheless, Ms. Warren continued to interview Beth in a suggestive manner. For example:

Ms. W   Has he ever made you touch him?

BETH   Huh uh [a negative reply].

Ms. W   Huh? Have you ever seen his private parts?

BETH   Huh uh [another negative reply].

Ms. W   Huh? Someone told me that he's making you touch him?

BETH   He did.

Ms. W   It wouldn't be your fault if he did, Beth. Has he ever tried to get you to touch him anywheres? Huh?

BETH   Yeah.

Ms. W   And where has he tried to get you to touch him?

BETH   On the private parts and I don't.

Ms. W   Okay. Have you ever seen his private parts?

BETH   No.

Ms. W   Now let's tell the truth here.

BETH   No.

The question-and-answer exchange immediately above reveals how Ms. Warren expected Beth to tell her she had seen and touched Mr. Noble's "private parts." When Beth initially denied doing so, Ms. Warren continued to question her in a very suggestive manner—"Someone told me that he's making you touch him." Beth then complied with Ms. Warren's suggestion—"He did." Ms. Warren proceeded to ask Beth more leading questions regarding what Mr. Noble supposedly said to her.

Ms. W   What did he say to you when he tried to get you to touch his private parts?

BETH   He didn't say nothing.

Ms. W   Now he had to say something to you. How did he ask you?

BETH   He says come here and we say no and then he walks up and, just all the time walks, and then he comes in the house and sets until me and Theresa's done playing, and there he is standing right beside the door, see we was going home one day and he grabbed it.

In asking these leading questions, Ms. Warren responded to her own expectations—pedophiles try to gain a child's trust, attempting to reduce her resistance to complying with his demands for sexual gratification. Consequently, Ms. Warren attempted to elicit information regarding this issue from Beth. In her attempts, she resorted to leading questions directly suggesting to Beth what she expected to hear—"Now he had to say something to you. How did he ask you?" Beth, however, never indicated Mr. Noble saying anything to gain her trust and break down her resistance to the alleged abuse.

Despite Beth previously reporting she never saw Mr. Noble's "privates," Ms. Warren continued directing leading and suggestive questions to her about this issue.

> Ms. W   Someone says they've seen Andy's private parts. Wonder which little girl has seen his private parts?
>
> BETH   Who said it?
>
> Ms. W   Well, I don't know who said it.
>
> BETH   Who told you?
>
> Ms. W   Don't know that either.
>
> BETH   Don't know it, I don't know it either.

Telling Beth that another child saw Mr. Noble's "private parts," and suggestively implying the same thing happened to Beth, severely contaminated the entire interview. Throughout this interview, Ms. Warren continually questioned Beth in a manner designed to confirm her (Ms. Warren's) expectations. As the interview with Beth progressed, she disclosed information that can only be considered implausible.

Magical Fingers

> Ms. W   How do you know he stuck his fingers up your putty cat?
>
> BETH   Because I seen him.

Children who have been sexually abused would respond to a question such as this by specifying what they felt, not what they saw.

> Ms. W   Well, what was you wearing that day?
>
> BETH   Clothes.
>
> Ms. W   Okay.
>
> BETH   Pink clothes.
>
> Ms. W   Well, how did he get to your putty cat?
>
> BETH   Fingers.
>
> Ms. W   Well, you've got pants on right now, what did he do, stand up here and show me. What was you wearing, pants or a dress?
>
> BETH   Pants.

Ms. W   Okay, and how did he get to your putty cat?

BETH   He stick his finger right through them.

Ms. W   Now, show me.

BETH   Right through them.

Ms. W   Really, through your pants, hum?

In other words, Beth claimed Mr. Noble fondled her vaginal area, and that he did so *through* the pants she wore. In view of the impossibility of these allegations, Ms. Warren continued to question Beth about them.

Ms. W   Hum? Does he feel your putty cat underneath your panties or on top of your panties?

BETH   On top.

In her determination to attribute some degree of logic and coherence to Beth's report, Ms. Warren transformed her statement regarding "pants" to mean "panties." Nevertheless, Beth never used the word "panties" until Ms. Warren had done so.

Ms. W   On top of panties? What about you said he stuck his finger up your butt, was that underneath your panties?

Ms. Warren again attempted to elicit details from Beth consistent with her allegations—"was that underneath your panties?" Beth, however, only partially complied with what Ms. Warren suggested.

BETH   Just with panties on, in me, pants on.

Though Beth mentioned "panties," she also continued to insist her "pants" were "on." Ms. Warren asked more biased questions of Beth, stereotyping Mr. Noble as a generally undesirable person.

Stereotype Induction

Ms. W   What do you think we should do to a man like that?

BETH   Put him in jail.

Ms. W   Put him in jail. And your daddy went and jumped on him?

BETH   Daddy said if he laid a hand on me, if he lays a hand on me and Colleen, daddy said he would beat him up.

Ms. Warren's questions encouraged Beth to think of Mr. Noble as a bad man who deserved to be in jail. Stereotyping people in this manner motivates children Beth's age to attribute all kinds of other negative characteristics to them. Consider, for example, a study in which children between 4 and 6 years old played with a man named "Dale," who was actually a confederate cooperating with the experimenter.[12]

In the course of playing with the children, Dale also asked them for their help in taking off his sweater. Half of the children were later interviewed in a neutral manner about Dale and their interactions with him. The remaining children encountered a biased interviewer who incriminated Dale. The incriminating interviewer made statements to the children such as: "He wasn't supposed to do or say that. That was bad. What else did he do?" All of the children were then asked a series of direct questions about what happened with Dale. Children in the incriminating condition gave significantly more inaccurate responses than children in the neutral condition. One-third of the children in the incriminating condition moreover embellished their incorrect responses in an incriminating manner.

For example, asked if Dale ever touched other kids under incriminating conditions, the children indicated: (1) He touched Jason, Toni, and Molly, (2) he touched them on their legs, (3) he kissed them on the lips, and (4) he took their clothes off—"Yes, my shoes, my socks, and my pants. But not my shirt." In comparison with children in the neutral condition, children in the incriminating condition were also more likely to make negative statements about Dale: "The guy came in and did some bad things." These children also agreed that Dale intended to misbehave, fool around, neglect his job, and act mean. Quite obviously, these were the very effects Ms. Warren created by encouraging Beth to stereotype Mr. Noble in undesirable terms.

When Saying Is Believing

Det. Brown then asked Beth for more details related to her allegations. Beth's replies revealed a remarkable facility for imagination.

DETECTIVE B   You said that Andy has touched you how many times?

BETH   Three.

DETECTIVE B   Now these three times, is this on the same day or is this different days?

BETH   Different days.

DETECTIVE B   Has he touched you on three different days?

BETH   Three, three different days.

DETECTIVE B   Okay.

BETH   On Monday, Tuesday, and Saturday.

DETECTIVE B   How do you remember those days?

BETH   I just said them.

In responding to Det. Brown's questions, Beth invented answers attempting to satisfy what she thought he expected of her. It is quite unlikely that a child Beth's age could accurately remember the days of the week when Mr. Noble supposedly abused her. The interview with Beth then proceeded to address other allegations directed at Mr. Noble.

BETH   But when I was a baby I used to, I bited his dangle dang.

Ms. W   You what?

BETH   That's what I told you.

Ms. W   What about his dingly dang, what did you say?

BETH   That I bited his dangle dang when I was a baby.

DETECTIVE B   We can't understand you baby.

BETH   I bited his dangle dang when I was a little baby.

Ms. W   You bit what?

BETH   I bite his dangle dang when I was a little baby.

Ms. W   You bit whose dangle dang?

BETH   Andy Noble's dangle dang.

Ms. W   How long ago was you a little baby?

BETH   I don't know.

Beth later reported that when she supposedly bit Mr. Noble's "dangle dang," she was 1 year old. She furthermore indicated that Mr. Noble did not say anything to induce her to bite his "dangle dang" because "he was asleep."

COLLEEN'S INTERVIEW

Ms. Warren began her interview with Colleen by reassuring her and encouraging her forthrightness. Very rapidly, however, Ms. Warren fell back into her penchant for leading and suggestive questions.

Ms. W   No, don't be scared, we talk to boys and girls every day.

Colleen   He plays with my putty cat.

Ms. W   He plays with your putty cat. Now when you say play with your putty cat, I don't know if I know what a putty cat is. Okay you say he plays with your putty cat, he pulls down your britches, where are you when he does this?

Colleen   At his house.

Ms. Warren again resorted to a very suggestive statement—"he pulls down your britches." This statement originated with Ms. Warren. Colleen had not previously said anything to even imply that Mr. Noble pulled down her "britches." Ms. Warren likely suggested the "britches" episode wanting to avoid the unlikely scenario described by Beth (Mr. Noble supposedly touched Beth by putting his finger *through* her pants). Ms. Warren then asked about the frequency of the alleged abuse.

Ms. W   How many times has he touched your kitty cat? One time? Now are you telling me the truth? Okay.

These multiple questions indicate that Colleen nonverbally replied that Mr. Noble allegedly touched her one time, and that she thought she was telling the truth about this issue. Subsequent questions led to Colleen indicating that when Mr. Noble allegedly abused her, she was in the "back room" of his house, and Beth was with her. To say the least, these were curious claims, because Beth insisted that all episodes of the alleged abuse occurred on the front porch of Belinda's home. Ms. Warren then proceeded to ask Colleen:

Ms. W   And he grabbed you with his cane? Where was his wife at?

COLLEEN   In the house.

Ms. W   Okay. Did she tell him to stop or anything? Did she see what he was doing? Well, what did she say to him?

COLLEEN   Let them kids go.

This question-and-answer exchange indicates that though aware of her husband's allegedly inappropriate behavior, Mrs. Noble limited herself to telling him, "let them kids go." In turn, she supposedly stood by passively as her husband took Colleen and Beth into the "back room." Most alarming is how Ms. Warren and Det. Brown neglected to clarify these unlikely claims with appropriate follow-up questions. Ms. Warren then proceeded to subject Colleen to more leading and suggestive questions.

Ms. W   Let them kids go. Okay. So you all were in the back room? He pulled down your pants? Okay. Did he make you do anything to him? Well someone was telling us that he did make you girls do something to him, touch him somewheres?

Ms. Warren again suggested to Colleen that Mr. Noble pulled down her pants, and apparently, Colleen compliantly agreed with her suggestion in a nonverbal manner. The manner in which earlier suggestions can influence a child's subsequent responses is seen in Colleen's response to a question asked by Det. Brown.

> DETECTIVE B   Did he pull your pants down? Did he pull them all the way down, off, or what did he do?
>
> COLLEEN   He pulled them down.

After the suggestions conveyed by Ms. Warren and Det. Brown, it is not surprising that Colleen told them that Mr. Noble supposedly pulled her pants off. In doing so, she demonstrated the normal inclination of children her age to satisfy the expectations expressed by the adults interviewing them.

Inventing Answers

Det. Brown then attempted to obtain more detail from Colleen regarding her allegations.

> DETECTIVE B   Let me ask, let me ask you, if you know how many different days that he touched you?
>
> COLLEEN   Touched me Sunday, Monday, Tuesday.

Colleen previously said Mr. Noble had touched her on only one occasion. Then when asked these questions, despite her earlier statement, Colleen altered her previous answer, likely assuming she had answered incorrectly. Otherwise, why would Det. Brown have asked her the question if her previous answer had been correct? Ms. Warren then attempted to determine why Colleen supposedly waited so long before reporting the alleged abuse.

> Ms. W   Well, Andy should not have touched you. You didn't do anything wrong. I think you feel bad don't you? And you didn't do anything wrong. And your sister didn't do anything wrong. If anyone ever touches you again then you need to tell someone right then. Do we know why we waited so long to tell? Was you scared?
>
> DETECTIVE B   Why were you scared to tell?
>
> COLLEEN   I don't know.
>
> DETECTIVE B   Did anyone, did anybody tell you not to tell?
>
> COLLEEN   Yeah.

DETECTIVE B   Who told, who told you not to tell?

COLLEEN   Andy.

DETECTIVE B   What did Andy say?

COLLEEN   He said if you ever tell then I'll come and kill you.

Reviewing this question and answer exchange reveals how both Ms. Warren and Det. Brown influenced Colleen. They suggested she did not disclose her alleged abuse more promptly because she was "scared." Colleen originally indicated she did not know why she took so long to disclose. In response to the interviewers' influence, however, she reported a scenario consistent with what they suggested to her. Det. Brown then directed the interview to what Colleen saw when supposedly looking at Mr. Noble's "private part."

DETECTIVE B   Did you ever see anything come out of it? When did you see his dick?

COLLEEN   I never did.

Ms. W   But you told us what it looked like. How did you know that? Huh? Did somebody tell you that or have you seen it?

COLLEEN   I didn't see it.

Ms. W   Have you ever put your mouth on his dick? Has he ever tried to make you? Has he?

COLLEEN   Yeah, but I didn't do it.

Ms. W   Oh, but that's alright, but if you did Colleen, it would have been okay, it wouldn't be your fault.

DETECTIVE B   Did you see his dick when he tried to make you put your mouth on it? So you did see it? What, did he have his clothes off or on or what?

COLLEEN   On.

On two different occasions in the question-and-answer exchange cited above, Colleen said she never saw Mr. Noble's "dick." Det. Brown and Ms. Warren, however, continued to repeatedly question her about this issue, and in response to their suggestive influences, Colleen indicated she did see Mr. Noble's "dick." The interview then moved in the direction of attempting to determine what Mr. Noble supposedly said to Colleen.

DETECTIVE B   How did you, what did he, how did you see his dick?

COLLEEN   Pulled down his britches.

DETECTIVE B   He pulled down his britches? Did he pull his britches, how far did he pull them down?

COLLEEN   To his knees.

DETECTIVE B   To his knees. Now what, what did he do when you saw him do this? Tell us what all he did.

MS. W   What did he say to you, honey?

COLLEEN   He said I'll get a knife on you and Beth if you ever tell.

DETECTIVE B   Do what?

COLLEEN   If you ever get a knife on, if you ever tell anybody I'll get a knife on you and Beth.

Colleen's response was rather implausible. Pedophiles do not threaten their victims before abusing them. Instead, they typically solicit the victims' cooperation by plying them with gifts or promises. Pedophiles will sometimes resort to threats after abusing children and attempting to coerce them into silence, but rarely before abusing them.

Colleen's reply to the questions cited above indicates that in response to Ms. Warren's question—"What did he say to you, honey?"—she could only recall what had previously been suggested to her. Det. Brown and Ms. Warren previously suggested to Colleen that she did not immediately disclose the alleged abuse because she was scared. At that time, Colleen invented a scenario consistent with this suggestion. Then when asked what Mr. Noble said to her, Colleen reports the scenario she created in response to the previous suggestive questions. In fact, however, what Colleen describes Mr. Noble saying simply does not fit the context in which he supposedly said it.

More Implausible Claims

The interview then addressed what Mr. Noble supposedly did when his pants were allegedly down to his knees.

DETECTIVE B   Okay, but now when you saw him pull his pants down, how many times did you see him pull his pants down? Just once, okay, what did he do after he pulled his pants down?

COLLEEN   He tried to make us kiss his dick.

It is important to remember that this response had previously been suggested to Colleen by Ms. Warren and Det. Brown.

DETECTIVE B   Okay, did either one of you kiss it?

COLLEEN   Beth bited it.

MS. W   Beth bited it? Gosh, I bet that hurt didn't it?

DETECTIVE B   What did, tell us more about that, what happened? Did she bite it more than once? Twice? Well, how long did she bite it?

COLLEEN   About two minutes.

DETECTIVE B   Okay, what happened after she bit it for two minutes?

COLLEEN   She went [demonstrating a bite], he went ohhhhh!, and Beth ran out of the house.

During Beth's interview, she said the above incident supposedly occurred when she was 1 year old! Det. Brown and Ms. Warren seemed to ignore how impossible Beth's claims were. Instead, they appeared to accept Colleen's secondhand account of her younger sister's imaginative story as legitimate.

SUMMARY OF BETH'S AND COLLEEN'S INTERVIEWS

While interviewing Beth, Ms. Warren and Det. Brown pressured her into saying: (1) Mr. Noble told her not to say anything about what he allegedly did—despite Beth initially reporting that Mr. Noble said nothing to her. (2) Mr. Noble touched her "putty cat" by putting his fingers *through* her pants. (3) Mr. Noble was a generally undesirable person as she stereotyped him negatively. (4) She remembered the days of the week on which Mr. Noble allegedly abused her. (5) She remembered biting Mr. Noble's "dangle dang" at the age of 1 year.

While interviewing Colleen, Ms. Warren and Det. Brown pressured her into saying: (1) Mrs. Noble merely told her husband, "Let them kids go," while supposedly observing his attempts at abusing Colleen and Beth. (2) Mr. Noble pulled her pants down. (3) She was scared to disclose the alleged abuse to anyone. (4) She saw Mr. Noble's penis. (5) Mr. Noble attempted to make her kiss his "dick." (6) She saw Beth bite Mr. Noble's "dick."

I testified on Mr. Noble's behalf at a pretrial hearing. Carolyn Clark, Mr. Noble's public defender, petitioned the court to review the interviews of Beth and Colleen. My testimony carefully detailed the many errors committed by Ms. Warren and Det. Brown. I moreover explained how the evidence obtained in such interviews is inherently unreliable. After my testimony, the prosecutor offered Mr. Noble a plea arrangement. If he pled guilty to a misdemeanor, the court would sentence him only to the 10 days he had spent in jail since being arrested. In other words, Mr. Noble would serve no more time in jail. Because a guilty plea would have no impact on Mr. Noble's life under these circumstances, he accepted the prosecutor's offer.

CHILDREN'S MEMORY AND SUGGESTIBLITY

Our review of Mr. Noble's case demonstrated how children will tell adults what they think the adults expect to hear. More importantly, however, what happens when children make these grossly mistaken claims and allegations? Don't these children know they are merely telling stories to satisfy the expectations of adults, or could the children actually come to believe their own fabrications? Unlikely as it may seem, children can readily believe their own imaginative tales given the proper conditions.

Leading and suggestive questions, corresponding to the many examples in this chapter, can profoundly distort the memory of children to the degree they report imaginary events as if they happened.[13,14] In response to leading and suggestive questions directed to them by a trusted adult, children can experience considerable confusion.[15] When subjected to repeated questioning that arouses their imagination, children are especially inclined to confuse actual events and imaginary events.[16]

Confusion between actual events and imaginary events transpires because of what is known as the "postevent information effect."[17,18] After witnessing an event, all people—children included—sometimes encounter new information that can actually alter their recall. This new information can profoundly contaminate memory, including the incorporation of fictional details into what we think we remember.

Postevent Information Effects

For example, Jean Piaget, the internationally respected psychologist, reported the following example of how postevent information had distorted his memory:

> one of my first memories would date, if it were true, from my second year. I can still see, most clearly, the following scene, in which I believed until I was about 15. I was sitting in my pram, which my nurse was pushing in the Champs Elysees, when a man tried to kidnap me. I was held in by the strap fastened around me while my nurse bravely tried to stand between me and the thief. She received various scratches, and I can still see vaguely those on her face. Then a crowd gathered, a policeman with a short cloak and a white baton came up, and the man took to his heels. I can still see the whole scene, and can even place it near the tube station. When I was about 15, my parents received a letter from my former nurse saying she had been converted to the Salvation Army. She wanted to confess her past faults, and in particular return the watch she had been given as a reward on this oc-

casion. She had made up the whole story, faking the scratches. I, therefore, must have heard, as a child, the account of this story, which my parents believed, and projected it into the past in the form of a visual memory.[19]

It is important to note the wealth of details that could be interpreted as supporting the veracity of Piaget's "memory": (1) He was sitting in his pram, (2) held in by a strap, (3) as the nurse stood between him and the kidnapper, (4) he could still vaguely recall the scratches on the nurse's face, (5) a crowd gathered, (6) a policeman with a short cloak and white baton arrived at the scene, and (7) the kidnapper then fled. Impressive as these details may seem—and as persuaded as Piaget was by them—the fact remains, he imagined this scene. It never occurred as he remembered it.

Mousetraps and Touching

In a more recent study done at Cornell University, Steven Ceci and his colleagues dramatically demonstrated the effects of postevent information on children between the ages of 4 and 6.[20] These children were asked, "Do you remember when you got your finger caught in a mousetrap and had to go to the hospital to get it off?" Without exception, every child participating in this experiment initially denied any such encounter with a mousetrap. The "interviewers," however, responded to the children by suggesting: "Well I think it happened. I think it did. And I'm going to see you again in a few days to see if you can remember when you got your finger caught in a mousetrap and had to go to the hospital."

In response to frequent repetitions of this question, 58% of the children who participated in this experiment eventually reported remembering this fictional incident. These children also described a wealth of details related to this imagined event. One boy reported:

My brother Colin was trying to get Blowtorch (an action figurine) from me, and I wouldn't let him take it from me, so he pushed me into the wood pile where the mousetrap was. And then my finger got caught in it. And then we went to the hospital, and my mommy, daddy, and Colin drove me there, to the hospital in our van, because it was far away. And the doctor put a bandage on this finger (indicating).[21]

Moreover, the children continued to insist they remembered the "mousetrap incident" even when their own parents subsequently told them no such event ever occurred. Ethical considerations necessitated that the experimenters explain to these children how and why they had been deceived. Initial attempts at satisfying this ethical obligation by debriefing the children alone often failed. The children responded to these debriefings by continuing to insist they remembered the mousetrap incident. Consequently, the experimenters then included at least one parent in the debriefing sessions to assist them. Despite the debriefing participation of one of their parents, some children continued to claim vividly recalling the mousetrap episode.

The mousetrap experiment distorted and confused the recall of children by creating what is known as source-monitoring problems.[22] In these instances of distorted memory, the "interviewers" became the source of what the children remembered rather than the event in question. For example, another study investigated memories for performed actions versus imagined actions (e.g., "did you really touch your nose, or did you just imagine yourself touching your nose?"). Compared with adults, 6-year-olds were far more likely to confuse memories of imagining and memories of doing.[22] Similarly, 8-year-olds also experienced difficulty discriminating between actions they imagined another person doing and actions they saw that person do.[24]

Perhaps even more dramatic is a study demonstrating how easily children can be misled regarding where on their bodies they were touched.[25] In this study, 4- and 10-year-olds watched a slide presentation. In the early stages of the experiment, the experimenter touched each child—for a duration of 10 seconds—on either the hand or shoulder. Approximately 15 minutes later, half of the children were given misleading information. If they had been touched on the shoulder, they were told they had been touched on the hand—or vice versa. After another 10 minutes elapsed, the children were asked questions about the slides they had seen and where they had been touched.

For both age groups, 4- and 10-year-olds, more than 25% of the children misled by the experimenters complied with the misleading suggestions. If told they had been touched on the hand, but actually touched on the shoulder, the majority of the children reported being touched on the hand—or vice versa. This experiment compellingly demonstrates how easily children can become confused and mistaken about where on their bodies someone touched them. Quite obviously, then, children can recall an affectionate hug, or a friendly pat, in a very mistaken manner—and real-life instances of mistaken recall can lead to tragic consequences.

When asked suggestive questions—Did he touch your private? Did he make you touch his private? When he touched you what did he say?—

children imagine scenarios corresponding to the questions they hear. Suggestive questions asked repeatedly lead children into feeling increasingly familiar with the scenes they imagine. In other words, the more children imagine an event, the more familiar it becomes. And as an imagined event becomes more familiar, children are more inclined to think they are remembering it—rather than dismiss it as imagination—because of its familiarity.

Therefore, the research examining the effects of suggestibility on children's memory dramatically demonstrates: (1) it is quite easy to distort a child's memory via leading and suggestive questions and (2) once the child's memory is distorted, the child genuinely believes the distortion.

OVERVIEW

Because children use their imaginations to embellish their reports of misremembered events with persuasive sounding details, their accounts of these "nonmemories" sound very compelling. Not surprisingly, then, the relevant research demonstrates that the accuracy with which various professionals identify children who report factually accurate information— compared with those who do not—is at a level less than chance performance.[26] Specifically, this particular study reported:

> Experts who conduct research on the credibility of children's reports, who provide therapy to children suspected of having been abused, and who carry out law enforcement interviews with children, generally failed to detect which of the children's claims were accurate and which were not, despite being confident in their judgments. . . . Similarly, it may become difficult to separate credibility from accuracy when these children, after repeated interviews, give a formal videotaped interview or testify in court.[27]

To say the least, these are sobering considerations. If children can be so profoundly mistaken in what they think they remember, but appear so compellingly persuasive, how many innocent people are serving time in prison for crimes they never committed? In Chapter 5, we review recently recognized legal hearings designed to protect innocent people from false allegations of sexual abuse. Relatedly, we will also examine the necessity of videotaping all interviews of children in cases of possible abuse.

5

Misinterpretations, Misunderstandings, and Videotapes

In response to the outrageous miscarriage of justice in the Kelly Michaels case, the New Jersey Supreme Court established a procedure to prevent similar tragedies from occurring. The court ruled that in cases of alleged sexual abuse of children, defendants can request a pretrial taint hearing. Taint hearings review the evidence against a defendant, specifically examining it to determine whether it is defective as a result of the kinds of interviews we discussed in Chapter 4. Courts in other states have also adopted this procedure to protect the legitimate rights of defendants charged with sexually abusing children.

The State of Ohio, for example, has defined criteria for determining whether to allow the out-of-court statements of a child into evidence at a criminal trial. This is a particularly important issue, because in cases of alleged sexual abuse prosecutors frequently attempt to bolster their case by relying on the testimony of a professional who interviewed the child. In some criminal trials, the child never testifies in court. The professional who interviewed the child testifies instead. Given the exceedingly biased interviews we reviewed in Chapter 4, the potential for this kind of secondhand testimony to convict innocent people looms ominously over any trial in which it is allowed.

In determining whether to allow a child's out-of-court statements into a trial, the Ohio Supreme Court specified the issues a trial judge must consider. The court ruled these statements are admissible via another person "as long as such statements have indicia of reliability." The court further held that in those cases where "there is no particularized guarantee of trustworthiness, then the child's out-of-court statement is not admissible."

In other words, the Ohio Supreme Court demands that trial judges carefully review the evidence in cases of alleged sexual abuse. Trial judges must determine whether the evidence has been contaminated or tainted. In comparison, for example, consider a criminal case charging a defendant with driving while intoxicated. Assume that a police laboratory accidentally contaminated the defendant's blood sample with the blood of another person. Quite obviously, the blood evidence is tainted, and consequently, it cannot be presented at trial. In cases of alleged child sexual abuse, Ohio courts—and courts in various other states—are obligated to determine whether the evidence against the defendant is so tainted that it cannot be admitted at a trial.

In the case of *Ohio v. Hubert Johnson*, Judge Ed Lane of the Washington County Common Pleas Court addressed this issue of tainted evidence. The importance of this case and of Judge Lane's conclusions deserve a detailed review. Other than the defendant, the judge, and the attorneys, the names of all of the other figures in the case have been changed.

OHIO V. JOHNSON

In late spring, the hills of southeastern Ohio turn a lush green. The afternoon sun radiates throughout the valleys below, inviting people out of their homes and offices to enjoy its warmth. On just such a day, Hubert Johnson relaxed in his parked car, with its windows down, watching his girlfriend's granddaughter, 3½-year-old Brittany. Now retired and in his mid-60s, Hubert felt content to wait patiently while his girlfriend completed various errands in downtown Marietta, Ohio. This tranquil scene was about to be abruptly disrupted.

Behaving as the active child she was, Brittany moved about energetically while playing with her toys and eating a banana. Across the street in a beauty shop, three women observed Brittany and Mr. Johnson sitting in his car. Though the afternoon sun reflecting off the car's front window partially obscured their view, they thought they saw Brittany's head darting rapidly above and below the dashboard. For reasons that will never be clearly understood, they leapt to the conclusion that Mr. Johnson was sexually abusing Brittany. Convinced of what they thought they saw, one of the women called the Marietta Police Department. Within minutes, three police cars with flashing lights and screeching brakes converged on Hubert's vehicle.

Not knowing where Brittany's grandmother was, the police officers removed the girl to the Washington County Children's Services Agency. Hubert was arrested and held overnight in jail. The police also undertook a thorough search of Hubert's car, going over its interior with the proverbial fine-tooth comb. In particular, the officers searched for any physical evidence of sexual abuse such as semen or pubic hair. Despite their determination, they found nothing except for Brittany's scattered toys and her partially eaten banana. In the early evening of that same day, Ms. Moore, a social worker with Washington County Children's Services, videotaped her interview with Brittany. Ms. Moore concluded that Brittany's behavior during the interview confirmed that Mr. Johnson had sexually abused her.

As a man of modest means, Mr. Johnson could not afford to retain an attorney of his own; consequently, the court appointed counsel for him. Rolf Baumgartel, Mr. Johnson's court-appointed attorney, reviewed the videotaped interview of Brittany. Though relatively young and inexperienced, Mr. Baumgartel found what he considered evidence of a poorly conducted interview. Not only did Ms. Moore seem to respond to Brittany in a leading and suggestive manner, she sometimes appeared overtly coercive. Disturbed by what he saw, Mr. Baumgartel contacted me to review the videotape and other related documents in this case.

Never-Ending Interviews

Ms. Moore's interview with Brittany lasted approximately 1 hour and 12 minutes. For the first 22 minutes of the interview, nothing of much significance occurred until Brittany began removing the panties of an anatomically detailed doll. She then proceeded to bite the vaginal area of the doll. At that point, Ms. Moore directed a series of questions at Brittany: (1) "Who did that to your pee-pee?" (2) "Who does that to your pee-pee?" (3) "Is it somebody I know who does that to your pee-pee?" (4) "Did it hurt?"

These questions were exceedingly suggestive and leading because they assumed that Brittany had been sexually abused. Repeatedly directing such questions to Brittany pressured her to find the answers Ms. Moore wanted. Ms. Moore seemed to assume she already knew what happened, and then set out seeking details to confirm her preconceived expectations.

Twenty-five minutes into the interview, Ms. Moore asked Brittany: "Can you show me what Hubie did in the car that wasn't very nice?" This question was so leading and suggestive that it could have motivated Brittany to revise and ultimately distort her memory. Nonetheless, Ms. Moore continued to direct more leading questions at Brittany: (1) "If you won't tell me what happened in the car, will you tell your mother?" and (2) "Remember when you and Hubie were in the car, was Hubie sitting or standing?" Though less obvious than the previous questions, these questions were also leading and suggestive. In particular, Ms. Moore persistently directed Brittany's attention to a particular topic—Hubie and what supposedly happened in the car.

At the 31-minute mark, Brittany clapped the hands of an adult doll together in response to Ms. Moore's prompting. Ms. Moore asked, "Did anybody ever do something to your pee-pee?" Brittany unhesitatingly replied, "No." Ms. Moore then pointed to the doll's penis asking, "What else do you do with that?" Brittany seemed to ignore this question, and she did not reply. It is important to note that when directly asked, "Did anybody do anything to your pee-pee?" Brittany clearly answered, "No." Ms. Moore, however, blithely disregarded Brittany's negative reply, focusing instead on pulling the information from her she expected to hear.

After being interviewed for 33 minutes, Brittany put her finger in the doll's anus and Ms. Moore asked, "Anybody do that to you?" Brittany replied, "No." Apparently dissatisfied with this answer, Ms. Moore repeated the previous question, "Somebody do that to you?" Brittany again replied, "No." Therefore, when asked directly—on two occasions—if anybody ever put anything in her anus, Brittany clearly indicated, "No." As the interview proceeded, however, it became increasingly evident that Ms. Moore simply disregarded what Brittany said unless it conformed with her expectations.

At the 35-minute mark, Ms. Moore asked Brittany, "Do you like sitting in the car with Hubie?" and "What happened while you were waiting in the car?" In what amounted to classic understatement, Brittany replied, "The cops came." Ms. Moore then asked, "What were you and Hubie doing?" Brittany answered, "Nothing." At this point, Ms. Moore took a 3-minute break after which her interview with Brittany continued.

Interviewer Bribery

Immediately after the break Ms. Moore told Brittany, "Talk about the car, then we go get mommy." Ms. Moore then took her watch off saying to Brittany, "So you can see what time it is." Brittany, however, appeared less than impressed and put the watch back on Ms. Moore's wrist. Ms. Moore then suggested, "Let's talk about the car, and then you can play with my watch." At this point, Ms. Moore was resorting to outright bribery attempting to direct Brittany to the topics she wanted her to discuss. Ms. Moore promised Brittany, "we go get mommy" if you "talk about the car." Next Ms. Moore indicated, "you can play with my watch" if "you talk about the car."

Despite Ms. Moore's blatant attempts at manipulating a child who felt increasingly tired and bored, Brittany ignored her efforts. While turning a deaf ear to Ms. Moore's questions, Brittany stood on a chair in the interview room. Ms. Moore responded by insisting, "You have to talk to me." Brittany emphatically replied, "No, no, no." Ms. Moore countered by again promising, "Talk to me and we'll go get mommy" and "A few more questions and we'll go get mommy." Brittany essentially ignored these pleas, finding her reflection in a one-way mirror more interesting than Ms. Moore's begging and pleading.

Ms. Moore's promises about seeing "mommy" likely accomplished little more than to bewilder Brittany. She did not live with her mother, nor had she even seen her mother in a long time. Brittany lived instead with her maternal grandmother. Nevertheless, Ms. Moore neglected to obtain this important background information. Therefore, she was promising an outcome that made no sense to Brittany. Rather than reassure her to any degree, this promise likely confused her. Brittany expected to see her grandmother, not her mother.

At 45 minutes into the interview, Ms. Moore's frustration became increasingly evident. She asked Brittany, "Who told you not to tell?" still assuming there was something to tell. Brittany again ignored this accusatory inquiry, prompting Ms. Moore to raise her voice as she asked, "Did Hubie do something to you?" When Brittany continued not to respond, Ms. Moore resorted to multiple questions: "Did you and Hubie play games in the car, what happened in the car, something good or bad?" Confronted with this never-ending cross-examination, Brittany replied, "Something bad."

At this point, Ms. Moore exited the interview room, quickly returning with a package of cookies for Brittany. Whether intentional or not, the timing of this gift was rather uncanny. When Brittany finally suggested that "Hubie" had done something "bad," she immediately found herself rewarded with a package of cookies. Regardless of what Ms. Moore did or did not intend, the effects of her actions involved outright manipulation and bribery.

Ms. Moore then suggested to Brittany, "Remember you were going to tell me and mommy what Hubie did to you. Did Hubie do something bad in the car?" Brittany replied by simply shaking her head "no." Nevertheless, this statement was so leading and suggestive that it amounted to coerciveness. The question assumes—without any basis for doing so—that Hubie did "something bad" to Brittany.

Is This What You Want?

Ms. Moore then asked: "What about Hubie . . . Hubie bad guy or good guy? Can you show me what you and Hubie did in the car? Good thing or bad thing?" Brittany hestitated a few moments before replying, "Bad thing." Asked repeatedly about the supposedly "bad thing" Hubie "did in the car," Brittany finally began to sense what Ms. Moore expected of her. Ms. Moore followed up her previous question by asking, "What bad things did Hubie make you do?" Brittany answered, "Hubie pooped in the car—back of the car." For a $3\frac{1}{2}$-year-old who is still learning proper toilet etiquette, "pooping" in a car would be a very bad thing. Consequently, we have compelling evidence of Brittany inventing a scenario in an attempt at satisfying Ms. Moore.

Not surprisingly, however, Ms. Moore was less than satisfied with Brittany's "disclosure." As a result, she proceeded to ask, "What else did he do? Did he play with his pee-pee? Did you touch Hubie's pee-pee? Did he touch you with his pee-pee?" In response to this series of questions Brittany replied, "No, no, no." Despite the emphasis with which Brittany answered these questions, Ms. Moore would not accept her replies. Instead, she continued to ask Brittany, "What did he do with his pee-pee, did you touch it?" Brittany responded, "No, no." Ms. Moore then asked, "Did you touch his pee-pee with your eyes, nose, fingers, mouth?" Brittany again replied, "No, no, no."

Disinclined to accept Britany's answers, Ms. Moore continued to ask questions designed only to confirm her hypothesis of sexual abuse. She neglected to ask questions that could have disconfirmed this hypothesis. At the 1-hour mark of the interview, Ms. Moore asked Brittany, "When your head was in his lap, show me what your head was doing, and then we'll go find mommy." Ms. Moore repeated this statement at least three times. In doing so, she assumed as fact what amounted to guesswork on her part—Brittany's head had been in Mr. Johnson's lap. This alleged event had not been corroborated by anyone, it only existed as a rumor having originated with what the trio in the beauty shop thought they saw. Determined to find what she expected to find, however, Ms. Moore ignored any distinctions between facts and rumors that might interfere with her self-appointed mission.

At 65 minutes into the interview, Brittany went to the door of the interview room, pulling on the handle indicating she wanted to leave. Given Brittany's demonstrated desire to terminate the interview, Ms. Moore should have concluded it herself. Prolonging the interview beyond this point merely invited more unreliable information as a result of Brittany's fatigue. Nonetheless, Ms. Moore disregarded these considerations and persisted in her inquisition.

Brittany then began to pull on the penis of the male doll. This development provoked Ms. Moore's eager interest leading her to ask: "Tell me what happened?" and "Who did that—pants fastened or unfastened?" These rapid-fire questions neglected to consider the relevant research demonstrating that nonabused children also react in this manner to anatomical dolls.

Though the interview had now lasted more than 70 minutes, Ms. Moore remained determined in her quest. She rapidly asked a series of questions despite Brittany retreating into a corner of the room: (1) "Did somebody pee in your face?" (2) "Did somebody pee on your face in the car?" (3) "Who peed on your face in the car?" (4) "Are you going to tell me?" (5) "Somebody told me you were in the car with Hubie." At this juncture, the interview deteriorated from leading and suggestive to manipulative and coercive. This sequence of questions fired at Brittany amounted to outright demands. In other words, Ms. Moore shrilly insisted that Brittany answer her questions.

Who's in Charge?

Demonstrating uncharacteristic assertiveness for a $3\frac{1}{2}$-year-old, Brittany responded to Ms. Moore's demands by beginning to exit the interview room. Ms. Moore countered by saying, "Help me put the clothes on the baby, then we can go." Less than elated with this offer, Brittany initially responded by turning the lights off and on in the interview room, but she then complied with Ms. Moore's request.

While dressing the anatomical doll, Ms. Moore subtly moved it closer to Brittany. Brittany responded by repeatedly pushing her own face into the doll's genital area. Ms. Moore then promptly asked, "Who made you do that, did Hubie make you do that?" Brittany did not respond with any clear answer, but in reply to the first question—"Who made you do that?" she appeared to point her finger at Ms. Moore. Simultaneously, the videotape ended as apparently the interview did also.

In the event this case went to trial, the prosecution wanted to show a jury only the last 5–10 minutes of the videotaped interview. Ms. Moore would have testified on behalf of the prosecutor, concluding that Brittany's response to the anatomical doll was "consistent with" children who have been sexually abused. In fact, Brittany was not available to testify at a trial. She refused to talk with the prosecutor, and she would not respond to Ms. Moore's most recent attempts at interviewing her again. Brittany apparently wanted as little to do with Ms. Moore as possible, perhaps anticipating another interrogation ordeal. As a result, the prosecution wanted to feature Ms. Moore as its star witness.

The prosecution preferred that a jury never see the many times Brittany emphatically denied any abuse, or hear her claims indicating that Mr. Johnson "pooped" in the back of the car. Because the police never found any physical evidence consistent with this claim, a jury would have considered it rather incredible. Had the prosecution proceeded in the manner it wanted, Mr. Johnson almost certainly would have become a ward of the Ohio Department of Corrections. Defending against the biased evidence the prosecution wanted to present bordered on the impossible.

Taint Hearing

On November 8, 1996, I testified in the Common Pleas Court of Washington County, Ohio, with Judge Ed Lane presiding. Having carefully reviewed the videotape of Ms. Moore's interview and other related documents, I felt well-prepared. Mr. Johnson's attorney, Mr. Baumgartel, began his direct examination of me by asking about my professional background and history. In response to Mr. Baumgartel's motion, Judge Lane ruled that I qualified as an expert witness. Legally, this ruling is an important one. In most legal proceedings, witnesses can only testify about what they know on a firsthand basis. The typical witness is not allowed to express personal opinions regarding a matter before the court. Expert witnesses, however, can express their professional opinions about the disputed issues in a legal proceeding.

I began my testimony by outlining how children should be interviewed in cases of alleged sexual abuse. Compared with appropriate interview procedures, I bluntly characterized Ms. Moore's interview as an interrogation. I further clarified how her questioning style was initially leading and suggestive, and then deteriorated into outright coerciveness. I outlined the many problems associated with repeatedly directing the same questions at children, and how repeated questions can skew a child's answers. I moreover summarized the accumulated research demonstrating the unreliability of anatomically detailed dolls. I also explained how an unbiased, objective interviewer would attempt to both confirm and disconfirm these kinds of allegations. Finally, I concluded that Ms. Moore had essentially held Brittany hostage, promising her she could see her mother after she talked about the "bad things" Mr. Johnson supposedly did.

In contrast to my lengthy testimony in response to Mr. Baumgartel's direct examination, the prosecutor's cross-examination was brief and perfunctory. Mr. Rings, the prosecutor, seemed relieved by the opportunity to accommodate my tight schedule necessitating I make my return plane flight. As I left the witness stand, he appeared more relieved than I that the hearing had concluded. Judge Lane announced that he would review all of the evidence from the hearing, watch the videotape of Brittany's interview, and then issue his written decision as promptly as possible.

Judge Lane's Decision

Exactly 1 week later, on November 15, 1996, Judge Lane issued an 11-page decision.[1] He ruled that the prosecution could not present Brittany's out-of-court statements at trial either via the videotape or through Ms. Moore's testimony. Judge Lane also directed harsh criticisms at the "interrogation" Brittany endured. He moreover pointed out how severely skewed the interview was, emphasizing:

> It is apparent to this Court that based on the testimony of Dr. Campbell and upon a review of the tape of the interview, that Ms. Moore interrogated the child with only one objective in mind. That objective was to obtain information that could only lead to an indictment of the defendant. Her objective was never to obtain the truth of the matters alleged.

Judge Lane was also very disturbed by the manner in which Ms. Moore essentially held Brittany hostage. He pointed out how:

> This interview was conducted in such a manner that it is obvious to this Court that this child eventually realized that she was not going to be allowed to see her grandmother/mother, or to leave the room, until she told Ms. Moore what Ms. Moore wanted to hear. Early in the interview, Ms. Moore stated to the child, "We are almost done." How-

ever, the interview continues for well over three-quarters of an hour after this point in time.

In his overview of the interview, Judge Lane emphasized:

> Bribing a three-year-old with cookies is not a valid interview procedure whether it is done intentionally or unintentionally. Continually restraining a three-year-old and promising her to be able to see her mother/grandmother once she gives the right answers are not valid interview techniques. The techniques used in this interrogation are not valid for any age level, especially for a child of such tender years.

In concluding his opinion, the judge indicated:

> Neither the safety of child victims, the rights of the Defendant, nor the interest of the Court in the pursuit of justice are served by this type of interrogation technique.

In response to Judge Lane's emphatic opinion, the Washington County Prosecutor's office dropped all charges against Mr. Johnson. This case never went to trial, and Hubert Johnson walks the streets of his community as a free and grateful man. Fair and just as the outcome was in this case, the specter of innocent people mistakenly convicted of child sexual abuse too often remains a chilling possibility. For example, Judge Lane also commented directly on Ms. Moore's interview skills stating, "There has been no evidence presented to this Court that Ms. Moore has the training to conduct these types of interviews."

In other words, Judge Lane leveled some rather stinging criticisms at both Ms. Moore and the Washington County Children's Service Bureau. Many people might expect such reactions would motivate an agency like the Children's Service Bureau to undertake wholesale changes in its interview practices. Typically, however, sharply critical reviews of their work merely leave these agencies more deeply entrenched in their prevailing practices. The personnel of these agencies rationalize their resistance to change claiming what they do is misunderstood and unappreciated. Most alarmingly, there are many agencies involved in assessing allegations of sexual abuse that are determined to avoid scrutiny. They do so by refusing to videotape their interviews of children. Practices such as these reflect deliberate policy, and are not the result of ill-informed oversights.

VIDEOTAPING INTERVIEWS

The following organizations and well-respected authorities have emphasized the absolute necessity of videotaping—or at least audiotaping—

investigative interviews in cases of alleged child sexual abuse: the American Academy of Child and Adolescent Psychiatry,[2] the U.S. Attorney General's Task Force on Family Violence,[3] the California Attorney General's Office, Steven Ceci of Cornell University,[4] and Lucy McGough of the Louisiana State University Law School.[5]

In the typical case of alleged sexual abuse, however, investigative interviews are neither videotaped nor audiotaped. Consequently, there are no verbatim transcripts available in these cases. Too often, then, it is impossible to determine whether interviewers contaminated the memories of children via leading and suggestive questions. Imagine, for example, what would have happened to Hubert Johnson without the videotape of Ms. Moore interviewing Brittany. Circumstances such as these have convicted a shocking number of innocent people accused of sexually abusing children.

Dr. John Yuille, a well-respected psychologist on the faculty of the University of British Columbia, and his colleagues recognize the necessity of recording investigative interviews in cases of alleged child sexual abuse. They emphasized:

> The number of interviews can be minimized by recording the interview. Preferably, the interview will be videotaped but, in the absence of video equipment, an audiotape will suffice. If no electronic equipment is available, a verbatim record must be kept. There are many advantages to recording an interview, although having such an objective record of their interview performance may be intimidating for some professionals. It has come to our attention that, in the wake of the McMartin case, a number of professionals have decided not to record interviews. Since poor interview quality was a central feature of the McMartin case, many have decided that it is better not to have a record of an interview. It would seem that such a decision is based on the fear of having one's work publicly scrutinized. This is a most unfortunate development. Our goal should not be to hide poor interviews, for it is important that the adequacy of the methods used to obtain children's evidence be assessed. A more appropriate goal would be to educate interviewers in order to enable them to conduct interviews that can withstand public scrutiny.[4]

Yuille's position is supported by evidence of interviewers reaching their conclusions very early in their interviews, and then clinging to those premature conclusions even when confronted with contrary evidence.[7,8] As a result, interviewers commonly overestimate the amount of information they process during their interviews. They assume they weigh multiple factors in reaching their conclusions, but the relevant evidence demonstrates they rely on minimal data.[9] In fact, they frequently arrive at their diagnostic impressions within the first 2 to 3 minutes of an interview, and sometimes as rapidly as 30 seconds.[10] Not surprisingly, then, there is no relationship between the confidence that interviewers express in their opinions and how accurate those opinions really are.[11]

Frequency of Interviewer Bias

As would be expected, interviewers typically insist they avoid directing leading or suggestive questions at children. The relevant research, however, does not support these claims. Interviewers typically question interviewees in a manner that biases the information they obtain.[12,13] Assumptions about a child's supposed abuse history, for example, increase the frequency of questions directed at that topic—and asking enough questions allows interviewers to think they have found the answers they expected.[14] These processes are known as "one-sided questioning" or "confirmatory questioning."

The expectations of interviewers can also lead them to believe that evidence consistent with their initial impressions was exhibited during an interview, when in fact, it was not.[15] Conversely, they are also less likely to recall evidence actually present during an interview, but inconsistent with their original impressions. These judgmental errors are known as "confirmatory bias."[16] As a result of their confirmatory biases, interviewers neglect to consider hypotheses other than sexual abuse. Questions designed to test alternative possibilities, such as "Did your mommy or daddy tell you that this happened, or did you see it happen? Who else besides your teacher has touched your private parts—has your mommy touched them too?"[17] are never asked.

Additionally, related research has demonstrated that psychiatric trainees overlook 50% of the important issues transpiring during their interviews.[18] Furthermore, another 50% of what these trainees did report to their supervisors was also distorted. These data suggest that the total accuracy of a non-recorded interview approximates 25% (0.5 × 0.5 = 0.25). Moreover, related research has demonstrated that experienced therapists also do not accurately recall their own behavior during interviews.[19,20] In particular, interviewers typically cannot recall the specific questions that elicited the reported responses of the child. Focused intently on what the child says, interviewers characteristically disregard what they ask and its corresponding influences on the children they interview. Without videotapes of an interview, then, we can never know the extent to which the interviewer might have influenced the child who was interviewed.

Examples of Interviewer Bias

One study in particular dramatically demonstrated the effects of biased interviews on children. In this study, 5- and 6-year-olds viewed a staged event that could be considered as either abusive or innocent.[21] "Chester," a confederate of the experimenter, interacted with the children by either (1) cleaning dolls in a playroom or (2) handling the dolls roughly in a mildly abusive manner. The children were interviewed about this event several times on the same day by interviewers who were: (1) *accusatory*—suggesting that Chester had been playing with the toys rather than working, (2) *exculpatory*—suggesting that Chester had been working rather than playing, or (3) *neutral*—nonsuggestive.

When questioned by a neutral interviewer, or by an interviewer whose interpretations were consistent with what the child observed, the children provided factually accurate reports. When the interviewers contradicted what the child had seen, however, the reports of those children promptly conformed to the suggestions and beliefs of the interviewer. By the end of the first interview, 75% of these children responded in a manner consistent with the interviewer's point of view. Eventually, 90% of the children answered questions in a manner suggested by the interviewer.

Another study also demonstrated the effects of interviewer bias when interviewing young children.[22] This study examined how interviewers' expectations influenced their style of questioning, and the subsequent accuracy of children's reports. Three- to five-year-olds participated in a staged event, and they were interviewed about this event 2 weeks later. Some interviewers received accurate information about the event before beginning their interviews. Other interviewers were misinformed about this event, and still other interviewers received no information. All interviewers were instructed to: (1) question each child until they found out what had happened and (2) avoid leading and/or suggestive questions.

The interviewers asked the children an average of 50 questions during interviews typically lasting 20 to 30 minutes. Despite the warning to avoid leading questions, 30% of all questions were leading, and half of those misled the children. Misinformed interviewers asked four to five times more misleading questions than the other interviewers. Consequently, the children encountered considerable pressure during the interviews. The children agreed with 41% of the misleading questions, and those interviewed by misinformed interviewers provided the most inaccurate information. Therefore, what interviewers think they know about a case significantly influences how they question children. In turn, their manner of questioning children profoundly affects what the children report.

Rather than obtain spontaneous narratives from children, too many interviewers seek confirmation of their preexisting expectations. For example, an analysis of child sexual abuse investigative interviews, done by child protective professionals in the State of Tennessee, produced sobering results. This analysis revealed that the interviewers spent little time asking children open-ended questions. Instead, 90% of the questions were highly specific, requiring one-word answers.[23] In response to circumstances such as these, children become very passive in contrast to active interviewers.

Prosecutors' Responses to Videotaping

Despite the overwhelming evidence underscoring the absolute necessity of videotaping interviews with children in cases of alleged sexual abuse, it appears that prosecutors are becoming progressively disinclined to do so. In a particularly enlightening study, 297 surveys were mailed to prosecuting attorney's offices nationwide.[24] One hundred fifty-three offices (52%), representing 41 states, responded. The survey was designed to answer the following the questions: (1) What innovations are being utilized in cases involving children? (2) Which innovations are no longer employed, and why not?

Surprisingly enough, over half of the responding prosecutor's offices indicated they no longer used videotaped statements of children at trial. The percentages of responses citing their reasons for discontinuing videotaping were as follows: lack of funds = 28%, defense challenge or appeal = 18%, hurts case = 40%, not needed = 22%, other = 9%. The fact that "hurts case" was the primary rationale expressed for not videotaping interviews is shocking to say the least.

Given the prosecutors' related concerns regarding "defense challenge or appeal," a combined total of 58% of those responding to this question apparently prefer to keep juries uninformed about how children are interviewed. Quite obviously, convictions are more likely in cases of alleged sexual abuse if juries never see the work of interviewers such as Ms. Moore. It seems that many prosecutors are determined to keep juries in the dark regarding these kinds of problems.

Prosecutors and others who resist videotaping interviews typically attempt to rationalize their position. They argue that videotaping makes it more difficult for children to express themselves. Nevertheless, a demonstration project sponsored by the California Attorney General's office found no evidence to support this argument.[25] In particular, the California project found that videotaping did not inhibit children's readiness to respond. This project moreover found that the professionals involved responded enthusiastically to videotaping. The opportunity to observe themselves interviewing children allowed these professionals to correct their errors and rapidly increase their overall interview skills.

Prosecutors, and the professionals with whom they prefer to work, have also claimed that videotapes give defense attorneys "too much ammunition." This argument contends that defense attorneys exaggerate the significance of minor errors in interview procedure. Again, however, the California project found no evidence to support this claim. The professionals participating in this project reported that juries understood minor discrepancies and confusion in what children reported. These professionals further emphasized that when interviews are conducted competently, there is nothing to hide.

CLAIMS OF SPECIALIZED TRAINING

Many professionals who interview children in cases of alleged sexual abuse make claims about their specialized training. They insist that their training allows them to avoid interviewing children inappropriately. In fact, however, no one knows how effective specialized training is in the areas of child abuse and child maltreatment. For example, one study in particular assessed the effectiveness of a comprehensive, 10-day training seminar. This was a seven-module curriculum—"Child Sexual Abuse Curriculum for Social Workers"—developed by the American Association for Protecting Children (AAPC), a division of the American Humane Association.[26]

The study obtained "before" measures of assessment skills from the professionals prior to their participating in the training seminar. On completing the training, the study also obtained "after" measures of assessment skills from the participating professionals. The results of this study failed to support the hypothesis that overall assessment skills would improve subsequent to training. For a sample of 12 experienced Kentucky social workers, the average posttest score was slightly, but not significantly, higher than the pretest score. Therefore, training did not result in any reliable improvement for the Kentucky sample completing it.

In a sample of 24 experienced California social workers, however, the opposite occurred. Pretest scores were higher than posttest scores. In other words, the assessment skills of the California sample declined slightly, though not significantly, as a result of this training. The results of this study are especially important because most training programs related to child sexual abuse are not this intensive. The usual training program in this area lasts 2 to 3 days at the most.

Various professionals frequently testify in courts claiming their "specialized training" affords them unique expertise. These overconfident claims deserve persistent challenge. In particular, professionals who make these claims should be asked the following questions:

1. Would you agree that an objective evaluation of the effectiveness of the training program you completed would necessitate: (1) an assessment of the participants' skills prior to the program and (2) another assessment of the participants' skills after completing the program?

2. And if the training program is effective, we would expect that the participants' skills would increase subsequent to completing the program. Correct?

3. Do you know whether the effectiveness of the training program you completed has ever been objectively evaluated in this manner?

4. Would it surprise you to know that an evaluation of a comprehensive, 10-day, seven-module curriculum—"Child Sexual Abuse Curriculum for Social Workers," developed by the American Association for Protecting Children, a division of the American Humane Association—found that the participants' skills did not increase as a result of training?

5. Would it moreover surprise you if you knew that the skills of 24 experienced California social workers undergoing this training actually declined?

6. Without any objective evaluation of the training program you completed, and in view of the demonstrated lack of effectiveness for the training program I just cited, is it still your opinion that the training you completed provides you with special expertise in assessing allegations of child sexual abuse?

Interviewing Children Effectively

Obtaining Background Information

As previoulsy pointed out, interviewing children effectively in cases of alleged sexual abuse necessitates obtaining relevant background information before undertaking the actual interview. In particular, interviewers need to know: (1) How did the allegation originate? (2) Did the child spontaneously disclose that she was abused? (3) Or did someone else suspect the child had been abused, and question the child accordingly? (4) Who has discussed these allegations with the child, and what was discussed? By the time a child is initially interviewed, she is frequently surrounded by a network of adults who already assume that the alleged abuse did occur. Consequently, the child may encounter enormous pressure to conform her reports to the collective thinking of this adult network.

Obtaining critically important background information necessitates an interviewer initially meeting with one of the child's parents, or an adult who serves as the child's primary caretaker. In addition to learning about the allegations, an interviewer should also obtain other information about the child. An interviewer needs to know: (1) With whom does the child live? (2) Does the child attend school, and if so, in what grade? (3) Does the child have siblings, and if so, what are their ages?

While speaking with a parent or caretaker, an interviewer should inquire about one or two known events that recently transpired in the child's life. If the child attended a recent birthday party, for example, the interviewer can determine: (1) Whose birthday was celebrated? (2) Who else attended the party? (3) Where was the party held? (4) What kinds of gifts were given? (5) Did the children eat at the party, and if so, what? (6) Did the children participate in some activity, such as riding a pony, going to a zoo, or watching a magician? A well-prepared interviewer will then use this information when questioning a child who may have been sexually abused.

Avoiding Acquiescence

Once the necessary background information has been obtained, the interview begins by establishing rapport with the child. The interviewer can draw the child into discussing the school she attends, or her family, or her hobbies, for instance. Very early in the interview, it is necessary to deal with the problem of acquiescence.

Children perceive the adults with whom they converse as well-informed people who question them only to test their knowledge. Children find it difficult to understand how they could possess important information unknown to an adult. In response to an interview, children attempt to determine what the adult expects to hear and then answer accordingly. They exhibit what is known as acquiescence—responding "yes" to questions in an attempt to satisfy the expectations they attribute to the adult interviewing them.

Interviewers can reduce the contaminating effects of acquiescence by explaining to the child, "I may say something, or ask something, where I am wrong. If I am wrong about something, will you promise to tell me?" Children typically agree to "help" an interviewer in this manner; to this end, the interviewer can ask the child to practice. In particular, I ask children to practice saying, "No, Dr. Campbell, that's wrong!"

Lavishly praising children for their willingness to correct the interviewer reduces the effects of acquiescence. Approximately 5 or 10 minutes after children have practiced correcting a mistaken assumption of mine, I will ask a question that presumes erroneous information. For example, I often ask children about a nonexistent sibling—"How old is your younger brother?"—and then wait for the child to correct me. In response to being corrected, I emphatically applaud the child for "helping me." In response to this praise, children pay close attention to any other errors I might commit over the course of the interview. Even more importantly, the child is less inclined to acquiesce in response to my questions.

Assisting the Child's Recall

The interview then moves to asking children about the one or more known events that have recently occurred in their lives. If the child recently attended a friend's birthday party, I will ask the child to tell me about this event. In particular, I want the child to spontaneously describe what happened at the party. When the child finishes her description, I explain that maybe I can help her remember some more things.[27] I then introduce her to four simple drawings to aid her recall. The drawings correspond to: (1) *participants*—who was there? (2) *setting*—where did the event occur? (3) *actions*—who did what at this event? and (4) *conversations*—who said what to whom? I then ask the child to tell me about the known event while specifically referring to these four issues.

Quite obviously, this portion of my interview is more than leading or suggestive—it is directive. However, I am directing the child about *how* to most effectively remember past events. I am not directing the child regarding *what* she recalls. My influence limits itself to defining a strategy that enhances the accuracy of her recall. In particular, I ask the child to again tell me about the known event focusing on the participants, the setting, actions of the participants, and conversations of the participants.

Organizing the memories of children in this manner allows them to recall more information about past events without influencing *what* they remember. The details children report about known events also serve as a baseline of comparison when obtaining details about the alleged abuse. In other words, I assess whether the child describes the alleged sexual abuse with the same quantity and quality of details that she describes the known event.

By the time I direct the interview to the critical issues of alleged sexual abuse, the child feels relatively comfortable with me. We have spent time discussing benign events while the child "assists" me. Therefore, the child is responding to me with a sense of trust and comfort when the interview addresses the allegations of sexual abuse. I do resort to a slightly leading question to raise the issue of possible sexual abuse, asking: "I was told that someone might have touched your privates, *but I don't know what happened, can you help me?*" (This question is asked after the child's "private areas" have been identified.) As the child spontaneously describes the alleged abuse, I confine myself to asking, "And what happened next, what happened after that?" After the child finishes her narrative, I reintroduce the pictures directing her to the issues of (1) participants, (2) setting, (3) actions, and (4) conversations.

Depending on their age, children who have been sexually abused can provide numerous details related to the abuse. For example, a 5-year-old described how her uncle would sit her on his lap, telling her how much he liked her. She continued to explain how he started stroking her vaginal area, suggesting to her "this is what special friends do." She additionally reported her uncle saying, "special friends who do this keep it a secret." When she agreed to keep these secrets, her uncle would give her candy. This little girl moreover described the abuse she experienced with the same quantity and quality of details that she described her friend's recent birthday party. After the attorney representing the defendant uncle saw the videotape of this interview, he promptly began discussing a plea arrangement with the prosecutor. The attorney knew it would be futile for his client to plead not guilty and proceed to trial.

In another case, a 6-year-old girl described a family picnic she recently attended with considerable detail. When asked about the alleged sexual abuse, however, she responded with what amounted to a sketchy outline—"He touched me there." Beyond this statement, this child found it difficult to answer questions about the specifics of the setting. She could only say the alleged abuse occurred at the alleged perpetrator's house, but could not specify where in the house.

Asked about what conversations had transpired related to the alleged abuse, she initially became puzzled, and then replied, "Ask my mom, she knows." In response to other questions, she replied "I don't know" or "I don't remember." The profound discrepancies between her recall of the family picnic and her recall of the alleged abuse indicated that the abuse amounted to an imaginary event. Nevertheless, this little girl seemed to genuinely believe her own statements about the abuse. As so often happens in false allegations of sexual abuse, what this child thought she remembered had been severely contaminated by her imagination.

There are other cases, however, where children and/or the adults who influence them engage in premeditated fabrications alleging sexual abuse. Rare as these cases are, they too often result in criminal convictions of innocent people. In Chapter 6, then, we will examine cases of alleged sexual abuse that amount to outright lies.

6

Sometimes They Just Lie

False Allegations as Fabrications

In July, the rising sun races across the flatlands of northern Ohio. Climbing rapidly above the horizon, it quickly overwhelms the soft twilight of dawn. On a July morning in 1995, in the small town of Delta, Ohio, bright daylight woke Duane Carlson and he rose to ready himself for work. While going about his morning rituals, he felt relieved knowing that his daughters were about to spend the next month visiting their mother. Ever since he and his first wife divorced 6 years ago, Duane had been the custodial parent for 14-year-old April and 11-year-old Betsy. As a result of numerous unstable relationships with various men since their divorce, his former wife's lifestyle would not have offered the girls much stability.

Though Duane's remarriage to Sharon 5 years earlier created an intact family for his daughters, parenting them presented an increasing frequency of challenges. As a teenager, April was becoming particularly difficult especially since falling in love with 16-year-old Jamie. Jamie identified closely with the "punk look," shaving half his head and dyeing the remaining hair a shade best described as screeching orange. The odd assortment of metal objects stuck through his nose, lips, and eyebrows further complemented the appearance of his hair. Duane characterized Jamie as looking like the south end of a rooster headed north. April, however, did not appreciate this description of her first love.

IF LOVE IS BLIND, SHE NEEDED A DOG AND CANE

April recently disappeared for almost an entire day without telling anyone of her plans. She and Jamie spontaneously decided to venture off to an amusement park. This incident followed a dramatic drop in April's school grades. Her relationship with Jamie had left her as disinterested in school as he was. Duane and Sharon then grounded April, prohibiting any contact with Jamie, and confining her to the house until she left for the month's stay with her mother. Outraged at what he considered a horrible injustice, Jamie used a beer can opener to inflict superficial cuts on the inside of his arms. Duane wondered whether Jamie intended this dramatic gesture to demonstrate how much he missed April, or if it simply was another attempt at maintaining his avant-garde appearance.

As he emerged from the shower on this July morning, Duane thought he heard muted voices downstairs. Wearing only a towel about himself, he went to investigate. Much to his surprise, April was up and sitting in the living room. This was a teenager who often slept until noon, but on this particular morning, she said she awoke and could not fall back asleep. Duane sat down with April, talking about various activities she had planned while visiting her mother. In an uncharacteristic moment of responsibility, April suggested to her father that he might be late for work unless he resumed dressing. Duane explained he was starting work later than usual, and wanted to take advantage of the available time to talk to her about Jamie.

April became increasingly irritated as her father told her that her mother knew about the many problems involving Jamie. April especially protested when informed that both her parents agreed Jamie was not welcome to visit during the month's stay at her mother's. Aware that her protests were falling on deaf ears, April sullenly crossed her arms over her chest insisting she no longer wanted to discuss the issue. Duane agreed there was little else to discuss; he only wanted April to understand she would not be seeing Jamie while visiting her mother. April responded by further retreating into silent pouting.

Strained silence briefly prevailed until footsteps were heard in the hallway outside of April's first-floor bedroom. Moving from the living room to identify these unexpected sounds, Duane discovered Jamie trying to tiptoe from April's room. His obligatory combat boots, however, reduced his efforts to futility. Jamie briefly froze as Duane bellowed, "What in the hell are you doing here?" Convinced that the situation precluded any acceptable response, Jamie bolted for the outside door. Duane promptly pursued him, losing his towel but managing to collar Jamie. By the time Duane delivered a few kicks to Jamie's posterior, they were both halfway outside the front door. Jamie's shrill protests combined with Duane's stark nakedness amounted to an interesting sight to say the least. Finally aware of his awkward circumstances, Duane yelled, "I don't ever want to see your blanking face again," and retreated back into the house.

Removed from what could have been embarrassing scrutiny, Duane directed his full attention to April. He emphatically informed her, "April, that weirdo is history. You will not have anything to do with him in the future." April insisted that her father was being grossly unfair, further claiming this was another example of his misunderstanding her. Duane countered that he understood all too well what was going on between that "asshole" and his daughter in her bedroom. April challenged Duane, rhetorically asking what Jamie must have thought about her father walking around the house half-naked. Duane replied he seriously doubted whether Jamie possessed the intellectual capacity for well-defined thought. April huffily terminated this exchange by exiting to her bedroom.

Duane returned to the upstairs bedroom he shared with Sharon, discovering her awake as a result of the events downstairs. He summarized for her what had happened, seeing at least some humor in the situation. Explaining how he found himself simultaneously reaching for Jamie with one hand while frantically grabbing for his towel with the other, he chuckled about knowing what it was like "to be a one-legged man in an ass-kicking contest." Sharon, however, could only respond by shaking her head in numb disbelief. Duane reminded her that his ex-wife planned on picking up the girls prior to his returning home from work. Given the circumstances, he appreciated the opportunity to avoid another confrontation with April before cooling off. Sharon promised to call him should any more crises develop prior to the girls leaving with their mother.

THE ABUSE EXCUSE

Duane called his ex-wife the day after she had picked up the girls. He explained the most recent episode involving April and Jamie, advising she watch April closely to prevent her contacting the "beloved rooster." April's mother responded by suggesting Duane was coming down too hard on April. Duane angrily reminded her that he carried the burden as April's primary custodian, and he did not appreciate her comments. Their phone conversation terminated as they simultaneously hung up on each other.

Exactly what transpired over the next 2 weeks still remained unclear until April, her mother, and Jamie all appeared at the Fulton County (Ohio) Sheriff's office. There they were interviewed by Det. John Preston and Karol Klauss of the Ohio Department of Child Protective Services. Throughout much of the interview, April sat on Jamie's lap giggling in response to the attention lavished on her. Her response was particularly curious because she alleged that her father had sexually abused her—including penile–vaginal intercourse—since the spring of 1993. Adolescent girls who suffer this kind of gross abuse—especially if perpetrated by their own father—rarely disclose it while giggling. Apparently, however, this consideration never occurred to Det. Preston or Ms. Klauss.

In response to April's allegations, Det. Preston arranged for April to call her father the following day at work. While Det. Preston recorded the call, April responded to his cues trying to lead her father into incriminating statements. Without anything incriminating to say, however, Duane confined himself to demanding that April undertake wholesale changes in her behavior—otherwise, she might want to consider living with her mother. Their father–daughter dialogue then deteriorated into accusatory exchanges about Jamie sneaking into April's bedroom. Disappointed as Det. Preston was in the outcome of the phone call, he remained determined in what he considered his pursuit of justice.

Det. Preston contacted Duane at work, and asked that he come to the Sheriff's Department for an interview. When Duane arrived there, he also met Lieutenant Carey of the local police department. Det. Preston assumed the primary responsibility for interviewing Duane, and Lt. Carey functioned more as an observer. Despite Det. Preston's subsequent denials, Duane recalled how the detective immediately ripped him with accusations. He characterized Duane as beyond despicable for what he had allegedly done to April. Det. Preston did not begin audiotaping this interview until after his preliminary attack on Duane.

The audiotape of the interview clearly documented Duane's emphatic and understandably angry denials. Interestingly enough, however, Lt. Carey later testified claiming, "I was watching the defendant's actions and he made an indicator that he was—it was time to confess his crimes." Lt. Carey then betrayed his own unwarranted confidence by subsequently admitting, "I don't remember what his [Duane's] words were." Exactly how Lt. Carey knew that Duane was ready to confess, without remembering what he said, was never clarified. Nonetheless, both Lt. Carey and Det. Preston remained steadfast in their opinions.

EXCULPATORY EVIDENCE

As a result of the evidence presented at a preliminary hearing, Duane was charged with seven separate counts of sexually abusing April. If convicted of these charges, he could spend the rest of his life in prison. Duane's ex-wife also went to family court obtaining an order placing April and Betsy in her custody. Duane retained the services of an excellent Toledo-area attorney, Gerald Baker. In response to Mr. Baker's advice, he and Sharon searched April's room looking for anything relevant to his defense. What they found left them both in shocked disbelief. They discovered a number of letters April had written to her friend, Carol, in the spring of 1995. One of the letters said:

> what if Richie wanted to fuck me over the weekend and he found out that I wasn't a virgin! Then he would get mad at me for cheating on him! Cause he knew I was a virgin the last weekend I saw him! Well gotta go! Yes, I still love Robert, but he only took my virginity then left. [This letter predated April's relationship with Jamie.]

April's letter clearly established that she had fabricated her allegations. If Robert took her virginity in the spring of 1995, then the allegations contending her father vaginally penetrated her beginning in 1993 were transparently false. Duane and Sharon could only conclude that April had fabricated these allegations to protect her relationship with Jamie. Duane and Sharon understood how April thought she had found the love of her life, but they never expected her to resort to premeditated lies to protect him. They kept asking themselves and each other, "How could she do this?" Reviewing the research related to group conflicts provides answers to this nagging question.

In-Groups and Out-Groups

Both adolescents and adults typically participate in various social groups. People identify with their family groups, the groups with whom they work, the neighbors residing near them, and their own ethnic background, to cite a few examples. When closely identified with some group, people respond to considerations of "in-group" versus "out-group" status. People who identify themselves with the same group share in-group status. In-group individuals also define themselves as different from the out-group individuals who do not identify themselves with their group. In circumstances of pronounced conflict between groups, the interactions between them can become very hostile and aggressive. Too often, for example, relationships between blacks and whites in this country have been characterized by hostile and aggressive exchanges because of in-group versus out-group influences.

People characteristically think in positive terms about their own in-groups, and simultaneously, they regard out-group individuals in negative terms.[1] In-group members exaggerate the differences between themselves and out-group individuals. These exaggerated differences are then attributed to conditions identifying the in-group as supposedly superior.[2] In particular, out-group individuals are often stereotyped as untrustworthy, deceitful, and hostile.[3] When struggling with a crisis, in-group members also typically blame the crisis on out-groups.[4] Though oblivious to these effects of in-group versus out-group conflicts, April nonetheless responded to them.

Dehumanizing Out-Groups

April's feelings about Jamie motivated her to view their relationship with a persistent in-group bias. While regarding Jamie in unrealistically idealized terms, April reacted with increasing hostility to her father's ridicule of "the rooster who looked like an odd duck." April also stereotyped her father in generally negative terms, blaming him for all of the problems undermining her relationship with Jamie. Consequently, April no longer responded to her father and Sharon as a family in-group; she instead reduced them to the status of an out-group undeserving of any empathy or compassion. In other words, April dehumanized her father, and in doing so, she even altered how she referred to him. Previously she proudly called him "Daddy," but now she spoke sarcastically of him as "daddy dearest."

Persistently dehumanizing people reduces the usual feelings of obligation to treat them in a fair and decent manner.[5] Regarding people as very much unlike ourselves, and inferior to us as a result, makes it easier to aggress against them in various ways, even including lying. We can ask ourselves, for example, how obliged we feel to respond truthfully to a friend compared with an enemy. Given the degree to which April thought of her father as an out-group enemy, it was much easier to lie about him.

Unfortunately, these issues never occurred to the criminal justice system determined to both prosecute and vilify Duane Carlson.

THE TRIAL

After I had been qualified as an expert witness, my trial testimony focused on childhood development and what is called "satellization."[6] In response to the helpless dependency of a newborn child, parents function as satellites revolving around that child's needs. Parents defer their needs and preferences in order to meet the needs of their vulnerable newborn. Over time, however, these satellization characteristics undergo substantial change. By the child's third birthday, the processes of satellization begin to dramatically reverse themselves as the child encounters various expectations and demands. Parents insist that children of this age conform with expectations regarding what they should do, and comply with limits specifying prohibited behaviors. In other words, children evolve as satellites revolving around their families' collective welfare between the ages of 2 and 3.

From the ages of 3 years until approximately 12, children typically relate to their family as stable satellites. They identify closely with the family unit, demonstrating loyalty and respect for their parents. Adolescence, however, brings profound changes into the lives of parents and teenagers alike. In response to adolescence, the loyalty of teens shifts from family to peer group. For the typical teenager, the opinions of their friends are infinitely more important than their parents'. As a result, teenagers identify more with their peer groups than their families.

My testimony outlining the processes of satellization helped the jury understand how adolescence changes the loyalties of children. I then continued to testify about the effects of conflicts between in-groups and out-groups. The defense attorney asked me whether people were more inclined to tell the truth about a friend or an enemy. Already anticipating my reply, some of the jurors began nodding their heads affirmatively. Nonetheless, this jury was not about to rush to judgment. It deliberated more than a day before returning its unanimous verdict of not guilty.

Duane Carlson's ordeal dramatically demonstrates how people can find their lives ripped apart by fabricated allegations of sexual abuse. Angry adolescents single-mindedly pursuing their selfish agenda, for example, can subject innocent people to horrible injustices. Parents who are divorced, or estranged without having married each other, also encounter the divisive influences of in-group versus out-group effects. Could these circumstances motivate angry, vindictive parents to knowingly direct false allegations of sexual abuse at their parental counterparts? Unfortunately, firsthand experience with such cases necessitates answering with an emphatic "Yes."

THE RELATIONSHIP FROM HELL

If some relationships can be described as turbulent, then Ed Bielaska and Laura Orley's amounted to a destructive tornado. Ed and Laura met in 1986 in suburban Detroit and began dating each other regularly. In the spring of 1987, Laura discovered she was pregnant and their daughter, Ginny, was born in December. Though they never married, Ed and Laura lived with his parents for approximately 6 weeks in early 1988. Both Laura and her mother, however, found it difficult to adjust to this situation. Until she began living with Ed, Laura rarely spent so much as a night away from her own family's home. In response to her mother's frequent encouragement, Laura took Ginny and returned to her family in the spring of 1988.

After Laura moved back home, the relationship between her and Ed deteriorated into hostile, accusatory exchanges, and she began refusing Ed's requests for visitation with Ginny. When Ed moved to California, however, Laura's animosity gradually diminished until she actually missed him. After learning that Ed's sister was planning on visiting him in California, Laura phoned Ed suggesting she might also make the trip. Though initially hesitant about resuming their relationship, Ed relented and told Laura he would like to see her again. The romantic atmosphere of southern California rekindled their passion, and while visiting Ed in the summer of 1988, Laura became pregnant with their second child.

Without yet knowing she was pregnant, Laura involved herself in a serious relationship with a Paul Newton shortly after returning to Michigan. By October 1988, Ed had also returned to Michigan, and he filed a petition with the Wayne County Circuit Court seeking physical custody of Ginny. Disturbed by the frequency with which Laura left Ginny at her mother's while living with Paul, Ed concluded he could offer Ginny a more stable home. The court responded to Ed's petition by ordering a split custody arrangement with Ginny staying with him from noon on Sundays to Wednesday mornings. Laura was to assume Ginny's custody for the remaining portion of each week.

Despite the court's clearly defined order specifying shared custody, Ed frequently encountered circumstances of Laura or her mother denying him access to Ginny. Ed responded to these arbitrary denials by filing written complaints with the court. In response to Ed's complaints, the court would order Laura to appear at a formal hearing and explain herself. At these proceedings, Laura typically remained silent while her attorney shielded her from the judge's displeasure. The judge would then threaten to find Laura in contempt of court unless she complied with the existing visitation order. Laura quickly learned these were empty threats, and consequently, she continued denying Ed's visitation whenever she felt so inclined.

Laura gave birth to her and Ed's second child, Louise, in March 1989, and she married Paul Newton in early April of that year. As a result of the court's order of March 31, 1989, both Ed and Laura were to undergo a psychological evaluation at the University of Michigan Center for the Child and Family. Laura did attend one evaluation session on May 30, 1989, but she neglected to keep subsequent appointments. During her only interview, Laura expressed her hope and expectation that Ed would withdraw from his daughters' lives.

The psychologist involved in this evaluation emphasized how "Ms. Orley communicated in word and action that she feels she has little to gain by cooperating with this evaluation, and through extension, with the Court." This psychologist further characterized Laura as "passively obstructing" Ed's attempts at establishing a relationship with his daughters. As this case continued to run its convoluted course, too many "experts" overlooked the findings of this critically important, though incomplete, first evaluation.

Parental Alienation Syndrome

By the summer of 1989, Laura had undertaken a campaign to entirely exclude Ed from the lives of his daughters. Parents who pursue this agenda engage in what is known as the "parental alienation syndrome."[7] These attempts of one parent to alienate their children from the other parent are often motivated by feelings of betrayal. After their romantic interlude in California, for example, Ed chose not to pursue Laura when he returned to Michigan. Laura's ensuing feelings of betrayal likely served as the force driving her attempts at alienating the girls from Ed. Laura also discovered how effective allegations of sexual abuse could be in pursuing this agenda.

Disregarding how she stonewalled the University of Michigan Clinic in June, Laura called them in August 1989 claiming she had found evidence of Ed sexually abusing Ginny. She specifically alleged Ginny telling her, "Ed tickle me there" while pointing to her vaginal area. The U-M psychologist advised Laura not to overinterpret this apparently ambiguous event. The psychologist also recommended that Laura and Ginny return to the clinic allowing a more adequate assessment of these most recent developments. Apparently, however, this recommendation failed to satisfy Laura's expectations, and she went shopping for a professional who would meet her needs.

In early September 1989, the court received a letter from a social worker, Linda Merkle. She summarized her professional contacts with Laura, Ginny, and Mr. Newton that began in mid-August. Ms. Merkle reported Laura alleging that Ginny had said her father and her father's dog "tickled [my] private parts." Ms. Merkle also clarified how Ginny had not expressed any such statements directly to her. Nevertheless, Ms. Merkle blithely ignored how these secondhand allegations were incredible enough to defy imagination. She instead characterized Laura and Mr. Newton as concerned parents who were "in tune" with Ginny.

Ms. Merkle also never obtained any information from the U-M clinic; therefore, she knew little about the events preceding her involvement in this case. Laboring under the effects of incomplete information, Ms. Merkle recommended supervised visitation for Ed. Of course this was an altogether curious recommendation because Ms. Merkle had never seen Ed at the time she made it.

Transparently false as these allegations were, the court did not dismiss them as unfounded until early December 1989. Another hearing addressing the issue of visitation was held over 3 days in late January 1990. As a result of this hearing, the court ordered visitation for Ed with Ginny on two afternoons per week and every other Sunday. It is important to remember that previously the court awarded split custody to Ed—he would care for Ginny from noon on Sunday until Wednesday mornings. In January 1990, however, the court substantially reduced the time Ed could spend with Ginny. These developments likely encouraged Laura to continue pursuing her agenda.

Contempt with an Attitude

Despite the reduction in Ed's visitation time, Laura continued to deny him even the limited visits he did have. Ed responded to these developments by filing more complaints with the court. In May 1990, the court finally issued a warrant for Laura's arrest as a result of her blatantly defying its orders. Consistent with its previously established pattern, however, the court again responded too slowly to a situation demanding more immediate action. Laura exploited the court's persistent passivity by surreptitiously moving with Paul and the girls to a destination that remained unknown at that time.

For more than 3 years, besides not seeing his daughters, Ed did not know where they were. He hired private investigators attempting time and again to locate the girls, but they found nothing. Then in May 1993, Ed learned that after separating from Paul, Laura and the girls had returned to Michigan from North Carolina where they previously lived for 3 years. As a result of an emergency court order, Ed visited with Ginny on May 22, 1993, and he visited with Louise for the first time ever the following day. At this time, the court awarded Ed supervised visitation with his daughters on Sunday afternoons. The court also ordered that one or more members of Ed's family would be responsible for being present at all times and overseeing his interactions with his daughters.

Expert Shopping

Aware that the Wayne County Circuit Court was beginning to lose its patience with her, Laura again sought out professional allies hoping they might assist her. On June 17, 1993, she took Ginny to a social worker—Karen Schulte—claiming her daughter was finding it difficult to adjust to visiting her father. Ms. Schulte reported that Ginny felt disinclined to visit her father because of what he supposedly said to her. Ms. Schulte continued to see Ginny for scheduled appointments on June 22, 26, and 29. Despite seeing Ginny twice a week, Ms. Schulte never specified what about her psychological condition necessitated this frequency of appointments. Seeing children this often for counseling typically corresponds to an acute crisis threatening their psychological stability. Ms. Schulte, however, never identified exactly what in Ginny's condition justified such frequent appointments.

Ms. Schulte did report that Ginny "appeared to be overwhelmed and confused about what had happened since her move to Michigan and the issue of the identity of her father." In other words, Ginny's feelings of confusion and turmoil were well accounted for by known events. The man whom she had long considered her father, Paul Newton, had disappeared from her life. Another man who seemed a veritable stranger to her, Ed Bielaska, now identified himself as her father. Moreover, we can safely assume that Laura felt less than enthusiastic about Ed assuming a paternal role in his daughters' lives. Without Laura accepting and endorsing Ginny's relationship with Ed, we would expect Ginny to feel apprehensive and awkward about this stranger who called himself "Daddy."

Circumstances such as these create a difficult impasse for children and parents alike. Custodial parents typically reject noncustodians assuming a significant role in their child's life until they know the child and noncustodian enjoy a good relationship. Nonetheless, children and noncustodial parents find it difficult to establish a comfortable relationship without the custodial parent's acceptance and approval. A competent therapist recognizes that helping children in these situations necessitates reducing the frequency and intensity of conflicts between their parents.[8] As long as children find themselves caught in the middle of their parents' ill-tempered exchanges, their psychological welfare will suffer.

Unfortunately, however, Ms. Schulte neglected to respond effectively to Ginny's welfare. She instead responded to Laura's suspicions regarding the August 1989 allegation of sexual abuse. Ginny responded to Ms. Schulte's interests by supposedly telling her, "Ed talked about wanting to touch bottoms, mine's and Louise's." One week later on June 29, 1993, Ms. Schulte reported more allegations directed at Ed. Ginny told her that during a visit with her father, he supposedly touched her bottom while she was changing into her bathing suit. Responding to her naive thinking that advocated "believe the children," Ms. Schulte concluded Ed had abused Ginny.

Ill-Informed Recommendations

As a result of these most recent allegations, Ms. Schulte wrote Laura's attorney a letter making three specific recommendations: (1) Ed's visits with Ginny and Louise should be terminated until further notice, (2) Ed should undergo an evaluation at Ms. Schulte's clinic, and (3) Ginny should continue in therapy with Ms. Schulte to further assess the allegations directed at Ed. There was a great deal about this case, however, Ms. Schulte did not know when she made her recommendations. She did not know about the August 1989 evaluation at the University of Michigan clinic, which was never completed because of Laura's noncooperativeness. Ms. Schulte moreover did not know that it was virtually impossible for Ed to have abused Ginny on the date in question—June 27, 1993.

On June 27, 1993, Ed called a Kelly Beveridge who was renting his home at that time. He asked Kelly if he could bring Ginny and Louise to the house to use the swimming pool. Kelly said yes, and Ed took the girls along with his mother to go swimming. Kelly subsequently testified that during the entire time Ed was there with the girls, he never went inside the house. His mother spent time in the house overseeing Ginny and Louise, but not Ed. Ginny claimed that Ed fondled her in the "pink bedroom." Kelly, however, also testified that during the hour that Ed and the girls were at the house, her girlfriend was also in the "pink bedroom." Because Laura was Ms. Schulte's only source of information, the social worker remained unaware of these facts that made it impossible for Ed to have molested Ginny on the day he allegedly did so.

Even more importantly, Ms. Schulte did not know that on June 24, 1993, Laura telephoned her sister-in-law, Carol Rivera. Outraged by what she considered the cruel injustices Ed had suffered, Carol later testified about Laura telling her, "They [Laura and her family] had planned to accuse Ed once again of abusing the children." In other words, Carol's testimony demonstrated beyond any doubt that Laura was engaged in a deliberate, systematic campaign to falsely accuse Ed of sexual abuse.

This was not a situation of Laura overreacting to her own elevated anxiety and jumping to mistaken conclusions. Instead, Laura knew exactly what she was doing. Unfortunately, however, the testimony of Kelly Beveridge and Carol Rivera was not heard by the court until February 1994. As a result, the judge responded to Ms. Schulte's ill-informed recommendations and suspended Ed's visitation privileges. Following the visit of June 27, Ed did not see Ginny and Louise again until mid-October 1993.

After the court allowed Ed to resume visitations with Ginny and Louise—as long as one or more members of his family supervised his visits—he was again accused of sexual abuse. This time the allegation involved Louise. Having embraced Laura's cause as a naive but loyal ally, Ms. Schulte reported Louise saying that her father had taken her into the bedroom, shut the door, locked it, laid down on the bed next to her, and touched her bottom with his finger.

Subsequent testimony, however, established that during most of the time the children were visiting on this date (November 28, 1993), Ed was outside hanging Christmas lights. Both of his parents were present supervising this visit, and they later testified that Ed was never alone with either Ginny or Louise on that day. In other words, if Ed had abused either girl, his parents had involved themselves in a conspiracy with him trying to conceal it.

Self-Appointed Experts

The court then ordered that Ed, Laura, and the girls undergo an evaluation at the Family Assessment Clinic, a clinic affiliated with the University of Michigan. This clinic operated independently of the U-M Center for the Child and Family involved in the 1989 evaluation. Dr. Kathleen Faller, who practices as a social worker and is the director of the Family Assessment Clinic, was less than well respected for her work related to allegations of sexual abuse. For example, Dr. Elissa Benedek, a past president of the American Psychiatric Association, had testifed in other legal proceedings describing the work of Dr. Faller and her clinic as biased and one-sided. After reviewing videotapes of interviews done at Dr. Faller's clinic, Dr. Benedek found numerous instances of the interviewers resorting to leading questions while not allowing children to express themselves in their own words.

Because of the poor reputation of the Family Assessment Clinic, and in response to his attorney's advice, Ed decided not to participate in its evaluation. Like Ms. Schulte, Dr. Faller knew nothing about the attempted 1989 evaluation at the Center for the Child and Family. Dr. Faller moreover did not know that Ed's parents were present during the entire visit on November 28. Nonetheless, the Family Assessment Clinic did interview and evaluate Laura, Ginny, and Louise.

I subsequently reviewed videotapes of the Faller group's interviews of Ginny and Louise, and like Dr. Benedek, I found evidence of them resorting to severely biased tactics. In particular, the interviewers repeatedly asked one-sided questions designed only to confirm the theory that the children had been sexually abused. The interviewers did not seek any information that could have disconfirmed the assumption of sexual abuse. Subjected to this kind of questioning, Ginny and Louise both said that Ed had touched their vaginal areas. The Faller group specifically concluded that the allegations of June 27, 1993, were founded in fact.

Throughout the interviews done by Dr. Faller's group, Ginny and Louise responded quite passively compared with the interviewers, who did most of the talking. As a result, the interviewers never obtained a verbatim, uninterrupted narrative from the children expressed in their own words. Neglecting to obtain verbatim statements from Ginny and Louise left the interviewers in the dark. They did not know whether the girls were describing imaginary events or instances of actual abuse.

These interviewers also neglected to assess if what the girls thought they remembered had been suggested to them by their mother, their maternal grandparents, and/or Ms. Schulte. The interviewers furthermore failed to consider issues of innocent touching. To belabor the obvious, all parents touch their children, and their memories of innocent touching can be distorted by adults who question them expecting to find evidence of abusive touching.

Dr. Faller's group committed their most outrageous errors when they allowed Laura's presence during most of their interviews with the girls. During Louise's interview, for example, she often responded to questions from the interviewer by looking at her mother. Louise clearly sought her mother's guidance when feeling unsure of how to respond to various questions asked of her. Consequently, how Laura responded to Ginny and Louise's uncertainty when removed from the scrutiny of a video camera was a sobering consideration.

Finally, a Competent Expert

The court next ordered that Ed, Laura, and the girls undergo an evaluation conducted by Dr. Patricia Wallace. Dr. Wallace is a Detroit-area psychologist with extensive experience related to custody and visitation disputes and allegations of sexual abuse. Dr. Wallace discovered that Ginny and Louise underwent diligent preparation for her evaluation. She reported Ginny nervously responding to a question by exclaiming, "Oh oh, I forgot what Mommy told me to say." Dr. Wallace further explained how Ginny "was clearly confused and hesitant to discuss topics, other than those for which she had been specifically coached by her mother."

Dr. Wallace moreover described the girls running to Ed and hugging him when she interviewed them together. This was an exceedingly significant event, being the first and only time any mental health professional involved in this case had observed Ed and the girls interacting with each other. Ms. Merkle and Ms. Schulte reduced themselves to relying on second- and thirdhand information regarding Ed's relationships with Ginny and Louise. Without observing the girls' responses to Ed on a firsthand basis, they simply stereotyped him in ways consistent with Laura's thinking. For example, Laura stereotyped Ed by calling him "the jerk" in the presence of Ginny and Louise.

Dr. Wallace also learned that when Laura and the girls lived in North Carolina, Laura did not respond very effectively to her daughters' educational and health care needs. At 6 years of age, Ginny could not count beyond three or read a book written at her age level. In fact, Ginny was never enrolled in school in North Carolina despite turning 5 in December 1992. After enrolling in school subsequent to returning to Michigan, Ginny continued to struggle. Her teacher testified that as a 6-year-old, she was still learning the letters of the alphabet. Laura had also neglected to have the girls properly inoculated, and she frequently missed scheduled medical appointments for them.

As a result of Dr. Wallace's comprehensive evaluation, she recommended that the court place Ginny and Louise in Ed's custody. In making this recommendation, Dr. Wallace specified that Laura appeared more committed to alienating the girls from Ed than properly caring for them herself. Dr. Wallace moreover emphasized how Laura persistently disavowed any responsibility for the chaotic lifestyle her daughters had endured. Laura preferred to blame all of her difficulties on Ed and Paul, characterizing them as if they were somehow interchangeable parts in her life. Laura claimed: "They were both excessive drinkers. They both forced [her] into sexual relationships. They both were big liars." Without Laura taking any responsibility for her own problems, Dr. Wallace worried she would continue struggling from one crisis to another. Such an outcome would obviously compromise the welfare of Ginny and Louise.

CUSTODY TRIAL

The custody trial to determine whether Ed or Laura could most effectively respond to the needs of their daughters began on February 7, 1994. Judge Colombo, who had presided over most of the many hearings in this case, was unavailable for this trial. In what would eventually prove to be a horrible example of bureaucratic irresponsibility, a court administrator assigned retired District Judge Daniel Van Antwerp to replace Judge Colombo. This was not a jury trial; instead, Judge Van Antwerp alone would make the decisions regarding the contested issues of custody and visitation.

Beyond having no firsthand knowledge of the previous developments in this long and convoluted case, Judge Van Antwerp also had not previously heard a custody case. Michigan's upper-level circuit courts retain jurisdiction in all cases of custody and visitation disputes. Judge Van Antwerp's experience as a lower-level district judge was limited to misdemeanor cases such as shoplifting and disorderly conduct. Unfortunately, his inexperience with family law matters became painfully evident throughout the course of this trial.

As a result of the evidence presented at the trial, Judge Van Antwerp knew how Laura refused to cooperate with the first custody evaluation in May 1989. The judge also heard ample evidence demonstrating Laura's persistent determination in attempting to alienate the girls from Ed. Carol Rivera testified about Laura telling her—on June 24, 1993—how she planned to falsely accuse Ed of abusing the girls. Kelly Beveridge also testified how it would have been impossible for Ed to have abused either of his daughters on June 27, 1993. Judge Van Antwerp furthermore knew that Laura had blatantly defied the court's orders when she moved to North Carolina in 1990. He also heard the expert testimony of Dr. Wallace and myself, explaining how children can report nonexistent events by contaminating their memories with imagination.

Despite all of the evidence presented to Judge Van Antwerp, he concluded that Ed had sexually abused his daughters. Consequently, the judge ruled that the girls should remain in Laura's custody. Judge Van Antwerp moreover ordered that Ed have no visitation with the girls for 8 months, and during that time, the judge wanted Ed to undergo treatment.

In reaching his decision, the judge emphasized: "Discarding what was said and the leading questions, the children still hold to the premise that Edward molested them." This reasoning suggests that Judge Van Antwerp was napping when Dr. Wallace and I explained how suggestibility can undermine the accuracy of what children think they remember. Rather than carefully weigh the expert testimony he heard, the judge appeared to dismiss it entirely. He commented: "The experts seem to throw mud at one another and poke holes in each other's positions. So you have to wonder if these so-called experts are really experts at all. . . . It's kind of hard to hold them in the same esteem as you would have held them prior to listening to them."

THE APPEAL

Incensed by the horrible injustices Ed had suffered, attorney Demosthenes Lorandos took his appeal for the sum of one dollar. Legal fees for the numerous hearings and the previous trial had entirely depleted the resources of Ed and his family. Nevertheless, Mr. Lorandos was more than a bargain. Prior to graduating from law school, he had practiced as a doctoral-level psychologist for almost 20 years. As a result, Mr. Lorandos was well prepared to argue the many complex issues before the appeals court panel of three judges.

On July 19, 1996, the appeals court issued its written decision after hearing the lengthy arguments and voluminous evidence in this case. The court unanimously overturned Judge Van Antwerp's decision, finding numerous instances of his mistaken reasoning. The appeals court emphasized:

> We conclude that the trial court [Judge Van Antwerp] discounted or disregarded most of the trial testimony which supported that plaintiff [Ed] had not sexually abused the children, and that the Schulte and the Faller group interviews and evaluations were unreliable in that they proceeded from the presumption that plaintiff had sexually abused the children and relied to a great extent on unsubstantiated representations made by defendant [Laura].

The appeals court was also less than impressed with the objectivity of Ms. Schulte. It pointed out how: "The trial court based its finding of sexual abuse largely on statements the children made to Schulte, a social worker hand-picked and hired by defendant to substantiate that sexual abuse had occurred, and the children's statements in the videotapes." Addressing the many issues related to the videotaped interviews done by the Faller group, the appeals panel emphasized: "There was expert testimony by Drs. Campbell and Wallace that the Faller group's questioning was coercive and suggestive. Our independent review of the tapes leads us to the same conclusion."

The appeals court further criticized the Faller group for allowing Laura's presence at most of the interviews:

> The propriety of the defendant [Laura] sitting in on most of the interviews conducted by the Faller Group was seriously questioned at trial. Drs. Wallace and Campbell testified defendant encouraged certain answers, and that her presence would affect the interview. Again, our independent review is in accord.

The appeals panel moreover commented on the bias evident in the Faller group's interviews of Ginny and Louise:

> When the tapes are viewed in their entirety, it is clear that the interviewer assumed the veracity of the defendant, and assumed that the abuse had occurred. The focus was on getting the children to describe the abuse. The children were subjected to repeating questioning until the desired response was obtained.

The appeals court ruling overturning Judge Van Antwerp's decision necessitated another hearing in front of Judge Colombo regarding custody. Attorney Lorandos persuasively summarized all of the evidence in this case, and Judge Colombo placed Ginny and Louise in Ed's custody. The girls rapidly adjusted very well to living with Ed and his wife, Claudia. They now understand that the previous allegations of sexual abuse directed at their father were imagined.

This case dramatically demonstrates how vindictive parents can rip apart the lives of innocent people. It also illustrates the too-often counterproductive effects of therapy for children in situations of sexual abuse. Though Dr. Faller and her group repeatedly betrayed appropriate standards in evaluating these allegations, Ms. Schulte's supposed "therapy" with Ginny and Louise made the greatest contribution to contaminating their memories. In the next chapter, then, we examine how therapy can distort and contaminate the recall of children in cases of alleged sexual abuse.

7

---⌇∿⌇---

The Persuasiveness of Play Therapy

*Children Remembering What
Their Therapist Thinks*

Though dwarfed by the witness stand surrounding her, 9-year-old Rachel commands hushed silence from the entire courtroom in which she testifies. A jury, three attorneys, and a judge fix their undivided attention on her. Rachel details the repeated episodes of sexual abuse she supposedly suffered at the hands of her mother and stepfather. Reactions of shock and sympathy flash across the face of every juror as Rachel recalls the fellatio and vaginal penetration she apparently endured.

Dramatic and compelling as Rachel's narration of her alleged nightmare was, her testimony also evoked images of an iceberg—only one-seventh of an iceberg is visible, the rest being submerged beneath the water's surface. My testimony in this case helped the jury understand issues they might have otherwise overlooked. They knew that many assumptions underlying Rachel's sordid revelations demanded closer scrutiny. After a trial of 11 days, the jury returned verdicts of not guilty in response to all of the charges against her mother and stepfather.

BACKGROUND AND CHRONOLOGY

Subsequent to Rachel's parents separating in September 1986, her father, Daniel, became increasingly suspicious that she had been sexually abused by his estranged wife's live-in boyfriend, Mark. As a result of

125

Daniel's suspicions, he sought a physical examination of his then 5-year-old daughter in August 1987. Despite the fact that the result of the initial examination was negative, Daniel obtained another examination for Rachel in September 1987, which also yielded a negative result. In mid-September of that year, Daniel obtained Rachel's custody, and by mid-October, he solicited the counseling services of a master's-level psychologist, Ms. England, for Rachel.

During 13 treatment sessions between October 1987 and February 1988, Rachel never disclosed any experience of sexual abuse to Ms. England. She did report feeling overwhelmed by the simultaneous demands for her loyalty from each parent. Rachel described her ensuing conflicts in physical terms explaining, "My stomach hurts when I feel a pull from both sides." She clarified, "The hurt starts when I see Mommy and Daddy fight," while exclaiming wistfully, "I just wish they would stop." Like so many other children of divorce, Rachel could not choose which parent she preferred because she wanted to live with both.

In early July 1988, Rachel's mother, Cindy, and Mark married. By mid-July, Daniel filed a complaint with Children's Protective Services (CPS) accusing Mark of striking Rachel so hard that he left a hand-print on her back. CPS undertook a comprehensive investigation, and found no cause for substantiation after interviewing both Cindy and Mark. The investigator closed this matter, suggesting her agency would likely see this family again because of their ongoing custody dispute. Subsequent events verified the investigator's prediction: CPS conducted another investigation related to allegations of Rachel's sexual abuse beginning in mid-August 1988. Like the previous investigation, this inquiry also discovered no basis for substantiation. The second investigator also issued an ominous warning, namely, that the frequency with which Rachel was undergoing interviews threatened the reliability of anything she might say in the future because of suggestibility effects.

EFFECTS OF BIASED THERAPY

By September 1988, Daniel had met Kathy, a divorced psychiatric nurse. Kathy responded sympathetically to Daniel's view of Rachel's problems because she had been sexually abused herself as a child. Kathy recommended therapy for Rachel with Dr. McKay, a psychologist at the facility where she worked. Approximately 1 month after initiating this course of treatment, Dr. McKay's notes indicated Rachel reporting that Mark had sexually abused her. Rachel's recall of this supposed abuse included her description of how "Mark squirted sticky stuff on my face from his thing."

Obviously, however, problems of suggestibility and memory contamination undermined what Rachel thought she remembered. What would account for Rachel recalling this alleged abuse in October 1988 after reporting nothing to Ms. England between October 1987 and February 1988? Rachel's October 1988 report likely responded to Dr. McKay's influence more than anything else. In response to Dr. McKay's recommendations, the court terminated Cindy's visitation except for supervised visits confined to her former husband's residence.

In February 1990, Dr. Will, a child psychiatrist employed at the same facility as Dr. McKay, assumed the responsibility for Rachel's treatment. Dr. Will also advocated expressive therapy for Rachel, confident that such procedures facilitated necessary "disclosure work." While eagerly advocating this "disclosure work," Dr. Will overlooked a fundamental principle regarding memory; namely, memory never improves with the passage of time. It either remains the same, or more often it fades and decays. Dr. Will nevertheless assumed that beginning in February 1990, she could assist Rachel in remembering events supposedly transpiring before September 1987. Over the next 2 years of therapy with Dr. Will, Rachel's "disclosures" grew at an exponential rate. In fact, she eventually alleged that her mother had participated with Mark in sexually abusing her.

Treatment for What?

Both Drs. McKay and Will insisted they were treating Rachel for sexual abuse. Carefully considering the many issues involved, however, indicates that it is inappropriate to treat children for sexual abuse *per se.* Sexually abused children exhibit a wide range of symptoms and reactions as a result of their abuse.[1] Some children respond to experiences of sexual abuse by becoming depressed and withdrawing into themselves. Other children react with demonstrations of anger and aggressiveness.

Treating children who respond so differently to abuse as if they are basically alike is grossly mistaken.[2] In other words, effectively meeting the needs of sexually abused children necessitates identifying the clinical condition they exhibit that warrants treatment. Specifically, we need to know whether this child is depressed and withdrawn, or angry and aggressive.

Neglecting to clearly identify the child's clinical condition is tantamount to physicians claiming they treat people for automobile accidents.

In fact, many people involved in such accidents never require medical treatment, and when they do, treatment is a response to their clinical condition (e.g., fractures, concussions, internal injuries) rather than the event responsible for the clinical condition. Neither Dr. Will nor Dr. McKay, however, clearly identified a clinical condition necessitating therapy for Rachel.

Even when sexually abused children do exhibit a clinical condition warranting treatment, relying exclusively on individual therapy is ill-advised. Children respond more positively to therapy when it consistently includes their parents. Parents understandably struggle with considerable worry and self-doubt as they attempt to aid their child in circumstances of abuse. Because worried, self-doubting parents suggest to their children that their condition is a serious one, they can unintentionally impede the child's recovery.

Children cannot recover age-appropriate, normal behavior until they know their parents feel comfortable and self-confident about their situation—but the parents cannot feel comfortable and self-confident until they see their child behaving normally. Therefore, treatment for sexually abused children often involves a challenging impasse: The child cannot be "OK" until the parents are "OK," but the parents cannot be "OK" until the child is "OK." Considerations such as these, however, never occurred to Dr. Will while treating Rachel.

In response to Dr. Will's encouragement, Rachel kept diaries of her thoughts and feelings. Between May 1, 1990, and February 2, 1992, she made 246 separate entries in her diaries. Rachel described her mother negatively on 121 occasions, and Mark was described negatively in 120 entries. Her portrayals of her mother and Mark involved increasing anger and fantasized retribution. In response to Dr. Will's influence, Rachel wrote about wanting to yell at her mother and poke Mark with sharp objects.

Dr. Will responded by lavishly praising Rachel for venting her feelings. Rachel's ventilating eventually led her to conclude that calling her mother "Cindy"—rather than "Mom"—would afford her enormous relief and comfort. Rachel decided to reserve the designation "Mom" for Kathy, and Dr. Will endorsed her decision—even though she had met Cindy only briefly on one occasion after which she refused her any future appointments.

To belabor the obvious, the sequence of events outlined in this case staggers the imagination. At 5 years of age—shortly after Rachel's father assumed her custody—she reported the kinds of loyalty conflicts that often inundate children of divorce. Three years later, after residing continuously in her father's custody, Rachel insists she endured frequent sexual abuse at the age of 5 that was so cruel that it bordered on the sadistic. Rachel's profound revision of her own history underscores the powerful persuasiveness of therapy for children.

Source-Monitoring Errors

Unfortunately, child therapy can distort and confuse the recall of children by creating source-monitoring problems associated with memory.[3] In these instances of distorted memory, the therapist becomes the source of what children remember, rather than the event in question. Therapists can profoundly distort the memory of children by suggesting interpretations of what they supposedly encountered or experienced. In response to the therapist's influence, children accept these interpretations as legitimate. They then resort to their imaginations—though convinced they are searching their memories—inventing anecdotes of past events that appear to validate the therapist's interpretations.[4]

Consider, for example, the case of 4-year-old Susan whose parents thought she had been sexually abused at the day-care center she attended. Despite her parents' suspicions, the supposed perpetrator had never been identified, and Susan claimed the abuse occurred while she was asleep. Moreover, Susan had not exhibited any behavioral or emotional problems indicating a need for treatment. Nonetheless, a child therapist eagerly began therapy with Susan, assuming she had been sexually abused.

With considerable pride, the therapist reported teaching Susan to say, "Don't touch my private." In response to this development, the therapist then led Susan into talking about her supposed abuse. The therapist specifically noted how she "affirmed the client for telling about sexual abuse." In other words, the therapist praised Susan for thinking she had been sexually abused. In subsequent sessions, the therapist continued encouraging Susan to describe the "scenario of sexual abuse." As a result of source-monitoring errors, these kinds of therapist influences can lead children into reporting imaginary experiences of abuse as if they were real.

In still later sessions, the therapist used dolls with Susan to "reenact the abuse scene." The therapist described how she assisted Susan to use a female doll "to scream and run after the male doll approaches." This is another example of a therapy procedure that can mistakenly persuade children about having been sexually abused. Every time the child uses the female doll to "scream and run," she vividly imagines herself experiencing these events. In turn, the child ends up thinking she remembers what actually amounts to imagination.

Therapy Books

Child therapists also frequently rely on books that depict various abuse scenarios. The booklet *What Every Kid Should Know About Sexual Abuse*, for example, identifies children's private parts as their "chest, breasts, genitals (sex organs), and anus (opening to your intestines)."[5] This booklet then defines how "sexual abuse is when: (1) Someone wants to look at your private parts, and/or (2) Someone wants you to look at his or her private parts."

For children under age 8, the information about "private parts" is often ambiguous. For instance, how accurately do young children discriminate between their chests or breasts and their shoulders and stomachs? How accurately do they discriminate between their sex organs and their abdomens? And how accurately do they discriminate between their anuses and their hips?

In response to booklets such as these, young children can misinterpret innocent touching of the shoulder, abdomen, or hip as sexual abuse. The potential for such misinterpretations becomes even more evident when sexual abuse is defined as "someone looking at your private parts." Consequently, books such as these can persuade children that an adult looking at them amounts to sexual abuse. The likelihood of children misinterpreting how an adult looks at them further increases when they learn: "Anyone might be a sexual abuser—someone you know, or a stranger." In other words, this book suggests that almost anything amounts to sexual abuse, and practically everyone is capable of committing sexual abuse.

Reading these books with their therapists creates source-monitoring problems for children. They find themselves confused about what they imagine versus what they remember. Children can easily reinterpret an innocent touch as sinister, and revise innocuous statements as threatening. In fact, the use of such books has led to the reversal of criminal convictions. Concluding that a child's allegations of sexual abuse against her father were "improperly influenced" by a "highly suggestive book on sexual abuse," the Supreme Court of Minnesota overturned a father's conviction for criminal sexual assault.[6]

PERSUASIVENESS OF CHILD THERAPISTS

Returning to Rachel's case, the circumstances of her parents' divorce obviously subjected her to considerable duress. In psychological terms, she struggled with a double approach–avoidance conflict. Her feelings of affection and loyalty for both parents motivated her to approach them. Nevertheless, sustained closeness with either parent also aroused Rachel's anxiety—and corresponding avoidance responses—anticipating censure from the other parent. In other words, Rachel expected disapproval from her father and Kathy if she enjoyed a close relationship with her mother and Mark. Rachel also expected similar responses from her mother and Mark for enjoying a close relationship with her father and Kathy.

When conflicts such as these assume chronic proportions, the child endures an emotionally painful situation. A therapist who responds sympathetically to such a child's plight, and offers hope for alleviating it, profoundly increases her influence with that child. Dr. Will responded in this manner to Rachel, encouraging her to engage in whatever activity she found appealing. Child therapists characteristically seek a warm and understanding relationship with their clients. Doing so allows them to assume a role of central significance in a child's life.

When Dr. Will testified in the criminal trial on behalf of the prosecution, she disclosed relying on a treatment known as play therapy. Dr. Will also eagerly described how play therapists think about their endeavors.

> In the early part of therapy, I was getting to know Rachel and she was getting to know me and trust me. We worked on identifying feelings, and I let her guide where we went. It was done initially with playing, drawing, a fairly unstructured kind of therapy.

Play therapists regard the spontaneous play activities of children as possessing impressive therapeutic value. Play therapy presumably helps children because:

> play is the child's natural medium of self-expression. It is an opportunity which is given to the child to "play out" his feelings and problems just as, in certain types of adult therapy, an individual "talks out" his difficulties.[7]

The effusive confidence with which play therapists, such as Dr. Will, describe their work seems almost inspiring. Of course, play therapists can only rely on self-inspired confidence given the dismal state of play therapy outcome research.[8]

Ethical obligations and intellectual honesty demand that relevant research prevail over intuitive appeal when assessing the value of any ther-

apy method. In the case of play therapy, these obligations result in sobering conclusions. Helpful as play therapy may appear, the evidence available to verify its effectiveness is quite unimpressive. For example, play
therapy does not appear to enhance academic or intellectual achieve-
ment.[9,10] Treatment effects for play therapy are conspicuously absent when
dealing with specific behavioral disorders.[11,12] Moreover, play therapy
does not improve the interpersonal adjustment of children who participate in it.[13,14] Reviews of play therapy consistently comment on the unavailability of outcome data to support this treatment approach.[15]

As long ago as 1975, an overview of treatment for children emphasized that the era of blind faith in the activities of play therapy had
ended.[16] In other words, play therapy amounts to, at best, an experimental
treatment not known to be effective. Even more sobering are the data
demonstrating that play therapy does not effectively aid children who
have been abused. The study supporting this conclusion reported: "No
consistent support was found for the hypothesis that time-limited play
therapy would improve the adjustment of maltreated preschoolers who
already were attending a therapeutic preschool. This lack of support was
evident at both post-test and follow-up."[17]

While summarizing a comprehensive review of play therapy research
reporting mostly nonsignificant outcomes, and some equivocal results, a
reviewer lamented:

> This is a disheartening state of affairs for those who feel strongly
> about play therapy. The data lead to a puzzling paradox.—Why is it
> that clinical wisdom regarding the value of play therapy is unsubstan-
> tiated by the empirical results? Is a clinical activity being utilized
> whose value is at least suspect?[18]

Instead of conceding the limited value of play therapy, this reviewer
advocated additional research seeking evidence of its presumed effectiveness. Of course, one can always call for more research to avoid the obvious
conclusions associated with the existing evidence. If this reviewer's comments accurately reflect the attitudes prevailing among play therapists,
then play therapy finds itself in a crisis of enormous proportions. Rather
than accept the obvious conclusions to which the accumulated data lead,
play therapists cling tenaciously to their blind faith regarding the supposed benefits of play therapy. Consequently, their position reminds one of
Hegel's tongue-in-cheek observation: "If the facts do not agree with the
theory, so much the worse for the facts."

FEELINGS AND EMOTIONS IN PLAY THERAPY

Like any other psychotherapy orientation, the direction of play therapy responds to the theoretical convictions of its practitioners—and play therapists want children to dramatically express their feelings and emotions. Play therapists are particularly interested in the emotional experiences of children that seem to involve anger. Consequently, they attend selectively to their clients' behavior, reserving their greatest interest for responses they interpret as corresponding to angry feelings or emotions.

As a result of the therapist's influence, children in play therapy learn when they are expressing "angry feelings" and how significant such expressions supposedly are. Dr. Will, for example, frequently reassured Rachel "that the feeling of anger was okay." Thus, play therapy encourages children to actively express themselves as a necessary condition of treatment. To the degree that children demonstrate imaginative improvisation in play therapy, they typically encounter lavish praise for the creativity with which they ventilate their feelings. Interestingly enough, related data have demonstrated that improvised, active behavior influences changes in attitudes and beliefs.

Enhanced Persuasiveness

In 1956, college students were asked to argue that 90% of college graduates should be drafted immediately after their graduation. The students were assigned to one of three experimental conditions: (1) They used an outline to improvise a speech that was tape-recorded, (2) they read a prepared speech into a tape recorder, or (3) they merely read the prepared speech to themselves. The students who could actively improvise (Condition #1) exhibited the greatest attitude change in the direction of the speech they made.[19]

Like the college students in the previous experiment, children in play therapy respond to their treatment in an "as if" manner. In response to their therapist's praise, they act *as if* they are angry, and this kind of pretending can influence children to conclude they actually are angry. In fact, we often infer what we believe about ourselves from our most recent actions.[20]

Considerations such as these, however, never constrained Dr. Will's imaginative interpretations. She blithely disregarded her own influence while describing Rachel as "expressing a lot of anger toward Mark and talked about hating him, wanting to tear him and poke him, and wished that he was dead." Unless children in these circumstances define themselves as angry, they must contend with why they are acting in a manner so inconsistent with what they think and feel.

Reconstructing the Past

Children who act as if they are angry are also motivated to reconstruct past events in accordance with their apparent anger. Otherwise, they would endure persistent conflicts as a result of recalling pleasant memories involving someone with whom they are supposedly so enraged.[21] In turn, leading questions and suggestive interpretations can assist children in finding the proper details for a revision of the past that is more consistent with their here-and-now behavior.

As a vehicle of therapist influence altering attitudes and beliefs, play therapy becomes progressively more persuasive over time. Though children appear to control the course of play therapy, therapists actually exercise ultimate control via their interpretive comments. Play therapists regularly attribute a child's overt behavior to some underlying feelings. Simultaneously, they influence children to amplify and exaggerate the intensity with which they express those feelings. The therapist then labels the child's feelings as anger or some other similar emotion, and attributes those feelings to an alleged history of sexual abuse.

For example, Dr. Will described how Rachel felt that other children in her school thought badly of her. She then explained to Rachel, "Many kids who have been through sexual abuse will think that the abuse is their fault and believe that they are bad." Rachel initially rejected this particular interpretation, but make no mistake, Dr. Will eventually prevailed. She persistently attributed various experiences reported by Rachel to her alleged history of sexual abuse.

Again and again, Dr. Will explained to Rachel that she suffered nightmares because she had been sexually abused, and she endured unpleasant thoughts because she had been sexually abused, and she related to others in a controlling manner because she had been sexually abused. Inundated by this unrelenting propaganda week after week and month after month, Rachel eventually succumbed. She began reconstructing events from her past in accordance with the indoctrination of her play therapy.

For children assumed to have been sexually abused, the interpretive endeavors of play therapy correspond to a rigid formula: You are undergoing experience A because of experience B—and experience B almost inevitably equates to a supposed history of sexual abuse. Thus, play therapists arbitrarily define the formative experiences of children for them—even patronizing them with wildly speculative interpretations. In view of the therapist's reputation as a kind and gentle figure, children accept these interpretations as legitimate. They then resort to their imaginations—though convinced they are searching their memories—inventing anecdotes of past events that appear to validate the therapist's interpretations.[22,23]

NETWORK FORMATION AND GUILT INDUCTION

More often than not, custodial parents serve as gatekeepers for their children's health care, and therefore, they usually select a therapist for them. As gatekeepers, custodial parents can influence the decisions therapists make regarding who participates in their children's therapy. As a result, play therapy with children of divorce often excludes noncustodial parents, and these circumstances lure play therapists into sympathetic alliances with custodial parents.[24] As happened in Rachel's case, false allegations of sexual abuse frequently evolve in response to the influences of biased play therapists who overidentify with custodial parents.

Because a "harmony of minds" between two or more people affords them mutual feelings of comfort,[25] play therapists accommodate themselves to the influences of custodians. In turn, they interpret a child's relationship with her noncustodial parent in a manner that corresponds to the custodian's agenda. While progressively endorsing each other's thinking, play therapists and custodians proceed to interact more frequently because of the views they share.

In their determination to create a "therapeutic alliance" with a custodial parent, play therapists may go beyond a genuine and understanding relationship to the extent of coalition formation. A critic of these coalitions has described how they develop—and the problems they create—while summarizing the shortcomings of one-sided custody evaluations:

> It is possible for psychologists to become slowly compromised by the "us/them" mentality that pervades each side of an adversarial legal dispute [or nonlegal dispute]; to become tainted by having only half the data pertinent to the case; or to be influenced in some way by financial remuneration. An insidious process may occur through which psychologists gradually lose their objectivity and unwittingly become partial as advocates for one parent.[26]

As an example of committing the kinds of mistakes cited above, Dr. Will explained:

> The history that I was given by the stepmother and the father was
> that Rachel had been sexually abused by Mark, that he had touched
> the genitalia, and that there was a concern about oral sex. They de-
> scribed having gone to the emergency room and having this evalu-
> ated.

Unfortunately, Dr. Will neglected to obtain the emergency room records
clearly indicating no substantiation—nor even any suspicion—of sexual
abuse. Her error likely corresponded to her penchant for overidentifying
with the cause espoused by Rachel's father and stepmother.

Complex social networks often develop in response to allegations of
sexual abuse—even when those allegations are false. For example, Rachel
lived in a three-generation household that included her father, stepmother
(Kathy), and both paternal grandparents. As a result of her working relationship with Dr. Will, Kathy frequently spoke with her about Rachel's behavior at home and her response to treatment. Kathy also shared the
details of these conversations with Rachel's father and grandparents. In
turn, any one of these adults would discuss issues related to Rachel's
treatment directly with her. As Dr. Will sympathized with Kathy about the
ordeals Rachel had supposedly endured, Kathy reciprocated by reassuring Dr. Will that her wisdom was aiding Rachel enormously. Consequently, Rachel was well aware that her father's family and Dr. Will
viewed each other with considerable respect.

Ultimately, then, play therapists often find their work enthusiastically
supported by a social network. A child who attempts to resist the influence of a play therapist in these circumstances encounters the conformity
pressures of a powerful majority. If another respected adult were available
to support the child's resistance, the play therapist's influence could diminish accordingly. Typically, however, the readiness with which these
networks reject any views deviating from their own guarantees that no
such support is available to the child. Not surprisingly, then, children conform and comply with the influences of play therapists to avoid the guilt
their nonconformity would provoke.

ISOLATION AND INFORMATION CONTROL

Play therapists often isolate children from sources of information
that might challenge their influence. For example, when they recommend
limitations or suspensions of a noncustodian's visitation rights, noncustodial parents obviously find it more difficult to defend their reputations.

Play therapists may also resort to "blame-and-change" maneuvers as a means of justifying their arbitrary visitation recommendations. When play therapists indulge in these maneuvers, children learn that therapy *blames* your father (or your mother if she is the noncustodian) in order to *change* you.[27]

Blame-and-Change Maneuvers

Blame-and-change maneuvers triangulate a child's relationship with the noncustodial parent. Once triangulated, that relationship is subjected to critical comments by a variety of third parties (i.e., custodial parent, custodial stepparent, grandparents, and the ever kindly play therapist). These third-party observers assume they know more about the child's relationship with the noncustodial parent than the child does. Consequently, the child and the noncustodial parent can no longer manage their own relationship. Instead, their relationship responds to the influences of various third parties who are often less than committed to maintaining their parent–child bond.

Dr. Will, for example, unhesitatingly influenced Rachel's relationship with her mother by directing ill-informed comments at her about it. She explained:

> On one occasion Rachel talked about being bothered that Mommy, or Cindy, had talked about Mark during a visit, and I talked with her about letting Mommy know that she was bothered by this. And we talked about what she could do; that—if Mommy talked about Mark, that she could leave, and that she could tell Mommy that she [Rachel] would leave.

This is a particularly chilling example of a play therapist intruding on how a child relates to a noncustodial parent. Though Dr. Will never observed Rachel's relationship with her mother on a firsthand basis, she attempted to alter that relationship in accordance with her own biases.

When play therapists triangulate a child's relationship with a parent via blame-and-change maneuvers, they ignore the research relevant to children of divorce. Above all else, the postdivorce adjustment of children is directly related to the quality of their parents' postdivorce relationship.[28-30] Children who enjoy stable relationships with both custodial and noncustodial parents adjust more effectively to their parents' divorce. Play therapists too often disregard this research and triangulate a child's relationship with a parent via blame-and-change maneuvers. As a result, their treatment efforts frequently deteriorate into an iatrogenic outcome—the attempt to treat the child's distress only increases its severity.

To better understand how play therapists influence children, we can consider the work of Edgar Schein.[31] He studied the indoctrination procedures used on American POWs by the Chinese during the Korean war. Schein referred to those procedures as "coercive persuasion," but they are more commonly known as "brainwashing." Regardless of the term chosen to describe such tactics, Schein emphasized they are neither novel nor unique. Brainwashing isolates people from other influences, coerces them into acting as if they agree with their captors, and leads them into revising their memories of the past.

While acknowledging differences in substance related to the agenda of various influence agents, Schein also cautioned against overlooking similarities in method shared by those agents. He specifically insisted:

> There is a world of difference in the content of what is transmitted in religious orders, prisons, educational institutions, mental hospitals, and thought reform centers. But there are striking similarities in the manner in which influence occurs.[32]

In view of the similarities between play therapy and other persuasive endeavors, one can argue that play therapy too often amounts to "brainwashing."

Play Therapy and Its Marketing Appeal

Surprisingly enough, the American Psychological Association (APA) enthusiastically endorses play therapy despite the accumulated evidence demonstrating its ineffectiveness. Above and beyond its traditional commitment to scholarly and professional journals, the APA has expanded the diversity of its publications. APA ventured into the areas of public information and marketing in 1990 by publishing *A Child's First Book About Play Therapy*.[33]

First Book prepares children for play therapy by describing what they can expect from that experience. It is written expressly for youngsters between the ages of 4 and 7 using simple language they can easily understand. Because the authors encourage parents to read this book with their children, it also influences how they react to their child's treatment. *First Book* perceptively assumes that parents who understand and accept the principles of play therapy are more inclined to endorse it for their children.

First Book portrays play therapy in a manner that effectively solicits parental approval for this treatment. It discusses the problems of children so as to normalize them; consequently, neither parents nor children feel stigmatized by the difficulties supposedly requiring the services of a play therapist. The authors acknowledge that parents can help their children with some problems. Nevertheless, there are other problems so difficult and persistent that they demand the "special help" of "child therapists."

Readers also learn that child therapists assist youngsters to "understand their feelings while they play." The authors emphasize the importance of this understanding by explaining, "Children's problems seem to get better when they understand their feelings." Nevertheless, children and parents are advised to be patient because "getting better is hard and it takes a long time."

First Book promotes play therapy so convincingly that it qualifies as a marketing dream. It indicates that the problems that burden children often leave them severely distressed, therefore arousing a sense of need for a particular service. *First Book* then informs its audience about the expertise of play therapists who assist youngsters to overcome their difficulties, thus promoting a service that supposedly meets the previously cited need.

First Book evokes images of increasingly secure children triumphing over troublesome feelings, and then sharing a final hug with their therapist who will not forget them. In turn, one can readily imagine parents smiling gratefully out of appreciation for the good works of perceptive therapists who relate to their children with such warmth and understanding. If produced as a TV commercial with appropriately scored background music, these scenes could provoke misty-eyed smiles from millions of deeply touched viewers.

Despite its many shortcomings, APA seemed sufficiently pleased with *First Book* to vigorously publicize it. Advertisements touting it as an "invaluable resource" appeared in scientific and professional journals such as the *American Psychologist, APA Monitor, Clinical Psychology Review, Journal of Consulting and Clinical Psychology, Professional Psychology,* and *Psychotherapy.* One can only assume that APA's publication office saw considerable sales potential in *First Book.* Perhaps its sentimental impact will prompt sequels titled *Second Book, Third Book,* and so on, as inspirationally moving as their predecessor.

Overview of Play Therapy

At best, play therapy provides children with a pleasant relationship that appeals to them as an enjoyable pastime. Nevertheless, whenever psychotherapy deteriorates into mere companionship, it assumes the characteristics of an enjoyable luncheon engagement—the affable exchanges between friends are more important than the substance of their meeting. One could argue that play therapy offers children little more than the supportive understanding of an adult friend. Thus, many play therapists merely operate "rent-a-friend" agencies, and unlike spontaneous friendships with older companions, play therapists often promote long-term leases.

Play therapy's appearance of effectiveness can lead to serendipitous outcomes.[34,35] When children speak positively of a play therapist, parents may begin to feel competitive with this semianonymous figure who seems so important to their child. Determined to restore themselves as *the* significant adults in their youngsters' lives, parents undertake greater involvement with their children so as to compete more effectively. Developments such as these allow play therapists to claim credit for improvements in parent–child relationships.

At worst, play therapy exacerbates the circumstances ultimately responsible for the psychological distress of children. When play therapists pursue supportive, affectionate relationships with their clients, they encourage maintaining the status quo in their familial environments. In other words, play therapists can unwittingly encourage parents to continue responding to their children as they have done before. The parents do so because they think this therapy is meeting their children's needs. Therefore, the illusion of treatment effectiveness decreases the probability of parents altering how they relate with their children. The relevant research, however, demonstrates that children respond better to treatment when their parents exhibit specific changes in their behavior.[36]

Guild-Driven Agenda

At a time when considerations of cost containment and treatment efficiency increasingly influence health care policy, play therapy stands out as an anachronistic luxury that health care systems can ill-afford. Without data demonstrating play therapy's effectiveness, health insurers could legitimately designate it an experimental procedure and refuse to recognize it for reimbursement. If insurance carriers were to adopt such a position, one wonders if APA would officially protest on behalf of play therapists. Should this scenario actually ensue, it would reduce ethically responsible psychologists to head-shaking disbelief.

The readiness of APA to promote play therapy via its publication of *First Book* corresponds to its persistent disregard of relevant research. APA has endorsed a treatment modality without sufficient empirical support to verify its effectiveness. As a result, APA leaves itself open to charges of neglecting its scientific responsibilities. At the very least, APA should have published *First Book* with the same responsible caution it expresses in its journals. All APA journals contain the following statement or one similar to it:

> The opinions and statements published are the responsibility of the authors, and such opinions and statements do not necessarily represent the policies of the APA or the views of the editor.

Surprisingly enough, this kind of disclaimer appears nowhere in *First Book*.

By virtue of publishing *First Book* without an appropriate disclaimer, APA seems so preoccupied with *who* to market and *how* to market, it blithely overlooks *what* it is marketing. If *First Book* amounts to an advertisement for play therapy, then APA has irresponsibly ignored requirements for truth in advertising. APA's vigorous promotion of *First Book* reduces it to the status of a myopic organization unable to see beyond its self-serving interests as a professional guild. As a result, this kind of ill-advised, public relations venture can only jeopardize the reputation of APA as a scientific–professional organization.

PLAY THERAPY AND MALPRACTICE CONSIDERATIONS

Above and beyond the ethical oversights committed by many play therapists who treat children of divorce, the malpractice considerations are even more sobering. A 1990 review outlined how the exacerbation of a client's presenting symptoms and the development of new symptoms (i.e., "disruption of previously solid relationships") increase the malpractice risks for psychotherapists.[37] When therapy for children of divorce deteriorates into a triangulated relationship, their symptoms frequently worsen and their relationships with one or both parents are often disrupted.

In treating children of divorce, play therapists sometimes include the noncustodial parent after having already established a loyal coalition with the custodial parent. In these situations, the therapist often remains aligned with the custodian and subjects the noncustodian to accusatory interpretations. Rather than address *what* needs to be done to resolve the parental conflicts of the present, the therapist suggests *why* the noncustodian committed alleged transgressions in the past—and these suggestive interpretations often reflect the custodian's agenda. Therapists who commit these errors merely fuel the fires of parental conflict that burn between divorced spouses. This outcome can result in such parental polarization that only supernatural intervention could reverse it.

When noncustodial parents endure the biases of a therapist aligned with their ex-spouse, they may overgeneralize their experience to all psychotherapists. As a result, they reject psychotherapy as hopelessly counterproductive, resign themselves to the continued inevitability of disrupted relationships with their children, and bring renewed vigor to future confrontations with their custodial counterpart. These circumstances also create fertile ground for growing malpractice litigation. Disillusionment with psychotherapy that leads to feelings of hopelessness is another cause for legal action against psychotherapists.[38]

OVERVIEW

Whether fanning the flames of false allegations of sexual abuse, or neglecting the welfare of children with more conventional problems, play therapy has long avoided responsibility for its frequently counterproductive outcomes. Therapists who portray themselves as kindly figures playing gently with children appear at least committed to a worthy endeavor—or seem merely benign at their worst. Obviously, however, this charitable conclusion qualifies as another example of how appearances can be exceedingly deceptive. Nevertheless, the discovery procedures of malpractice litigation would shed sorely needed light on the massive shortcomings associated with play therapy.

Therapy for children can dramatically alter their memories, persuading them they suffered horrible episodes of sexual abuse that never actually occurred. If therapy can so profoundly contaminate the memories of children, could it have the same effects on adults? Can therapists persuade adults that they were sexually abused when, in fact, no such abuse ever happened? Surprising as it may seem, the answer to this question is yes. We address these issues of therapy and adults in Chapter 8, which starts Part II of the book. There we will examine claims of repressed memories.

II

Claims of Repressed Memories

8

---⟨∽⟩---

Adults Recalling
What They Forgot to Remember?

Assume that the parents of a young woman in her mid-20s receive the following letter from their daughter.[1]

BEFORE

Dear Mom and Dad:

I want you to know how much it means to me that you have made it possible for me to have this house and the help you've been to me fixing it up is something I'll never forget. I am so lucky to have had you beside me this last couple of years. I really don't know what I would have done without you. I love you very much and am so lucky to have such wonderful parents. Thank you for everything.

Your daughter

Approximately 6 months later, these same parents receive the following letter from their daughter.

AFTER

Dear Mom and Dad:

I love and respect you but it can't erase the hurt and pain I endured as a child. I cannot be around you without going into the depth of depression. The lies and secrets must end. I feel betrayed. Everything you do for me feels like a lie. If you want to help me heal, the secret must end. I need to hear "yes" it happened. I want Daddy to cry and admit the secret. I want Mom to say "I failed you. I didn't protect you." I am not crazy. This happened. I was sexually abused by my father for years. My mother failed to see the abuse and allowed it to happen. The burden is too much so let's speak the truth. We don't need to fix a divorced, poor, sick daughter. We need to fix a 36 year old woman carrying scars from her childhood. The abuse has affected my life in every way.

If you cannot help me, then please leave me alone.

The "night and day" differences in the tone and content of these two letters raise the question: What is going on here? Subsequent to writing her "before" letter, this young woman sought out the treatment services of a mental health professional. Over the course of numerous therapy sessions, her therapist "assisted" her in uncovering memories of her father's alleged sexual abuse—memories that presumably had been repressed. Consistent with the doctrines of Freudian theory, the therapist assumed that this young woman's current problems originated from some childhood trauma (or traumas) motivating the use of repression as a coping mechanism. In particular, this theory-driven thinking presumes that the human psyche frequently deals with horrific traumas by wiping out—or repressing—any memories of those traumatic experiences.

THEORETICAL FOUNDATIONS OF REPRESSION

Current theories regarding childhood trauma and repression were substantially influenced by Jeffrey Masson's 1984 book *The Assault on Truth: Freud's Suppression of the Seduction Theory.*[2] Masson worked as the projects director of the Sigmund Freud Archives before being fired in 1981. In his 1984 book, Masson returned to Freud's original theory claiming that psychological disorders of adults frequently developed as a result of childhood sexual abuse.

Freud originally thought his adult patients could not remember the sexual abuse they supposedly endured. Recalling those childhood experiences of abuse would presumably leave them overwhelmed. Motivated to avoid the emotional devastation associated with remembering such events, Freud theorized that his patients repressed—or forgot—these traumatic experiences. In treating his patients, Freud initially sought to assist them in recovering these apparently repressed memories. He later revised this theory, insisting that the scenarios his patients recalled amounted to fantasies rather than memories of actual abuse.

Masson vehemently criticized Freud for abandoning his original theory, contending he did so to avoid the disbelief and censure of his nineteenth-century Victorian contemporaries. Throughout the mid- and late

1980s, Masson's position regarding childhood sexual abuse received considerable attention and endorsement. In her 1988 book *Healing the Incest Wound*, Christine Courtois insisted: "Survivors [of incest] with the most severe memory deficits often describe almost complete amnesia for childhood but report experiencing jarring, recurrent, intrusive symptoms, particularly flashbacks and body sensations."[3] Bassel van der Kolk, a psychiatrist who also endorses this thinking, claimed that adult victims of childhood sexual abuse "experience the original trauma without conscious awareness of the historical reference."[4]

Recovered Memory Therapy

The eagerness with which therapists embrace classical Freudian assumptions regarding trauma and memory loss influences the experiences of many clients in psychotherapy. Numerous therapists now practice what is known as "recovered memory therapy." For example, a 1992 article in the journal *Psychotherapy* summarized the "memory reconstructions" a therapist undertook with four of her clients.[5] This therapist reported:

> Client A, a 30-year-old female, who initiated therapy 2 years ago to work on relationship issues. Under the stress of therapy she began having flashbacks of abuse. She now remembers being physically and sexually abused and tortured by several family members.

> Client B is a 42-year-old male who entered therapy 10 months ago. Recent work with another therapist had led him to suspect that he had been sexually abused. He is finding it necessary to disentangle himself from some abusive relationships in order to tolerate returning memories of physical torture and sexual abuse by several family members.

> Client C is a 29-year-old who has worked intermittently with several therapists over a 4-year period. Her therapy focused on sexual dysfunctions and abusive relationships, without exploring the possibility of childhood abuse. Memory reconstruction work over a 6-month period has brought partial recall of physical and sexual abuse by several family members.

> Client D is a 20-year-old female, who entered therapy 4 months ago, stating that she wanted to break the emotional hold her parents had on her. When discussing her parents, her train of thought was often interrupted by dissociative episodes. She now has fragmentary recall of sexual abuse by several family members.

It is important to note that not one of these clients entered therapy with any childhood memories of physical or sexual abuse. As a result of their treatment experiences, however, these clients began struggling with horrifying memories of cruel maltreatment. Consider, for example, the following "before" and "after" letters:[6]

BEFORE THERAPY

Mom and Dad:

Just thought I would drop you a line to say hi! I have been so busy lately I have forgotten to tell you guys how much I love you. You two have done so much for me. . . . You have continually supported me, loved me, and helped me work through my various problems and adventures. . . . I just wanted you guys to know that you are appreciated. I seldom tell you how I feel or how much you guys mean to me. . . . I love you more than words can say.

AFTER THERAPY

Dear First name and Last name:

Why am I writing this letter: To state the truth—Dad I remember just about everything you did to me. Whether you remember it or not is immaterial—what's important is I remember. I had this experience the other day of regressing until I was a little child just barely verbal. I was screaming and crying and absolutely hysterical. I was afraid that you were going to come get me and torture me. That is what sexual abuse is to a child—the worst torture—I experienced what professionals call a "body memory." My body convulsed for hours—the pain started in my vagina and shot up and out my mouth . . . I felt I was a small child being brutally raped. I knew I was remembering what I had experienced as a child . . . I asked who could have done such a thing—initially I thought Mom, since I had a vague dream about her—but that did not fit—then I blurted out, "Oh, my God, my father repeatedly raped me . . ." I needed your protection, guidance and understanding. Instead I got hatred, violation, humiliation and abuse . . . I don't have to forgive you . . . I no longer give you the honor of being my father . . . I'm not the victim anymore.

Shocking as the above examples are, other clients report remembering even more sadistic experiences of mistreatment. These clients think that therapy assisted them in remembering past episodes of satanic ritual abuse.

Claims of Satanic Ritual Abuse

Numerous therapists believe that many of their clients have been victimized by worldwide, systematically organized, intergenerational cults. These cults supposedly harbor multiple perpetrators who subject their victims to quasi-religious rituals involving sexual assault, human sacrifice, cannibalism, and the consumption of human blood and waste. A group calling itself "Survivors of Incest Anonymous" claimed ritual abuse involves two components:

> The physical component usually includes torture, at times maiming and disfigurement, and even death. The sexual component of ritual abuse is often violence, purposefully painful, intended to degrade and dehumanize, and to orient the victim towards sadism.[7]

Therapists who think their clients struggle with repressed memories of ritual abuse insist they must eventually recall it. Otherwise, the client's "recovery" supposedly remains incomplete.

Consider, for example, the case of Lucey Abney who was hospitalized in a Texas psychiatric facility for depression.[8] By the time she left the hospital after nearly a year's stay, she thought she had more than 100 different personalities. She attributed these personalities to her history of childhood abuse supposedly perpetrated by a satanic cult. Another young woman, hospitalized in a Texas psychiatric facility, recalled how she was placed in restraints, and threatened with the restriction of her hospital privileges unless she recalled her alleged cult activities.[9] This woman's therapist accused her of killing babies as part of cult rituals, and then repressing her memory of those acts. The therapist also told her that both of her parents had sexually abused and tortured her.

Gina Smiley sought treatment for an eating disorder.[10] A therapist persuaded her that all of her problems originated with satanic abuse. Her family allegedly forced her to bear children who were then murdered and devoured in a satanic ritual. As part of her therapy, Ms. Smiley insists that treatment personnel regularly pinned her to the floor, performing exorcisms on her in front of other patients. Another treatment facility in Michigan not only subjected a client to an exorcism, it also billed her health insurance for the procedure!

Satanic Ritual Abuse and Conspiracy Theories

Therapists who contend that many of their patients suffer the effects of ritual abuse also embrace conspiracy theories about their work. Dr. Corydon Hammond, a prominent figure in treating clients he describes as survivors of ritual abuse, has claimed an international conspiracy drives these cults. When interviewed on an Arlington, Virginia, radio station in June 1992, Dr. Hammond said:

> My best guess is that the purpose of it [satanists] is they want an army
> of Manchurian candidates—tens of thousands of mental robots who
> will do prostitution, do child pornography, smuggle drugs, engage in
> international arms smuggling, do snuff films, all sorts of lucrative
> things and do their bidding. And eventually, the megalomaniacs at
> the top believe, [they will] create a satanic order that will rule the
> world.[11]

More recently, Dr. Hammond has reportedly sought to distance himself
from the position he expressed in June 1992. Nevertheless, his position at
that time continues to influence numerous other therapists.

In the spring of 1993, David Calof, a hypnotist with no formal training beyond a bachelor's degree, presented his views regarding ritual
abuse to the Menninger Clinic. Calof claimed:

> In ritual abuse especially you will see "triggering programs" that are
> literally installed by the perpetrators to potentiate self-harm. . . . You
> will find the possibility of disguised contact—or clandestine contact—
> with perpetrators that will then potentiate self-harm.[12]

As an example of "disguised" or "clandestine" contact, Calof cited the
following letter sent to a supposed survivor of ritual abuse by her sister:

> Dear Sis,
> Mom and I have been thinking about you. Can't wait to see you again.
> . . . In the meantime, take care of yourself.
> Love, Sis

While characterizing this letter as "insidious," Calof insisted it influenced
the client in various unexpected ways. He interpreted the first sentence as
persuading the client that people can read her mind. Calof also claimed
that this letter cryptically warned the client, "No matter where you are, or
what you are doing I will know if you tell." More than anything else,
Calof's impressions demonstrate the talent of many therapists for finding
what they expect to find when drawing conclusions about ambiguous
statements open to various interpretations.

Calof continued to interpret "Can't wait to see you again" as indicating a "presupposition" by the "perpetrating group" that the client would
inevitably return to them. He then concluded that the final sentence really
amounted to a demand for the client to kill herself. While indulging in his
symbolic conjecture, Calof neglected to consider the gross inconsistency of
his interpretations. If the client were to kill herself, then her return to the
"perpetrating group" would be anything but inevitable.

INTERPRETIVE LIBERTIES

When reaching their conclusions about who has been sexually abused as children, therapists act as if they enjoy interpretive license limited only by their imaginations. While discussing victims of sexual abuse on CNBC in April 1992, Dr. Brenda Wade claimed:

> It's so common that I'll tell you, I can within 10 minutes, I can spot it as a person walks in the door, often before they realize it. There's a trust, lack of trust, that's the most common issue. There's a way that a person presents themselves. There's a certain body language that says I'm afraid to expose myself. I'm afraid you are going to hurt me.[13]

As she indulged in her overconfident conclusions, Dr. Wade likely never considered whether two or more of her colleagues would share her conclusions after observing the same person. Disregarding this fundamentally important consideration reveals more about the ignorance of too many therapists than anything else.

Unfortunately, however, many therapists resort to the kind of nonsense cited above. For example, a Jean McCauley misinformed the listening audience of National Public Radio in December 1995. Like Dr. Wade, Ms. McCauley insisted:

> I can almost spot these patients [survivors of abuse] as they walk in the door. There's a certain pattern of both physical and psychological complaints. There's a way that they fail to meet eye contact. There's a certain distress and depressed look about them, or anxious look about them that it's almost like I can tell as they walk in the door.

If Ms. McCauley really thinks she can accurately assess her clients before they so much as utter a word, then anxiously retreating from her suggests good judgment from those who do so.

Behavioral Indicators of Supposedly Repressed Memories

Various therapists have developed symptom lists related to their thinking about repressed memories. These lists claim to identify people who have supposedly repressed their memories of childhood sexual abuse. In her book *Repressed Memories: A Journey to Recovery from Sexual Abuse,* Dr. Renee Fredrickson describes her checklist consisting of various symptoms related to seven general areas.[14] In particular, Fredrickson specifies the following symptoms (and many others) as indicating repressed memories of child sexual abuse:

Sexuality: 1) I began masturbating at a very early age. 2) As a child, I used to insert objects into my bottom, and I do not know where I learned to do this. 3) I seemed to know some things about sex even before they were explained to me.

Sleep: 1) I often have nightmares. 2) I have difficulty falling or staying asleep. 3) I sometimes wake up feeling as if I am choking, gagging, or being suffocated.

Fears and Attractions: 1) I am frightened of one or more common household objects. 2) I would never go into a closet or any dark, confined place. 3) There are certain things I seem to have a strange affection or attraction for.

Eating Disturbances: 1) I have had periods in my life when I couldn't eat, or I had to force myself to eat. 2) Sometimes I binge on huge amounts of food. 3) Certain foods or tastes frighten me or nauseate me.

Body Problems: 1) I do not take good care of my body. 2) I hate my body. 3) I have odd sensations in my genitals or rectum.

Compulsive Behaviors: 1) I sometimes hurt myself in a way that marks or scars my body. 2) I have an addiction to drugs or alcohol. 3) My drug or alcohol use started before I was 13.

Emotional Signals: 1) There have been times when I was very suicidal. 2) I feel a sense of doom, as though my life will end in tragedy or disaster. 3) I have unexplained bouts of depression.

Barnum Effects

Claims for indicator lists such as Fredrickson's flounder as a result of the "Barnum effect."[15] The latter term refers to showman P. T. Barnum's cynical observation suggesting that "there's a sucker born every minute." The accumulated data related to the Barnum effect demonstrate how it heightens people's gullibility. People are highly predisposed to endorse reasonable-sounding descriptions of themselves if: (1) those descriptions seem personally tailored to them and (2) are expressed by an authority figure.[16] In particular, Barnum-like descriptions can appear valid because they specify characteristics frequently found in the general population (high base rates), while defining those characteristics in vague terms.[17]

It is clear and evident that Barnum-like descriptions undermine the value of Fredrickson's symptom list. Her symptom list cites conditions characterized by high base rates (e.g., "I have difficulty falling or staying asleep," "I do not take good care of my body") and vague definitions (e.g., "I seemed to know some things about sex even before they were explained to me," "There are certain things I seem to have a strange affection or attraction for"). In other words, this symptom list can fit almost any client as a result of relying on high base rates and vague definitions.

Confirmatory Bias

The Barnum-like characteristics of indicator lists such as Fredrickson's lead therapists who rely on them into committing errors of "confirmatory bias." Confirmatory bias is the "tendency to seek supportive data for one's hypothesis and to underweight or disregard nonsupportive data."[18] Fredrickson's list encourages therapists to focus excessively on confirming cases of supposedly repressed memories of childhood sexual abuse. Simultaneously, this list neglects to specify how claims of repressed memories can be disconfirmed.

Confirmatory biases also motivate therapists to limit their questioning of clients to queries that can only confirm hypotheses of repression and sexual abuse. Simultaneously, they avoid questions that could elicit disconfirmatory responses.[19] Related data, for example, demonstrate that attempting to determine whether an individual is an extrovert leads subjects into asking mostly one-sided questions—"What would you do if you wanted to liven up a party?"[20] Regardless of how people answer this question, their responses can be interpreted as consistent with their assumed status as extroverts. Similarly, then, assumptions about a client's presumed history of sexual abuse can increase the frequency of confirmatory questions directed at that issue—and asking enough confirmatory questions allows therapists to conclude they found the answers they were expecting.

In view of the high base rates and vague definitions characterizing Fredrickson's list of indicators, the probability of false-positive errors—mistakenly confirming repressed memories—far exceeds the probability of false-negative errors—mistakenly ruling out repressed memories. Therapists who rely on these indicators in a legal proceeding rapidly flounder in response to the cross-examination questions for indicator lists found in Chapter 3 of this book.

PARENTAL REACTIONS

Assume that you have received a totally unexpected letter from your daughter or son directing horrible allegations of sexual abuse at you. Prior to the letter, you felt comfortable about your relationship with this child.

You knew you were not a perfect parent, but then how many parents can claim such perfection? Now, however, you find yourself accused of the ugliest, most unthinkable acts. How do you respond? What do you do? Parents confronted with these nightmare accusations often react with shocked disbelief. The following letter from an accused father details such a reaction.

> The charges made against us have been devastating. My sleepless nights have gone on and on as if forever. Life has lost all meaning for me. One reason, I had hoped my children would continue to bring me joy and comfort in my "golden years." This hope has been shattered. The only thing that has kept me sane is the fact that I truly believe this is the fantasy of a highly disturbed individual. No one, not even my wife, will ever know the living hell I have gone through.[21]

Legal Actions and Criminal Investigations

Other families have found themselves threatened with legal actions and subjected to criminal investigations. The following letter from a mother summarizes such experiences.

> Our daughter had a restraining order issued against her father. The charges were incest, rape, and murder. She claimed she was molested from the age of three months on. She also accused him of murdering three women, one of which he was to have cut up and put through a meat grinder and made her watch. She even drew pictures of the three women.
>
> My husband was thoroughly investigated by investigators in two counties. We were unaware of the investigations until we were called down to the Sheriff's office. They interviewed us separately, and at the conclusion agreed that something was definitely unstable about our daughter.
>
> They [Sheriff's investigators] were upset at the cost involved in the investigations, and seemed to think that her psychologist and psychiatrist were at fault. My husband had to take a lie detector test which he passed with flying colors. Absolutely nothing turned up in the investigations. . . . Since that time my daughter informed me that I would never be able to see the grandchildren. I continue to write her little notes but receive no response. We are continuing our prayers for a resolution to this bizarre situation.[22]

Maintaining Contact

Despite the allegations directed at them, parents often put forth persistent efforts trying to maintain contact with their accusing child. Consider, for example, a mother who still attempts to communicate with her daughter after 7 years.

> It has been seven years since Dr. H stopped all family contact. I'm allowed to write him [Dr. H], then he passes them to my daughter. She mentioned that she didn't read the last two letters—I believe he [Dr. H] reads parts of them to her. He said she would get too upset.
>
> She lives alone in an apartment. She said it is very hard. The last time we spoke, her speech was so slurred I had to concentrate to understand her. She said she can't read or watch television because she can't concentrate (This is a woman who graduated from college with honors). She also said she can't do much during the day. She shocked me when she said that she is now Bulimic. My youngest grandson, 9-years-old (I last saw him at three), now gets therapy four times a week for a fractured psyche because of my daughter's problems.
>
> My family's entire life has been ruined by Dr. H's treatment and isolation of my daughter. I've missed my grandson's childhood. Dr. H wouldn't even give me the courtesy of an office visit to try to understand her illness or to be of help in some small way and yet he answers to no one!
>
> My daughter was a well educated woman of 31. She had a wonderful professional husband and a beautiful home, two beautiful sons, loving family, and many friends. She was a teacher and full of life and love. After the shock of her father's death, and a depression following the birth of a baby, she went into therapy. She is now a non-working, drugged, lonely, divorced bulimic vegetable who has been torn from her family and friends.[23]

Meeting the Therapist

Some parents manage to meet with their accusing child and the therapist. The outcomes of such meetings, however, can leave unsuspecting parents feeling ambushed. Consider, for example, the following letter from an overwhelmed mother.

> The meeting with my daughter and the therapist was the most devastating and numbing experience I remember ever having experienced. My daughter was supported by the therapist in a very emotional and angry tirade directed at me. The therapist insisted that I had had an abused childhood, that I was either deliberately or unwittingly withholding painful episodes of abuse involving myself, relatives or family friends. The more the therapist made these statements, suggesting things that I was 'denying,' the angrier and more unreasonable became my daughter's tirade.
>
> It broke my heart to sit and watch and hear my daughter, whom I love with all of my being, hurting so very deeply. And I was unable

to hug her or say anything, except to feebly express my total bewilderment. The therapist in my presence, as though I was not there, pointed out to my daughter that not only was I a person who needed to control everything and everyone, I was also a 'great denier.'[24]

Threatened Lawsuits

Other parents accused of having sexually abused their adult child first learn of the accusations via an attorney's letter. These letters often threaten them with a lawsuit. The following is an example of the letters some parents have received.

Dear Mr. and Mrs. R,

Please be advised that this Law Firm represents your daughter. She has consulted with me regarding the effects she is suffering from severe childhood trauma resulting from the abuse inflicted by all of you. The trauma described is unspeakable.

As a result of this trauma, without relating all of the details in this letter, she has been unable to hold a full-time job. Further, her condition requires intensive therapy and frequent hospitalizations. Although she has been suffering the financial burden of this condition alone, at this time, she can no longer afford to do this and is seeking compensation from you.

Without filing a Court action, Ms. R has authorized me to make the following demand letter for settlement.

1. You assume responsibility for Ms. R's medical and therapeutic expenses including any hospitalization for the remainder of her life.
2. Reimbursement to Ms. R for therapy and hospitalization expenses incurred during 1990 and 1991, in the estimated amount of $10,000.00.
3. Payment of $250,000.00 to help, in some small way, to compensate her for the disabilities, pain, suffering, humiliation, and severe lifetime trauma that she has suffered and is expected to suffer.
4. A life insurance policy to be taken out on your lives with Ms. R to be named beneficiary to ensure that the settlement be paid.
5. That you agree to never contact her or her children in any way. Ms. R's therapists and I are familiar with the details of her childhood trauma. We all agree that any contact with her family would be detrimental to her recovery.

I am therefore requesting that you address all communication to my office. If you wish to enter into settlement at this time without the necessity of Court action, please contact my office. If I do not hear from you within 10 days, I will assume that you do not intend to enter into settlement and will advise Ms. R regarding the appropriate judicial relief. Rest assured, however, that if you do not settle this matter, in any lawsuit, Ms. R will be requesting substantially larger sums and her attorney's fees. As a lawyer, I have dealt with many of these cases, and the facts that have been related to me and which will be related to a jury, warrant the imposition of substantial punitive and compensatory damages.[25]

Some attorneys apparently consider claims of repressed memories as potentially lucrative sources of business. In early 1994, a Tallahasee law firm sent a form letter to numerous mental health professionals throughout Florida. This letter informed them of changes in the Florida statue of limitations allowing "surviviors of physical, sexual, or mental abuse occurring in childhood" to pursue legal action against the alleged perpetrators. The letter further claimed that the "victims" of such abuse "often do not discover their injury and its causal connection until their adult years." This same letter continued by stating:

> As a professional who may come into contact with persons recovering from various forms of childhood abuse, elder abuse, and incest, you are in a position to raise the legal awareness of those survivors whose rights might potentially be affected. . . . For those for whom confrontation and restitution would provide empowerment and closure, it could be an important final step in the healing process. If someone you know, currently treat, or have treated in the past is an abuse or incest survivor, please make them aware of [Florida] Chapter 92-102.[26]

Defending against Lawsuits

Parents who must defend themselves against these outrageous allegations face a demanding, uphill battle. Even when the parents prevail in a court of law, their victories leave them feeling empty and hollow. Consider, for example, the following case.

> A little more than four years ago, our daughter initiated a lawsuit against both of us, accusing us of the most bizarre and unbelievable acts of sexual abuse and satanic ritual abuse. There was no truth to any of her claims, nor was there one scintilla of evidence against us. If the therapist or her attorney had made any attempt to corroborate the "memories" which were uncovered in therapy, they would have seen

pediatric records and a gynecological examination report verifying that there was no trauma (some of the horrendous things she accused us of would have left scars).

Our daughter's lawsuit against us has just been dismissed with prejudice, meaning that she can never initiate another suit against us on these charges. We strongly proclaimed our innocence from the beginning, and defended the lawsuit vigorously. At what cost? Monetarily, it has cost in excess of $80,000.00, and the final bills are not yet in (we were fortunate in not only getting excellent legal representation, but an attorney who discounted legal fees by 25% or else the cost would have been substantially higher). Emotionally, there is no figure that can represent that cost to us. But perhaps the cost to our daughter is the highest. She has dismissed her entire "family of origin," saying that they are all "in denial," and that she has the only "reality" of her entire childhood and adolescence. She has gained widespread acceptance as "victim," and this will be hard for her to give up.

We are reluctant to let her go, but perhaps we must come to the realization that she may never return to us and reality.

Letting Go

Heartbreaking as it is to do so, other parents finally come to the conclusion that they have no choice but to say good-bye to their accusing child. The following letter from a father—to his accusing daughter—explains the decisions he and his wife felt forced to make.

I am writing this to wish you a Happy 40th Birthday. For a normal family, one that has not been destroyed by bad therapy, this would be a special occasion. In our case, it will just be a day for your mother and me to remember all of the happy times we had together when you were growing up and after you first had children. These we will have always. We will never forgive the profession for what it did to you.

So you won't be shocked when the time comes, we have set up a trust to provide for our grandchildren when they reach adulthood. The only stipulation is that they view some videos and read some articles that present our side of this tragedy.

We have always loved you and were proud of you. We could not have asked for more than you were—a sharp mind, an engaging personality, a loving person who was in turn loved by many friends.

We have fought for you in the only way we have known how, and we will continue to do so—if for no other reason than to help others. I hope that you enjoy your birthday. Who knows, someday we may meet and be a family again. I'll always love you.[27]

Recovering from the Allegations

With the passage of time, some parents and families gradually recover from the ugly allegations directed at them. Through persistent determination, they regain a sense of direction in their lives, and simultaneously, they often decide to disclose the allegations to people outside their immediate family. A mother wrote about making this decision for herself.

> For two and one-half years whenever friends asked, "How are the children?," I've lied and said, "They're OK." But I can't do that any more. Now when people ask, I tell them the truth. Although I am sorry that they are shocked and saddened by the story that my daughter "recovered memories of abuse," I confess that I feel liberated, as though a great weight had come off my shoulders. We love our daughter and don't want to harm her or make it difficult for a potential reconciliation, but pretending to others that this did not happen really would be "in denial."[28]

Another mother reported how she responds to people asking about her daughter.

> I have finally found a way that is comfortable for me to explain to neighbors and friends who ask where my daughter is. I tell them that she has joined a sort of therapy-cult that is obsessed with sexual abuse. People seem to understand cults.[29]

When disclosing their children's allegations to long-time friends, other parents have encountered totally unexpected reactions. The following letter from an accused father describes such a situation.

> Last Friday I met an old friend and colleague for lunch. We have not met since my daughter made her accusation because I didn't feel I could see him without telling him about this crisis in my life. I have felt so perplexed that I just didn't want to talk about it. Now that I understand how this happened, I was finally able to call my friend.
>
> We began with the ordinary pleasantries when suddenly he broke off with—"But that's not what I want to talk about. I have to tell you that there's been a terrible problem with my daughter she has accused me of sexual abuse." As he began his narrative, I interrupted, "I don't want to stop you but I have to tell you first that I have exactly the same problem. . . ." The startling thing to me was to hear him say that he has learned that his neighbor across the street has the same problem. In that, he was luckier than me because he did not have to live with this alone.[30]

Tragic Endings

Unlike the cases cited immediately above, other parents and families
are faced with tragic endings related to these accusations.

> My husband and I were in attendance at the Memory and Reality
> conference last April [1993]. The conference meant so much to him. It
> was a real help. He died June 10th—he just couldn't hold on any
> longer for the heart transplant. The hardest thing about his death for
> me is that he died without this terrible accusation being resolved.[31]

Another widow wrote a similar letter.

> It is with regret that I inform you of the death of my husband.
> Our daughter, who was estranged from us, came home after her fa-
> ther had a massive heart attack. He never regained consciousness. She
> was by his bed for the 10 days before his death. No one will ever
> know if he knew she was there. Not one word about the false accusa-
> tions has been mentioned. I am sure that the stress of the last two
> years led up to the heart attack. It was something he could not under-
> stand, but he had forgiven her.[32]

And still another widow reported similar circumstances.

> My husband died about three months after our daughter's con-
> frontation which was, of course, absolutely devastating. I'm afraid
> now that the truth will be even more painful to our daughter, if or
> when she finally realizes that her memories are false. It's so sad and
> there is no way I can help her.[33]

Facing the inevitability of death has led other parents to seek help
with difficult questions.

> Lately I have been wondering how accused parents are handling
> the names of their estranged children and grandchildren in their obit-
> uary (That gives you some idea of how much hope we have for retrac-
> tion or reconciliation!). The most satisfactory thing we have come up
> with so far is to name the ones who are still a part of our lives, and
> then simply add: "Other members have been lost to the 'recovered
> memory' craze." What are other families doing?[34]

RETRACTING CLAIMS OF REPRESSED MEMORIES

Despite the strong convictions of many clients regarding their recovered memories of childhood sexual abuse, other clients have retracted
their allegations. The cases of "retractors" who emphatically reject their

previously "recalled memories" raise questions regarding their prior treatment. Consider, for example, the letters of the following retractors.

> Dear Daddy,
>
> I love you very much. I am writing to say that I am sorry for what I've done to you and our family. I have made a grave mistake. I finally realize how deceiving our minds can be. My life back then was in a turmoil and I was very confused.
>
> I will not pass the blame to any other. I take full responsibility because God has given each of us a will and choices to make. I made a bad choice. It has saddened me to see you crushed by my actions. And I'm sorry that all this time has gone by to get me to this place of humility and honesty. God vindicates the innocent. He sees your innocence and I finally see it too. *I love you very much.*[35]

Another woman wrote her parents retracting her "memories," emphasizing how bewildered she feels by what happened to her.

> Dear Ma and Dad:
>
> I cannot seem to let go of my so heavy guilt for everything. Nothing was true except that I was very ill and being controlled by drugs and doctors. I have looked over copies of letters I sent and received. A horrible nightmare for which I beg your forgiveness. It may sound like a cop-out although it is true, but there is so much I do not remember, and I ask your forgiveness for those things too. Never again will I allow myself to lose control of me. I thank you for being here at my 'awakening,' I look forward to returning to the rich, wonderful family life we enjoy, although I question my worthiness. I am proud to be a part of you. I hope someday soon you can feel the same way about me.
>
> The best way I can communicate is through my writing. This letter does not even touch the depths of my pain, nor does it erase even an inch of the pain that I caused you. Please read this with an open mind, and give me a chance. Believe I am off the medications, believe I am me. And most of all, please believe that monster was NOT me. That monster is dead.[36]

Therapist Attention

The following retractor's letter reveals how clients can fall victim to the attention their "memories" receive. Fascinated by what they think they have discovered, therapists respond by pressuring clients for more memories.

> My psychiatrist was understandably fascinated with my various personalities—however fictional—a book was being written, videos

were made. My intermittent cries of denial about the abuse were rejected as "an unwillingness to co-operate." The interpretation that "she must be hiding more of these repressed memories" led to even more intensive psychotherapy and hypnosis.

Seven years, including lengthy stays in hospitals and countless emotional crises, brought about loss of job, husband, children, and any feelings of self-worth I had ever possessed. Five years later, I am in the process of rebuilding my shattered life.[37]

Loss of Rationality

Another retractor describes the manner in which she lost all ability to think for herself as a result of therapy. Consequently, she felt increasingly trapped in a treatment experience from which she could see no escape.

> I watched my parents go through hell and it's difficult to even try to make it up to my Dad. I pray everyday that if a person like me can break away from that craziness so can others. . . . If anyone had told me when I was in therapy that I was wrong and the therapist was wrong, I would have defended the "truth" as I saw it as fiercely as I'd defend my own children. There's no rationality when you're there, no sense of reality outside the therapist's belief and support, nothing to fill up the longings you feel except to immerse yourself completely in the falsehoods you so truly believe. There feels like there is no escape once you're in it, nowhere to go.
>
> My Dad, even knowing what I believed about him, never cut me off when I wasn't speaking to him and was so afraid of him. . . . He was devastated, of course, but he simply waited for 6 years for me to come back to him and I finally did. . . . The question I had the most difficulty with was: "Did I in all honesty ever stop loving my parents?" . . . The sad fact is that the parents you "remember" in therapy are lies, and the parents you remember before therapy are, in fact, the loving parents you've loved all your life. So, no, I never stopped loving my "real" parents. The ones I hated were only fakes made up in therapy sessions by a therapist who used all the wrong techniques. Time will wear away the "imposter parents" and you find the real parents still there just like you truly remember them—and still loving them despite all the therapist's attempts to destroy that love.

MALPRACTICE LITIGATION

Overwhelmed by feelings of betrayal and exploitation, other retractors take legal action against their former therapists. They claim that the therapists who treated them relied on grossly inappropriate therapy techniques. The outcomes in these malpractice cases demonstrate that when subjected to careful scrutiny, the practices of recovered memory therapy are repeatedly discredited.

Texas Case

For example, Lucy Abney—whose case was discussed earlier in this chapter—and her husband filed suit against her former psychologist and the hospital where she was treated in Harris County, Texas, in October 1993. Their petition alleged negligence regarding the therapist's diagnosis, and fraudulently misrepresenting Ms. Abney's condition to her health insurance carrier. The complaint also made claims of civil conspiracy and deceptive trade practices.

Ms. Abney claimed her former therapist and the hospital convinced her that her family had participated in satanic ritual abuse including rape, torture, and human sacrifice. Her therapy further persuaded her that her husband was a high-ranking member of the cult. Ms. Abney also contended she was hospitalized solely to "extract from her medical insurance carrier the maximum amount of money that was available under her insurance policy."[38] As the hospital pursued this blatant fraud, Ms. Abney claimed it "devised a scheme whereby it paid the insurance premiums surreptitiously, telling the insurance company they were being paid by Lucy Abney."

Ms. Abney and her husband's lawsuit was settled via mediation in April 1995, one month before it would have gone to trial. The terms of the settlement remain confidential.

Washington Case

Laura Deck filed suit against her former therapist, his supervisors, and the clinic where she underwent treatment in King County Superior Court in the state of Washington in January 1994. Ms. Deck originally sought therapy for her feelings of depression and sleep-related problems. She told her therapist of recently suffering a concussion, and feeling depressed since the birth of her youngest child a year earlier. Ms. Deck also disclosed her long-term concerns regarding other members of her family.

Rather than address her presenting problems, Ms. Deck's therapist immediately "embarked on a course of treatment involving hypnosis, guided imagery, and related techniques." The therapist repeatedly suggested she "imagine various scenarios and report what she saw."[39] Ms. Deck claimed these procedures led her into believing an uncle had brutally raped her and that she had participated in gruesome satanic rituals as a child. Her suit further indicated that before entering therapy, she had no memories of any such experiences.

In a pretrial deposition, Ms. Deck's former therapist insisted it was "reasonable" to assume she had endured the satanic abuse she thought she remembered. Nonetheless, the therapist also acknowledged that Ms. Deck initially disbelieved her "memories" of satanic abuse. As a result, he labeled her disbelief as "denial" while engaging in persistent efforts aimed at "wearing down her resistance." Ms. Deck contended the therapist eventually prevailed in his efforts at overcoming her "resistance" and in turn, she developed false memories of horrific abuse.

Prior to trial, the therapist and the other defendants made an acceptable settlement offer to Ms. Deck. She accepted that offer, and the terms of the settlement remain confidential.

Minnesota Case

In January 1996, a jury in Ramsey County, Minnesota, returned a verdict in excess of $2.5 million against psychiatrist Diana Humenansky.[40] The plaintiff in this case, Elizabeth Carlson, complained that Dr. Humenansky used hypnosis and sodium amytal to convince her she suffered from multiple personalities. Her many personalities supposedly developed as a result of her parents, other relatives, and neighbors sexually abusing her as a child. In response to her treatment, Ms. Carlson also believed she had participated in an intergenerational satanic cult.

In attempting to defend Dr. Humenansky, her attorneys sought to introduce testimony that hypnosis, drugs, group pressure, and suggestion could not create false memories. The presiding judge, Bertrand Poritsky, severely limited this defense strategy. He ruled there was insufficient scientific evidence to support claims of repressed memories. The jury was also less than impressed with the defense claims on behalf of Dr. Humenansky. They awarded Ms. Carlson $2,278,300 for past and future pain and suffering, and another $83,000 for past and future medical expenses. Ms. Carlson's husband also received $150,000 for his loss of companionship with his wife.

The jury award in the Carlson case was the second multimillion dollar verdict against Dr. Humenansky in less than a year. In July 1995, another jury awarded Vynnette Hammane more than $2.6 million in response to Dr. Humenansky's grossly inappropriate treatment.[41] Ms. Hammane alleged that Dr. Humenansky told her that she "must have been" sexually abused by her father, mother, uncle, grandfather, grandmother, and possibly other family members. According to Ms. Hammane, Dr. Humenansky insisted she had no memories of this abuse because of her own "repression and denial." Ms. Hammane further alleged that during her more than 5 years of treatment, Dr. Humenansky threatened her with abandonment, incarceration, and the loss of her child. Ms. Hammane detailed how her false memories left her terrified, and persuaded her to break off relationships with various family members.

Florida Case

In December 1996, Sue Tinker settled her lawsuit against Dr. Alan Tesson, a Florida psychiatrist, for $650,000. Ms. Tinker complained not only about the memories of satanic ritual abuse that Dr. Tesson created, but also alleged that he lured her into an affair while treating her. Dr. Tesson vigorously denied inducing Ms. Tinker's false memories. Videotapes of his sessions with her, however, demonstrated otherwise. Ms. Tinker's attorney—Don Russo—also demonstrated that Dr. Tesson frequently consulted with self-proclaimed experts in satanic ritual abuse such as Dr. Cory Hammond. Court records revealed that Tesson attended one of Hammond's lectures. In the course of this lecture, Dr. Hammond resorted to particularly outrageous claims. He insisted Nazi scientists introduced a satanic cult into the United States for purposes of mind control, ritual sacrifices, and child pornography.

OVERVIEW

Claims of repressed memories frequently involve accusations so bizarre and outrageous that they stagger the imagination. Shocked parents vehemently dispute these allegations, insisting they never abused their children. Numerous retractors undertake wholesale shifts in their thinking, claiming they and their families have been victimized by colossally incompetent therapists. Jury verdicts and out-of-court settlements demonstrate how difficult it is for recovered memory therapists to defend their practices. Particularly alarming is the fact that recovered memory therapy can only rely on Freudian theory to support its basic assumptions.

This consideration then raises questions regarding the contemporary status of Freudian theory.

For more than 40 years, legions of critics have rejected claims that Freudian theory is legitimately scientific. A 1985 overview of Freudian theory characterized it as scientifically untested, and criticized it for an excessive reliance on the intuitive impressions gleaned from its case studies.[42] Because of how poorly defined it is as a theory, Freudian thinking provokes unbridled conjecture and wild speculation from its disciples.[43] As a result, Freudian theorists regularly distort data to conform with their theoretical convictions.[44]

In 1970, a definitive text outlined the glaring deficiencies of Freudian theory, emphasizing: "the question then arises as to why psychoanalytic [Freudian] theory is taken seriously by anybody and why it was not relegated to oblivion long ago?"[45] Paradoxically, the vague and imprecise features of Freudian theory protect it from scientific scrutiny. Ill-defined theories resist scientific testing because it is so difficult to falsify or discredit them. Advocates of the theory persistently resort to some alternative explanation when objective evidence disconfirms one or more of its assumptions.[46] Thus, others have observed that Freudian theory amounts to a doctrine of faith,[47] and as a result, it manages to perpetuate itself by rejecting its critics as heretics.

Quite obviously, then, practitioners of recovered memory therapy cannot adequately defend themselves by relying on Freudian theory. Like too many other theories of behavior, Freudian conceptualizations are long on rhetoric and short on facts. Rather than resorting to theoretical speculation, the chaotic problems associated with recovered memory therapy necessitate a review of the relevant psychological research. We turn to Chapter 9 for that review.

9

Repressed Memory Claims

Scientific Fact versus Science Fiction

Surprising as it may seem, carefully examining the relevant research finds practically no support for theories of repression. Dr. David Holmes, of the University of Kansas, published a major review of repression-related data in 1974.[1] Long before the current controversies surrounding repression developed, Holmes concluded that any evidence verifying the existence of repression was characterized by its conspicuous absence. In 1990, Holmes published a subsequent review emphasizing he was yet to find any data indicating he should revise his 1974 findings. He concluded:

> Despite over sixty years of research involving numerous approaches by many thoughtful and clever investigators, at the present time there is no controlled laboratory evidence supporting the concept of repression. It is interesting to note that even most of the proponents of repression agree with that conclusion. However, they attempt to salvage the concept of repression by derogating the laboratory research, arguing that it is contrived, artificial, sterile, and irrelevant to the "dynamic processes" that occur in the "real world."[2]

Does Trauma Create Memory Loss?

Though Holmes's critics argue to the contrary, "real world" evidence demonstrates that if repression does occur in response to trauma, it is an exceedingly rare event. A 1986 study, for example, examined the reactions of 5- to 10-year-olds who had witnessed the murder of one of their parents.[3] Quite obviously, these children had endured horrible traumas. Consequently, the investigator anticipated that some of them might show evidence of repression of those memories. In fact, however, not one of these children exhibited any indication of repression. They instead continually struggled with vivid and painful recollections of what they had seen. This study is also quite consistent with an earlier study published in 1984. The 1984 study reported another group of children reacting in essentially the same manner to the murder of their parents.[4]

A 1985 study examined the reactions of 38 children who survived a lightning strike killing 3 of their playmates.[5] Except for one boy hospitalized as a result of his injuries, the other children clearly remembered this event when interviewed 9 months later. Despite the severe trauma associated with witnessing their friends' deaths, none of these children exhibited any evidence of repression. The electrical effects of the lightning strike itself most likely accounted for the one child's memory loss. He was described as a "side-flash victim."

A related case study reported the reactions of a 3-year-old girl who had been kidnapped, sexually abused, and left to die in a mountain outhouse.[6] When found and later interviewed by the police, she clearly described what had happened, and identified the perpetrator in a lineup. The perpetrator ultimately confessed, thereby verifying the accuracy of the child's description. Obviously, then, this case presented no evidence of repression despite the brutal trauma endured by the child.

Studies of concentration camp survivors also fail to support an assumed relationship between trauma and memory loss.[7] Follow-up interviews in 1984 and 1988 were compared with the information concentration camp survivors gave police investigators between 1943 and 1948. Despite enduring and witnessing horrible atrocities perpetrated by their Nazi captors, these survivors accurately remembered what they had experienced. They vividly recalled episodes of mistreatment, various punishments, and the characteristics of their guards. Though an average of 66 years old when most recently interviewed, these former captives described their ordeals in great detail. Once again, then, this study found no evidence to support theory-driven assumptions regarding trauma and memory loss.

Revised Claims Regarding Trauma and Memory Loss

In her 1990 book *Too Scared to Cry*, psychiatrist Lenore Terr reported the experiences of 26 children who were kidnapped and held captive for

27 hours in Chowchilla, California.[8] Though not physically harmed, these children suffered a frightening ordeal. Their kidnappers drove them around in darkened vans, and subsequently buried them in a trailer hidden in a rock quarry. When Terr interviewed these children 7 to 13 months after this episode, and then 4 to 5 years later, they accurately recalled numerous details related to this harrowing event. In other words, these children exhibited no evidence of repression despite the traumas of this experience.

Curiously enough, Terr has emerged as a staunch proponent regarding childhood trauma and repression, especially the trauma of sexual abuse. Her 1994 book *Unchained Memories* contends that adults who endured childhood sexual abuse commonly repress their memories of those experiences.[9] In advocating her position, Terr insists that single episodes of trauma rarely result in repression. She claims, however, that repression is commonly associated with multiple traumas.

Similarly, psychiatrist Judith Herman's 1981 book *Father–Daughter Incest* did not even cite the term "repression" in its index.[10] In 1981, Herman reported how the incest survivors she interviewed experienced persistently intrusive memories of their abuse. By 1992, though, Herman also revised her previous position. She now insists that the trauma of childhood sexual abuse frequently motivates repression.[11]

Quite clearly, then, advocates of the trauma-repression theory have dramatically shifted their position over time. This consideration raises the following questions: What evidence is available supporting these assumptions of trauma-induced memory loss? Can the therapists who practice recovered memory therapy rely on anything other than their own theory-driven thinking?

STUDIES CITED IN SUPPORT OF REPRESSION

Herman and Schatzow (1987)

Judith Herman and her psychiatric colleague, Emily Schatzow, reported the experiences of 53 adult clients participating in a 12-week treatment program addressing childhood sexual abuse.[12] Because 64% of these clients disclosed new memories of childhood sexual abuse during their therapy, Herman and Schatzow concluded this was evidence of their previous memory losses. In particular, they emphasized how:

> Participation in group proved to be a powerful stimulus for recovery of memory in patients with severe amnesia. During group therapy,

more than a quarter of the women experienced eruption into consciousness of memories that had been repressed.[13]

When clients begin therapy wondering about past sexual abuse, can they persuade themselves they were abused? Therapy groups inevitably pressure clients to conform their thinking with what the other clients think. Therefore, clients in a recovered memory group who decide they were never abused can feel ostracized as "denying" deviants. For example, consider the case of "Doris" reported by Herman and Schatzow in their 1987 article.

> In group, Doris initially reported almost complete amnesia for her childhood. She spoke little until the sixth session when she began to moan, whimper and wring her hands. In a childlike voice she cried, "The door is opening! The door is opening!" . . .
>
> In the three weeks following this session, Doris was flooded with memories which included being raped by her father and forced to service a group of her father's friends while he watched. The sexual abuse began at about the age of six and continued until the age of twelve, when she was impregnated by her father and taken to an underground abortionist.[14]

Disregarding the effects of group pressure on Doris's supposedly recovered memories is so ill-informed as to border on the naive. Doris likely responded to the group as a "powerful stimulus" for creating memories via her own suggestibility. Dramatically recalling her memories shifted her status from out-group observer to in-group participant. Her "memories" also prompted considerable attention and approval from other group members and her therapist. Therefore, this study does not support the assumptions of recovered memory therapists regarding trauma and memory loss. Instead, it demonstrates how clients in group therapy respond to the group's demands for conformity and compliance.

Briere and Conte (1993)

In 1993, Briere and Conte reported their survey of 450 clients who reported sexual abuse histories.[15] When asked if there was ever a time they could not remember their abuse, 59% of this sample responded "Yes." Other therapists have interpreted this finding to conform with their own theoretical preferences. They conclude, for example, that 59% of sexual abuse victims "went through periods of amnesia when they were not aware of their prior abuse."[16] Such conclusions, however, are ill-advised because the entire sample of this study was in therapy. As a result, the therapists likely persuaded these clients that repression is a common experience associated with sexual abuse. In turn, the clients reported experiences of repression merely in response to their therapist's influence.

Williams (1994)

Williams's more recently reported study interviewed 129 women whose histories of sexual abuse were verified by hospital records.[17] These women had all been sexually abused approximately 17 years earlier, while between the ages of 10 months and 12 years. Williams reported that 38% of the sample—none of whom were in therapy—did not remember their previous abuse at the time of the interview. These results, however, do not necessarily support conclusions regarding the assumed prevalence of repression.

Many of the women in Williams's study reported multiple incidents of childhood sexual abuse. As a result, two raters assessed whether the women did or did not disclose the "index event." By "index event," Williams was referring to whether the women recalled the specific episode of sexual abuse documented by hospital records. Williams reported that 49 of the women (38%) in the study did not recall the index event. Of these 49, however, 33 reported experiencing one or more other incidents of childhood sexual abuse.

In interpreting her data, Williams neglected to consider the influences of the "serial-position effect."[18,19] The serial-position effect refers to the impaired recall of events not well isolated in memory—because they were preceded and/or followed by similar events. If your history of dental care includes only one especially painful experience, for example, you remember the details of that visit more vividly. In response to numerous painful episodes in your dentist's office, it is more difficult to remember the details associated with any one particular visit. Memories associated with many painful visits become confused and contaminated with each other.

In view of the serial-position effect, it becomes evident that earlier sexual abuse can interfere with recall of later abuse. Conversely, later abuse can also interfere with recall of earlier abuse. A single episode of sexual abuse is more readily recalled, other factors being equal, because it stands out in memory. Therefore, the women in Williams's study who suffered multiple episodes of childhood abuse found it difficult to recall the details of any specific episode, including the "index event." The serial-position effect, then, also undermines Terr's claims that compared with single episodes of trauma, multiple traumas result in repression. In reporting her observations in this regard, Terr actually cited the serial-position effect without realizing it.

Williams also neglected to acknowledge that the serial-position effect likely accounts for the memory deficits of the women she interviewed. Instead, she tacitly encouraged those so inclined to leap to unwarranted conclusions regarding repression as they interpret her data. Moreover, a closer examination of Williams's data reveals that only 16 women (12%) of the total sample reported no memory for *any* episode of childhood sexual abuse. In other words, the widely publicized 38% figure related to this study—supposedly indicating a substantial number of women without any memory for their own childhood sexual abuse—is in fact 12%.

For her total sample, Williams reported that the younger her subjects were at the time of their abuse, the less likely they were to recall the index event. Quite possibly, then, the vast majority of women who reported no recall of any abuse were less than 5 years old when it occurred. If this were the case, the lack of recall for these 16 women would best be understood in terms of normal childhood amnesia. Adults typically find it very difficult to remember events that occurred before the age of 4 or 5.[20]

For example, Williams cited the example of one of her subjects who was asked whether anyone in her family was ever in trouble for his or her sexual behavior. This subject initially answered "No," but proceeded to clarify:

> I never met my uncle (my mother's brother), he died before I was born. You see, he molested a little boy. When the little boy's mother found out that her son was molested, she took a butcher knife and stabbed my uncle in the heart, killing him.[21]

Williams reported that this subject's hospital records, and corresponding newspaper accounts, documented how the subject herself (age 4), her cousin (age 7), and another playmate (age 4) had all been abused by her uncle. This particular subject, however, demonstrated no evidence of remembering her own abuse.

The inability to recall at age 21 an episode of your own sexual abuse—occurring 17 years earlier—does not support conventional assumptions regarding trauma and repression. This woman's report seems to reflect the effects of infantile amnesia, combined with the influences of what she later heard about this incident. In other words, what adults think they remember from very early childhood corresponds to what they hear as older children.[22] In summary, then, careful evaluation of Williams's study clearly indicates it is seriously flawed. It cannot support the conclusions about repression that too many therapists want to draw from it.

Loftus, Polonsky, and Fullilove (1994)

A more recent study surveyed 105 women undergoing treatment for substance abuse.[23] In response to an interview, 57 of these women reported a history of childhood sexual abuse. Of these 57, only 52 responded to the interview question addressing the persistence of their memory related to the abuse. Ten of these women (19%) reported they had forgotten the abuse for a period of time until the memory later returned. Another 6 women (12%) claimed to have remembered portions of their abuse but not all of it. In total, then, 16 of the 52 women (31%) reporting a history of sexual abuse also indicated there was a period of time they could not remember any, or parts, of the abuse.

In view of the substance abuse histories of these women, even suggesting that their self-reported memory failures involve repression is ill-informed. Memory deficits, for example, have been characterized as "the hallmark of alcoholism."[24] Others have found that the long-term memories of alcoholics remain impaired even after years of abstinence.[25] Related research has demonstrated that compared with male alcoholics, women more frequently report problems related to memory.[26] Consequently, it is not surprising to find that 31% of females, involved in substance abuse treatment, report memory deficits related to their childhood years.[27] Compared with any hypothetical mechanisms of repression, the memory impairments associated with substance abuse appear more responsible for these findings.

Feldman-Summers and Pope (1994)

A 1994 study surveyed 330 psychologists, asking if they had been sexually or physically abused as children.[28] Almost one-quarter of the participants reported a history of childhood abuse. Of this subsample, approximately 40% indicated that there was a period of time they could not remember all or some of the abuse. Of the 40% who claimed a period of forgetting, slightly more than half (56%) of those psychologists attributed the recall of their memories to psychotherapy, or to a combination of psychotherapy and other circumstances.

However persuasive they may appear, the findings of this survey are severely limited by the characteristics of its sample. These psychologists all belonged to one or more of seven divisions of the American Psychological Association primarily associated with professional practice endeavors. Related data demonstrate that therapists belonging to these divisions endorse Freudian theories with considerable frequency. Specifically, 70% of a sample of the Psychotherapy Division members, surveyed in late 1991, identified some variation of Freudian theory as their primary or secondary theoretical orientation.[29] An even greater endorsement of Freudian theories would be expected from members of the Division for Psychoanalysis who participated in this study.

Given the prevalence of Freudian thinking within the ranks of therapists, the findings of this survey reflect their theoretical preferences more than anything else. Freudian-oriented therapists can be expected to endorse repression as a viable concept, and in turn, it is not surprising when they interpret some of their own life experiences vis-à-vis repression. This study concluded that its findings "lend further support to the observation that many people forget, for various periods of time, some or all of the trauma they have experienced." The many problems associated with this study's sample, however, indicate its conclusion goes far beyond the data available to support it.

Theoretical Inadequacies

Above and beyond the unavailability of reliable evidence to support assumptions regarding trauma and memory loss, there is no theory that even adequately explains such events. Human memory involves three related processes: (1) encoding information, (2) storing information, and (3) retrieving information.

The encoding stage refers to whether we consider some event important enough to remember. As I write this, I cannot remember the make and color of the automobile parked next to mine at the restaurant where I ate lunch yesterday. That information was not important enough to even register—or encode—in my memory. Events distinctive or important enough for encoding are stored in what amounts to the complex filing system of memory. Our memory files are organized in meaningful categories associated with one another. Suddenly remembering jokes and stories, while listening to the jokes and stories of others, illustrates how memories are stored in files related to each other.

Retrieving information from memory depends on identifying the label for a particular memory file. An old friend, with whom I attended both high school and college, recently described a humorous event we shared. At first, however, I could not recall the episode because I mistakenly thought he was talking about a high school experience. Searching through my high school memory files left me unable to recall an event that actually occurred during college. Once I identified the anecdote as a college experience, I "opened" the appropriate file and remembered it.

If traumatic experiences lead to memory loss, then any theory advocating this position must clearly identify the memory processes involved. Do traumatic experiences interfere with the encoding stage of memory, and if so, how does this interference occur? Or do traumatic experiences intefere with the storage stage of memory, and if so, how does this interference occur? Or do traumatic experiences interfere with the retrieval stage of memory, and if so, how does this interference occur? Current theories of trauma and memory loss neglect to answer these important questions. These theories suggest *why* people might engage in repression, but they fail to specify *how* repression supposedly occurs.

The heated debates regarding repression too often distract us from a more compelling issue. If trauma leads to memory loss, how can recovered memory therapists claim they assist clients in retrieving those supposedly repressed memories? Any recall of repressed memories would necessarily depend on retrospective memory—our memory for the past events of our own lives. The accumulated evidence, however, clearly demonstrates that retrospective memory is notoriously inaccurate.

RETROSPECTIVE MEMORY

Can We Trust Childhood Memories?

Research examining human memory consistently indicates that after the age of 10, people rarely remember events that occurred before the age of 3 or 4.[30,31] In another study, for instance, very few subjects less than 4 years old at the time of John F. Kennedy's assassination could remember where they were when they learned of it.[32] The majority of subjects who were 9 and older in November 1963 could recall some firsthand information associated with JFK's death. These findings indicate that people rarely remember much from before the age of 4, and moreover, memories between the ages of 4 and 8 tend to be quite inaccurate.

Even when people recall events from their childhoods, the accuracy of what they remember is often poor. A study done in New Zealand interviewed a sample of more than 1000 children at ages 7, 9, 11, 13, and 15.[33] Over the course of this study, the mothers of these children were also asked questions regarding: (1) the extent of conflict in their families and (2) the degree to which the mother felt depressed. At ages 13 and 15, the children were also asked how attached they felt to their families. At age 18, these same children were interviewed again and asked questions about their childhoods.

Their responses to these questions are expressed in terms of a correlation coefficient, which can range from 0.00 to 1.00. A correlation of 1.00 corresponds to an exact 1:1 relationship between earlier responses and present replies. A correlation of 0.00 corresponds to no relationship whatsoever between earlier responses and present replies.

These 18-year-olds were specifically asked:

1. Between the ages of 7 and 15, how much conflict was there in your family? Mean correlation = 0.19.
2. When you were between the ages of 7 and 15, how often did your mother seem depressed? Mean correlation = 0.16.
3. When you were about 13–15 years old, how close did you feel to your parents? Mean correlation = 0.36.

The very limited accuracy with which these 18-year-olds recalled the events in question demonstrates the unreliability of retrospective memory. In particular, retrospective memory is especially unreliable when trying to remember ambiguous circumstances open to interpretation. Adults attempting to recall childhood instances of family conflict, maternal depression, and parental closeness must rely on conjecture and imagination. Attempts at remembering these events ultimately amount to guesswork because memory and imagination are so intertwined with each other. Brain imaging studies, for example, demonstrate that both memory and imagination involve essentially the same areas of the cerebral cortex.[34] Therefore, people can find it very difficult to accurately discriminate between what they think they remember and what they imagine.

Past Memories and Present Influences

When therapists attempt to reconstruct the childhood and adolescent experiences of their clients, they focus on the kinds of subjective experiences that defy accurate recall. For example, therapists frequently try to determine the extent of family conflict their clients encountered while growing up. Therapists also want to know if the mothers of their clients were depressed, and how close those clients felt to their parents. The relevant research, however, clearly demonstrates that attempting to reconstruct these subjective experiences of the past is a futile endeavor. What clients think they recall from that period amounts to a combination of client imagination and therapist suggestion.

With the passage of time, adult memories of childhood and adolescence often change enormously. People frequently reinvent their past in response to contemporary needs and circumstances.[35] Another study, for example, surveyed 1669 high school seniors in 1965.[36] These students were asked questions about five issues: (1) guaranteed employment, (2) the rights of criminal defendants, (3) aid for minorities, (4) legalization of marijuana, and (5) equal rights for women. These same students were again interviewed regarding these issues in 1973 and 1982. In 1982, they were also asked to recall how they responded to the 1973 interview. Relying on their retrospective memories, these subjects remembered their 1973 attitudes as essentially the same as their 1982 attitudes. In fact, however, their attitudes of 1973 and 1982 were quite different.

Not surprisingly, then, two separate volumes, published by the National Academy of Sciences, emphasized that retrospective methods have contributed nothing of scientific value to psychology.[37,38] Consequently, reports from clients in therapy claiming to remember subjective events from childhood deserve considerable skepticism. They are more likely reporting the effects of therapist influence than accurate recall.[39]

THERAPIST FAMILIARITY WITH MEMORY RESEARCH

The previously outlined evidence dramatically demonstrates how human memory is much more fragile—and prone to distortion and decay—than most people realize. This consideration raises the question of whether therapists understand the basic research regarding memory. Throughout 1992, Michael Yapko, a well-respected psychologist specializing in hypnosis, surveyed 864 therapists about their attitudes and assumptions regarding memory.[40] These therapists were attending the conferences of various professional groups such as the American Association for Marriage and Family Therapy, the Family Therapy Network, the American Society of Clinical Hypnosis, and the Milton H. Erickson Foundation.

The therapists participating in this survey reported the following information regarding the highest degree they had earned.

Degree	Number	Percent
Master's	553	64.0
Ph.D.	210	24.3
M.D.	37	4.3
B.A./B.S.	41	4.7
Other	10	1.2
No answer	13	1.5

The educational background of this group is essentially the same as therapists in general. Consequently, the responses of this group can be generalized to practicing therapists. Yapko asked the therapists the following background question and obtained the responses cited below:

Is your knowledge of the workings of memory:

below average = 149 (17.2%); *average* = 574 (66.5%); *above average* = 102 (11.8%); *no answer* = 39 (4.5%).

Overall, then, 78.3% of the practicing therapists in this study considered their knowledge of memory as average or above. Yapko then proceeded to ask the following ten questions, for which he obtained the responses summarized below:

1. The mind is like a computer, accurately recording events as they actually occurred.

Agree strongly	Agree slightly	Disagree slightly	Disagree strongly	No response
107 (12.4%)	179 (20.7%)	220 (25.5%)	349 (40.4%)	9 (1.0%)

Approximately one-third of these therapists agree, or strongly agree, that the "mind is like a computer, accurately recording events as they actually occurred." In other words, one-third of these therapists are misinformed regarding this particular assumption about memory. The previously cited evidence related to retrospective memory clearly demonstrates how the mind does not store memories with anywhere near the accuracy of a computer.

2. Events that we know occurred but can't remember are repressed memories, i.e., memories that are psychologically defended against.

Agree strongly	Agree slightly	Disagree slightly	Disagree strongly	No response
187 (21.6%)	326 (37.7%)	244 (28.2%)	89 (10.3%)	18 (2.1%)

Even more shocking is the fact that 59.3% of these therapists agree or strongly agree with mistaken assumptions regarding repression. As previously emphasized, the availability of evidence supporting Freudian notions of repression is characterized by its conspicuous absence. Rather than lead to repression, traumatic experiences are more often remembered clearly and vividly. Nonetheless, almost 60% of these therapists demonstrated how unaware they are of the relevant research.

3. Memory is a reliable mechanism when the self-defensive need for repression is lifted.

Agree strongly	Agree slightly	Disagree slightly	Disagree strongly	No response
103 (11.9%)	316 (36.6%)	281 (32.5%)	144 (16.7%)	5 (2.3%)

The therapists' responses to this question are also cause for alarm. More than 48% of these therapists assume that once the presumed effects of repression are alleviated, clients can accurately remember previous events from their lives. Again, however, the accumulated data related to retrospective memory clearly demonstrate how grossly mistaken such assumptions are.

4. If someone doesn't remember much about his or her childhood, it is most likely because it was somehow traumatic.

Agree strongly	Agree slightly	Disagree slightly	Disagree strongly	No response
81 (9.4%)	291 (33.7%)	276 (31.9%)	193 (22.3%)	23 (2.7%)

In response to this question, more than 43% of the therapists demonstrated they were misinformed. Because retrospective memory is so often distorted, people cannot accurately recall the subjective experiences of their childhoods. The replies to this question, however, indicate that substantial numbers of therapists disregard the evidence underscoring the limitations of retrospective memory. Simultaneously, these therapists leap to ill-informed conclusions. They presume childhood traumas in the lives of clients who simply do not remember much about their formative years. A client of mine, however, perceptively explained her faint recall for the events of her childhood. She said, "My adult life has been so much more interesting than my childhood. I think what I remember from childhood is limited by how boring it was."

5. It is necessary to recover detailed memories of traumatic events if someone is to improve in therapy.

Agree strongly	Agree slightly	Disagree slightly	Disagree strongly	No response
27 (3.1%)	138 (16.0%)	300 (34.7%)	388 (44.9%)	11 (1.3%)

Fortunately, more than 79% of these therapists knew that effective therapy does not necessitate recovering detailed memories of presumed childhood traumas. When psychotherapy assists clients to resolve their problems, it aids them in the here and now. To belabor the obvious, clients cannot change how they previously managed their lives or coped with difficult circumstances. The changes clients undertake in response to therapy are always limited to their current life situations.

6. Memory is not significantly influenced by suggestion.

Agree strongly	Agree slightly	Disagree slightly	Disagree strongly	No response
17 (2.0%)	66 (7.6%)	294 (34.0%)	461 (53.4%)	26 (3.0%)

In response to this question, more than 87% of the therapists knew that memory is significantly influenced by suggestion. Laboratory research has clearly demonstrated that eyewitness memory, for example, can be altered by the suggestions of interviewers. After watching films of an automobile accident, people can report seeing stop signs that never existed—but were suggested to them.[41] Quite obviously, then, what clients think they remember in psychotherapy is also influenced by their therapists' suggestions. Too many therapists, however, remain oblivious to how they suggestively influence clients.

7. One's level of certainty about a memory is strongly and positively correlated with that memory's accuracy.

Agree strongly	Agree slightly	Disagree slightly	Disagree strongly	No response
35 (4.1%)	173 (20.0%)	310 (35.9%)	310 (35.9%)	36 (4.2%)

Remember the children in Chapter 4 who thought they recalled their hand caught in a mousetrap, and going to a hospital? Despite the fact that it never occurred, many of these children continued to insist they remembered this imaginary event—even when their own parents explained it never happened. Adults who report seeing stop signs they only imagined also confidently conclude their recall is accurate. Therefore, the degree of confidence with which people report memories is not necessarily associated with their accuracy. Nevertheless, more than 24% of these therapists mistakenly assumed a relationship between memory accuracy and reporting confidence.

8. I trust my client such that if he or she says something happened, it must have happened, regardless of the age or context in which the event occurred.

Agree strongly	Agree slightly	Disagree slightly	Disagree strongly	No response
44 (5.1%)	176 (20.4%)	351 (40.6%)	278 (32.2%)	15 (1.7%)

Despite qualifying this question with the consideration "regardless of the age or context in which the event occurred," more than 25% of the responding therapists were willing to naively trust the memories of their clients. In other words, these therapists neglect to consider the extent to which client memories can revise the past in response to here-and-now needs. Some clients, for example, revise their memories of the past to avoid accepting responsibility for their current problems. Therapists who endorse such memory revisions too often fail to effectively assist their clients.

9. I believe that early memories even from the first years of life are accurately stored and retrievable.

Agree strongly	Agree slightly	Disagree slightly	Disagree strongly	No response
106 (12.3%)	244 (28.2%)	272 (31.5%)	228 (26.4%)	14 (1.6%)

Well-informed psychologists have long recognized the severe memory limitations associated with infantile amnesia.[42] Forgetting events that occurred before the age of 3 or 4 is a universal experience. Young children store memories using verbal classifications consistent with their tender years.[43] The verbal classifications of adults, however, are quite different from the classifications they used as 3 or 4 year-olds. Consequently, adults cannot recall events stored via the language classifications of a young child. Adults no longer use these language classifications, and without the ability to identify a particular "memory file," adults cannot "open" it. Therefore, the responses to this questions are shockingly ill-informed. More than 40% of these therapists neglected to consider the limitations of infantile amnesia on adult memory.

10. If a client believes a memory is true, I must also believe it to be true if I am to help him or her.

Agree strongly	Agree slightly	Disagree slightly	Disagree strongly	No response
110 (12.7%)	204 (23.6%)	260 (30.1%)	274 (31.7%)	16 (1.9%)

Clients seek the services of therapists because how they think about their problems is not helping them. In other words, clients are looking for a different direction in solving their problems. Had their previous attempts at problem solving been effective, clients would not need a therapist's services. Consequently, it is folly for therapists to assume they must endorse what clients *think* they remember in order to aid them. Nevertheless, more than 36% of these therapists are willing to uncritically assume what their clients assume—even though these assumptions have not assisted the clients in solving their problems.

Combining the responses of these therapists across all ten questions leads to a sobering result. An average of 33.8% are misinformed regarding fundamental mechanisms of memory. Additionally, 59.3% of these therapists mistakenly assume that traumatic experiences motivate the use of repression. More than 48% of these therapists also assume that once the presumed effects of repression dissipate, clients can recall events previously unavailable to their memory. If therapists understand so little about memory, how could their limited understanding influence clients?

CLIENT MEMORIES AND THERAPIST INFLUENCES

Blame-and-Change Maneuvers

Many therapists assume that people endure psychological problems because their families in general—or their parents in particular—previously betrayed them.[44] These assumptions encourage therapists to leap to negative conclusions about the families of their clients. This kind of thinking suggests to clients that psychotherapy must *blame your family* in order to *change you.*

Related data indicate that "blame-and-change" maneuvers are alive and well in psychotherapy. When therapists described various members of their clients' families in the articles of a well-respected journal, for example, more than 90% of the descriptions were negative and less than 10% were positive.[45] The family members were portrayed as intellectually dull, critical and intrusive, and cold and withholding to cite but a few examples. Especially alarming is the fact that the therapists arrived at these conclusions without ever having seen the people whose character they irresponsibly assassinated.

Too often, then, mental health professionals assume the worst about the families of their clients. As a result, they question clients in a biased, one-sided manner. In turn, they eventually find "evidence" that they interpret as verifying their original assumptions.[46] The tenacity with which some therapists pursue verification of their theoretical convictions related to sexual abuse should not be underestimated. For example, a California psychologist described blatant examples of biased assumptions regarding the prevalence of childhood sexual abuse:

> In the past two years, many patients have told me that previous therapists have presumed that they must have been sexually molested as children. If the patient had no such recollection, that was taken as evidence of severe "repression," or that the molestation must have happened very early in life, causing unusually great harm. Such therapists employed similar logic if the patient recalled a pleasant, loving family life. Such therapists repeatedly attempt to elicit fragmentary memories or fantasies, often with the aid of hypnosis, to confirm their preconceptions. Several patients told me their therapists went so far as to say, "I am certain you were molested because you have all the classic characteristics of adults molested as children."[47]

The potential for these kinds of tactics resulting in false allegations of sexual abuse is so obvious as to be alarming; consequently, they can only reduce more responsible mental health professionals to head-shaking disbelief. As we are about to see, the biased expectations of therapists can lead them into profoundly distorting the memories of their clients.

Suggested Memories

While undermining the bonds of trust and affection previously existing between client and family via blame-and-change maneuvers, a therapist can ask various suggestive questions. In view of the extent to which suggestive questions can distort memory, the degree of the therapist's influence should not be underestimated. For example, assume you are asked, "The last time you were at the airport, did you see the team of three elephants pulling the passenger jet down the runway with two clowns dancing on each wing?" Most people respond to this question by vividly imagining three massive, gray mammals lumbering down a runway, laboring against the weight of the plane, with two outrageously costumed figures prancing vigorously about each of its wings. Despite our facility for imagining this scene, however, it is unlikely that anyone would actually think they remembered it. The scene itself is so implausible that it immediately provokes rejection as a legitimate memory.

On the other hand, however, assume that a therapist asks a client questions such as: (1) "Maybe there was a time when your father looked at you in a seductive way?" (2) "Possibly he spoke to you in a suggestive manner?" (3) "Might he have touched your arm or face rather sensuously?" Each of these questions also arouses corresponding imagery suggested by the therapist. In turn, clients can confuse this imagery with emerging memories because they consider these scenes as plausible events. These questions also correspond to universal experiences. Practically everyone has encountered cirumstances of their father looking at them, speaking to them, and touching them.

Clients can begin to think they are recovering memories of their fathers' seductive glances, or suggestive remarks, or sensuous touches because of the therapist's influence. The New Zealand study demonstrated how these are the kinds of subjective events—open to varying interpretations—that people cannot recall accurately. Therefore, directing enough questions at clients about subjective circumstances can easily lead them into both revising and distorting memories of benign events. Moreover, they can create other memories for which there is no basis whatsoever in fact. Related research has dramatically demonstrated the relative ease with which false memories can be created.

Laboratory Research and False Memories

A 1986 study asked college students to keep extensive diaries for a 4-month period.[48] After all of the diaries had been collected and typed, the authors interspersed false diary entries in between actual entries. The students were then asked to identify which memories were real and which were false. Some false memories were written to express themes similar to the original memories, while others were not. If students wrote about examination anxiety or relationship problems, for example, some of the false entries corresponded to those themes. Other false entries were written in a manner unrelated to any of the actual diary themes.

The results indicated that the longer the delay between diary entry and recall, the less accurately subjects discriminated false from real memories. Even more importantly, the greater the thematic consistency between a false entry and an actual entry, the greater the likelihood of students mistakenly identifying a false entry as one they wrote. If students wrote about examination anxiety, for instance, they were more inclined to mistakenly identify false entries with that same theme as their own. In other words, these students thought they remembered writing numerous entries they never actually wrote.

Basically, then, this study demonstrates how we organize our memories in a thematic manner. Considering the frequency with which therapists resort to "blame-and-change" themes in therapy, the likelihood of clients reporting false memories is shocking to say the least. Because there is no such thing as a perfect parent, almost everyone can remember instances of their parents' arbitrary demands or selfish impatience. Recalling what typically amounts to infrequent episodes of parental harshness can also lead clients into creating memories of abuse that are entirely false. The false memories seem quite genuine to clients as a result of their thematic consistency with rare instances of previous parental insensitivity.

Related research has demonstrated remarkable levels of false memory when people try to recall words from a list they saw.[49] Assume, for example, that you have studied a list of words including: "bed, rest, awake, tired, dream, wake, snooze, blanket, doze, slumber, snore, and nap." Five to ten minutes after studying this list, you are asked whether you remember the word "sleep" from the list. The chances are substantially greater than 50–50 that you would report having seen the word "sleep" even though it was not on the original list. People report this false memory because of the thematic consistency between the original word list and the word "sleep." Not surprisingly, this study concluded: "The results reveal a powerful illusion of memory: People remember events that never happened."

Lost in a Shopping Mall?

The potential for therapists altering and/or distorting the memories of their clients cannot be underestimated. Elizabeth Loftus, of the University of Washington, investigated this issue enlisting some of her laboratory assistants as confederates in an experiment. She wanted to determine if it was possible to create childhood memories for events that had never occurred.[50] Loftus's confederates selected a target person from their own family, who was younger than them, and requested they participate in a memory experiment. The confederates asked the target subjects if they remembered being lost in a shopping mall when they were 5 years old. In fact, however, no such episode had ever occurred.

Initially, the target subjects denied any such memory, but they were asked to try and remember anything they could about this supposed incident. Within 2 days, the target subjects began to report memories related to this fictitious episode. One of them indicated, "That day I was so scared that I would never see my family again. I knew I was in trouble." The next day he thought he recalled a conversation with his mother, "I remember mom telling me never to do that again." Two days later, this same subject reported, "I sort of remember the stores." Though never actually lost in a shopping mall, this subject's persuasive statements to the contrary demonstrate how imagination can undermine memory.

Critics of Loftus's study might question its applicability to therapy, objecting specifically to how being "lost in a shopping mall" corresponds to the childhood experiences of many people. One could argue that as children, many adults encountered situations where they were told, "Hold my hand so you won't get lost." Or they briefly thought they were lost only to be promptly located by a caretaker. If a variety of childhood experiences can approximate "being lost," then the reports of Loftus's subjects may have involved more than suggestibility. Perhaps these subjects recalled actual events involving "near-lost" experiences.

On the other hand, however, numerous childhood experiences also approximate sexual abuse—they amount to "near-abuse" events. Toweling off a child's genitals after a bath, examining a child's anal or vaginal orifice for hygienic purposes, and even assisting children with clothing themselves, all approximate child sexual abuse. Whether such activities actually amount to child sexual abuse depend solely on the intent of the adult. Therefore, remembering oneself as having been lost—or sexually abused—frequently involves subjective interpretations of approximate experiences—or "near events." These considerations indicate that Loftus's research should be applauded—not indicted—for its relevance to therapy.

Historical Truth versus Narrative Truth

The potential for creating pseudomemories via suggestibility is a factor in all psychotherapy. Rather than uncover the "historical truths" of their clients' lives, psychotherapists construct "narrative truths."[51,52] The narrative truths of psychotherapy develop when therapists organize the information clients present them into consistent—but potentially distorted—themes. Subsequently, these themes are outlined for clients via the interpretations, summaries, and reflections of their therapist.

In turn, clients respond to their therapist's influence just as Loftus's subjects responded to her experiment. They report new information that appears to verify the preliminary versions of narrative truth previously constructed with their therapist. In other words, the narrative truths of psychotherapy evolve as clients "discover" information consistent with their therapist's suggestions. To belabor the obvious, narrative truths can substantially distort the historical truths of a client's formative history, and moreover, they may result in false allegations of childhood sexual abuse.

SOURCE MONITORING AND MOOD-CONGRUENT MEMORY PROBLEMS

Remembering versus Imagining

Experimental investigations of source-monitoring processes related to memory demonstrate that what people remember, and the source of a memory, exist independent of each other.[53] For example, 6-year-olds find it difficult to accurately discriminate between actual events and imagined events.[54] These children confused memories for what they actually did versus what they imagined doing (e.g., "Did you really touch your nose, or did you just imagine yourself touching your nose?"). Adults also find it difficult to remember what another person actually said versus what they imagined that person saying.[55]

Therapists seeking to uncover supposedly repressed memories can create source monitoring problems for their clients. Between therapy sessions, clients think a great deal about what their therapist said—or what they think the therapist said. As a result, these clients can encounter considerable confusion regarding what they heard versus what they think they heard. Even more importantly, clients can find themselves confused about what someone in their family actually did versus a therapist simply suggesting the family member engaged in those actions.

Mood-Congruent Memory Effects

Clients whose memories are distorted by source-monitoring problems readily recall events suggested by their therapist. Nevertheless, they mistakenly attribute the source of their "memories" to their own past experiences. Clients also feel depressed and discouraged in response to learning how their families supposedly betrayed them. They then recall more anecdotes consistent with their family's alleged "toxicity" as a result of how mood influences memory.[56,57] Depression, for example, increases the probability of people remembering their parents as rejecting and relying on negative controls. This effect, however, promptly disappears as the level of depression diminishes.[58]

In other words, contemporary circumstances influence our memory of the past more than any other factor,[59] and therapists who embrace "blame-and-change" maneuvers with a vengeance are especially powerful sources of contemporary influence. Determined to alleviate repression and recover memories of childhood sexual abuse, for example, therapists can encourage clients to inventory their past searching for anecdotes that seem important. Motivated to cooperate with their therapist, clients begin reporting imaginary events, but consider them legitimate memories because of source-monitoring failures.

Mutually determined to reduce the ambiguity surrounding the client's past, both therapist and client leap to ill-advised conclusions. They attribute unwarranted significance to what is actually conjecture in the service of rumor formation. Step by step, then, the speculative exchanges between clients and therapists converge into a commonly shared conviction—the client suffered episodes of formative sexual abuse that remained repressed until uncovered by the therapist. Once they construct conclusions such as these, clients and therapists typically cling to them tenaciously. Both therapists and clients can insist, "We agree, therefore we must be right."

OVERVIEW

The accumulated data fail to support the frequently assumed relationship between childhood sexual abuse and repression. In particular, the established scientific evidence can be summarized in the following manner:

- There is no accumulated body of evidence demonstrating that trauma—such as childhood sexual abuse—motivates people to repress events associated with that trauma.
- The reliability of studies suggesting that childhood sexual abuse leads to repression rapidly falls apart when examined closely. These studies characteristically overlook considerations such as normal childhood amnesia, everyday forgetting, and the influences of therapists.
- Retrospective reports recalling subjective psychological states and related family dynamics are inherently unreliable.
- Psychotherapy frequently results in clients and therapists constructing memories that involve more fiction than fact. Indeed,

the biases of too many therapists lead them into profoundly distorting the memories of their clients.

Unfortunately, too many therapists disregard this accumulated evidence and patronize their clients via wildly speculative interpretations suggesting that "even though you experienced it [alleged sexual abuse], you don't understand it. And even though I didn't experience it, your misunderstanding allows me to understand it better than you." These interpretive tactics suggest that Lewis Carroll's Mad Hatter would have enthusiastically endorsed recovered memory therapy. He might have described it as "a particularly illuminating exercise—you learn fascinating things about your past that never really happened. This proves that while truth may be stranger than fiction, fiction can be stronger than truth."

Above and beyond ripping families apart, allegations of repressed memories can result in innocent people facing criminal charges. Ill-informed therapists and irresponsible prosecutors too often lock arms while directing the most horrible accusations at decent, caring parents. In Chapter 10, we will examine such a case in detail.

10

Creating Repressed Memories

Imagination Inflation

On a gray, overcast day in November 1994, Jim Bauer faced the most excruciating ordeal of his life. Criminal charges alleging he had sexually abused his daughter came to trial in Michigan's Allegan County. The prosecution claimed that Terri Richards—30 years of age and Mr. Bauer's oldest child—repressed her memories of the abuse she suffered, between ages 4 and 16, until recovering them in psychotherapy. Mr. Bauer, however, emphatically denied these charges from the outset, pleading not guilty and demanding a jury trial.

EARLY TREATMENT HISTORY

The sequence of events leading to this situation originated in August 1988 when Ms. Richards entered a psychiatric hospital. At time of her admission, she was married and the mother of four children, with the youngest child having been born in February of that year. Hospital records indicated that Ms. Richards:

> has struggled with depression with withdrawal, irritability, remaining in bed but with sleep problems at night, feeling tired, no energy, increasing tearfulness, much more impatient and irresponsible with her children, anorexia with a 15 pound weight loss and lack of ambition.

These treatment records also noted:

An added stressor has been a motor vehicle accident in December [1987] in which her husband was seriously injured and had suffered a head injury. . . . She had a brief postpartum depression after her third child. At that time she also felt suicidal with reduced impulse control and received outpatient therapy.

In individual sessions the patient worked on issues surrounding past history of sexual acting out and impulsivity to deal with difficult feelings as well as revealing a past history of sexual abuse at the hands of a cousin and grandfather. She was also raped by two men when 19 years of age and was unable to identify who these men were.

Important as Ms. Richards's history of sexual abuse may seem, overemphasizing it would be mistaken. Her original need for treatment coincided with the birth of her third child—more than 8 years after her last episode of abuse. Her postpartum depression responded to the here-and-now issues involving her burdens of responsibility as a mother. Women who develop postpartum reactions do not experience the sense of elation they think they should feel about their baby. Their profound disappointment in themselves quickly develops into guilt, self-recrimination, and depression. Quite obviously, then, effective treatment for postpartum reactions must address these issues.

By August 1988, Mr. Richards likely felt overwhelmed by the responsibilities of caring for four children. As a result of her husband's closed head injury, Ms. Richards knew he could not assist her very well. Circumstances such as these understandably leave people feeling betrayed, abandoned, angry, and depressed. As a firstborn child, Ms. Richards also likely found it difficult to ask for help and assistance. Firstborn individuals tend to be quite independent and autonomous, preferring to rely on themselves to solve their problems.

Ms. Richards also was clearly willing to report previous episodes of sexual abuse. This consideration indicates that if her father had sexually abused her in the past, she would have reported it. Consequently, one need not have hypothesized any repressed memories of sexual abuse to account for her psychological condition in August 1988.

Initial Consultation with Ms. Smith

On September 9, 1988, the psychiatric hospital discharged Ms. Richards with a diagnosis of major depression. Ten days later she consulted with Ms. Smith, a therapist with a Master in Social Work degree, practicing at an outpatient clinic providing psychotherapy services. Ms. Smith completed a standardized form identifying the problems with which Ms. Richards was struggling:

- Makes own plans but without considering the needs of other family members
- Seldom holds job, or attends some classes, or does limited housework
- Seldom able to get along with others without quarreling or being destructive, or is often alone
- Almost always feels nervous or depressed, or angry and bitter, or no emotions at all
- Only occasional recreational activities, or engages in the same activity over and over again
- Severe problems most of the time
- Negative attitude toward self most of the time

Beyond this initial consultation, however, Ms. Richards did not undertake therapy with Ms. Smith at that time. Her condition continued to deteriorate, and she was readmitted to the same hospital on December 1, 1988. Ms. Richards was discharged from the hospital on January 13, 1989.

Ms. Smith Undertakes Therapy

On January 23, 1989, Ms. Richards began therapy with Ms. Smith, the therapist she saw in September 1988. Ms. Smith's treatment plan indicated that Ms. Richards "was sexually abused by her paternal grandfather and a male cousin. There may have been other sexual abuses in her past as well." The statement suggesting "other sexual abuses in her past" revealed more about Ms. Smith's biased expectations than anything else. She was eagerly prepared to venture off into a fishing expedition, looking for supposedly repressed memories of sexual abuse.

Ms. Smith specified the following treatment goals for Ms. Richards:

- To identify the impact of sexual abuse on her life
- To identify the issues within her marriage that need to be resolved
- To promote and increase self-esteem

At best, these treatment goals were ill-defined, and at worst, they were irrelevant to Ms. Richards's welfare. In September 1988, Ms. Richards presented as an isolated, self-centered, disorganized young woman who struggled with persistent anxiety, depression, and self-rejection. Rather than "identify the impact of sexual abuse on her life," Ms. Richards needed assistance in dealing with the isolation, anxiety, depression, and other negatives undermining her psychological welfare. She also needed to identify what to do to resolve the problems in her marriage. In other words, considerations of *what* needed to be done, as opposed to *why* her problems existed, would have been more appropriate to Ms. Richards's welfare.[1]

The notes for Ms. Smith's January 23, 1989, session with Ms. Richards indicated:

> [Ms. Richards] . . . Seen with husband Dave. . . . Dave wants to be involved in all the therapy—I [Ms. Smith] set limits. Terri to be seen individually 2 times a week. Dave to attend individual [therapy] with Kate C. Occasional joint sessions to keep the two connected and marital sessions "down the road." Terri resistant to Dave knowing everything.

Despite the fact that Mr. Richards was genuinely committed to his wife's welfare, Ms. Smith reduced him to a peripheral role in her treatment. Simultaneously, she appointed herself to a position of excessive significance in Ms. Richards's life. Nevertheless, Ms. Smith neglected to consider how she could resolve a two-person, marital conflict while focusing most of her efforts on only one of the spouses (Ms. Richards).

BAIT-AND-SWITCH TACTICS

Ms. Smith's notes for her January 31, 1989, session with Ms. Richards indicated:

> Brought little notebook and read off thoughts and issues she'd thought of. Many acknowledged fears re: trusting me. Talked in depth about them and gave [her] permission to feel hesitant.

At this point, Ms. Richards found herself subjected to what is known as the "bait-and-switch" tactic in psychotherapy.[2] She sought treatment to deal with the seven issues outlined in September 1988, but Ms. Smith "switched" her to examining how she felt about her as a therapist. In effect, Ms. Smith told Ms. Richards: Before you can solve your problems, you must understand your relationship with me. Therefore, your relationship with me is more important than solving your problems.

Issues of Ms. Richards's relationship with Ms. Smith were also evident in the notes for February 16, 1989:

Focused on her resistance. Fears of my not liking her revealed. Able to acknowledge that she feels pressure building and is fearful of returning to the hospital. Explored some perceptual disturbances connected to trust. To write in notebook.

If Ms. Richards's fears of Ms. Smith not liking her had assumed major importance, then Ms. Smith allowed herself to become too important to Ms. Richards. When therapists emerge as such central figures in their clients' lives, they typically accomplish little more than gaining their dependency. Related data indicate that therapists frequently acquire substantial prominence in the lives of their clients. For example, one study reported that more than 80% of clients experience thoughts, feelings, or images involving their therapist between sessions.[3] These experiences occurred most frequently when the clients found themselves contending with difficult situations or feeling discouraged. Not surprisingly, then, other data indicate that lonely and isolated clients may depend excessively on therapy while idealizing their therapist as a result.[4]

Blame-and-Change Maneuvers

Ms. Smith's notes for February 23, 1989, indicated:

addressed how dynamics with Dave replicate family dynamics, particularly regarding being ordered about and her needs ignored.

In this session, Ms. Smith suggested to Ms. Richards that she grew up in a family where she "was ordered about" and "her needs ignored." This tactic is another example of the "blame-and-change" maneuver in psychotherapy. This maneuver suggests to clients that treatment must "blame your family in order to change you." Ms. Smith's affinity for blame-and-change maneuvers is also seen in her notes of March 20, 1989. On this date, she recorded how Ms. Richards reacted to her canceling a previous therapy appointment because of illness.

Focused on her anger regarding my illness. Discussed abandonment issues from mother's frequent headaches—differentiated that mother did not take care of her even when well. Terri projected I called in sick only to test her and she contemplated acting out by calling secretary and screaming. Also touched on changes in relationship with David.

Ms. Smith had again resorted to more "blame-and-change" maneuvers. Rather than take responsibility for her own actions and apologize for canceling a session, Ms. Smith suggested that Ms. Richards was really angry at her mother. She characterized Ms. Richards's mother as a hypochondriac who neglected her children even when feeling well. In Ms. Smith's thinking, clients ought to blame the maladjusted parents who betrayed them. Curiously enough, however, Ms. Smith arrived at these conclusions without ever meeting Ms. Richards's mother. While preoccupied with "blaming and changing," Ms. Smith also merely "touched on" the more important issues related to Ms. Richards's relationship with her husband.

Ms. Smith's notes for March 30, 1989, indicated:

> [Ms. Richards] brought in photo album and teenage journal and letters. Looked at pictures—identified family members. Little reaction to grandfather. Picture not like she thought of him. Discussed seeing him in person. Some intimation of fear of memories—possibly father abused.

This is the first time Ms. Smith's notes indicated any suggestion that Ms. Richards's father had sexually abused her. Entertaining this possibility necessitated she rely on unsupported theories regarding trauma and memory loss. During her testimony at a pretrial hearing, Ms. Smith revealed her willingness to endorse ill-informed assumptions related to repression. While outlining her thinking about trauma and memory, she claimed: "If there has been a traumatic memory that has been suppressed as a defense mechanism of the psyche, then that usually stays suppressed until it reappears." Unfortunately, Ms. Smith was not asked to explain this convoluted statement. If challenged to do so, her floundering attempts would have probably sounded like Abbott and Costello's "Who's on first?" routine.

Preliminary Suspicions of Sexual Abuse

After returning to her office from a 2-week vacation, Ms. Smith's notes for May 24, 1989, indicated:

> Terri cried first—stated she missed me and talked about her panic last week. Also related she suspects her father sexually abused her—hard to admit. Also questioned her re time and loss of memories.

Ms. Smith's willingness to blame Ms. Richards's parents has already been identified. When Ms. Richards reported suspicions of her father having sexually abused her, these suspicions likely reflected Ms. Smith's influence. Without ever having seen Mr. Bauer on a firsthand basis, Ms. Smith was predisposed to view him in more extreme terms.[5,6] Depending on secondhand information about others encourages observers to stereotype them in an exaggerated manner.[7,8] Consequently, in addition to influencing how Ms. Richards viewed her father, Ms. Smith's influence was also ill-informed.

BIAS, PREJUDICE, AND STEREOTYPING

Relying on secondhand information about other people is the basis of prejudice and stereotyping. Examining the characteristics of prejudice and bigotry allows us to better understand how Ms. Smith influenced Ms. Richards. In turn, we will apply the accumulated research regarding these issues to Ms. Richards's therapy.

Examples of Prejudice and Stereotyping

Prejudice and bigotry can be considered particularly ugly blotches staining the pages of our nation's history. African Americans, Jewish Americans, Hispanic Americans, and Arab Americans are among the many groups who have endured cruel experiences of prejudice and bigotry motivated by ill-informed stereotypes. We are all familiar with the ugly stereotypes endorsed by substantial numbers of people at one time or another. For example:

- African Americans are dangerous because of their violent and aggressive nature.
- Jewish Americans regularly walk over other people pursuing their ambitions of upward mobility.
- Hispanic Americans are lazy and unreliable employees who use any excuse to avoid work.
- Arab Americans are religious zealots whose affinity for terrorism poses a persistent danger to our welfare.

Stereotypes motivate very rapid impressions of other people. Rather than think about someone as an individual, we think about characteristics associated with the stereotype—aggressive, status seeking, lazy, or zealot.[9] In response to stereotypes, people selectively attend to examples they can interpret as confirming the stereotype, and they disregard other examples inconsistent with the stereotype.[10] Correspondingly, then, people overestimate the frequency of some circumstance if that circumstance is consistent with the stereotype.

People also reject as atypical circumstances any situations discon-firming a stereotype they endorse. For example, prejudices against African Americans motivate people to overestimate the frequency of black crime. Simultaneously, they underestimate the frequency with which African Americans demand a greater police presence in their own communities to reduce crime.[11] Therefore, it is not surprising that negative stereotypes vigorously resist change. Any evidence inconsistent with the stereotype is discounted as an unusual exception.[12]

Contact Theory

Interestingly enough, contact with members of another ethnic group substantially reduces the extent of prejudice and bias directed at them.[13] Whites who have black friends or acquaintances, for example, are less likely to say they preferred living in an all-white neighborhood. Whites with black friends or acquaintances were also more willing to advocate equality in housing, education, and employment.[14] In other words, contact with another ethnic group leading to friendships or acquaintances signifi-cantly reduces expressions of prejudice directed at that group.[15]

To belabor the obvious, language labels can encourage reliance on bi-ased stereotypes.[16] For example, consider the three groups—African Amer-icans, homosexuals, and women, and also consider that they can be labeled "niggers," "faggots," and "bitches." These latter terms activate more nega-tive stereotypes in how people think compared with the former terms. Therefore, ethnic slurs can be considered shortcut devices for arousing bi-ased stereotypes—and all of the prejudices associated with those biased stereotypes. These considerations then raise the following question: Do therapists resort to biased stereotyping in how they view the families of their clients? Unfortunately, the answer to this question is an unqualified "yes."

STEREOTYPING AND RECOVERED MEMORY THERAPY

Prejudices of Therapists

Therapists regularly respond to the families of their clients in a biased and prejudiced manner. For example, Dr. Hans Strupp of Vanderbilt Uni-versity, one of the most respected figures in psychotherapy research, claims that most clients endured a childhood history of "emotional deprivation and empathic failures."[17] When he uses such terms, Strupp is indulging in biased and prejudiced conclusions about the parents of his clients.

A 1990 article that appeared in the *American Psychologist*—the flagship journal of the American Psychological Association—insisted that psychological distress originates in "an interpersonal environment that is disrespectful, psychologically avoidant, unempathic, and punitive."[18] Ultimately, then, this thinking presumes that the parents of clients are disrespectful, psychologically avoidant, unempathic, and punitive.

A 1991 article also emphasized that "psychopathology stems from unconscious pathogenic beliefs that usually develop from traumatic childhood experiences."[19] Such assumptions lead therapists into regularly contending that the parents of their clients either: (1) subjected those clients to traumatic childhood experiences, (2) neglected to protect them from traumatic childhood experiences, or (3) both of these assumptions are correct. These considerations then lead to the following question: How do these stereotypical assumptions influence what happens in psychotherapy?

Cruel Stereotypes

The biased prejudices of too many therapists encourage them to rely on tactics we previously called "blame-and-change" maneuvers. Consider, for example, the therapist who portrayed a client's husband as "an inept, passive, affable man of small physique, whose intellectual dullness kept him from discerning that the family might profit from a trace of order."[20] This therapist, however, had never met the client's husband. The male client of another therapist was described as enduring a "childhood spent with a highly critical and intrusive mother that prompted his attacks on his demanding and possessive partner."[21] Again, this therapist had never met the client's mother or partner.

Another male client was described as originating "from a segmented family where his father had been distant and emotionally barren. His mother was loving and nurturing, but emotionally undemonstrative and withholding."[22] As you now probably suspect, this therapist also never saw the parents whose characters he irresponsibly assassinated. A female client's parents were described as "withholding and abandoning," which, in turn, supposedly resulted in the client viewing the therapist as "prohibitive and rejecting like her parents."[23] Once again, this therapist had never met the parents of this particular client.

Rapid Impression Formation

As previously explained, stereotypes motivate very rapid impressions of other people. Rather than think about someone as an individual, we think about the characteristics associated with the stereotype—aggressive, status seeking, lazy, or zealot. Similarly, therapists can resort to stereotypes of "dysfunctional family" or "toxic parents" rather than think about those people as individuals. While responding to their own biased thinking, therapists selectively attend to examples allowing them to characterize their clients' families as "dysfunctional" or "toxic." In turn, they disregard any examples of family life inconsistent with these stereotypes.

Also as previously indicated, people overestimate the frequency of some circumstance if it is consistent with a stereotype. They also discount as atypical circumstances any situations that disconfirm the stereotype. Therefore, the stereotypical thinking of many therapists leads them into overestimating the frequency with which their clients endured harsh, nonsupportive responses from their parents. Correspondingly, examples of families responding to clients in an affectionate and encouraging manner are disregarded as atypical circumstances.

The many negative stereotypes of therapists about the families of their clients vigorously resist change. Any evidence inconsistent with the stereotype is discounted as an unusual exception. At this point, then, you might be inclined to ask: Are you saying that therapists regularly resort to "family slurs" that are equivalent to racial slurs? Once again, unfortunately, the answer to this question is an unqualified "yes."

Language Influences

We previously considered how language labels can encourage reliance on biased stereotypes. Therapists are exceedingly familiar with terms portraying the families of their clients in a negative manner. Consider, for example, the adjectives "inept, passive, intellectually dull, critical and intrusive, demanding and possessive, distant and emotionally barren, undemonstrative and withholding, and prohibitive and rejecting." In other words, therapists rely on socially undesirable terms in portraying client families, and they do so more frequently than thinking about them in positive terms.

Related research has also demonstrated that the more available any particular category is in our memory, the greater likelihood of us classifying events using that category. Applied to therapists, we can begin to understand how their thinking regularly categorizes client families in negative terms. These are the terms most available to them when they think about the families of their clients. Therapists can therefore trap themselves in their own stereotypical thinking. Preoccupied with how the families of clients supposedly betrayed them, they overlook the positive influences of those families. As an example of this kind of skewed thinking, consider the following riddle.

> Early on a Saturday morning, a father and his 6-year-old son drive off to complete various errands. As they wait at a red light, an out-of-control speeding truck slams into their car. The collision instantly kills the father, and the son suffers life-threatening head injuries. EMS personnel rapidly transport the child to the emergency room of a local hospital. Preliminary examination reveals that the boy's condition necessitates immediate surgery. The chief neurosurgeon happens to be at the hospital, and immediately begins preparing for surgery. On seeing the child, however, the surgeon exclaims, "I can't proceed, this is my son."
>
> In view of the father's death in the accident, how could this be? How could the surgeon exclaim, "this is my son"?

The simplest answer to the riddle, of course, is that the surgeon was the child's mother. For many people, however, thinking about the term "surgeon" in stereotypical ways prevents them from thinking about a female. Surgeon tends to be stereotypically associated with males. Similarly, thinking about their clients' families in stereotypically negative ways also skews the opinions of many therapists. Their stereotypical thinking prevents them from considering how clients have benefited from positive family experiences. These considerations then lead to the following question: How do the biases and stereotypes of therapists influence their clients?

Influencing Clients

In response to blame-and-change maneuvers—or the family slurs—preferred by so many therapists, clients are left feeling bitter and resentful about their parents. Persuaded they were regularly betrayed by their parents, clients begin to deal with them more guardedly as a result of their therapist's influence. These circumstances leave parents bewildered by an adult child who inexplicably becomes defensive and moody. In turn, it is not surprising that parents become rather distant and aloof in response to situations such as these.

While updating their therapist about these recent developments, clients describe their parents as remote and unapproachable—and the therapist sympathizes with them about the enormous burdens they supposedly bear. In response to this support, clients gravitate into an increasingly dependent relationship on their therapist. Simultaneously, they reduce the frequency of face-to-face contact with their parents. These considerations then lead to the next question: What happens when therapists pull clients away from their families?

As we previously discussed, limited contact with members of another ethnic group substantially increases the likelihood of prejudice and bias directed toward that group. Basically, then, we are talking about how the biases of therapists influence client perceptions and opinions about their parents by reducing the client's family contacts. The most important distinction here is whether clients think of their parents in stereotyped and prejudiced terms, or as individuals.

Thinking of their parents as individuals allows clients to view them more accurately and objectively. But thinking in the stereotypical terms preferred by too many therapists—toxic parents and dysfunctional families— leads clients into viewing their parents in a biased and prejudiced manner. Therefore, when therapists pull clients into more distant relationships from their families, they create potentially difficult problems. In response to these circumstances, clients may stereotype their parents in ways so biased and prejudiced that they are similar to the ugliest kinds of racism.

STEREOTYPING AND MEMORY DISTORTIONS

Availability and Automaticity

In response to their therapists' influences—and most especially in response to distancing themselves from their families—clients begin to stereotype their families relying on the terms they learn in therapy. As a result of their therapist's indoctrination, negative stereotypes are readily available to them when they think about their families. Clients begin finding what they consider evidence of their families as critical, intrusive, demanding, possessive, and so forth, because those stereotypes are so prominent in their thinking. As clients engage in more and more stereotyping of their families, they do it in an increasingly automatic manner. They respond to their own stereotypical thinking so automatically, they remain unaware they are doing it.

Betrayal Scripts and Expectancies

All of us recall some of our memories in response to "memory scripts." Memory scripts involve general assumptions about past events leading us to believe "things must have happened that way." For example, I might say I remember brushing my teeth, shaving, and showering on the morning of November 22, 1963—the day of John F. Kennedy's assassination. Rather than actually recalling the events of that morning, however, I am reporting a memory script. I am simply reconstructing what I usually did on weekday mornings as a college student.

While automatically and effortlessly stereotyping their families, clients develop "betrayal scripts." These scripts assume that all of their problems originated as a result of mistreatment by their families. Previously led into stereotyping their families, clients assume the accuracy of their betrayal scripts because "things must have happened that way." Betrayal scripts become so familiar to clients that their very familiarity increases their persuasiveness. The betrayal script "feels" quite familiar after stereotyping their parents; thus, clients begin to unhesitatingly accept the script as accurate. Betrayal scripts also create expectancies, and these expectancies profoundly influence memories of ambiguous events.

As pointed out in Chapter 9, the accuracy with which we remember past events open to varying interpretations is quite poor. More than anything else, here-and-now attitudes influence our memories for such events. Betrayal scripts acquired in therapy are especially powerful influences distorting what clients think they recall from the past. In response to their betrayal scripts, clients expect to uncover evidence of previous parental misdeeds. When finding evidence they interpret as confirming their expectations, clients experience a surprising sense of relief. Though increasingly convinced of their families' prior betrayals, they feel relieved thinking that their expectations—and those of their therapist—have been verified. The apparent verification of their expectations seems to make their lives more understandable and less unpredictable.

Imagination Inflation

Increasingly familiar betrayal scripts encourage clients to think about their families in otherwise unimaginable ways. Betrayal scripts allow them to imagine themselves enduring the most horrible kinds of parental cruelty. Such experiences seem plausible as a result of the stereotypes suggested by their therapist. Interestingly enough, simply imagining some event also leads people into concluding the event might have happened.

Elizabeth Loftus asked college students how likely it was that as children they had broken a window with their hand. Two weeks later, some of these students were asked to imagine this event had actually occurred. In particular, they were asked to:

> Imagine that it's after school and you are playing in the house. You hear a strange noise outside, so you run to the window to see what made the noise. As you are running, your feet catch on something and you trip and fall. . . . What did you trip on? . . . As you're falling you reach out to catch yourself and your hand goes through the window. As the window breaks, you get cut and there's some blood. . . . What are you likely to do next? How did you feel?[24]

Compared with the students who did not imagine the above scene, students who did were more likely to think they had experienced something like putting their hand through a window. In other words, simply imagining a childhood event leads people into thinking the event might have happened to them.

CREATING MS. RICHARDS'S MEMORIES

In response to Ms. Smith's recommendation in early 1989, Ms. Richards began reading the book *Courage to Heal*.[25] This book has been called the "Bible" of the recovered memory movement. The following quotations, however, clearly demonstrate the extent to which *Courage* can exploit suggestible clients via the dissemination of "junk science."

- "I am not academically educated as a psychologist ... But none of what is presented here is based on psychological theories" (p. 14).
- "If you don't remember your abuse you are not alone. Many women don't have memories, and some never get memories. This doesn't mean they weren't abused" (p. 81).
- "If you maintained the fantasy that your childhood was `happy,' then you have to grieve for the childhood you thought you had . . . you must give up the idea that your parents had your best interests at heart" (p. 119).
- "If you're willing to get angry and the anger just doesn't seem to come, there are many ways to get in touch with it" (p. 124). "Create an anger ritual (burn an effigy on the beach). . . . Visualize punch-

ing and kicking the abuser when you do aerobics. . . . You can be creative with your anger . . . you can heal with anger" (p. 129).

- "If your memories of the abuse are still fuzzy, it is important to realize that you may be grilled for details. . . . Of course such demands for proof are unreasonable. You are not responsible for proving that you were abused" (p. 137).
- "Monetary compensation, even if it cannot undue the damage, is a form of justice, of being vindicated by society while the abuser is blamed and punished" (p. 309).
- "[G]et strong by suing" (p. 310).

On p. 311, the reader finds a list of attorneys to consult for pursuing civil litigation.

Influences of Courage to Heal

Claiming that none of the issues addressed by *Courage* involve psychological theory is colossally naive. This claim also urges readers to disregard the accumulated scientific evidence related to memory. Like too many therapists, the authors of this book—Ellen Bass and Laura Davis— find their own intuitive theories more compelling than scientific evidence.

Insisting that "if you don't remember your abuse you are not alone" suggests that readers can recover memories of abuse they currently do not recall. This suggestion further leads readers into expecting that giving "up the idea that your parents had your best interests at heart" will assist them in recovering such memories. Quite obviously, however, this suggestion also encourages readers to stereotype their parents in a manner consistent with "blame-and-change" maneuvers. Such stereotyping profoundly influences what readers think they remember when "getting angry" to retrieve presumably repressed memories.

"Getting angry" also leads readers into thinking they recall particularly ugly memories by encouraging "imagination inflation." Nevertheless, readers are advised they are not responsible for the veracity of the allegations they express. Instead, they can simply sue someone if they feel so inclined.

Ms. Smith's Influence

Because Ms. Smith recommended *Courage,* we can assume she endorsed its horribly ill-informed assumptions. This consideration also indicates that Ms. Smith led Ms. Richards into the kinds of exercises recommended by *Courage*. Though Ms. Smith never documented such exercises in her notes, she acknowledged many events transpiring in Ms. Richards's therapy that were not recorded. For example, Ms. Smith admitted using hypnosis with Ms. Richards despite never reporting it in her treatment notes.

Ms. Smith's notes indicated that on July 20, 1989, Ms. Richards:

> Talked of memory of being a child and hiding in bathroom at campground all day. Mother found her and dragged back to campsite. Adult relatives sitting around fire, Terri wet her pants as she was pulled into the camp. Put to bed, but first her father grabbed her teddy bear and said she was too old for it, then threw it on the fire. The adults were silent. Terri remembered no further information.

Childhood memories such as these are notoriously unreliable. This particular memory of Ms. Richards likely reflected the "blame-and-change" influences of Ms. Smith. In response to the latter maneuvers, we can assume Ms. Richards developed "betrayal scripts" leading her into recovering false memories via the effects of "imagination inflation." In particular, for example, consider the effects of imagination inflation combined with asking clients the kinds of questions we discussed in Chapter 9: (1) "Maybe there was a time when your father looked at you in a seductive way?" (2) "Possibly he spoke to you in a suggestive manner?" (3) "Might he have touched your arm or face rather sensuously?" These kinds of questions can easily lead clients into creating false memories of childhood sexual abuse.

Family Experiences of Therapists

What accounts for the eagerness with which therapists stereotype the families of their clients in such negative terms? Surprisingly enough, therapists recall their own childhoods more negatively than do other professional groups. For example, compared with graduate students in business, education, engineering, and health sciences, therapists in graduate school reported more problems in their childhood families.[26] Another study reported that compared with other female professionals, female therapists reported greater levels of distress, trauma, and conflict with their families of origin.[27]

Related data demonstrate that compared with research psychologists, therapists chose their careers in response to (1) their own experiences of psychological distress and (2) their desires to resolve their own personal problems.[28] These studies collectively support a conventional stereotype of therapists, namely, that they are a maladjusted lot who wander into their calling in a misdirected attempt at solving their own problems. Other data, however, challenge this stereotype. The female therapists who reported frequent problems with their families or origin also exhibited high levels of satisfaction with their lives and low levels of psychological disturbance.

The characteristics of the female therapists cited above raise the question of whether therapists more often grow up in troubled families. Or do they only think this is the case as a result of their education and training as therapists? What they remember about their families is at least partially influenced by their encounters with Freudian theory as students. These experiences could lead them into revising their memories of childhoods that were actually happy and content. Regardless of whether their memories about their families are biased and distorted, therapists nonetheless *think* they grew up in troubled families. This thinking obviously influences their readiness to direct blame-and-change maneuvers at the families of their clients.

A FAILING THERAPY

On August 17, 1989, Ms. Smith interviewed Ms. Richards's three oldest children. When she asked Jimmy, "what problems could I help fix for him?" Jimmy replied: "Mom and Dad fighting." Susan's response to this question "was the same as Jimmy's—Mom and Dad fighting. Martha—same answer about fighting."

Continuing Marital Conflicts

In other words, after almost 7 months of therapy at two sessions per week, Ms. Richards still found herself involved in frequent and intense disputes with her husband. This development corresponded to Ms. Smith neglecting to deal appropriately with Ms. Richards's marital conflicts. Rather than respond effectively to these issues, Ms. Smith was much more interested in recovering Ms. Richards's supposedly repressed memories. The relevant research, however, demonstrates that the acrimony and turmoil inundating Ms. Richards's marriage severely jeopardized her psychological welfare.[29] Therefore, this is another example of Ms. Smith neglecting to respond effectively to Ms. Richards's needs.

Family Alienation

Ms. Smith's notes for November 6, 1989, reported:

> Mother has called. Terri freezes, mother demands and Terri can't
> speak. She's to decide with David whether they want their children to
> see them [Terri's parents] at Xmas or not, then set limits.

Persuasive as this report may seem, it warrants closer examination.
Ms. Smith was reporting the dynamics of a two-person relationship she
never saw. Without directly observing the interactions between Ms.
Richards and her mother, Ms. Smith was indulging in inappropriate speculation—speculation guided by her assumptions related to "blame-and-
change" maneuvers. Even more outrageous was Ms. Smith's willingness
to alienate Ms. Richards, and her own children, from her parents. This
kind of alienation can create enormous problems, leading to despair of
suicidal proportions. The French sociologist Emil Durkheim first discussed these issues in 1897.[30] Apparently, Ms. Smith remained unfamiliar
with this well-established thinking in 1989.

Speculative Exchanges

Ms. Smith's notes for her session of January 8, 1990, indicated that
Ms. Richards:

> Got thru holidays OK. Had list to start—some confrontation with
> mother in dreams—labeled herself as psychic then discounted. Started
> to reveal memory of hiding under porch, being quiet and mom calling
> her and crying. Stopped self—confronted. Also confronted regarding
> lost memories and looking for others.

It is important to note that Ms. Smith did not specify exactly what she
confronted Ms. Richards about, and in particular, what memories she
questioned her about. It is quite possible Ms. Smith confronted Ms.
Richards about memories she thought Ms. Richards should be recalling. If
so, Ms. Smith was encouraging Ms. Richards to speculate about childhood
events. Speculative exchanges between therapists and clients, however,
also readily lead into overconfidence.

The relevant data demonstrate that conjecture addressing why some
event might have occurred leaves people more confident that the event
did occur.[31] Despite the unavailability of any evidence to support such a
conclusion, the effects of "imagination inflation" lead people into their
overconfidence. Furthermore, these speculative exchanges frequently re-

spond to the effects of leveling and sharpening.[32] Both therapist and client can sharpen their impressions related to what seems significant about the client's past, and simultaneously, they level what seems less than significant. Often, however, the processes of sharpening and leveling respond more to the theoretical convictions of the therapist than reflecting an accurate assessment of the client. Nevertheless, the consensus shared by therapist and client can create unwarranted confidence in their conclusions.

More Blame-and-Change Maneuvers

Ms. Smith's notes of February 6, 1990, reported Ms. Richards's growing frustration with the frequency with which Ms. Smith was canceling her therapy appointments:

> Focused on anger re my absence. Reviewed pros and cons of any close relationships—set limits re anger—repeated reassurances that I'm not trying to dump her. She wanted me to make decision re: her staying or not—I refused. Stressed need to resolve transference issues re: mother's sickness.

In a little more than 1 year of treatment, Ms. Smith had canceled a total of seven sessions: 2-9-89, 6-1-89, 8-8-89, 9-6-89, 9-18-89, 12-5-89, and 2-5-90. Ms. Richards's increasing intolerance of these cancellations was altogether understandable. Ms. Smith, however, again attempted to avoid responsibility for her own actions, instead blaming Ms. Richards's mother for how Ms. Richards reacted. Unfortunately, there is an alarming likelihood that Ms. Smith's actions also led Ms. Richards into disavowing responsibility for her own behavior, and instead blaming others.

IMAGINATION CONTAMINATING MEMORY

Ms. Smith's notes for March 1, 1990, indicated how Ms. Richards:

> Started with memory of white garage and green door, fears she set fire to it—feels fear. Blocked going further. Discussed some of the process to recovery of memories. We planned to meet Monday at the house to explore possible feelings.

Ms. Smith's notes for March 5, 1990, reported some of Ms. Richards's reactions as they met at her childhood home.

> Met at childhood home. Retraced memories she has—fear occurred during some memories—acknowledged blocking. Biggest discovery for self was how small the house actually was—could her mother re-

ally have not heard the abuse? More details regarding the bondage in the dining room.

By March 1990, Ms. Smith had persuaded Ms. Richards that her father had sexually abused her as a child. Nevertheless, Ms. Smith's own notes disclose how unreliable retrospective memory is—Ms. Richards's childhood home was much smaller than she remembered it. Even more importantly, Ms. Richards expressed her doubts about whether her father could have abused her without her mother hearing it. Ms. Smith, however, chose not to respect Ms. Richards's doubts. She regarded her theoretical convictions as substantially more important than Ms. Richards's welfare.

In mid-March 1990, Ms. Richards told Ms. Smith how her younger brother and younger sister emphatically challenged what she thought she remembered. Her younger siblings both insisted they did not recall any memories related to what Ms. Richards thought she was recalling. The younger sister's position was especially compelling because she and Ms. Richards had shared the same bedroom as children and teenagers. Ms. Smith, however, simply dismissed these considerations as involving "denial" on the part of the sister and brother.

Mechanisms of Created Memory

Ms. Richards's created memories did not suddenly appear in an overnight manner. It took somewhere between 6 and 9 months to acquire these memories in response to Ms. Smith's influence. Consequently, creating memories in therapy is a gradual, insidious process involving the sequence of events outlined below.

1. In response to the blame-and-change maneuvers of a therapist, clients begin stereotyping their families in negative terms.
2. In particular, clients learn to think of their families as critical, intrusive, demanding, possessive, and the like.
3. Preoccupied with how their families allegedly mistreated them, clients find it difficult to recall previous episodes of family support and encouragement.
4. Clients then begin to distance themselves from their families, and their reduced family contacts lead them into even more exaggerated stereotyping.
5. In response to stereotyping their families in cruel and vicious terms, clients develop betrayal scripts. These scripts lead clients

into assuming that all of their problems originated with their families' supposed betrayals.

6. Betrayal scripts also motivate clients to imagine outrageous scenarios regarding how their families might have betrayed them.

7. As a result of imagination inflation, what clients imagine can strike them as more than plausible. Because they expect to retrieve memories of previously repressed betrayals, clients think what they merely imagine amounts to recovered memories.

Disavowing Responsibility

When confronted regarding how she could have influenced Ms. Richards's "recovered memories," Ms. Smith protested any such suggestion. While testifying at a hearing prior to Mr. Bauer's trial, Ms. Smith vehemently denied ever influencing Ms. Richards's memory. In particular, she claimed:

> I'm not active in that recovering of memory process . . . memories do not come back before [the] psyche is ready to handle it [sic]. . . . So I am not active with my clients in terms of trying to make them remember.

Without having video- or audiotaped her sessions with Ms. Richards, Ms. Smith's claims regarding how active she was in treatment are not supported by the relevant data. In fact, psychotherapists do not accurately recall how they influence clients.[33,34] They are characteristically oblivious to the influences they exercise in therapy. Rather than monitor their own behavior, therapists focus their attention on what their clients say. As a result, it is difficult for them to accurately remember how they respond to their clients.[35]

Ethical Dilemmas for Therapists

In the typical case of recovered memory, therapists contend that clients endured horrible experiences of childhood sexual abuse. They also insist the clients had no memories of that abuse before undertaking therapy. To belabor the obvious, these therapists have succumbed to outrageous examples of prejudice and stereotyping. Their biased conclusions can also create difficult ethical problems for those who indulge in them. This is especially true if the therapist is a psychologist.

In particular, any therapist who concludes that therapy has assisted a client to recall previously repressed memories of childhood sexual abuse—

supposedly perpetrated by one or both parents—must acknowledge that this outcome creates potential forensic or legal consequences. Principle 7.02 of the American Psychological Association's Ethical Code addresses issues related to "forensic assessments." The relevant sections of the code state:

> (a) Psychologists' forensic assessments, recommendations, and reports are based on information and techniques (including personal interviews of the individual when appropriate) sufficient to provide appropriate substantiation for their findings.
> (b) Except as noted in (c), below, psychologists provide written or oral forensic reports or testimony of the psychological characteristics of an individual only after they have conducted an examination of the individual adequate to support their statements or conclusions.
> (c) When, despite reasonable efforts, such an examination is not feasible, psychologists clarify the impact of their limited information on the reliability and validity of their reports and testimony, and they appropriately limit the nature and extent of their conclusions or recommendations.[36]

When therapists conclude that a client has recovered previously repressed memories of childhood sexual abuse perpetrated by a family member, the ethical principles cited above raise the following questions:

- Has the therapist undertaken a personal interview of the alleged offender to substantiate his or her findings?
- Is the therapist willing to testify about the alleged offender in a legal proceeding without ever examining him or her?
- Without having personally interviewed an alleged offender, does the therapist clarify the consequences of the limited information available to him or her?

Therapists too often ignore these considerations while indulging in theoretically in-vogue terms such as "dysfunctional family" and "toxic parents." Ultimately, however, these terms amount to little more than family slurs. Therefore, these family slurs deserve the same disrespect that slurs such as "racially inferior" and the "weaker sex" have justly earned.

EPILOGUE

Ms. Richards remained in treatment with Ms. Smith throughout 1990 and into mid-1991. During the preliminary hearing related to the criminal charges against her father, Ms. Richards claimed she had no clear memories of him allegedly raping her until the spring of 1991. Ms. Richards's testimony, combined with that of Ms. Smith, resulted in her father undergoing trial. The prosecution charged Mr. Bauer with numerous counts of first-degree criminal sexual contact, a life sentence felony in the State of Michigan.

My expert testimony on behalf of Mr. Bauer emphasized, among many issues, the following four points outlined in the previous chapter:

1. There is no accumulated body of evidence demonstrating that trauma—such as childhood sexual abuse—motivates people to repress events associated with that trauma.
2. The reliability of studies suggesting that childhood sexual abuse leads to repression rapidly falls apart when examined closely. These studies characteristically overlook considerations such as normal childhood amnesia, everyday forgetting, and the influences of therapists.
3. Retrospective reports recalling subjective psychological states and related family dynamics are inherently unreliable.
4. Psychotherapy frequently results in clients and therapists constructing memories that involve more fiction than fact. Indeed, the biases of too many therapists lead them into profoundly distorting the memories of their clients.

After the presentation of closing arguments, the jury began its deliberations. Disinclined to engage in any rush to judgment, the panel of 12 jurors deliberated over 3 hours before it reached its unanimous verdict of not guilty. Relieved as Mr. and Mrs. Bauer were, this verdict has not eliminated the continuing pain and emptiness they feel for their firstborn child who still alienates herself from them. In early 1993, Ms. Richards left her husband and four children to live with another man. Mr. Richards filed for divorce and the court awarded temporary custody of the children to him.

Quite obviously, then, recovered memory therapy amounted to a disastrous outcome for Ms. Richards. It left her estranged not only from her parents and siblings, but also from her own children. The extent to which recovered memory therapy betrayed Ms. Richards's welfare raises questions regarding the general effects of this treatment approach. Is it possible that this therapy mistreats clients so horribly that it invites malpractice litigation? In Chapter 11, we will address this question and many other related issues.

11

Clients Suing Recovered Memory Therapy

In 1990, the State of Washington amended its Victim Crime Act. The changes allowed clients to seek reimbursement for therapy expenses if they claimed previously repressed memories of sexual abuse. Between 1991 and 1995, Washington residents filed 670 repressed memory claims, of which 325 were approved for reimbursement. Thirty of these cases were selected for developing "a preliminary profile" of the effects of recovered memory therapy.[1]

Of the 30 randomly selected cases, 29 (97%) involved female clients. The same percentage of the sample was white, their ages ranging from 15 to 67 years (average age 43). These clients saw mostly master's-level therapists (26 of 30, 87%). Two clients saw doctoral-level psychologists, and two were treated by M.D. psychiatrists. In 26 of the 30 cases, the first memory of alleged childhood sexual abuse emerged in psychotherapy. The entire sample of 30 clients remained in therapy 3 years after their original memories first developed. Over half of the sample (18 of 30, 60%) continued in treatment 5 years after recovering their memories.

Prior to recovering their memories, only 3 (10%) of the clients experienced suicidal thoughts and/or engaged in a suicide attempt. After thinking they had recovered their memories, however, 20 of the 30 clients (67%) struggled with suicidal thoughts and/or had attempted suicide. Before recovering their memories, only 2 of the 30 clients (7%) had been hospitalized in a psychiatric unit. After recovering their memories, however, 11 of the 30 clients (37%) had been hospitalized. Before reporting recovered memories, only 1 of the 30 clients had engaged in self-mutilating behavior, i.e., cutting of the hands, arms, legs, or other body parts. After reporting their memories, 8 of the clients (27%) engaged in self-mutilation.

These 30 clients were fairly well-educated, and most had been employed before entering therapy (25 of 30, 83%). After 3 years of therapy, however, only 3 of the 25 (12%) still continued to work. Twenty-three of the thirty clients (77%) were married when they began therapy. Within 3 years after starting their therapy, 11 of the formerly married clients (48%) were separated or divorced. Seven of the eleven divorced or separated clients (64%) had lost custody of their children. All 30 clients were estranged from their extended families.

These data are more than just shocking, they dramatically underscore the horrible damage suffered by clients in recovered memory therapy. They lose their jobs, their marriages, and their children, and they lose the support of their families. Their psychological condition deteriorates to the point of needing hospitalization—often as a result of suicidal urges or self-mutilating impulses. To belabor the obvious, the incompetent therapists responsible for these tragedies invite lawsuits for malpractice. To better understand how such mistreatment can result in legal action, we will examine one such case in depth.

RECOVERING MEMORIES AND DAMAGING CLIENTS

Though only 19 years of age, Sandra Green had found her life filled with problems and disappointments. In the summer of 1989, she left her parents' home in Indiana and moved to Michigan with friends who had recently relocated there. Sandra viewed her parents as stubborn and arbitrary in demanding she comply with their rules and expectations while living at home. Not too long after moving to Michigan, Sandra discovered how much she missed the familiarity of friends and family. She even realized she missed her mother and father. Her sense of pride, however, prevented her from disclosing these feelings to her parents. When feeling especially lonely, Sandra was also drinking excessively.

In October 1990, Sandra sought out the services of an outpatient psychotherapy clinic. She completed a standardized intake form reporting her "problems with relationships, and anxiety and depression." Sandra further revealed, "I know I have a problem drinking alcohol," and added she wanted to "figure out how to deal with my parents." After completing this form, clinic personnel admitted Sandra into a partial hospitalization program. Sandra would spend 2 to 3 days a week, between 9 AM and 3 PM, participating in this program. Additionally, she was placed in a therapy group for people with multiple personality disorder—or what is now known as "dissociative identity disorder."

Diagnosing for Bait and Switch

Sandra's placement in a dissociative disorders group was grossly inappropriate. This treatment decision was unrelated to the problems she identified when seeking therapy: (1) difficulties with relationships and anxiety and depression, (2) alcohol abuse, and (3) needing to "figure out how to deal with my parents." Nevertheless, the psychiatrist who assumed responsibility for her care—Dr. Irene Jones—considered herself a specialist in the treatment of dissociative identity disorder.

In a manner similar to other clients we previously discussed, Sandra encountered the "bait-and-switch" tactic in psychotherapy. She responded to the "bait" of therapy, expecting it would alleviate the psychological distress motivating her to seek it. Despite her expectations, she found herself "switched" to a treatment related more to her therapist's theoretical interests than responsive to her problems.

Diagnosing Sandra with a dissociative disorder also served to justify her placement in a partial hospitalization program. Her health insurance paid much more for partial hospitalization compared with the cost of one or two sessions of therapy per week. Sandra's insurance carrier would have likely rejected claims for partial hospitalization had she been diagnosed with an alcohol problem or an anxiety or depressive condition. A diagnosis of dissociative identity disorder, however, makes partial hospitalization services appear legitimate. As you might suspect, partial hospitalization programs and inpatient psychiatric facilities diagnose dissociative disorders with astounding frequency.

A nursing note of October 26, 1990, summarizing Sandra's participation in group therapy on that date stated:

> Sandra reports being tired because of having to work all night. She does not recognize having alter personalities. Reports experiencing flashbacks but unable to know memory at this time.

The comment about "alter personalities" refers to a common characteristic of dissociative identity disorder. People contending with this disorder exhibit sudden and dramatic changes in their behavior from one time to another. These behavioral changes are so profound because they actually involve different personalities influencing the person at different times. The nursing note quoted above, however, neglected to consider how simple fatigue can create some of the symptoms of a dissociative disorder. In particular, simple fatigue provokes sudden, unexpected shifts in mood and attitude. Disregarding these effects of fatigue amounted to what is known as "confirmatory bias"—the "tendency to seek supportive data for one's hypothesis, and to underweight or disregard nonsupportive data."[2]

Overdiagnosing Dissociative Identity Disorder

While indulging their own confirmatory biases regarding Sandra's diagnosis, Dr. Jones and her staff disregarded the accumulated evidence demonstrating that dissociative disorders are frequently overdiagnosed.[3-5] It seems rather curious, for example, that a condition supposedly as common as dissociative disorder is not diagnosed by a majority of psychiatrists in other countries.

Despite the considerable attention directed at dissociative disorders in the early 1900s in France, for example, the diagnosis is rarely reported there now.[6] The diagnosis of dissociative disorder is also very rare in Great Britain,[7] Russia,[8] and India.[9] A Japanese survey failed to find a single case of disorder.[10] These cross-cultural data identify the frequency of dissociative diagnoses in the United States and Canada as a pseudoepidemic. Dissociative disorder diagnoses are too often fabricated in order to collect exorbitant fees from health insurers. Dr. Jones and her staff, however, likely preferred to disregard this persuasive evidence.

To better understand the thinking of therapists about dissociative identity disorder, consider the description of this condition found in the 1994 *Diagnostic and Statistical Manual* of the American Psychiatric Association. This is the definitive reference for all diagnostic classifications used by therapists.

> Dissociative Identity Disorder reflects a failure to integrate various aspects of identity, memory and consciousness. Each personality state may be experienced as if it has a distinct personal history, self-image, and identity, including a separate name. Usually, there is a primary identity that carries the individual's given name and is passive, dependent, guilty, and depressed. The alternate identities frequently have different names and characteristics that contrast with the pri-

mary identity (e.g., are hostile, controlling, and self-destructive). Particular identities may emerge in specific circumstances or may differ in reported age and gender, vocabulary, general knowledge, or predominant affect.[11]

Suggesting Dissociative Diagnoses

Therapists can lead clients into creating the appearance of dissociative identity disorder. In response to their therapist's influence, clients begin exhibiting the characteristics of two or more personality states. Such states often seem dramatically different. A particular personality state may present as deferentially polite and mild-mannered, while another appears aggressively hostile and cynical. The relevant research, though, demonstrates how the appearance of a dissociative disorder frequently involves therapist influence combined with client suggestibility.

Consider, for example, research examining what people think they recall from a "past life." Assuming that "past lives" are entirely illusory, whatever people recall about them amounts to imagination heightened by suggestibility. The relevant data demonstrate that in response to suggestion, people imagine fascinating events about their supposed "past lives."

In a 1991 experiment, subjects undergoing hypnotic regression were told their past-life identities would probably emerge as a different sex and race from themselves, and also likely live in an exotic culture (experimental group). Subjects in the control group also underwent hypnotic regression, but they heard no suggestions about the details of their presumed past-life identities. Compared with the control group, subjects in the experimental group more frequently reported themes of different sex, different race, and exotic culture when describing their past lives.[12]

In another experiment, subjects participating in a past-life regression experiment knew they would be questioned about their past-life childhoods. Subjects in the experimental condition were told that children in past eras were frequently abused. Subjects in the control group did not hear this suggestion about abusiveness. The subjects in the experimental condition reported significantly higher levels of childhood abuse related to their past-life identities than subjects in the control group.[13]

If the suggestibility effects of hypnosis can influence what people think they recall from a "past life," then suggestibility effects can also lead people into creating the appearance of a dissociative disorder. The therapist need only suggest, for instance, that the client experiences contradictory feelings at different times, e.g., demure innocence versus bold seductiveness. Clients then respond to these suggestions by conforming their behavior to the therapist's expectations.

Applied to Sandra Green's case, these considerations are especially disturbing because Dr. Jones used hypnosis with her. One of Dr. Jones's treatment notes for Sandra reported: "In hypnosis talked with the part who feels she had to 'do anything' to save others." This supposed "part" of Sandra's personality likely developed in response to her heightened suggestibility as a result of hypnosis. Dr. Jones also resorted to role playing procedures that further suggested the symptoms of a dissociative disorder to Sandra. The following treatment note documents how Dr. Jones suggested to Sandra that there were different parts of her personality.

> Focused on her fear of a peer [another patient], did some role playing (with props)—she [Sandra] took the role of talking to the resistant, frightened part of her who is trained to "save" this peer. Talking regarding how fear triggers her to switch [presumably to another personality].

As Sandra spoke to the supposedly "resistant, frightened" parts of herself, she also vividly imagined these traits as corresponding to another personality. In response to the effects of "imagination inflation," Sandra became increasingly convinced that she suffered from dissociative identity disorder. Ultimately, however, she acquired her dissociative symptoms from the suggestions of her therapists.

Dissociative Disorder and Assumptions of Repression

Large numbers of therapists also assume that dissociative disorder diagnoses correspond to a history of childhood abuse. These therapists think that clients develop dissociative disorders to contend with the traumatic experiences they supposedly suffered as children. In particular, this theoretically driven thinking contends that dissociative disorders allow clients to repress their memories of the abuse they presumably endured. As a result, the therapists who naively embrace this thinking are also determined that clients recall their repressed memories in vivid detail.

Dr. Jones and her staff led Sandra into recalling memories of satanic ritual abuse so outrageous and unbelievable that they stagger the imagination. By November 2, 1990, a group therapy note for Sandra reported: "Client beginning to share memories of occult ritualistic abuse experienced as a young child and early adolescent." Dr. Jones and her staff continued to persuade Sandra that all of her problems began with the ritual-istic abuse she supposedly endured as a child and adolescent. What amounts to the effects of Sandra's brainwashing is seen in the following treatment notes recorded by Dr. Jones and her staff.

> 11-5-90: Client able to have a sense that mother is drawing her back into the family to become involved in ritualistic activities. Getting flashbacks about blood and babies. Remains withdrawn at times. Able to use art work to discuss issues on a minimal basis. Support & en-couragement given.
> 11-14-90: Remembering incidences when impregnated by father and then having baby sacrificed by rituals.
> 11-16-90: Client dealing with memories related to being held under water. Having choking and suffocating sensations.
> 11-28-90: Worked in group on being drugged and taken out of house during night. . . . Reports current time and memory loss. Amnesia from the past is still widespread. . . .
> 12-7-90: Client able to review many sexual experiences with parents and brothers with whom she slept with all of her preteen and some teen years. Realizing that all contact with parents is to persuade her to return to family and ritualistic activities. Able to use art work and journaling to deal with these issues.
> 12-10-90: Client dealing with memories of being forced to abort a baby at age 13 yrs—Able to cry and relive memory pain. Art work is very helpful to regain this dissociated material.
> 12-12-90: Client dealing with memories of trainer in cult rituals, being forced to perform rituals and eat and drink things that were not food . . . time and memory loss remains evident.

EVIDENCE OF SATANIC RITUAL ABUSE?

Despite the confidence of Dr. Jones and her staff to the contrary, law enforcement authorities have been unable to find any evidence corrobo-rating satanic cult activity. In response to the growing hysteria regarding claims of ritual abuse, numerous law enforcement agencies have under-taken massive investigations of these allegations. The enormous time and effort devoted to these investigations found no reliable evidence to sup-port such claims. For example, Kenneth Lanning of the Federal Bureau of Investigation has emphasized:

> Until hard evidence is obtained and corroborated, the American peo-ple should not be frightened into believing that babies are being bred and eaten, that 50,000 missing children are being murdered in human sacrifices, or that satanists are taking over America's day care centers.

No one can prove with absolute certainty that such activity has NOT occurred. The burden of proof, however, as it would be in a criminal prosecution, is on those who claim that it has occurred. As law enforcement agencies evaluate and decide what they can do or should do about satanic and occult activity in their communities, they might want to also consider how to deal with the hype and hysteria of the "anti-satanists." The overreaction to the problem can clearly be worse than the problem. An unjustified crusade against those perceived as satanists could result in wasted resources, unwarranted damage to reputations, and disruption of civil liberties.[14]

Ritualistic Abuse and Hysteria

In a subsequent article published in 1991, Lanning outlined how his unit spent 10 years in a nationwide search for evidence of satanic ritual abuse.[15] Despite their persistent efforts, they found nothing. Lanning contends that if satanic ritual abuse were occurring, his unit would have found some concrete evidence during their exhaustive search.

Lanning further emphasized that epidemic allegations of satanic abuse frequently follow conferences where therapists hear dramatic "survivor" stories. At one such conference, "survivors" talked about their abuse in detail. One "survivor" reported memories of sexual abuse on the day she was born, while also claiming recall of her mother's attempts to abort her. Another "survivor" told a detailed story of satanic ritual abuse that included a large number of prominent people from her hometown.

Though well-informed law enforcement agencies view claims of satanic ritual abuse as hoaxes, their evidence has not dissuaded substantial numbers of therapists. Jeffrey Victor, a New York sociologist, is pessimistic about therapists becoming more realistic in their thinking regarding claims of satanic abuse. He emphasizes how:

> The satanic cult scare can be seen as a form of deviant behavior which exists only in the preconceptions of a group of professionals who see what they expect to see. This collective behavior is likely to persist, despite the lack of corroborating evidence for satanic cult ritual abuse allegations, because it has become organized into volunteer organizations and regularly held conferences and because of the media attention given to the stories.[16]

Family Alienation

While indoctrinating Sandra about the satanic abuse she supposedly suffered, Dr. Jones and her staff also pulled her from her family. The following notes clearly document how Sandra distanced herself from her parents in response to the influences of her therapy.

> 12-17-90: Pt attended the full program. Has been working hard to break family ties.

> 1-4-91: Client experiencing much anxiety, fear, and submissiveness in regard to threats of parents to harm her if she does not do what they say. Given suggestions as to how to relocate and protect self from parents and their belief system. Feels very submissive and helpless to get away from being obedient to their wishes.

The notes of 12-17-90 and 1-4-91 underscore the extent to which the "blame-and-change" practices of Dr. Jones and her staff led them into alienating Sandra from her parents. In doing so, they compromised the level of social support available to her. Social support refers to the encouragement, assistance, and reassurance available to individuals from their network of relationships with other people.[17-19] Previous research has demonstrated that high levels of social support reduce the effects of stressful life events and chronic life strains.[20]

Accumulating research has also distinguished between social support that is actually enacted and perceived social support.[21] Perceived social support refers to an individual's perceptions, and corresponding expectations, regarding the social support available to them. Interestingly enough, perceived social support exerts a greater influence on psychological welfare than enacted support.[22,23] In other words, people who think they enjoy a network of supportive relationships—even if they may be mistaken—benefit from social support effects.

In view of the known effects of social support on psychological welfare, any reasonable standard of psychotherapy practice demands that therapists increase the availability of perceived social support in the lives of their clients. Effective therapy therefore mobilizes the families of clients into socially supportive networks responding to the client's needs. Conversely, effective therapy most certainly does not drive a wedge of alienation into the relationship between client and family.

A Mother Who Wanted to Help

Ripping Sandra from her family deprived her of the genuine support and caring they wanted to give her. Consider, for example, the following letter her mother wrote the clinic administrator explaining her concerns about Sandra's welfare. She wrote this letter to the administrator because her previous letters to Dr. Jones had gone unanswered.

I would like an appointment so I could meet with her psychiatrist—Dr. Irene Jones—or her social worker, or anyone involved with her case. I understand patient confidentiality, but why can't someone just listen. In the last five months that Sandra has been there, not one person has been interested in talking with her family, or trying to find out anything about her background or childhood.

I find it very hard to believe she's receiving the right kind of help unless the therapists know about her history. I always thought that therapists were willing to work with the patient's family. I find this not to be true in Sandra's case. All I'm asking is to let us provide information about her. Is that so wrong?

I love my daughter, and all I want to do is help her. I don't understand why no one at your facility is willing to listen, or let me help her. The least someone could do is listen to why she came to Michigan and how her problems increased after that. I don't want to lose my daughter. The last few months have been a nightmare. My every waking moment is on Sandra and what can I do to help her. What am I supposed to do? Put her out of my mind and forget her? What kind of mother could do that?

I feel like Sandra is a prisoner there, and I'll never get to see her again. I don't know what else to do, beg on my hands and knees, or camp out in your lobby until I'm thrown in jail? At least then I could tell someone that would have to listen. Please don't think I'm an overreacting mother. This has just went on so long, and I'm at my wit's end. Something needs to be done, and done now for Sandra's sake.

Neither Dr. Jones, nor any of the therapists working with her, ever responded to the mother's letter. The clinic administrator replied with a perfunctory letter claiming that considerations of confidentiality prevented the clinic's therapy personnel from contacting her. This claim amounted to unmitigated nonsense. Rather than seeking information about her daughter, Sandra's mother wanted to discuss what she knew about Sandra. Invoking issues of confidentiality merely allowed Dr. Jones and her staff to continue avoiding Sandra's mother. Despite her mother's sincere and genuine interest in Sandra's welfare, the nonresponsiveness of Dr. Jones and her staff conveyed an unmistakable message—Get lost!

Iatrogenic Outcomes

Throughout early 1991, Sandra's psychological condition continued to deteriorate in response to the persistent mistreatment of Dr. Jones and her staff. It is important to remember Sandra's problems in October 1990 versus what she endured by early 1991. In the fall of 1990, she struggled with substance abuse problems, feeling anxious and depressed, and wanting to determine how to deal more effectively with her parents. By January 1991, she thought she had suffered unimaginable ritualistic abuse including her father impregnating her, sacrificing that baby, being drugged, and consuming human waste. This brief overview of Sandra's therapy demonstrates how her treatment amounted to an "iatrogenic" outcome—the misinformed and misguided attempts at treating her made her condition worse.

During late 1990 and into 1991, Sandra continued to drink excessively. Intoxication seemed the only available relief allowing some respite from her horrible memories. In April 1991, while intoxicated and stumbling about the parking lot of a bar, Sandra was pulled into a car and raped. She was so intoxicated that it was difficult for her to remember many details about the rape. When she reported this assault to Dr. Jones, the doctor insisted it was Sandra's father who had raped her. She claimed he was attempting to intimidate her into leaving therapy. Dr. Jones further advised Sandra to report her father's alleged rape to the local police agency.

Claims of Cult Conspiracies

Characteristically complying with Dr. Jones's influence, Sandra reported her father allegedly raping her to the local sheriff's department. The detective assigned to her case, Sgt. Connors, immediately contacted the police agency in Indiana where her father lived. Indiana officers interviewed her father, and promptly verified his claim of relaxing in a bowling alley more than 250 miles away when Sandra was raped. Sandra reported this information to Dr. Jones, and she concluded that Sandra's father had sent a "cult messenger" to rape her.

After Sandra returned to Sgt. Connors's office to explain how she was the victim of a "cult messenger," he called Dr. Jones. Sgt. Connors's report of his phone conversation with Dr. Jones is as follows:

> This officer asked Dr. Jones if she believed everything that Sandra was telling her about the occult, the human sacrifices, and the rape. At that time Dr. Jones said, "That on a scale from 1–10 with 10 being the highest, that Sandra was a 10." This officer then asked, "you believe that her father has raped her along with many of his friends and they are also having human sacrifices?" Dr. Jones replied that there have been reported cases of this all over the world.

Sgt. Connors felt puzzled and rather bewildered after speaking with Dr. Jones. As a veteran of more than 20 years of police work, he had never encountered a single case involving claims of ritualistic cults. Determined to keep an open mind, however, he contacted the nearest FBI office. Agent Wood advised Sgt. Connors that the FBI had investigated some 400 complaints regarding alleged cult activity. Nonetheless, not a single case had ever been substantiated. Agent Wood further explained that allegations of ritual abuse typically originate in response to psychotherapy. Wood continued clarifying, "Somehow, these counselors and therapists pull this information out of their patients."

Wanting to thoroughly investigate Sandra's claims, Sgt. Connors also contacted the chief psychologist of the Michigan State Police, Dr. Kramer. Dr. Kramer indicated that their agency had encountered numerous allegations similar to Sandra's. He also emphasized that the Michigan State Police had never been able to substantiate those allegations. Dr. Kramer further explained that to the best of his knowledge, no physical evidence had ever been found of a human sacrifice committed by a supposed cult. In Dr. Kramer's opinion, some "wacko shrink" was jeopardizing Sandra's welfare more than any satanic cult.

Sgt. Connors next phoned Sandra asking her to return to his office so they could further discuss her allegations. While Sandra sat on the edge of her chair in his office, Sgt. Connors summarized his discussions with Agent Wood and Dr. Kramer. Carefully and deliberately, he explained how previous allegations similar to hers had always led to a dead end. Ever so politely, he asked Sandra whether Dr. Jones really knew what she was doing. Or was it possible Sandra needed to find another therapist? When Sandra reviewed this meeting for Dr. Jones, the doctor concluded there was only one explanation for Sgt. Connors's doubts and concerns— he was obviously involved in a cult himself!

INPATIENT HOSPITALIZATION

Persuaded that one or more police agencies were also part of the satanic conspiracy victimizing her, Sandra's psychological condition rapidly deteriorated. Simultaneously, the frequency of her alcohol abuse increased. On April 24, 1991, she felt overwhelmingly distressed and sought assistance from the emergency room of Hillside Hospital. The notes of the ER physician reported: "This is a 20-year-old female patient, with no history of systemic disease, who comes to the emergency room requesting detoxification." The ER report continued: "Patient drinks 3–4 times per week, often consumes as much as a fifth of whiskey on a weekly basis."

Dr. Jones responded to Sandra's ER visit by admitting her to the psychiatric unit of Hillside Hospital. Dr. Jones's admission note stated:

> This patient is admitted secondary to direct transfer from the adult partial hospitalization program. She is complaining of increased sleepiness, anxiety, fear, depression, increased episodes of time loss, and feeling overwhelmed with suicidal ideation.

It is important to note how Dr. Jones neglected to even mention Sandra's substance abuse problems. Her alcohol abuse obviously made an enormous contribution to her sleepiness, depression, time loss, and suicidal ideation. Nonetheless, Dr. Jones never addressed Sandra's alcohol abuse in her diagnostic formulations or treatment planning.

CONTINUING MISTREATMENT

Dr. Jones's note of April 30, 1991, regarding Sandra stated:

> Patient quite agitated, upset, frightened—got call from 'alleged' mother. Doesn't know how she got phone number. Said bad thing might happen if she wasn't out by Monday. Fearful of telling, just beginning to tell things that have been recent traumas.

Dr. Jones's reference to an "alleged mother" corresponds to the most outrageous example of her mistreating Sandra. She attempted to persuade Sandra that the woman she considered her mother was not her real mother. Being told that the person you have thought of as your mother for 20 years, actually is not your mother would leave anyone "agitated, upset, frightened."

Dr. Jones's note of May 6, 1991, regarding Sandra stated:

> Patient able to complete abreaction triggered by morning meeting—the terror, the fear, the feeling of being trapped. Had worked the majority of the day to complete memory of the ritual abuse by family at age 4 years. Difficulty balancing anger with need to smile and not show real feelings. Feeling very overwhelmed.

Dr. Jones's use of an "abreaction" procedure created more problems for Sandra than it solved. Such procedures encourage dramatic and intense expressions of anger and rage. Reacting in this manner often persuades clients that their emotional intensity confirms the childhood betrayals they supposedly endured, i.e., "If I'm this mad, something must have happened." In other words, Dr. Jones's abreaction procedure left Sandra's memory very confused and distorted.

On May 10, a social worker working in Hillside's psychiatric unit recorded the following note in Sandra's chart:

> Patient's mother, Susan Green, called to request an appointment to talk with Dr. Jones about patient. I informed her that the daughter wouldn't sign an authorization for release of information, but maybe Dr. Jones will meet with her.

This was an exceedingly important development related to Sandra's welfare. Her mother's continuing commitment to her daughter afforded Dr. Jones the opportunity to work with her on behalf of Sandra. Dr. Jones, however, again neglected to capitalize on this opportunity, and her neglect disregarded the level of social support available to Sandra.

Doubting Memories

Sandra was discharged from the psychiatric unit of Hillside on May 15, 1991. Her condition continued to progressively deteriorate, and she was readmitted to the hospital on May 24, 1991. At that time, she began questioning the accuracy of her memories. For example, a nursing note of June 5, 1991, stated:

> Client being flooded with memories which she has difficulty accepting. Realizing that many of her family members are/were involved in abusive situations and she is unable to keep them "good."

Memories such as these are notoriously unreliable, and more than anything else, this particular memory reflected the "blame-and-change" influences of Dr. Jones and her program. The traditional Freudian pursuit of insight has predisposed legions of therapists to lead their clients into detailed analyses of how their families supposedly betrayed them. Freudian therapists suggest that clients must understand the many effects of their family's alleged maltreatment in great depth and detail.

In their determination to promote these kinds of insights, therapists can prime their dialogues with clients.[24] Therapists exercise priming effects via leading questions, persistently examining particular topics, and resorting to slanted adjectives. In turn, the responses expected of clients—inventorying their supposed familial betrayals—receive greater therapist attention and corresponding reinforcement. Therefore, priming effects afford therapists the opportunity to lead clients into creating very distorted memories.

On June 13, 1991, Dr. Jones documented her ill-informed impressions regarding Sandra's supposed "body memories." Recovered memory therapists often assume that clients reexperience physical sensations related to the abuse they supposedly endured. The therapists think that these physical sensations confirm a history of abuse even when clients report no conscious recall of such maltreatment. Dr. Jones disclosed her naiveté regarding "body memories" in the following note:

> The patient admits to various somatic complaints related to memories as well as to recent trauma including headache, sore throat, and abdominal pain.

Dr. Jones's assumptions regarding "somatic complaints related to memories" overlooked the fact that:

> There is a high rate of "physiological and psychological noise" associated with everyday living. This base-rate noise, which refers to the minor physical, mental or emotional irritations or sensations associated with everyday living, is largely ignored in the course of everyday life. These phenomena can go undetected unless attention becomes focused on them.[25]

Dr. Jones persistently directed Sandra's attention to this "physiological and psychological noise." Via suggestibility effects, she attempted to persuade Sandra that this "noise" represented "body memories." In fact, though, what therapists consider body memories typically involve overinterpretations of frequently occurring but ambiguous physical sensations. Confused and bewildered clients, however, listen uncritically to their therapist's overinterpretations, and what they hear further influences what they think they remember.

The Revolving Hospital Door

Between June 14, 1991, and December 17, 1992, Sandra was admitted to, and then discharged from, Hillside's psychiatric unit on six more occasions. The colossal mistreatment she suffered left her increasingly confused and bewildered to the point of feeling persistently panicked. Her therapists continued to cruelly stereotype her parents as sadistic satanists. They insisted her father's letters were trying to lure her back into the cult by using "trigger phrases." The greeting cards she received from her mother were interpreted as filled with diabolical symbolism. Her therapists also repeatedly advised her to terminate all contact with her entire family.

The frequency with which Sandra was admitted, discharged, and then readmitted into Hillside revealed a grossly ineffective utilization review procedure. All hospitals must establish utilization review systems to monitor whether their services are used appropriately. The frequency of

Sandra's various admissions should have alerted the hospital—via its uti- lization review procedure—of serious problems related to her treatment. Despite the hospital's utilization review obligations, it never questioned Dr. Jones about Sandra's treatment.

ESCAPING RECOVERED MEMORY THERAPY

In early 1993, Sandra found a job she liked. Her working hours made it impossible for her to continue in the partial hospitalization program. Her responsibilities at work also forced her to substantially reduce the fre- quency with which she saw Dr. Jones. Much to her surprise, however, Sandra discovered that she seemed more stable, and less overwhelmed, as the frequency of her therapy decreased.

Falling in Love

While working, Sandra met a young man—Ken—to whom she felt moderately attracted. Ken more than reciprocated her interest. He found himself fascinated by this rather shy, petite brunette who appeared to be slowly emerging from some self-imposed shell. Though understandably guarded in the initial stages of their relationship, Sandra grew increas- ingly comfortable with Ken as they spent more time together. Slowly and ever so gradually, she began to reveal her nightmare of the past 2 years.

Ken initially listened empathetically and supportively to Sandra's mind-boggling stories about her therapy. He only insisted she refrain from any alcohol consumption during and after these heavy dialogues. Sandra began to notice how much better she felt without alcohol, and she decided on her own to stop drinking entirely. The more she disclosed her recent turmoil, the more she doubted the accuracy of her memories. Ken also doubted that anyone could have endured what Sandra supposedly en- dured and still relate to him in the warm, affectionate manner she did.

Over time, Sandra increasingly disbelieved the memories she thought she had recovered in therapy. Ken responded to her disbelief by outlining how normal and well-adjusted Sandra seemed to him. As diplomatically as he could, Ken suggested that perhaps Sandra's problems originated with "a bunch of wacko shrinks." Sandra giggled as she recalled how Sgt. Con- nors suggested the same possibility to her. Her laughter grew louder as she explained to Ken, "That poor man was so confused. He really wanted to help, and he tried so hard not to offend me. I should have listened to him."

As Sandra and Ken continued to talk about her previous therapy, he evolved into an appreciative audience laughing heartily at her outrageous tales. Sandra learned the more she laughed about her experiences with Dr. Jones and her staff, the more relieved she felt. Out of his genuine concern for Sandra's welfare, Ken also began urging Sandra to mend fences with her parents. Though she knew Ken was correct, the idea of contacting her parents sent Sandra's anxiety soaring. She appreciated Ken's willingness to deal with her patiently about this issue.

Reuniting with Family

While at lunch with Ken one day, Sandra observed a young woman, approximately her age, sitting with an older woman. As she watched them, Sandra surmised they were mother and daughter. This mother and daughter apparently had not seen each other for some time. They alternated back and forth provoking each other's delight with stories and anecdotes about friends and family. With misty eyes, Sandra held Ken's hand tightly asking if he would help her call her parents. Ken smiled warmly while reassuring Sandra he would be there for her, and applauding her decision.

With shaking hands, Sandra dialed her parents home in Indiana. Her mother answered, and soon burst into tears reassuring Sandra that she loved her and all was forgiven. Sandra wanted to explain to her mother what had happened, but her mother's tearful gratitude left her repeating, "It's alright, honey. I'm just so grateful to hear your voice." A brief conversation followed with her father emphasizing, "What happened doesn't matter. We just need to know you're OK." Though crying herself, Sandra smiled at Ken and told her father, "Daddy, I'm doing fine now."

Approximately a week later, Ken and Sandra drove to Indiana for a weekend visit with her parents. Despite her parents' ample reassurances expressed in subsequent phone calls, Sandra was still a bundle of nerves. Her anxiety promptly dissipated, though, when Ken pointed to the yellow ribbon tied around a tree in her parents' front yard. Sandra knew he was absolutely correct when he said, "Mom and Dad are welcoming the therapy hostage back home." Her parents' teary-eyed embraces and warm words further reassured Sandra she had done the right thing.

In practically no time at all, it seemed that Ken and Sandra's parents had known each other forever. Sandra finally had the opportunity to explain to her parents what she had endured since October 1990. They listened carefully knowing that Sandra was meeting her own needs, in addition to theirs, by pouring out this chronology of unbelievable mistreatment. When appropriate, Ken's comments brought humorous relief to Sandra's sobering accounts.

Sandra's mother then began talking about how Dr. Jones and her staff had treated her. Sandra reacted with shock and anger at hearing how her mother had been subjected to such cold contempt. Sandra's father added, "People shouldn't get away with this kind of thing. Doctor or not, you just don't do what they did to our family." The more they discussed this issue, the more Sandra, Ken, and her parents agreed that Sandra should contact an attorney in Michigan.

MALPRACTICE LITIGATION

It was not until the summer of 1995 that attorney Bill Read contacted me. Over the phone, he outlined the history of Sandra's mistreatment. He asked me to review all of the relevant documents and to then contact him. After reviewing Sandra's treatment records, I phoned Mr. Read. He requested an affidavit specifying the appropriate standard of care that should have been applied to Sandra's case. I responded by outlining the following issues.

Appropriate Standard of Care

The appropriate standard of care applicable to Ms. Green's condition necessitated that Dr. Jones and other Hillside treatment personnel respond in the following manner.

1. Appropriate assessment: Dr. Jones and other Hillside treatment personnel were obligated to systematically assess the complaints reported by Ms. Green in October 1990.
2. Specifically, Ms. Green's self-reported problems with substance abuse, and her problems related to her parents, should have been appropriately assessed. Additional assessment of her apparent anxiety and depressive conditions also should have been undertaken.
3. In particular, appropriate assessment of Ms. Green's clinical condition in October 1990 would have identified: (a) how often she consumed alcohol and what kind, (b) when, where, and

with whom she consumed alcohol, (c) the extent to which her abuse of alcohol was responsible for her anxiety and depressive conditions, (d) the extent to which her abuse of alcohol was responsible for the apparent conflicts with her parents, (e) what factors—other than alcohol abuse—played a role in her depressive and anxiety conditions, and in the conflicts between her and her parents, and (f) what social support resources, both actual and potential, were available to Ms. Green from her network of relationships with other people.

4. In response to the appropriate assessment outlined above, a comprehensive treatment program should have been developed for Ms. Green specifying well-defined treatment goals identified as a result of this assessment.

5. Well-defined treatment goals should have specified both "ultimate outcomes" and "instrumental outcomes" for Ms. Green's treatment.[26] Ultimate outcomes refer to the goals treatment seeks to achieve by the time therapy is terminated. Instrumental goals refer to interim goals related to the pursuit of ultimate goals (e.g., eliminating alcohol intake can be considered an instrumental goal related to the ultimate outcome of alleviating depression).

6. A critically important ultimate outcome for Ms. Green necessitated increasing the level of social support available to her. Reducing the frequency and intensity of conflicts between her and her parents—while assisting her in establishing more satisfactory relationships with them—would have served as an instrumental outcome designed to realize the ultimate outcome of increased social support.

7. Specific treatment methods—demonstrated to be safe and effective via appropriately conducted clinical trials research—should have been identified. These treatment methods would have defined exactly how therapy intended to realize the ultimate and instrumental goals of the treatment plan.

8. The treatment plan previously referred to, and the specification of ultimate and instrumental outcomes, should have been reviewed with Ms. Green in order to obtain her informed consent for treatment.

9. Over the course of Ms. Green's treatment, her progress vis-à-vis the treatment plan should have been regularly reviewed and necessary modifications undertaken.

Quite obviously, Dr. Jones and her staff repeatedly violated the standard of care outlined above. Though my written response to these violations appears rational and deliberate, I privately reacted with outrage. In a subsequent phone call, Mr. Read assumed the role of therapist allowing me to vent my anger about Sandra's horrible mistreatment. Once I was rational enough to listen, he requested another affidavit specifying how Dr. Jones and her staff violated the standard of care in Sandra's case.

Violations of the Standard of Care

1. In the records examined by me, I find no evidence of Dr. Jones, or other Hillside treatment personnel, executing an informed consent procedure with Ms. Green. An appropriately executed informed consent procedure would have clearly defined the proposed treatment, specified the risks associated with that treatment, and offered alternative treatment options.

2. The course of treatment Ms. Green underwent with Dr. Jones, under the auspices of Hillside Hospital—specifically her placement in a dissociative disorders group—was unresponsive to the clinical condition she presented at intake.

3. Dr. Jones and other Hillside treatment personnel subjected Ms. Green to profoundly ill-informed thinking regarding her supposed history of satanic ritual abuse.

4. Dr. Jones and other Hillside treatment personnel resorted to procedures such as "artwork" interpretation that are so subjective as to be inherently unreliable.

5. While leaping to ill-considered conclusions regarding Ms. Green's developmental history and related diagnosis, Dr. Jones and other Hillside treatment personnel repeatedly demonstrated evidence of confirmatory bias.

6. Dr. Jones and other Hillside treatment personnel persistently reduced the level of social support available to Ms. Green by systematically alienating her from her family. As they did so, they reduced her to suicidal despair.

7. While subjecting Ms. Green to repeated suggestions regarding the satanic ritual abuse she supposedly suffered as a child, Dr. Jones and other Hillside treatment personnel irresponsibly disregarded the relevant research related to retrospective memory.

8. While rushing to inappropriate diagnostic conclusions regarding Ms. Green's dissociative identity disorder, Dr. Jones and other

Hillside treatment personnel disregarded the published data demonstrating the extent to which that disorder is overdiagnosed.

9. The use of abreactive procedures, by Dr. Jones and other Hillside treatment personnel, severely undermined Ms. Green's psychological welfare—and distorted her memory—via the contaminating effects of induced mood.

10. Dr. Jones and other Hillside treatment personnel refused to even contact Ms. Green's family, and their conduct in this regard subjected her to exceedingly painful conflicts.

11. While alienating Ms. Green from her family, Dr. Jones and other Hillside treatment personnel encouraged her to become excessively dependent on them.

12. While subjecting Ms. Green to outrageously speculative interpretations regarding her developmental history, Dr. Jones and other Hillside treatment personnel disregarded how they distorted her thinking in general—and her memory in particular—via priming effects.

13. The interpretations of Dr. Jones and other Hillside treatment personnel regarding Ms. Green's supposed "body memories" neglected to consider the inherent suggestibility undermining the reliability of this procedure.

14. Dr. Jones and other Hillside treatment personnel suggested to Ms. Green that she should think of her natural mother as her "alleged mother." In doing so, they subjected her to an inordinate level of psychological distress.

15. While stereotyping Ms. Green's parents in exaggeratedly extreme terms, Dr. Jones and other Hillside treatment personnel disregarded the extent to which their opinions about her family relied on biased, secondhand impressions.

16. Despite the frequency with which Ms. Green was repeatedly hospitalized, neither Dr. Jones nor other Hillside treatment personnel considered the necessity of wholesale changes in their treatment planning for her.

17. Dr. Jones resorted to exceedingly ill-advised uses of hypnosis in her treatment of Ms. Green.

18. The utilization review procedures of Hillside Hospital neglected to respond adequately to the grossly inappropriate course of treatment endured by Ms. Green.

19. Because of the violations of the standards of care outlined above, Ms. Green's treatment resulted in a severe iatrogenic outcome.

The treatment attempts of Dr. Jones and other Hillside treatment personnel left Ms. Green more psychologically deteriorated than before undertaking this treatment.

Dr. Jones's Response

Dr. Jones's response to the lawsuit filed against her amounted to massive stonewalling. While testifying under oath at her own deposition, Dr. Jones denied ever hypnotizing Sandra. She claimed that Sandra would spontaneously drift into an "autohypnotic" state on her own. Rather than formally induce hypnois, Dr. Jones contended that Sandra "dissociated all the time, in the middle of a session, between sessions." Mr. Read responded to Dr. Jones by asking:

> MR. READ   Did you read the portion of her [Sandra's] deposition where she said that you would ask her to imagine, close her eyes, and you would count backwards, and she would imagine that she was in a balloon floating in the air? [In fact, this is a generally recognized and accepted procedure for inducing hypnotic trance.]
>
> DR. JONES   I read that.
>
> MR. READ   True or not true?
>
> DR. JONES   I doubt it.

Dr. Jones had previously admitted to no formal training in hypnosis. Consequently, her denying the use of hypnosis with Sandra was not surprising. Acknowledging her use of hypnosis would have invited harsh cross-examination about relying on a treatment procedure without adequate training. In hindsight, though, Mr. Read might have also asked Dr. Jones if she was familiar with the legal definition of perjury, and the penalties related to that offense.

Mr. Read continued to ask Dr. Jones about leading Sandra into referring to her mother as an "alleged mother."

> MR. READ   Did you ever refer to her mother as her alleged mother?
>
> DR. JONES   Yes, in—in connection with what she [Sandra] told me.

In other words, Dr. Jones denied influencing Sandra's references to her mother as an "alleged mother." She insisted that this designation originated with Sandra—not her.

Mr. Read then proceeded to ask Dr. Jones about her familarity with the research regarding repression.

MR. READ   Have you read any studies in regard to repressed memories?

DR. JONES   I can't recall any right now.

MR. READ   Okay. You can't recall reading any, or you can't recall the names of any?

DR. JONES   I can't recall reading any.

MR. READ   Do you know of any research studies concerning the repression of memories of people who have been abused as a child?

DR. JONES   Not specifically. Freud talked about repression, but I don't know any particular—

MR. READ   Other than Freud, anybody a little more recent?

DR. JONES   He just talked about repression in general. Not any studies.

MR. READ   So you can't quote from any studies, any recent studies?

Dr. Jones   No.

Quite clearly, then, Dr. Jones was unfamiliar with the voluminous research literature regarding repressed memories. She apparently found her own ill-formulated theories more persuasive than research evidence. Recovered memory therapists typically demonstrate abysmal ignorance regarding the basic mechanisms of memory. Tragically enough, however, they blithely disregard what they do not know while luring unsuspecting clients into making outrageous allegations.

Mr. Read then proceeded to ask Dr. Jones about satanic ritual abuse.

MR. READ   Do you believe in satanic rituals taking place now?

DR. JONES   I don't know.

MR. READ   You don't have a clue?

DR. JONES   I don't know.

Dr. Jones's response to this deposition revealed her determination to disavow any responsibility for her horrible mistreatment of Sandra Green. Like other recovered memory therapists in these circumstances, she persistently attempted to deny, minimize, and evade the overwhelming evidence demonstrating her neglect of Sandra's welfare. When asked about other important issues such as treatment planning and informed consent, Dr. Jones insisted she could not answer, lamely complaining about hospital records that were "incomplete."

While rapidly retreating in response to legal action against them, recovered memory therapists argue that their clients' memories and allegations originated with the clients. These therapists moreover insist they did nothing to provoke what their clients thought they remembered. The memories supposedly develop independent of the therapist's influence.

These self-serving claims overlook a fundamental consideration related to all psychotherapy. Psychotherapy inevitably responds to the theoretical orientation of the therapist. The relationship between therapist and client is not one of equals. Clients defer to the presumed expertise of therapists, and therapist influence is the common denominator of all therapy. Therapists contending they do not influence their clients, therefore, is tantamount to claiming they do not do therapy.

EPILOGUE

The massive evidence underscoring the irresponsible neglect of Dr. Jones and Hillside Hospital put their attorneys in a difficult position. Though Dr. Jones continued to rationalize her actions, the defense attorneys possessed enough objectivity to assess their case more dispassionately. They knew that trying to defend Dr. Jones and the hospital at trial would be a hopeless endeavor.

The defense attorneys considered me a formidable witness, but the prospect of Sandra and her mother testifying thoroughly intimidated them. Both Sandra and her mother would have easily won the sympathy of a jury and everyone else in the courtroom. Their firsthand accounts of the cruel mistreatment they suffered would have left any and all observers reaching for tissues. Not surprisingly, then, the attorneys for Dr. Jones and the hospital approached Mr. Read seeking an out-of-court settlement.

Hesitant to put herself and her family through another ordeal, Sandra accepted a settlement offered by the defense. The terms of that settlement prohibit the disclosure of the monetary figure involved.

The neglect and misconduct of Dr. Jones and Hillside Hospital obviously damaged Sandra more than anyone else. Nevertheless, her mistreatment also shattered the lives of her parents. The irresponsible allegations hurled at them, combined with temporarily losing their daughter, subjected Mr. and Mrs. Green to enormous distress. These issues lead us to the next chapter. There we will examine how two parents sued a recovered memory therapist not on behalf of their daughter, but on behalf of themselves.

12

Parents Suing Recovered Memory Therapy

With all four of their children grown and living on their own, John and June Thomas decided to build a new house. They discovered this was a far more challenging project than they expected. Coordinating the schedules of numerous tradespeople seemed as hopeless as trying to herd a dozen cats. Both species single-mindedly pursue their own agenda while disregarding everyone else's. Completing the new house consumed so much time and energy, John and June could not visit their adult children as often as previously.

John and June found it especially difficult to see their daughter Cathy, who lived almost 200 miles away with her husband and children. In the fall of 1991, June sensed an uneasy tension between herself and Cathy. Reacting as a concerned mother, June began phoning Cathy more frequently. When talking over the phone, June thought Cathy sounded alright. June had always thought of Cathy as basically well-adjusted. She sailed through school completing both bachelor's and master's degrees. Cathy also enjoyed a good reputation as a dedicated teacher, and her marriage to Mike appeared solid. Mike and Cathy moreover took great delight in parenting their two sons.

While at her parents' new home during Christmas of 1991, however, Cathy behaved strangely. She questioned her father at great length about his childhood, sometimes almost cross-examining him. While attempting to answer her many questions, John's amused smile prefaced his explaining, "Cathy, at my age those memories grow dimmer every year." Cathy replied that perhaps there were events in his past he preferred not to remember. June blurted out that Cathy's determination to "analyze everything" made her uncomfortable. She continued by adding, "Cathy, I'm afraid to say anything around you because you pick it apart."

In response to Cathy's abrupt silence, June regretted striking whatever sensitive nerve she had inadvertently hit. While looking at her mother with pointed disapproval, Cathy left the room without expressing another word. June followed Cathy, apologizing for however she offended her. As June attempted to resolve the situation, Cathy dismissed it as unimportant. Despite her words, however, her demeanor clearly conveyed how upset she remained. Knowing her daughter's facility for stubbornly entrenching herself in a position once she assumed it, June thought it best to return to the kitchen.

After Christmas and into early 1992, June and Cathy talked on the phone with moderate frequency. Cathy did not mention the events of Christmas, and June felt disinclined to broach them without knowing how Cathy would react. Nonetheless, they were rarely at a loss for topics of conversation. Updating daughter about her two brothers and her sister, and telling mother about the antics of her two grandsons, gave June and Cathy many events to discuss. While not yet entirely comfortable regarding her relationship with Cathy, June felt it was at least moving in the right direction.

DISTANCING DAUGHTER

In late February 1992, however, a phone call with Cathy left June worried and distressed. From the moment Cathy answered the phone, June knew she was upset and had been crying. Cathy spoke in vague generalities about "going through a hard time," but declined to discuss any specifics. Suspecting that Cathy still felt burdened by the Christmas episode, June responded reassuringly. June also shared with Cathy how concerned she was about their mother–daughter relationship. She further suggested they needed to meet in person and talk things out. Cathy hesitatingly agreed, but asked to postpone their meeting for the present time.

Feeling even more puzzled and disturbed in the aftermath of this phone call, June shared her concerns with John. He suggested they call their son George with whom Cathy had long been close. While talking with his parents, George briefly paused before disclosing that Cathy was seeing a therapist. He continued referring vaguely to her dealing with "issues in her past." George avoided clarifying the ambiguity of this statement. He obviously felt more comfortable telling his parents how he had urged Cathy to speak directly with them. Disinclined to put George in the middle between Cathy and themselves, June and John reassured him they would drop the topic if he preferred. George gratefully accepted their offer, and then remarked more ominously than he intended, "When she does talk to you, it'll probably be the hardest thing you've ever dealt with."

Bombs Camouflaged as Letters

On March 13, 1992, June and John received a letter from Cathy accusing them and their family of the cruelest atrocities imaginable. She began by stating she had been in therapy for the last 18 months. Cathy continued to allege that when she was between the ages of 7 and 12, her Uncle Fred sexually abused her. Then she leveled the accusations that left June and John reeling in bewildered disbelief. That portion of her letter said:

> When I started incest recovery therapy, I thought all I needed to do was get help for the memories I had of Uncle Fred abusing me. But as I worked through that trauma new memories started to haunt me.
> For the past six months, I've been remembering my life as a small child. I now know that I was violently, sexually abused as an infant up to at least age three by Dad. These memories have torn me apart—some days I would rather believe I was crazy than to believe they are true. But I can't deny it any longer.
> When I was too young for words, Dad used my body, pinned me down and almost strangled me. As an infant, I was choked by his penis jamming down my throat, until he ejaculated in my mouth. As a toddler/preschooler, my tense curled up body was pried apart and my legs were forced apart until my muscles could no longer resist. All of this was done in the dark with my mouth and eyes covered up. Dad is a child molester and the crime he committed against me has tormented my entire life.

Attempting to Respond

When John recovered enough to speak after reading Cathy's letter, he told June, "I won't even wait for you to ask. Just let me guarantee you, I never responded in any sexual way to Cathy. There is nothing about those accusations involving me that is true—nothing." Though relieved by

John's emphatic reassurance, June still felt overwhelmed by Cathy's allegations directed at June's brother Fred. Fred was only 8 years older than Cathy, and as a result, he related to June more as a mother than a sibling. Emotionally, June felt as if Cathy's allegations had been directed at her own son.

June called Fred, and as delicately as she could, confronted him regarding Cathy's allegations. Fred's long pause before replying seemed like an eternity, and then he tearfully admitted his past abuse of Cathy. While struggling with his choking voice to apologize again and again, he sunk deeper and deeper into a pit of guilt and self-recrimination. June's first impulse was to reach out and comfort her brother, but she knew her reassurance would be inappropriate. Though careful not to vilify him, she told Fred only Cathy could forgive what he did.

Fred reacted as if he alone could repair the horrible damages suffered by June, John, Cathy, and the rest of their family. In his thinking, this entire nightmare originated with his exploiting Cathy; therefore, he should be able to fix it. He wrote Cathy a long letter apologizing unequivocally for abusing her. He moreover offered to assist her in any way he could. Though Fred's letter provided Cathy some sense of closure related to him, it did nothing to change her thinking about her parents.

For the entire next day, June and John spoke with each other at great length. Still shocked and dumbfounded by Cathy's letter, they repeatedly asked themselves what could account for her ugly allegations. John wondered if she was mixed up as a result of childhood sexual abuse committed by someone else. June thought maybe Cathy's anger about what Fred did left her memory confused. John, however, had never tolerated indecisive passivity very well. Rather than persist in continued guessing, he insisted, "We've got to figure out what we are going to do." John and June both agreed they needed to meet with Cathy's therapist. In John's thinking, "That's where it all started, and that's where we need to go."

By the following day, June recovered sufficient composure to call Cathy. That call merely heightened her sense of desperation as she spoke only to Mike and Cathy's answering machine. The recorded message she left included a request to meet with Cathy's therapist. Mike returned June's call, saying Cathy could not talk at that time. June begged to know when she and John could see Cathy's therapist. Gently as he could, Mike reassured June that an appointment would be scheduled as soon as possible. After another 2 days elapsed, Mike again called June explaining that scheduling an appointment would be delayed because Cathy was undergoing hypnosis. June experienced a growing sense of resignation, wondering if she and John would ever meet the therapist.

Attempting to Recover

In response to a friend's suggestion, John and June made an appointment with a local psychologist, Mr. Wilson. He appeared sincere in wanting to help, but he also seemed to know little about the crisis inundating them. Mr. Wilson disclosed a secondhand familiarity with *Courage to Heal*, even acknowledging some of his colleagues frequently recommended it. After hearing John and June's trenchant criticisms of *Courage*—calling it the "Courage to Hate"—Mr. Wilson reconsidered mentioning the favorable review it received from a continuing education seminar he recently attended.

Mr. Wilson's firsthand relationship with the Thomases persuaded him John had not sexually abused his daughter. While expressing this conclusion to John and June, Mr. Wilson overlooked how he often indicted the parents of other clients without ever meeting them. His assistance limited itself to rather hollow-minded homilies advising John and June to "trust yourselves" and "be kind to each other." Frustrated by what he considered "pleasant platitudes," John expressed his reservations about seeing a therapist "who sounded like Barbara Walters." Agreeing they needed more than self-help inspirationals, John and June vetoed future appointments with Mr. Wilson.

John and June subsequently found another therapist, Ann Harmon, who helped them effectively. Having previously received her M.S.W. degree, Ms. Harmon had returned to school as a doctoral student. Whereas most therapists are woefully unfamiliar with important research, Ms. Harmon possessed a wealth of information. She explained the ill-informed thinking embraced by too many therapists about repression, and further clarified the impossibility of recovering memories from infancy. Ms. Harmon also effectively supported John and June's relationship with each other.

Exclusion and Separation

Between mid-March and early June 1992, Cathy persistently avoided her parents. June periodically spoke with Mike inquiring about Cathy's welfare. Mike felt increasingly bewildered by his wife's behavior. She would no longer speak with either of her brothers. Cathy had also never spoken about her therapy with her younger sister, Joan, convinced she would vehemently denounce her allegations. June asked Mike when she and John could expect to see Cathy's therapist, Dr. Mitchell. Mike sighed while replying he did not know what Cathy was waiting for, or how much longer it would take.

As June listened to Mike, the sound of futility in his voice was unmistakable. Concerned about his welfare also, June asked how he was managing. Mike sighed again, and then revealed that he and Cathy had separated in late May. Mike's unexpected disclosure briefly reduced June to verbally stumbling over herself. She tried inquiring about why, how, and who all at the same time. Mike explained he had challenged Cathy, outlining his doubts about the accuracy of her memories. Cathy responded by ordering Mike out of the house if he would not believe her. Mike clarified how he considered the entire situation so hopeless, he had no choice other than to leave.

More aware of needing to talk about his own turmoil, Mike opened up in response to June's support and understanding. He surprised her again while recounting how he had gone into therapy with Dr. Mitchell before Cathy did. Mike's individual sessions led to marital sessions for him and Cathy together, and it seemed in no time after that, Cathy was seeing Dr. Mitchell by herself. Mike described how Cathy and Dr. Mitchell's relationship rapidly developed to where they seemed like a "team" determined to exclude him.

When Mike detailed Dr. Mitchell's readiness to accept Cathy's memories premised on little more than blind faith, June's heart dropped. Mike related how he responded to Cathy's memories by repeatedly asking Dr. Mitchell, "How do we know this is true? How do we know this really happened?" With contempt too intense to suppress, Mike described Dr. Mitchell rhetorically asking, "Why would she say it if it wasn't true?" When Mike continued to press this issue, Dr. Mitchell played his ultimate trump card—suggesting Mike's protests were motivated by wanting to avoid his own repressed memories of childhood sexual abuse. Dr. Mitchell's barely concealed smugness provoked Mike's uncharacteristically blunt retort, "Bullshit."

Mike continued describing how he challenged Dr. Mitchell about considerations of corroboration. He felt someone should independently investigate these allegations to assess their legitimacy. Dr. Mitchell lamely countered, "The truth doesn't count. It's Cathy's truth that matters." This comment left Mike recalling something he read in college, "Imagination abandoned by reason produces impossible monsters."

As a result of Mike's phone call, June's previous pessimism deteriorated into desperate panic. Unwilling and unable to passively wait any
longer, June wrote Cathy a terse letter demanding a family consultation
with Dr. Mitchell. She warned Cathy, "Otherwise, you'll find me sitting on
your doorstep." Cathy responded to her mother's demands by scheduling
an appointment for them on June 11, 1992. June felt pleasantly surprised
when Cathy said that John was also welcome to attend the session.

AMBUSHING PARENTS

When John and June arrived at Dr. Mitchell's office after a long, anxious drive, Cathy was the first person they met. Cathy's distant and aloof
manner reduced her parents to feeling that, at best, she considered them
casual acquaintances. June sadly reflected on how this was the first time
ever they had greeted Cathy without mutual hugs and kisses. Cathy told
her parents to seat themselves in a waiting room; 5–10 minutes later, Dr.
Mitchell appeared introducing himself and inviting them into his office.

Soft Appearances versus Hard Allegations

Dr. Mitchell spoke so softly it was difficult to hear him. He seemed to
think how he sounded—especially his affectations of gentleness—was
more important than what he said. Even when expressing himself declar-
atively, his interrogative voice tone suggested he was asking questions.
Apparently determined to avoid confrontation, and maintain his kindly
appearance, Dr. Mitchell communicated with considerable ambiguity. He
seemed quite aware of how difficult it is to argue with someone you cannot understand. His double messages left June and John unsure as to
whether he was stating his opinions or soliciting their approval.

John and June's confusion would have surprised Dr. Mitchell had he
been aware of it. He assumed his manner of presenting himself reassured
clients of his "genuine authenticity." Curiously enough, he found it difficult to define "genuine authenticity" so others could understand it.
Nonetheless, he knew it was an important consideration for therapists
who wanted their clients to feel "grounded." Dr. Mitchell often spoke
earnestly about the necessity of "authenticity" and "groundedness" when
seeking "existential integrity." Not surprisingly, then, he resented his few
friends dismissing as "psychobabble" what he considered his sincere and
cogent observations.

In his persistently soft voice, Dr. Mitchell thanked John and June for their interest in Cathy's welfare. He continued, saying Cathy had been working very hard in response to some difficult problems. He asked John and June how much they knew about the issues of Cathy's therapy. They indicated their information was basically limited to the letter Cathy sent in March. Dr. Mitchell replied it seemed best to proceed by Cathy sharing her "story." Cathy began reading from what appeared to be a prepared script. Unlike Dr. Mitchell's soft mumbling, Cathy's shrill accusations could be heard with a cold clarity that left John and June in frozen disbelief.

Expanding Allegations

In addition to her previous allegations directed at John, Cathy claimed recovering memories of sexual abuse perpetrated by both grandfathers, two uncles, and her father's cousin. While barely missing a beat, Cathy's accusatory lyric shifted to indicting June for supposedly neglecting to protect her. When Cathy briefly paused for a breath, Dr. Mitchell added more ugly accusations in his incongruously polite voice. Looking directly at June and John, he ominously labeled them "a family burdened by a long legacy of incest." In Dr. Mitchell's solemn opinion, such a family desperately needed "professional help."

Seeking at least a temporary halt to the cross fire aimed at them, John and June tried to respond to these expanding allegations. Though Cathy alleged her paternal grandfather had penetrated her with his penis, John explained that such an event was virtually impossible. His father underwent prostate surgery—leaving him entirely impotent—prior to when Cathy claimed the abuse occurred. Looking at his daughter both plaintively and reassuringly, John told her he was certain he never abused her. June also explained her reasons for finding Cathy's accusations unbelievable. The more John and June spoke, the more they understood what they said made no difference. Cathy and Dr. Mitchell knew what they thought they knew, and they were not about to consider alternative explanations.

Disinclined to endure more character assassination in the guise of therapy, John and June ended the session as politely as they could. While standing and about to leave the office, June tentatively approached Cathy. Then overwhelmed by a surge of maternal instinct, she reached out with extended arms, hugging her daughter and saying, "I love you." Cathy's limp response passively resisted her mother's overtures. Her reaction left June feeling as if she was embracing Cathy's body with someone else in it.

When John and June walked out of Dr. Mitchell's consultation room, Cathy steadfastly remained behind. As June glanced at her, she looked like the surroundings provided her some kind of sanctuary.

Recovering from the Ambush

In his waiting room, Dr. Mitchell expressed his hopes for future sessions with John and June. Without committing themselves, they indicated perhaps it would be possible. June and John offered to pay for the session, and Dr. Mitchell unhesitatingly accepted. While driving home, June sought some humorous relief to at least partially alleviate what they had endured. With a faint twinkle in her eye, she asked John, "As bad as Barbara Walters?" John smiled sardonically as he replied, "Worse, all the warmth of Joan Lungen."

June also shared with John how she thought it rather odd that Dr. Mitchell did not give them a receipt. John tersely replied, "If I accomplish nothing else, I'll have the IRS in his office asking questions." Unable to shift her thinking from the day's earlier events, June remarked, "Watching Cathy made me think of Meryl Streep doing one of her victim roles. That woman loves playing the victim." John nodded agreeably, and then referring to Cathy's considerable weight gain since they last saw her, he said, "She's also starting to look like Roseanne Barr, in addition to sounding like her."

Over the next few months, June and John did the best they could to restore some degree of normalacy to their lives. In early July 1992, June was hospitalized for heart problems. Both she and John suspected her condition was precipitated by the stress of Cathy's allegations in general, and the ordeal of meeting with Dr. Mitchell in particular. Much to June's surprise, Cathy sent her flowers while she was in the hospital. The flowers aroused June's hopes for a phone call, but none transpired. In August, John and June contacted the False Memory Syndrome (FMS) Foundation of Philadelphia. The FMS Foundation was organized in March 1992. It serves as an information clearinghouse regarding the problems of psychotherapy and claims of recovered memories. The materials John and June received from the FMS Foundation further helped them understand their overwhelming ordeal.

In mid-September 1992, John and June received a note from Cathy requesting they meet again with Dr. Mitchell. A few days later, George gave · them a preview of that meeting. Cathy had shown him a videotape recorded while she was under the influence of sodium amytal—("truth serum"). Cathy expected the videotape would persuade George regarding the legitimacy of her allegations. She was less than elated when George persisted in his position insisting, "He's my father too, and I know he couldn't have done those things."

June and John spoke at great length about whether to accept the invitation for another session at Dr. Mitchell's office. They finally agreed June and Ms. Harmon would go together. John did not want June there by herself without support. He also decided, however, he would not attend the meeting. Explaining his decision to June he said, "I don't need homicide charges against me on top of everything else. A jury would probably give me a medal for shooting Mitchell, but I'd rather not risk it."

Truth Serum and False Recall

On October 22, 1992, June and Ms. Harmon met with Cathy and Dr. Mitchell in his office. Cathy began by indicating she had undergone a sodium amytal interview lasting 4 hours. She wanted them to watch selected portions of the videotape recorded during the amytal session. Ms. Harmon waited for June to respond, and she agreed to Cathy's proposal. Before seeing the videotape, June asked Cathy if she had recovered any memories of her father's alleged abuse prior to the amytal experience. Cathy replied, "No." Dr. Mitchell quickly added his opinion, claiming the use of sodium amytal was a "highly reliable" procedure. He moreover concluded that Cathy's response to the sodium amytal was "very consistent" with what had happened to her.

Ms. Harmon pointed out there is no scientific evidence demonstrating that memories recalled via sodium amytal are accurate. Dr. Mitchell cryptically replied, in a voice that practically whispered, "It depends on what you mean by scientific evidence." Dr. Mitchell did acknowledge that statements obtained from amytal interviews were inadmissible in legal proceedings. June asked Cathy exactly what kind of therapy she was receiving. Cathy responded, "Sodium amytal, hypnosis, and body work." In response to Cathy specifying "body work," June doubted it was anything like restoring a '65 Mustang. Beyond that, however, she remained unsure as to what "body work" involved. At this point, June did not know about "body memories."

June also asked Cathy what problems necessitated her going into therapy. Cathy replied she felt blocked from succeeding in her work as a teacher, and functioning effectively as a mother. Appearing almost disinterested in the problems that originally brought her into treatment, Cathy did not clarify them.

June thought to herself those are the "here-and-now" problems of an adult. Without at least some previous successes in their lives, people do not encounter career difficulties and parental problems. In other words, if you are a teacher and a mother, there are things you did effectively in the past to accomplish those outcomes. Therefore, how do "teacher problems" and "mother problems" lead you back into your childhood? Plowing through the past struck June as an odd way to deal with contemporary problems. Nonetheless, June kept these thoughts to herself, sensing her perspective would not be well-accepted.

Cathy then began reading from a spiral notebook she called her "journal." She prefaced her comments by explaining, "It feels like I am making this up." While entirely disregarding the significance of this comment, Cathy proceeded with her "story." She launched into a litany supposedly recalling how June removed her clothes and put her in a bathtub with John. Cathy continued by describing her father's hard penis, claiming he put it between her legs and ejaculated. She further contended this abusive incident, and all of the others she supposedly endured, occurred between the time she was an infant and 3 years old.

Cathy's allegations prompted Dr. Mitchell to declare, in a surprisingly clear and unmuffled voice, "This is a fatal disorder." Ms. Harmon wanted to ask whether this "fatal disorder" would necessitate surgery, chemotherapy, or radiation, but she managed to control herself. Ms. Harmon also found it interesting that Dr. Mitchell apparently had never heard of "infantile amnesia." Considerations of infantile amnesia make it impossible for anyone to recall memories of events occurring before the age of 3. Dr. Mitchell, however, would have likely dismissed this issue as another instance of superfluous scientific evidence.

Having previously learned not to wait for assistance from Dr. Mitchell, June sought clarification of her own unanswered questions. She realized that trying to rationally discuss Cathy's allegations was as futile as challenging them. Nevertheless, June wanted to know what to expect in the future. In particular, she asked Cathy if she and John could see their grandsons, Brian and Jimmy. Without hesitating, Cathy said "No," dramatically characterizing herself as a mother bear defending her two cubs. She appeared to think this metaphor justified her cruel decision despite breaking her mother's heart. June's chin dropped toward her chest as she sighed quietly, remembering how Brian and Jimmy loved her chocolate chip cookies.

June managed to pull herself together enough to ask Cathy her next question. Did she want other people in the family to leave her alone? Or would she be coming to various family events? Cathy coolly replied she might involve herself in selected family functions, but she most certainly would not remain silent about "the truth." Sounding like a novice over-acting her minor role in a high school play, Cathy declared, "The truth will set you free." This oratory moved Dr. Mitchell to vigorously nod his head in agreement, looking as if he belonged in a choir affirming the words of a come-to-Jesus preacher. Tragically enough, however, Cathy remained oblivious to how her "truth" had imprisoned her in a cell constructed of vicious rumors and cruel stereotypes.

Disinclined to confine himself to a supporting role in this saga any longer, Dr. Mitchell took center stage directing everyone's attention to the videotape. The tape revealed the physician, Dr. Kim, who oversaw the medical aspects of the procedure, and an exceedingly groggy Cathy. She appeared more interested in sleeping than anything else, and Dr. Mitchell had to frequently coax her into responding. During the amytal interview, Dr. Mitchell assumed a very active role compared with Cathy's passivity.

Ms. Harmon recorded nine instances of Dr. Mitchell responding to Cathy in an exceedingly leading and suggestive manner: (1) "Did he [John] do anything to touch you?" (2) "Are you little?" (referring to Cathy's age). (3) "What is Grandpa Thomas doing to you now?" (asked twice). (4) "And you can't get away or move." (5) "You're choking" (in response to Cathy coughing during the interview). (6) "What happened with Grandpa? He's touching you." (7) "And your Daddy won't leave you alone." (8) "And he takes you to bed at night." (9) Cathy mumbled there was someone in the room (presumably her bedroom as a child). Dr. Mitchell eagerly asked, "Is it Daddy?"

By this time, however, Ms. Harmon had already seen and heard enough. She knew how futile it would have been to point out these instances of Dr. Mitchell's leading suggestiveness. Instead, Ms. Harmon and June subtly signaled each other that it was time to leave. Before they left, June again reassured Cathy, "I love you and you can still come back. The door is still open." Cathy nodded silently indicating she understood. As Ms. Harmon and Cathy departed, Cathy again stayed in the office with Dr. Mitchell.

During the remainder of 1992 and throughout 1993, John and June saw no change in Cathy's situation. With few exceptions, she continued to isolate herself from them and the rest of the family. In early April 1994, June and John received a rare note from Cathy. She basically told her parents not to contact her unless she contacted them first. After rereading the letter numerous times, June looked at John while shaking her head and said, "I think she's closed the door forever. I don't see her coming back to us now." In a voice filled with resignation, John could only agree.

With the passage of more time, what Dr. Mitchell had done to them and their family continued to eat at June and John. In early 1995, they sought the names of attorneys who might advise them, and soon after that, they made an appointment with Bill Read. By this time, Mr. Read was already aware of what recovered memory therapy could do to families. As June and John summarized their own particular nightmare, however, they figuratively smacked Mr. Read in the face. Their case was different, very different.

Mr. Read had previously spoken to many outraged parents in John and June's situation. These were parents whose lives had been ripped apart by cruel, irresponsible therapists. Outraged at what they had endured, these parents desperately wanted Mr. Read to undertake legal action on their behalf. Again and again, however, Mr. Read had to explain there was no legal recourse available to them. The therapists who had torn their lives into shreds did not owe them a "duty of care." Though legally obligated to their clients, these therapists could hurl ugly accusations at the clients' families without having to answer for them. In June and John's case, however, the circumstances were quite different. When Dr. Mitchell saw them in his office and accepted payment from them, he assumed a "duty of care" in relation to them.

As a result of John and June's unique relationship with Dr. Mitchell, Mr. Read asked me to review their case. In particular, he asked me to assess whether Dr. Mitchell had violated his duty in relation to John and June, and if so, to detail the specifics of those violations. In reviewing Dr. Mitchell's conduct, it was necessary to rely on the now obsolete, 1990 ethical code for psychologists. The currently used 1992 code did not take effect until December 1, 1992—after June and John had seen Dr. Mitchell.

VIOLATING THE STANDARD OF CARE

I began my written assessment by specifying Dr. Mitchell's obligation to June and John. Over the course of his professional relationship with Mr. and Mrs. Thomas, Dr. Mitchell was obligated to respond to their welfare.

In particular, the relevant section of the Ethical Principles of Psychologists in effect at that time stated:

> **Principle 1: Responsibility:** In providing services, psychologists maintain the highest standards of their profession. They accept responsibility for the consequences of their acts and make every effort to ensure that their services are used appropriately.[1]

By encouraging the inappropriate use of his services, Dr. Mitchell repeatedly violated this particular principle, and many others, over the course of his professional relationship with Mr. and Mrs. Thomas. The specifics of his violations are detailed below.

Maintaining Professional Expertise

During his deposition taken as a result of the legal action filed against him, Mr. Read asked Dr. Mitchell:

> Q   In addition to your seminars, do you subscribe to any publications to keep you up to date in your field?
> A   I attend the library, the publications there, and I get a publication called Psychology. Psychology journal.
> Q   Do you know who publishes that?
> A   I'm not sure where it's out of.

Quite obviously, Dr. Mitchell could not accurately identify the one journal he said he received, nor did he identify the other journals he said he read. As a result, Dr. Mitchell violated the following ethical principle of the 1990 Code.

> **Principle 2: Competence:** The maintenance of high standards of competence is a responsibility shared by all psychologists in the interest of the public and the profession as a whole. Psychologists recognize the boundaries of their competence and the limitations of their techniques. They only provide services and only use techniques for which they are qualified by training and experience. In those areas in which recognized standards do not yet exist, psychologists take whatever precautions are necessary to protect the welfare of their clients. They maintain knowledge of current scientific and professional information related to the services they offer.[2]

Receiving one journal that he could not accurately identify, and supposedly going to a library to review other journals that he did not identify, failed to "maintain knowledge of current scientific and professional information related to the services" Dr. Mitchell offered.

Informed Consent

During Dr. Mitchell's deposition, the following question and answer exchange occurred regarding the status of his professional relationship with Mr. and Mrs. Thomas.

Q   On the top form, the top one, is that a form of your business?

A   Yes.

Q   You list Mr. and Mrs. Thomas as your patients, don't you?

A   Yes.

Q   And you billed them for that session, didn't you?

A   Yes, I did.

Q   And they paid you?

A   Yes.

Q   And they paid you for two other sessions, didn't they?

A   Yes, they did.

Q   Now did you bill someone else for those same sessions?

A   No.

Q   Why did you list them as your patients, if they weren't your patients?

A   I have to recall this session. Mr. and Mrs. Thomas did not come to me to be diagnosed, they did not come to me for any help with regards to themselves, did not come to me for any reason that had to do with any part of their own personal problems.

Q   So my question is, why did you list them as your patients?

A   This may have been a mistake, I don't know. There was never an understanding that Mr. and Mrs. Thomas were my patients.

Q   Well, when you have a person that comes in to see you, do they sign a contract and say they're going to be your patient and you're going to be their treating psychologist, and you both sign something? Do you do that in your practice?

A   Yes.

Q   Every time?

A   Pretty much.

Dr. Mitchell insisted he did not assume a duty of care in relation to Mr. and Mrs. Thomas. He specifically contended he did not define himself as their therapist. Quite clearly, however, Dr. Mitchell neglected to clarify for Mr. and Mrs. Thomas exactly what role he assumed in relation to them. Consequently, he violated the following principle of the 1990 code.

Principle 6: Welfare of the Consumer: Psychologists respect the integrity and protect the welfare of the people and groups with whom they work. When conflicts of interest arise between clients and psychologists' employing institutions, psychologists clarify the nature and direction of their loyalties and responsibilities, and keep all parties informed of their commitments. Psychologists fully inform consumers as to the purpose and nature of an evaluative, treatment, educational, or training procedure, and they freely acknowledge that clients, students, or participants in research have freedom of choice with regard to participation.

In particular, Dr. Mitchell neglected to "fully inform" Mr. and Mrs. Thomas "as to the purpose and nature" of his relationship with them. Dr. Mitchell also neglected to obtain Mr. and Mrs. Thomas's informed consent—despite testifying that he routinely executed an informed consent procedure with other patients. His neglect in this regard also amounts to a violation of Principle 6 of the 1990 code. As a result of creating a situation that could only confuse Mr. and Mrs. Thomas regarding the nature of his professional relationship with them, Dr. Mitchell also violated the following Principle of the 1990 code.

6(b). When a psychologist agrees to provide services to a client at the request of a third party, the psychologist assumes the responsibility of clarifying the nature of the relationships to all parties concerned.[3]

Sodium Amytal Interview

In response to deposition questions regarding sodium amytal interviews, Dr. Mitchell indicated:

Well, my feeling about your question is that you're asking me to talk about a procedure that I'm not an expert on, and about the impacts of sodium amytal and what sodium amytal does on patients, and that's not my expertise. So I feel very uncomfortable about trying to be definitive about it all.

If Dr. Mitchell did not know "the impacts of sodium amytal and what sodium amytal does on patients," then he was practicing beyond the limits of his training and experience. His conduct in this regard involves a violation of the previously quoted Principle 2 of the 1990 code. Specifically, Dr. Mitchell failed to "provide services and only use techniques for which [he is] qualified by training and experience." Dr. Mitchell moreover misinformed Mr. and Mrs. Thomas when he characterized sodium amytal interviews as "highly reliable."

Reliability of Sodium Amytal Interviews

A 1993 article appearing in the *Journal of Psychiatry and Law* reported an exhaustive search of the literature, between 1930 and 1992, regarding the effects of sodium amytal.[4] Written by psychiatrist August Piper of Seattle, Washington, this article emphatically concluded that sodium amytal is anything but a "truth serum."

Dr. Piper identified four major problems undermining the reliability of sodium amytal interviews: (1) Sodium amytal heightens suggestibility leaving patients more vulnerable to the contaminating effects of leading questions. (2) People do lie under the effects of sodium amytal. (3) Sodium amytal induces hypnosis, and the ensuing hypnotic state does not facilitate accurate recall of past events. People feel more confident in the accuracy of what they think they remember under hypnosis, but their confidence is unwarranted. (4) Sodium amytal provokes reality distortion to the degree that it can elicit floridly psychotic responses. Assuming that these psychotic responses correspond to past events is horribly mistaken.

Given the evidence cited above, characterizing sodium amytal as "highly reliable" revealed how misinformed Dr. Mitchell was. In expressing his ill-informed opinion to Mr. and Mr. Thomas, Dr. Mitchell failed again to "provide services and only use techniques for which [he is] qualified by training and experience." While misinforming Mr. and Mrs. Thomas about the effects of sodium amytal, Dr. Mitchell also violated another principle of the 1990 ethical code.

> 6(a). Psychologists are continually cognizant of their own needs and of their potentially influential position vis-a-vis persons such as clients, students, and subordinates. They avoid exploiting the trust and dependency of such persons. Psychologists make every effort to avoid dual relationships that could impair their professional judgment or increase the risk of exploitation.[5]

Dr. Mitchell exploited Mr. and Mrs. Thomas's vulnerability by subjecting them to misinformation regarding the reliability of their daughter's amytal interview.

Diagnosing Outside of a Professional Relationship

Before meeting Mr. and Mrs. Thomas for the first time on June 11, 1992, Dr. Mitchell concluded that Mr. Thomas was an exceedingly disturbed pedophile. Coming to such a conclusion prior to meeting Mr. Thomas violated Principle 4(k) of the 1990 code.

4(k). Individual diagnostic and therapeutic services are provided only in the context of a professional psychological relationship.

In other words, Dr. Mitchell arrived at diagnostic conclusions about Mr. Thomas without ever having met him. Dr. Mitchell's conduct in this regard further exploited Mr. and Mrs. Thomas's vulnerability. In response to the June 11 session with Dr. Mitchell, Mrs. Thomas wrote, "We both felt like we were there on trial being told that we both came from incest sick families and we needed to admit and get professional help."

Infantile Amnesia

The effects of infantile amnesia are generally recognized and accepted by appropriately trained and educated psychologists. Most empirical studies of childhood amnesia indicate that people's earliest recollection does not date back before the age of 3 or 4.[6,7] Other reviews of infantile amnesia have concluded: "Past the age of ten, or thereabouts, most of us find it impossible to recall anything that happened before the age of four or five."[8] Dr. Mitchell, however, was more than willing to endorse the supposed veracity of Cathy's memories prior to the age of 4. In doing so, he again misinformed Mr. and Mrs. Thomas and exploited their vulnerability.

Mr. and Mrs. Thomas's Status as Grandparents

Mike Hillman, Cathy's estranged husband, agreed to testify at a pretrial deposition. During this deposition, Mr. Read asked Mike about Mr. and Mrs. Thomas's relationships with his children.

A   He [Dr. Mitchell] was keeping the grandparents [Mr. and Mrs. Thomas] from their grandchildren.

Q   I'm sorry?

A   He [Dr. Mitchell] was keeping the family separated, with Cathy's help.

Q   In what way?

A   Interfering.

Q   How, in what way? Be specific, please.

A   The grandparents [Mr. and Mr. Thomas] couldn't see their grandchildren or their daughter.

Q   Why was that, now? Dr. Mitchell was not allowing it?

A   Cathy and Dr. Mitchell.

Q   Well, tell me how Dr. Mitchell was keeping the grandparents
from seeing the grandchildren.

A   He was advising Cathy not to let them get too close to her.

Q   Do you know why he was advising that?

A   It could hurt her emotionally.

Q   Did he tell you that?

A   Yes.

Quite obviously, then, Dr. Mitchell arbitrarily and capriciously disrupted Mr. and Mrs. Thomas's relationships with their grandchildren, and
as he did so, he further harmed Mr. and Mrs. Thomas.

Conclusions

Over the course of his professional relationship with Mr. and Mrs.
Thomas, Dr. Mitchell violated the appropriate standard of care via the following errors:

- Dr. Mitchell encouraged the inappropriate use of his services as a
  result of how he responded to Mr. and Mrs. Thomas, and as a
  consequence, he harmed them.
- Dr. Mitchell neglected to maintain an adequate level of knowledge of the current scientific and professional information related
  to the services he offered.
- Dr. Mitchell neglected to appropriately inform Mr. and Mrs.
  Thomas regarding the services he offered them, and as a consequence, he failed to protect their welfare and respect their integrity.
- While seeing Mr. and Mrs. Thomas with their daughter, Cathy,
  Dr. Mitchell neglected to clarify the nature of his relationships
  with these different individuals.
- Dr. Mitchell misinformed Mr. and Mrs. Thomas regarding the reliability of sodium amytal interviews. His use of a sodium amytal
  interview—and then reporting its supposed results to Mr. and
  Mrs. Thomas—exceeded the limits of his training and experience.
- Dr. Mitchell exploited Mr. and Mrs. Thomas's vulnerability by
  misinforming them regarding the results of sodium amytal interviews.
- Dr. Mitchell disregarded Mr. and Mrs. Thomas's welfare by
  reaching a diagnostic conclusion regarding Mr. Thomas before he

ever saw him. In doing so, Dr. Mitchell subjected Mr. Thomas to the same kind of stereotyping that leads to vicious racism.

- Dr. Mitchell harmed both Mr. and Mrs. Thomas by disregarding the generally recognized and accepted effects of infantile amnesia.
- Dr. Mitchell harmed both Mr. and Mrs. Thomas by disregarding the generally recognized and accepted limitations of retrospective memory.
- Dr. Mitchell harmed both Mr.and Mrs. Thomas by arbitrarily and capriciously intruding on, and disrupting, their relationships with their grandchildren.

EPILOGUE

After reviewing my written assessment of Dr. Mitchell's many errors, Dr. Mitchell's attorney knew his client was in a hopeless position. Quite simply, there was no defense available for Dr. Mitchell's numerous blunders. Consequently, Dr. Mitchell's attorney proposed an out-of-court settlement to Mr. Read. After consulting with Mr. Read, Mr. and Mrs. Thomas accepted the proposed settlement. The terms of that settlement prohibit revealing the monetary figure involved.

Dr. Mitchell's blatant violations of professional standards raise questions about the oversight responsibilities of professional organizations. Are these organizations even aware of the misconduct committed by their members? Do these organizations recognize the basic scientific evidence to which their members are obligated to respond? How do these organizations react to the horrible damages innocent people suffer as a result of recovered memory therapy? For answers to these questions and others related to them, we turn to Chapter 13.

13

Myopic Guilds and Flawed Evidence

Professional Organizations Defending Their Reputations

Recovered memory therapy has likely received more mass media attention than any other mental health issue. Since March 1992, the False Memory Syndrome (FMS) Foundation has also sought to inform the public regarding the crises of recovered memory therapy.

The FMS Foundation was originally organized by parents who insisted they were victims of false allegations, and psychiatrists at the University of Pennsylvania and Johns Hopkins University. The Foundation has persistently challenged the assumptions of recovered memory therapy. It has also directed extensive media attention to the tragedies of families torn apart by cruel allegations. Its monthly newsletters regularly expose the reckless irresponsibility of countless therapists. Not surprisingly, then, the Foundation's work has provoked frequent backlashes. Deeply committed to pursuing a favorable public image for themselves, practicing therapists often vilify it. They prefer the public remain unaware of the crises created by recovered memory therapy.

The professional organizations to which therapists belong have also reacted less than responsibly to this crisis. They ignore the frequency with which their members indulge in ill-informed therapy procedures. These organizations include—but are not limited to, the American Psychological Association, the American Psychiatric Association, the National Association of Social Workers, the American Counseling Association, and the American Association for Marriage and Family Therapy.

A 1995 study, reported by psychologist Debra Poole and her colleagues, demonstrated that substantial numbers of therapists indulge in potentially damaging treatment practices.[1] Despite the proneness of human memory to suggestion, these therapists assumed they could assist clients in recovering presumably repressed memories. Of the 195 doctoral-level psychologists participating in this study, 71% reported using at least one memory recovery technique. The techniques utilized included hypnosis, age regression, dream interpretation, guided imagery, use of family photographs, and clients writing journals. Of this same sample, 58% of the therapists disclosed using two or more of these techniques.

Interestingly enough, this group of therapists disagreed about which memory recovery techniques were appropriate and which were not. For example, more than one-fourth reported using hypnosis to recall presumably repressed memories of childhood sexual abuse. Another one-fourth of the sample, however, indicated that hypnosis should not be used for such a purpose. The disagreements between the theapists, regarding which techniques were appropriate, underscore how ill-advised it is to use any of them.

In the first stage of this survey, 80 therapists were asked: "Of the adult female clients whom you suspected were sexually abused as children, what percentage initially denied any memory of childhood sexual abuse?"[2] Seventy-five percent of the therapists indicated that some of the clients they suspected as having been abused as children denied any such abuse. Typically, however, the therapists continued to entertain their suspicions despite their clients' denials.

The results of this 1995 study are shocking to say the least. The majority of therapists resort to inherently unreliable procedures for recovering supposedly repressed memories. Even more alarming is the fact that these therapists are not limited to a fringe group of marginally trained practitioners. The therapists participating in this study were all educated as doctoral-level psychologists. If doctoral-level therapists regularly indulge in such ill-informed practices, what do the greater majority with master's degrees do? Generalizing from this 1995 study to all therapists leads to an unbelievable but frighteningly accurate conclusion. Dr. Robyn Dawes, of Carnegie-Mellon University, estimated that in any given year, as many as 750,000 clients are at risk for developing false memories in psychotherapy.[3]

ORGANIZATIONAL IRRESPONSIBILITY

Considering how recovered memory therapy can severely damage clients, attempts at recovering supposedly repressed memories amount to a public health hazard, as 750,000 people annually suffer the enormous risks associated with these ill-advised practices. This crisis demands decisive action from the various professional organizations to which therapists belong. The American Psychiatric Association, for example, vehemently criticized "past life regression therapy." In 1995, Dr. Mel Sabshin, medical director of the American Psychiatric Association, emphasized:

> The American Psychiatric Association believes that past life regression therapy is pure quackery. As in other areas of medicine, psychiatric diagnosis and treatment today is based on objective scientific evidence. There is no accepted scientific evidence to support the existence of past lives let alone the validity of past life regression therapy.[4]

Sadly enough, however, not one professional organization has denounced recovered memory therapy. Though there is also no legitimate scientific evidence supporting repression—or even suggesting that repressed memories can be accurately recovered—it is business as usual for recovered memory therapists.

Disregarding Research

The continuing practice of recovered memory therapy thrives in response to therapists disregarding research. Therapists regularly exhibit obsolete thinking because they rarely read legitimate journals. As a result, they neglect to inform themselves of new developments related to their work.[5] For example, less than 10% of 1100 therapists, employed in community mental health centers and state hospitals, relied on any professional publications in their treatment work.[6] Another study reported that none of the therapists in its sample could cite any research influencing how they practice.[7] This same study found that therapists prefer to discuss treatment issues with their colleagues rather than review the relevant literature.

Still another study examined 416 intake evaluations completed by various mental health professionals. Only 1 of these 416 evaluations developed a treatment rationale demonstrating any awareness of relevant research.[8] Related data indicated that therapists disregard relevant research and systematic decision making when: (1) choosing assessment procedures, (2) defining treatment goals, and (3) selecting treatment methods.[9] Rather than consider the legitimate research related to their work, therapists resort to ill-informed "pop-psych" and "self-help" books. A survey of 500 therapists, for instance, reported the book they most frequently recommend to clients is *Courage to Heal*.[10] The popularity of *Courage* within the ranks of therapists dramatically underscores their disdain for legitimate research.

Like the vast majority of their therapist members, the professional organizations representing them also ignore scientific evidence. In February 1993, the Council of Representatives of the American Psychological Association (APA) recognized the controversies regarding recovered memory therapy. It appointed a task force to study the many issues related to memories supposedly repressed but apparently recovered in psychotherapy. At that time, however, the APA Council voted 55 to 52 *against* obtaining input from its own Board of Scientific Affairs regarding who would serve on this task force.[11] Rather than carefully examine the scientific evidence related to recovered memory therapy, the majority of the Council considered clinical experience more compelling.

Clinical Experience

Clinical experience refers to the subjective impressions and opinions therapists develop over years of treatment work. In response to their therapy endeavors, they formulate intuitive theories about their clients and the problems they present. Unfortunately, however, clinical experience typically involves biased notions and skewed expectations reflecting the preconceived thinking of the therapist. These kinds of biases were first reported in 1929.[12]

The 1929 study examined the opinions of 12 interviewers who interviewed 2000 homeless men, attempting to ascertain the reasons for their homelessness. Co-workers described one of the interviewers as an ardent socialist. By an almost three-to-one margin, the socialist interviewer concluded the homelessness of the men he interviewed reflected economic conditions beyond their control (e.g., layoffs, plant closings). Another interviewer was described as a strong prohibitionist. Again by an almost three-to-one margin, the prohibitionist interviewer attributed homelessness to alcohol abuse. While relying on their clinical experience, these interviewers demonstrated a remarkable facility for finding evidence consistent with their pet hypotheses.

Subsequent research, published in 1979, also demonstrated the many shortcomings of clinical experience.[13] Therapists characteristically bring strong expectations to their work about the origins of client problems. They assume, for example, that some types of problems indicate repressed memories of childhood abuse. When interviewing clients, they selectively attend to information consistent with their preexisting thinking. While focusing on impressions that seem consistent with their preferred theories, therapists also overlook inconsistent evidence. Consequently, clinical experience leads therapists into finding what they expect to find.

Examining how psychologists interpret projective drawings further illustrates the many problems related to clinical experience. For years and years, legions of psychologists made inferences about clients based on their drawings of people. They frequently assumed that drawings with elaborate eye detail corresponded to suspicious, paranoidlike individuals.[14] In fact, however, these assumptions about eye detail and personality characteristics are horribly mistaken.[15]

Nonetheless, numerous psychologists still assume a significant relationship between eye detail and personality traits. They persist in their erroneous thinking because they vividly remember the few times their assumptions seemed correct. Simultaneously, they forget the many instances when their assumptions were clearly wrong. Therefore, clinical experience is inherently flawed because it rests on subjective impressions filtered through biased expectations.

Clinical Experience versus Scientific Data

Quite obviously, then, clinical experience can never substitute for—let alone compete with—scientific data. The vast majority of therapists, however, continue to confidently express opinions premised on clinical experience. While doing so, they disregard how their level of confidence is entirely unrelated to the accuracy of their judgments.[16] Therefore, therapists who preface their opinions by declaring, "In my many years of clinical experience . . ." deserve all of the skepticism these self-serving statements invite.

Despite the evidence outlined above, recovered memory therapists remain strong advocates of clinical experience. Lenore Terr, for example, insists clinical experience is more important than scientific evidence when evaluating claims of repression. In the 1993 criminal trial of *California* v. *Akiki*, the following dialogue transpired as Terr was cross-examined.

Q   . . . is there some question about the scientific validity of the theory of repression, Yes or No?

A   Yes. But I think that they are wrong. They are not clinicians, and they are not entitled to make that decision.

Q   Is it your position that only clinicians can make a decision concerning the scientific foundation of psychiatric or psychological principles?

A   Not all principles, but repression is a clinical principle, and I thought we were talking about repression.

Q   Is it your position that repression can only be addressed by clinicians and not by researchers?

A   The kind of researchers that are bringing this to question, sociology researchers, researchers who are doing cognitive psychology experiments, are not the ones who can make a value judgment on repression. It is the clinicians who can.[17]

The kind of thinking advocated by Terr is tantamount to practicing physicians concluding: "Biology and chemistry—we don't need those basic sciences to support our clinical work, we'll just wing it on our own." Unfortunately, this is also the kind of thinking embraced by the APA's Council of Representatives.

APA Task Force on Repressed Memories

When the APA eventually appointed its task force to study claims of repressed memories, it included three research scientists (Drs. Stephen Ceci, Elizabeth Loftus, and Peter Ornstein). The APA finally realized that excluding research psychologists from this work group would diminish the credibility of its findings. Three practicing therapists were also appointed to the work group (Drs. Judith Alpert, Laura Brown, and Christine Courtois). The therapists enthusiastically touted the value of clinical experience. They cited as "valuable," for example, "the large body of clinical case reports" claiming instances of repressed memories.[18]

Misinterpreting Data

The willingness of the therapists to rely on their clinical experience consistently undermined the efforts of the work group. The many discrepancies between objective data and their clinical experience led the therapists into misinterpreting relevant research. The therapists, for example, claimed that "Poole et al. (1995) do demonstrate that the minority (less than one quarter of those responding) of the therapists they surveyed described using techniques such as hypnosis."[19] This statement underscores how the therapists neglected to interpret data accurately. As detailed earlier in this chapter, the Poole study clearly reported that (1) 71% of the therapists in its sample used at least one suggestive technique for recovering memories and (2) 58% of the sample used two or more suggestive techniques.

The Poole study conservatively estimated that 25% of the therapists could be characterized as specifically focused on recovering memories of childhood sexual abuse. In particular, this subset of therapists assume that (1) memory recovery is critical to treatment outcome and (2) they can identify clients with repressed memories during the first therapy session. Quite obviously, then, the therapist members of the study group misinterpreted these data. The vast majority of therapists do use at least one memory recovery technique in their practices. The 25% figure refers to therapists who focus specifically on chilhood sexual abuse. It does not refer to the number of therapists who use suggestive techniques for recovering memories.

These same therapists expressed even more ill-informed comments about the 1995 Poole study. They argued: "The survey nature of the Poole study leaves us with no certainty regarding how therapists are applying these techniques because no such distinctions can be derived from the manner in which these data were collected."[20] A careful review of the Poole study, however, clearly demonstrates how mistaken this claim is.

In the first stage of this survey, the critical question asked of the therapists stated: "Some therapists use special techniques to help clients remember childhood sexual abuse. Check any technique you have used with abuse victims in the past two years."[21] In the second stage of the survey, this question was changed to clarify it. Poole and her colleagues made it quite clear that a technique should be reported only if it was used to retrieve memories of presumed sexual abuse. The second version of this question indicated: "Check any technique you have used in the past two years to help clients remember childhood sexual abuse."[22]

Changes in the wording of the above question did not affect the responses obtained from the therapists. For both versions of this question, the therapists reported using the same frequency of techniques to assist their clients' recall of supposedly repressed memories. Despite the APA work group therapists contending there is "no certainty how therapists are applying these techniques," they are again wrong. Quite clearly, therapists are using these techniques "to help clients remember childhood sexual abuse."

Minimizing and Rationalizing

The therapists of the APA work group persistently attempted to minimize and rationalize the many problems created by recovered memory
therapy. They insisted:

> The memory scenario that evokes the greatest debate and skepticism
> had to do with the apparent total loss of memory for an extended pe-
> riod of time and the delayed and detailed recollection years later.
> From the available research, which we review in this report, this ap-
> pears to be the least common memory scenario. Instead, it appears
> that the *majority* of traumatized individuals (including those sexually
> or otherwise abused as children) retain conscious memory (whether
> total, partial, or with fluctuating accessibility) whether or not they
> fully understand or disclose it. By implication, then, it appears to be
> the *minority* of traumatized people who have *total* memory loss and
> delayed recall.[23] [italics in original]

The therapists of the working group insist they consider total memory loss subsequent to trauma a rare event. One of their own members,
however, previously emphasized quite the contrary. In her 1988 book
Healing the Incest Wound: Adult Survivors in Therapy, Courtois claimed:
"Massive repression seems to be the main defensive operation available to
very young children and/or the violently abused."[24] "Massive repression"
means total memory loss, and "main defensive operation" indicates that
Courtois thinks of it as the most frequent outcome related to violent
abuse. Quite likely, then, Courtois finds evidence of massive repression
more frequently than she cares to acknowledge.

The working group therapists also chastised the research members
for asserting that therapists "hunt for buried memories." The therapists
insisted:

> We fail to understand where our colleagues [Ceci, Loftus, and Orn-
> stein] arrive at this assertion about the practices of "substantial num-
> bers" of therapists. We are fully aware, as noted in our main
> document, that there exist a number of poorly-informed therapists,
> untrained lay counselors, and self-help books whose authors endorse
> such an archeological strategy, which we have ourselves criticized.[25]

Again, however, the position quoted immediately above is exceedingly inconsistent with Courtois's 1988 book. In particular, Courtois
proudly described using the following procedure:

> Should the woman deny knowledge of abuse despite indications to
> the contrary, the therapist can gently probe, suggesting that the symp-

toms she has described are sometimes related to a history of abuse. The therapist might also describe what constitutes incest. At times, therapist and client will conclude that incest occurred even without conscious validation or memory on the part of the client.[26]

In view of her 1996 position regarding "poorly-informed therapists," Courtois is obligated to reject the procedure cited above as poorly informed. Nonetheless, it is likely naive to anticipate her doing so in the near future.

As previously discussed, the therapists of the working group argued that the researchers overestimated the frequency with which practitioners use suggestive techniques to recall memories. Once again, though, Courtois's 1988 book betrays her 1996 position. In 1988, she confidently concluded, "Hypnosis can assist in the recapturing of lost memories."[27] She further claimed, "Hypnosis can be used to assist clients in bringing material to consciousness."[28] Quite obviously, then, Courtois frequently uses hypnosis with her own clients, hotly pursuing the recall of presumably repressed memories.

Rank Hypocrisy

Courtois, and her fellow therapists with the working group, also scolded the researchers for suggesting that too many therapists are preoccupied with abuse issues. They specifically deplored how:

> the statement is made that the task of some therapeutic orientations is the "hunt for the missing memory." We suggest that this position is due to the misapplication and overgeneralization of material from the lay literature for abuse survivors to all psychotherapists, whatever their level of training and technique. We know of no professional program in Psychology that specifically trains graduate students in such a therapeutic strategy nor any mainstream approach to treatment to have this approach as a focus.[29]

As you likely suspect by now, Courtois's 1988 book provides another interesting contrast with the position quoted above. In 1988 she claimed: "Participation in an incest therapy group usually stimulates the memory recovery as members 'chain' from each other's experience."[30] Courtois and her colleagues suggest only poorly trained therapists, far removed from the mainstream of responsible practice, hunt for missing memories. Nevertheless, her 1988 book clearly reveals how she engages in those very practices herself. Interestingly enough, Courtois and her colleagues also cite her book as a "mainstream" resource.[31]

The therapists of the working group resorted to fallacious arguments, attempting to discredit data cited by the research members. On four separate occasions, the therapists challenged research published by members of the Scientific and Professional Advisory Board of the FMS Foundation.[32] They specifically identified the researchers' affiliation with the FMS Board, implying their findings were therefore suspect. Such arguments merely amount to a variation of *ad hominem* attacks, and they are intellectually dishonest as a result. Even if Adolph Hitler, for example, said that severely elevated anxiety interferes with learning, it would not alter the accuracy of this conclusion. The therapists, however, seemed to think *who* reports data is more important than *what* is reported.

To say the least, the contributions of the therapist members to the APA working group were abysmal. All deeply entrenched in their ill-informed thinking about trauma and memory loss, and eagerly embracing blame-and-change maneuvers, they repeatedly succumbed to their persistent biases.

In particular, they misinterpreted data that beginning students in psychology would find obvious. They suggested that recovered memory therapists rarely find evidence of massive repression, but Courtois's book demonstrates the contrary. They denied preoccupying themselves with hunting for memories, or using excessively suggestive procedures for recalling memories. Courtois's 1988 book also identifies these claims as rank hypocrisy. They additionally resorted to severely flawed reasoning when attacking the data cited by the working group's research members. More than anything else, this brief overview exposes how readily therapists deceive themselves. There is frequently a world of difference between what therapists actually do in therapy and what they say they do.

GUILD-DRIVEN AGENDA

Another sobering development involving the APA occurred in 1993. At that time, its Division of Family Psychology proposed the following amendment to the Ethical Principles of Psychologists and Code of Conduct: Psychologists discuss with clients or patients as early as is possible in the therapeutic relationship appropriate issues, such as . . . *the possible impact of therapy on close interpersonal relationships*"[33] (the italicized portion corresponds to the proposed amendment). Some members of the Division of Family Psychology responded positively to this proposed change in the ethical code. Others were, at best, lukewarm, but still others expressed grave concerns suggesting:

the proposed wording could leave the therapist open to all kinds of lawsuits by persons who might be negatively impacted by a change in relationship of a client who was working on relationship issues in therapy. The example of the False Memory Syndrome [FMS] Foundation was given.[34]

This proposed amendment to the ethical code was rejected. Apparently, then, political considerations provoked by the FMS Foundation can dictate the policies of the APA. In other words, APA seems compelled to revise its collective thinking if it finds itself aligned with the FMS Foundation. Doing otherwise would presumably amount to political incorrectness.

Marketing and Public Relations Priorities

In April 1995, another interesting development related to the APA transpired. Its monthly newspaper, the *APA Monitor,* announced a $1.5 millon public relations campaign to enhance the public image of psychologists.[35] More likely than not, this PR effort will avoid addressing the following issues: (1) Therapists prefer to rely on clinical experience while disregarding relevant research. (2) Clinical experience is typically limited to biased expectations and poorly formulated theories. (3) While rejecting relevant research and relying on clinical experience, the majority of therapists indulge in potentially damaging practices. These sobering problems correspond to a fundamentally more important question, namely, how did professional psychology deteriorate into a mindless guild responding more to its own agenda than the public's welfare?

Beginning in the late 1970s, the number of practicing therapists belonging to the APA grew at an exponential rate. These practitioners demanded that APA respond to issues such as insurance reimbursement, hospital privileges, and promoting psychological services. In other words, business considerations displaced the attention previously paid to the scientific considerations of practice. Dr. Scott Henggeler, of the Medical College of South Carolina, commented rather bluntly on this shift: "sometimes I feel that the name of the game in clinical psychology isn't really positive client outcome, it's acquiring and keeping clients."[36]

As you likely expect, research-oriented psychologists dismiss the business considerations of practitioners as irrelevant to their interests. Not surprisingly, then, Brendan Maher, former chairperson of the Psychology Department at Harvard, indicated: "it seems clear that the scientific interests of the clinical psychologist are likely to be focused in organizations outside the APA."[37] As more and more research psychologists abandon APA, its scientific credibility correspondingly suffers.

Without the influence of research psychologists, professional psychology may find itself dominated by marketing gurus frantically pursuing market share. Scientific progress can only suffer as a result of such developments, and in turn, the quality of professional education and training will deteriorate. Donald Peterson, of Rutgers University, insists this bleak state of affairs is already upon us. He observed:

> Resources for continuing education and postdoctoral training as they stand in psychology today are not a "system" at all. They are a chaotic disgrace, consisting for the most part of a potpourri of ill-conceived, empirically untested workshops.[38]

Fighting for Professional Survival

While crumbling from within, professional psychology also faces increasing challenges from other therapist groups. The number of therapists trained at a master's degree level—and belonging to organizations such as the National Association of Social Workers, American Counseling Association, and the American Association for Marriage and Family Therapy—now outnumber practicing doctoral-level psychologists. The relevant research clearly demonstrates that as therapists, doctoral-level psychologists are no more effective than their master's-level counterparts.[39] Health insurance companies, therefore, prefer to direct their subscribers to the less expensive services of master's-level therapists. As a result, doctoral-level psychologists struggle persistently attempting to maintain their private practices.

Doctoral-level psychologists desperately want to separate themselves from the ranks of their master's-level competitors. Consequently, the APA has undertaken a massive effort pursuing prescription privileges for practicing psychologists.[40] If APA's campaign succeeds, doctoral-level psychologists will be able to prescribe the medications now available only from D.O. or M.D. physicians such as psychiatrists. Considerable controversy surrounds this pursuit of prescription privileges for psychologists.

Dr. Wallace Tomlinson, a psychiatrist and associate dean at Tulane University's School of Medicine, emphatically denounced extending prescription authority to psychologists. While testifying before the Louisiana legislature, Tomlinson insisted that psychologists are insufficiently trained to prescribe medications "for the brain, heart, and all the organs of the body." He strongly advised that prescription privileges for psychologists be "unceremoniously buried." He further characterized this proposal as "a disgraceful attempt at experimenting on human subjects."[41]

Confronted with sharply critical statements such as Tomlinson's, there is little likelihood of APA acknowledging its problems related to recovered memory therapy. Candidly admitting this crisis would further undercut the image of a profession fighting for its survival. Instead, APA and all of the other professional organizations to which therapists belong respond to considerations of marketing and public relations while neglecting intellectual honesty. At a time when massive changes in our health care system occur so rapidly, marketing and public relations endeavors are compelling priorities for these organizations.

In other words, then, it seems evident that the APA and the other therapist membership organizations have responded to the crises engendered by recovered memory therapy demonstrating that: (1) clinical intuition takes precedence over scientific evidence, (2) political correctness prevails over ethical responsibility, and (3) marketing concerns triumph over the dissemination of accurate information. Basically, these are the agenda of a guild, and in particular, the APA's guild-driven agenda is not about to deal responsibly with the crises of recovered memory therapy.

DISSEMINATING MISINFORMATION

Rather than honestly examine the many scientific issues related to recovered memory therapy, the APA as well as the other professional organizations regularly retreat behind a smokescreen of misinformation. To illustrate how misinformation can distort facts and mislead, consider the laboratory work of Professor John Watson, done at Johns Hopkins University in 1920.

"Little Albert"

In what is now one of the most widely known studies in the history of psychology, Watson demonstrated the acquisition of a conditioned fear response using 9-month-old "Little Albert."[42] Little Albert was brought into Watson's laboratory, and every time he approached a white lab rat, Watson's assistant created a frighteningly loud noise behind Albert's head by banging a metal bar with a hammer. Albert subsequently exhibited a strong fear of the rat even when there was no banging on the bar behind him. Albert also exhibited a milder, but still pronounced, fear of various objects similar to the rat such as a rabbit, a white glove, cotton balls, and a white beard.

Interestingly enough, however, there are many other outcomes attributed to Watson's experiment with "Little Albert" that never occurred.[43] For example, a well-respected psychologist reported, "Albert developed a phobia for white rats and indeed for all furry animals."[44] In fact, however, this particular account is wrong—it never happened. Other textbooks reported Albert's fear generalizing to a cat,[45] his mother's fur coat, and even a teddy bear.[46] Wrong again, as a careful reading of Watson's original 1920 article establishes that these events never occurred. Other texts have reported that Albert's fears were subsequently eliminated via a "reconditioning" procedure. Again wrong, these accounts are science fiction. Watson never undertook any procedure attempting to alleviate Albert's acquired fear.

The misinformation related to Watson's experiment demonstrates the many shortcomings of anecdotal evidence. Anecdotal evidence involves second- and thirdhand accounts of an experiment or case study. Obviously, however, these second- and thirdhand recountings can be quite mistaken. Anecdotal evidence, like clinical experience, can also be misinterpreted in a manner consistent with a particular theoretical orientation. Many of the textbook authors who misreported Watson's experiment, for example, did so in a manner consistent with their theoretical preferences. Anecdotal evidence, therefore, always warrants persistent skepticism.

Recovered Memory Therapy and Anecdotal Evidence

Unfortunately, various professional organizations resort to anecdotal evidence when evaluating claims of repressed memories. Consider, for example, the "Statement on Memories of Sexual Abuse" issued in December 1993 by the Board of Trustees of the American Psychiatric Association.[47] Included in the various issues it addresses, this statement indicates:

> Children and adolescents who have been abused cope with the trauma by using a variety of psychological mechanisms. In some instances, these coping mechanisms result in a lack of conscious awareness of the abuse for varying periods of time. Conscious thoughts and feelings stemming from the abuse may emerge at a later date.

In view of how anecdotal evidence can misinform and mislead, we should ask: How did this anecdote originate, where was it first published, and what documentation, if any, is available to support it? Because this anecdote is not documented, and because we know nothing of its origins, it amounts to little more than secondhand information, and consequently, it should be considered potentially misleading. Obviously, this anecdote involves a secondary source. Possibly, it has been disseminated because it is consistent with a particular theoretical view, and as a result, it demands a good deal of skepticism.

This same statement of the American Psychiatric Association additionally discussed "implicit memory," referring to "behavioral knowledge of an experience without conscious recall." As an example of implicit memory, this statement cited an instance of "a combat veteran who panics when he hears the sound of a helicopter, but cannot remember that he was in a helicopter crash which killed his best friend."

Because this anecdote also is not documented, and because we know nothing of its origins, it also amounts to secondhand information. As in the case of the previous anecdote, this anecdote also involves a secondary source. Possibly, it has been disseminated because it is consistent with a particular theoretical view. And as a result, it also warrants a great deal of skepticism.

Finally, the previously cited statement of the American Psychiatric Association indicated: "Many individuals who recover memories of abuse have been able to find corroborating information about their memories." This statement raises many more questions than it answers, such as: (1) exactly who has recovered these memories and found corroboration (2) and what qualifies as corroboration (the agreement of other people sympathetic to the apparent plight of someone who supposedly recovered memories of childhood sexual abuse?).

Anecdotal Case Reports

Recovered memory therapists frequently cite anecdotal accounts of adults recovering presumably repressed memories of childhood abuse. A November 1993 article appearing in *U.S. News & World Report,* for example, detailed how a 38-year-old college professor supposedly recalled memories of the sexual abuse he suffered between ages 10 and 13. The article recounted how Ross Cheit:

> told his wife he thought their marriage was failing. He entered therapy. Then on August 23 [1992] while on vacation, he had something like a dream.
> He woke with the baffling sense that a man he had not seen or thought of in 25 years was powerfully present in the room. William

Farmer had been the administrator of the San Francisco Boys Chorus summer camp, which Cheit attended in the late '60s between the ages of 10 and 13. Cheit could picture him clearly—the big stomach and bent shoulders, the round head, wispy hair. Over the course of the day, he recalled still more. How Farmer would enter his cabin night after night, just as the boys were going to sleep. How he would sit on Cheit's bed, stroking the boy's chest and stomach while he urged him in a whisper to relax, relax. "I was frozen," says Cheit. "My stomach clenched against his touch. And then he would slowly bring his hand into my pants."[48]

Ross Cheit reportedly recalled these repressed memories in August 1992. We can assume he was interviewed for this article approximately a year or more later. Consider, therefore, the many events that transpired—between "recovering" his memories and being interviewed—influencing how Cheit interpreted what he remembered. At the time of his interview, Cheit's version of what he recalled approximately a year earlier relied on his retrospective memory. As discussed in Chapter 9, however, retrospective memory is notoriously unreliable. Cheit also apparently remained in therapy, leading to questions of how his therapist interpreted his recall experience. Did his therapist tell him he had recovered previously repressed memories? In other words, to what degree was therapist influence a factor in Cheit's thinking about his memories?

Unfortunately, Miriam Horn, the article's author, neglected to consider the influences of Cheit's therapist and the time elapsing between his reported recall and her interview. In fact, Horn disclosed a long-term acquaintance with Cheit predating her interviewing him. An obscure sidebar to her story—appearing in exceedingly small print—said:

The narrative in this story is based on Ross Cheit's account of his recovered memory experience, as described in interviews and legal documents. Cheit and Miriam Horn, the author, have been acquainted since junior high school.[49]

Responsible journalists avoid compromising their objectivity in this manner. Horn apparently considered herself exempt from this obligation.

Horn then continued her secondhand account:

For Cheit, there was no spectacular epiphany. The memory of Farmer was embarrassing and disgusting, but hardly momentous. It was not until October [1992], when at his therapist's suggestion Cheit went to the bookstore to buy Mic Hunter's Abused Boys, that he felt the full impact of what he had remembered. "As soon as I pulled the book off the shelf, I began to shake all over. I thought I was going to collapse. I looked at the title and thought, My God, that's me."[50]

Ambiguity of Anecdotal Case Reports

Unfortunately, this anecdotal narrative is ambiguous to say the least. If Cheit recalled his memories without a "spectacular epiphany"—"a sudden manifestation of the essence or meaning of something"[51] perhaps his memories were never repressed. Did reading *Abused Boys* simply result in him reinterpreting his past abuses as more significant than he previously thought? Had he always remembered this abuse but rarely dwelled on it? Or did reading this book lead him into concluding he had recalled previously repressed memories? Critically important as these questions are, Horn neglected to address them.

After Horn's article appeared in *U.S. News,* Mark Pendergrast—author of *Victims of Memory*—interviewed Cheit. Pendergrast reported how:

> Despite recalling his sexual abuse years after it occurred, Ross Cheit does not know whether to call his memory "repressed" or not, nor does he necessarily believe the kind of massive repression reported by other survivors in which years of abuse were supposedly siphoned off from consciousness.[52]

Quite possibly, then, Cheit always retained some memory of Farmer abusing him. What could have changed is how he interpreted this abuse, and the significance he attached to it.

Despite the many unanswered questions surrounding the Cheit case, recovered memory therapists enthusiastically cite it. They unequivocally describe it as an example of an abuse victim recalling previously repressed memories. In particular, for example, the therapists of the APA work group specifically referred to this case attempting to bolster their position.[53]

Cheit's case, however, ultimately amounts to anecdotal evidence. Those who use his experience to promote their own agenda typically neglect to mention: (1) Horn's compromised objectivity in detailing his recall, (2) the ambiguity surrounding what he reportedly remembered, and (3) Cheit's own doubts regarding repression. While overlooking these important issues, recovered memory therapists sharpen the details of the Cheit case consistent with theories of repression. Simultaneously, they level those details inconsistent with their theoretical allegiances.

Recovering Memories via Osmosis

Sylvia Fraser, a Canadian author and self-described incest survivor, is also frequently cited as an example of an abuse victim recovering previously repressed memories. In a March 1994 article in *Saturday Night Magazine,* Fraser insisted she recalled the memories of her father sexually abusing her independent of any therapist's influence. She specifically claimed:

> no therapist can be accused of misleading me, since none was involved in the initial recovery [of her memories]. I read no books on incest . . . and had no conscious interest in this subject.[54]

Despite the certainty with which she expressed herself, Fraser's 1988 book *My Father's House* entirely undermines her 1994 claims. In her book, she described how:

> I felt drawn to read about, and to experiment with, various psychological disciplines. Through Freudian and Jungian analysis, I learned how to interpret dreams as messages from my unconscious. Through primal and massage therapy, rolfing, bioenergetics, yoga, meditation, I grew more in touch with my body and emotions. . . . Unbeknownst to me, I was approaching a time when I would remember. The obsession of a lifetime was drawing to a close. My path of revelation was to be the path of dreams.[55]

Fraser's 1988 book further disclosed her consulting with a hypnotherapist. She reportedly told the hypnotherapist, "So far, most of my regurgitated memories are physical and emotional rather than verbal or visual. . . . I ask myself: did this really happen?" Quite clearly, then, Fraser felt less than confident about the veracity of her memories until undergoing hypnosis. In response to hypnosis, she thought she regressed to a time when:

> "I am a child in my father's house. My father sits on the bed in his underwear. . . ." On subsequent visits [to the hypnotherapist], I produce other childhood memories in which I express a growing sense of panic.[56]

Sylvia Fraser's example makes one wonder how often repressed memory therapists cite her 1994 article, and overlook its gross inconsistencies with her 1988 book. Fraser's self-description of herself recovering memories independent of any therapist's influence amounts to self-serving nonsense. Experimenting with Freudian and Jungian analysis inevitably exposes one to Freud's original seduction theory. Dream interpretation furthermore draws attention to Freudian assumptions regarding infantile sexuality. Fraser's claims are tantamount to an American diligently attending German class, but claiming she only learned that language via osmosis because of never actually visiting Germany.

The cases of Ross Cheit and Sylvia Fraser dramatically demonstrate how anecdotal evidence can mislead and misinform. Often conveyed by word of mouth from one person to the next, anecdotal evidence shifts and changes over time. Each time it passes from one person to the next, it conforms itself to the expectations and prejudices of those who report it. Therefore, relying on anecdotal evidence is both naive and gullible.

Tales of a Tail-Gunner

Despite the disreputable legacy of anecdotal evidence, the APA allows it to contaminate its journals. In August 1997, an article titled "Repressed Memories and World War II: Lest We Forget!" appeared in *Professional Psychology: Research and Practice,* published by APA.[57] This article reported a secondhand account of a Freudian therapist's treatment of a WW II veteran shortly after the war ended. Neither author of this article— Dr. Bertram Karon and Ms. Annemarie Widener—actually treated this veteran; the therapist was the senior author's brother working at the Veterans Administration (VA).

This article reported how the veteran suffered a hysterical paralysis of his right arm—a psychologically determined disability without any physical basis. After approximately 6 weeks of therapy at two sessions per week, the client reportedly said to his therapist, "You know, I once got a medal." When he appeared for his next session, the client showed the therapist a clipping of a newspaper article. The newspaper article detailed the story of a WW II plane crash.

The 1997 journal article continued, reporting how the client had served as tail-gunner in a two-man bomber. While returning from a mission and attempting to land, the client's plane crashed. Though the bomber's ruptured fuel tanks could have exploded at any moment, the client bravely disregarded this threat to his life. He instead struggled heroically in extricating the unconscious pilot from the plane. The journal article further described the client recovering his supposedly repressed memory of this harrowing event.

> During this psychotherapy session, he had remembered the details of his experience, including his heroic efforts and conscious terror. At the end of the session, his clothes were wringing wet with perspiration. But for the first time since that event, he had partial movement of his arm.[58]

Attempting to explain the client's presumed repression, Karon and Widener unreined their clinical experience to theorize speculatively:

> The hysterical paralysis psychodynamically represented a defense against ever experiencing the horror of that plane crash again. Like all of us would be, he was terrified and wanted to run from the plane to save himself. But his conscience could not let him abandon his friend, no matter how terrified he was or how dangerous the situation.[59]

In their determination to conform their interpretation of this case to their theory-driven thinking, Karon and Widener overlooked alternative explanations. For example, what is the likelihood of closed-head injury—more commonly called a concussion—accounting for the memory loss this client may have suffered? During WW II, Army Air Force personnel wore thin leather helmets affording them minimal protection from such injuries. Despite possibly suffering a concussion that might have neurologically incapacitated his memory, the client could have still undertaken his heroic efforts. Even though someone is "out on their feet," concussions do not necessarily preclude purposeful behavior.

It is also necessary to consider the newspaper clipping the client shared with the therapist. What that article reported could have substantially influenced the memories the client thought he recalled. The client's recall may also have been infuenced by his Freudian therapist's expectations more than anything else. In response to his therapist's influence, the client could have simply recalled a dramatic narrative consistent with the newspaper article.

Additionally, it is quite possible that the client's hysterical paralysis was unrelated to his combat experience. Karon and Widener indicated:

> This patient found it impossible to work at his occupation with a paralyzed arm. Being unable to work involuntarily was a way of expressing his hostility to his wife. . . . One year of psychoanalytic psychotherapy sufficed not only to remove his symptom, but also to enable him to function effectively at work and at home.

If this client struggled with feelings of hostility about his wife, then his inability to work may have been unrelated to his combat ordeal. The client's eventually regaining use of his arm and returning to work could have simply corresponded to the reduction of conflicts in his marriage. If this was the case, his therapy was entirely unrelated to such an outcome. VA therapists of this era never included spouses in the treatment of disabled veterans. Not one of these alternative explanations, however, received any consideration from Karon and Widener.

The blatant bias of this article also undermines the reputation of what was previously a well-respected journal. Do the editors of *Professional Psychology* really consider this anecdotal account, reported on a third hand basis and approximately 50 years removed from its occurrence, as reliable evidence? It appears the APA has now stooped to using a reputedly independent journal for disseminating its guild-driven propaganda. If this is the case, it amounts to a serious loss for those psychologists who still respect objectivity and intellectual honesty.

Contrary Anecdotal Evidence

My father, Dr. J. Frank Campbell, is a retired psychologist. Before completing his distinguished career at Wayne State University in 1982 as professor emeritus, Dad worked with the VA as a psychologist. Though he turned 86 in March 1998, Dad remains quite sound in both mind and body. As a result, he was an excellent resource to interview regarding the claims of Karon and Widener's article. This is especially so in view of another argument expressed by Karon and Widener. They contend the repressed memories of WW II veterans are overlooked because "there are very few living clinical psychologists who were working as therapists in the VA in the 1940s."[60]

Dad began working with the VA in early 1945 as chairman of the Department of Counseling and Advisement. Located at the Allen Park (MI) VA hospital, he supervised the work of 12 other counselors. He also carried his own caseload of approximately 30 clients per week. The disabled veterans with whom Dad and his staff worked had suffered very serious injuries. There were numerous paraplegics and amputees, for example, seeking assistance to repair and restore their lives.

Dad explained how these veterans "consistently recalled their combat experiences in vivid detail." Remembering their traumatic experiences frequently left them "unable to sleep, work, or travel any distance from their homes." Quite often, these veterans felt overwhelmed with guilt related to their combat experiences. Recalling the deaths of close friends, they would insist, "I should have done more. If I had been more careful, my buddy would still be alive."

I asked Dad if he, or anyone he supervised, ever encountered situations of a veteran repressing his memories of battle. Dad unhesitatingly shook his head while replying, "Never." He also pointed out that some veterans had no memories of wartime experiences because of head injuries, but "no evidence of repression." Dad continued to clarify how "sometimes we had problems getting them to talk because of how guilty they felt. They would simply say, 'I don't want to talk about it.' But they weren't dealing with repression, they were struggling with guilt."

In June 1946, Dad was promoted to Chief of Vocational Rehabilitation and Education for the Midwestern region of the VA. While in this position until 1950 when he left the VA, Dad supervised as many 300 professional personnel. He developed weekly in-service training seminars for his staff to review difficult and challenging cases. During this time, Dad never encountered any case of a veteran repressing memories of traumatic events.

Admittedly, this account of my father's VA experiences is also anecdotal. I can assure you, however, Dad was not about to alter his opinions in response to my influence. Instead, he frequently reminds me of how children should respect their parents, learning valuable lessons from those who are older and wiser!

OVERVIEW

In any given year, as many as 750,000 clients are at risk for developing false memories in psychotherapy. Not a single professional organization, however, has denounced recovered memory therapy. Like the vast majority of their therapist members, the professional organizations representing them also ignore scientific evidence. Rather than consider scientific data when evaluating claims of repression, recovered memory therapists resort to their clinical experience. Ultimately, however, clinical experience is inherently flawed because it rests on subjective impressions colored by biased expectations. Recovered memory therapists also frequently cite anecdotal evidence to bolster their position. Nonetheless, anecdotal evidence is as unreliable as clinical experience.

Preoccupied with fighting for their professional survival, therapists disregard the scientific issues related to their practices. As a result, progress in psychotherapy practice has suffered enormously. The time is long overdue for undertaking profound shifts in the practice of psychotherapy. In Chapter 14, we review the fundamental changes necessary for psychotherapy to effectively aid clients.

14

Changing Psychotherapy

In 1964, the *Annual Review of Psychology* introduced its evaluation of psychotherapy research declaring, "Chaos prevails."[1] After almost 35 years of subsequent research, the current evidence demonstrates that chaos is alive and well in psychotherapy. The number of different therapy orientations now exceeds 400, and quite likely, this number will continue to grow. Practicing therapists include: psychologists, psychiatrists, social workers, marriage and family therapists, professional counselors, substance abuse counselors, nurse practitioners, and pastoral counselors. These many diverse therapists use very different techniques, citing clinical experience to defend their choices. As a result, treatment practices often correspond more to a therapist's theoretical preferences than to the welfare of clients.

Despite this legacy of chaos, the relevant research indicates that psychotherapy usually helps clients. Since Hans Eysenck first challenged the efficacy of psychotherapy in 1952,[2] the accumulated data seem clear and evident: Clients in therapy fare better than those who do not undertake treatment.[3,4] Massive data analyses, reported over the previous decade, consistently demonstrated that the average effects of psychotherapy are superior to no treatment.[5,6]

Nevertheless, determining the average effects of treatment fails to specify how psychotherapy works.[7] We need to know: "What treatment, by whom, is most effective for this individual with that specific problem, under which set of circumstances?"[8] Without answers for this question, various reviewers remain pessimistic about the effects of specific therapy procedures.[9,10] They insist that comparisons of different therapy techniques lead to concluding: "Everyone has won and all must have prizes."[11]

In other words, there are enormous differences between the various treatment procedures different therapists use. Depending on their theoretical orientations, therapists may pursue insightful understanding, emotional awareness, or cognitive restructuring. Nevertheless, these specific treatment procedures are unrelated to psychotherapy outcome. Therefore, a paradoxical situation prevails undermining the fundamental assumptions of psychotherapy: *There is no evidence for the effectiveness of most therapy techniques despite their enormous variety.*[12-14]

Compared with any effects of its specific procedures, the quality of the client–therapist relationship accounts for the success or failure of therapy.[15-17] The degree to which clients perceive their therapist as a compassionately supportive figure is the best predictor of treatment outcome. In other words, psychotherapy is limited to offering clients the same supportive understanding they might otherwise obtain from a close, trusted friend.

Perhaps even more surprisingly, related data demonstrate that graduate school education and accumulated clinical experience are unrelated to therapist effectiveness. Professional therapists do not relate to clients any better than paraprofessionals.[18,19] Even college professors and housewives respond as effectively to clients as experienced doctoral-level therapists.[20,21] If practically anybody can practice therapy, then the substance of what therapists do seems quite limited.

SIX FUNDAMENTAL QUESTIONS

The continuing chaos undermining psychotherapy leads to six critically important questions: (1) Should therapists assume a *central* or *peripheral* role in relation to clients? (2) Should treatment focus on identifying client *deficits* or client *strengths?* (3) Should treatment primarily address events transpiring *within* clients or events that occur *between* clients and the other significant people in their lives? (4) Should treatment focus on the *historical* or *contemporary* events in the lives of clients? (5) Should therapists resort to their *clinical experience* or respond to well-defined *treatment manuals?* (6) Should training and supervision in psychotherapy rely on *secondhand information* reported by supervisees, or demand *firsthand information* obtained from live supervision?

CENTRAL VERSUS PERIPHERAL THERAPISTS

As previously indicated, therapy benefits clients more effectively when they feel comfortable with their therapist. Clients respond positively to therapists they regard as understanding, sincere, and warmly accepting. The research literature refers to these therapist characteristics as empathy, congruence, and warmth. Warm, congruent, and empathic experiences, however, are not limited to client–therapist relationships. People can enjoy such relationships with their friends and family on a regular basis.

Difficult Impasses

The sudden development of acute psychological distress can rapidly alter relationships that were warm, congruent, and empathic. Out of a concern for a distressed person's independence and dignity, friends and family may withdraw. Though more than willing to help, friends and family worry about appearing intrusive or pushy. Therefore, they wait for the distressed person to request their help. In response to these circumstances, distressed people can misinterpret the thoughtfulness of those close to them. They view these friends and family members as rejecting them.

Distressed, self-doubting clients who feel isolated readily gravitate into dependent relationships with their therapist. In situations such as these, therapists can acquire substantial prominence in the lives of those clients. The clients think of the therapist as a profound source of wisdom, affording them a unique relationship unavailable from family or friends. Therapists who emerge as such central figures in their clients' lives exercise considerable influence with them. In particular, excessively central therapists can use their influence leading clients into recalling false memories of childhood abuse.

Even when not attempting to recover supposedly repressed memories, excessively central therapists too often fail their clients. They specifically overlook their clients' needs for a broad spectrum of social support. They instead unwittingly exploit the impasses often prevailing between clients and their friends and family. Feeling abandoned and/or rejected by friends and family, clients think it hopeless to seek their help. These same friends and family members, however, maintain a respectful distance waiting for the request that would mobilize their assistance. Effective therapists recognize impasses such as these, and resolve them in order to increase the availability of social support in their clients' lives.

Social Support

Social support refers to the encouragement, assistance, and reassurance available to individuals from their network of familiar relationships.[22-24] Basically, there are four different types of social support: (1) *esteem support*—actions or statements reassuring people of their own worth; (2) *informational support*—input or guidance assisting people in dealing with problems; (3) *instrumental support*—sharing and helping behaviors that help people in their day-to-day lives; (4) *companionship support*—the support obtained from a sense of belonging related to shared activities.[25]

High levels of social support reduce the adverse effects of stressful life events and chronic life strains.[27] Elevated levels of social support related to familial relationships, for example, reduce the incidence of depression in adolescents.[27] The availability of familial social support also facilitates the adjustments of college students contending with the transition from adolescence to young adulthood.[28] Elderly adults seeking mental health services report deficits in the social support available to them.[29] Gay males, struggling with HIV-related conditions, reported less depression when they felt satisfied with their level of social support.[30] Victims of sexual assault also cope better when their family and friends respond supportively.[31]

Quite obviously, then, social support significantly influences overall psychological welfare. Consequently, any reasonable standard of practice demands that therapists increase the availability of social support in the lives of their clients.

Blame-and-Change Maneuvers

Unfortunately, psychotherapy frequently diminishes social support rather than enhancing it. Many therapists assume that people endure psychological problems because their families in general, or their parents in particular, previously betrayed them. As discussed earlier, these assumptions invite therapists to explain to their clients the effects of these alleged betrayals. The ensuing accusatory interpretations suggest to clients that treatment must "blame your family" in order to "change you."

To belabor the obvious, clients can sink into feelings of bitterness and resentfulness about the family members who allegedly betrayed them. Rather than inspire hope or optimism, bitterness and resentment result in pessimism and discouragement, which merely lead to more problems. Persuaded they have been regularly betrayed by their parents, for example, clients deal with them more guardedly. Bewildered by an adult child who seems defensive and moody, parents become more distant and aloof. Clients can then leap to the conclusion that their family rejects them and their treatment.

Victims, Villains, and Saviors

When friends and family appear to reject the client's treatment, they are likely to incur rejection from client and therapist.[32] Client and therapist begin to think of those people as cruel and cold, concluding they are villains. In turn, the client assumes the role of a beleaguered victim, and the therapist evolves as an altruistic savior, assisting the client to contend with the villains of a "toxic family."

Once anyone in a client's life who apparently threatens the therapeutic relationship has been designated a villain, client and therapist gravitate into a closer alliance with each other. Moreover, their designation as victims provides clients with an enhanced sense of potency that heretofore may have eluded them. Disregarding initial impressions to the contrary, a victim is actually more powerful than a villain. Victims enjoy a virtuous reputation that inspires them, villains endure a malevolent reputation that humiliates them.

When clients and therapists organize their relationship about the reciprocity of victim and savior, the identity of each demands the other persist in their role. Victims need saviors, and saviors need victims. Victims reassure saviors that they are in fact saviors, and saviors reassure victims that they they are in fact victims. When villains participate in the exchanges between victims and saviors, a triangulated relationship has developed.[33] These triangulated relationships typically organize themselves about the premise: "The enemy of my enemy is my friend," and as a result, they can persist for extended periods of time.[34]

When therapists emphasize the alleged deficits and shortcomings of a client's familial network, solutions for that client's problems are more difficult to find. Labeling clients as victims, and calling their families villains, also leads the clients into cruel stereotypes. This stereotyping insidiously plants the seeds for subsequent allegations of horrible childhood abuse. Consequently, therapeutically in-vogue terms such as "dysfunctional family" and "toxic parents" amount to prejudiced name calling ending in counterproductive outcomes. The therapists who resort to such slurs act as if they—and only they—can assist their clients. As a result, these therapists also lure their clients into depending excessively on the therapist.

Rather than solicit their clients' dependency, effective therapists resolve the impasses that alienate clients from friends and family. An effective therapist assesses clients to identify the types of social support relevant to their needs. Does the client need bolstered self-esteem, or information, or help with day-to-day living, or companionship? The therapist then involves friends or family members to increase the level of social support available to the client. In circumstances such as these, the therapist progressively assumes a more peripheral role in relation to the client. Simultaneously, friends and family emerge as the central figures they should be in the lives of the clients who need them.

Quite clearly, then, the determination of recovered memory therapists to alienate clients from friends and family is grossly inappropriate. The resulting dependency of clients can trap them into long-term therapy, and in turn, they end up underwriting the college tuition of a therapist's first-born child. The blame-and-change maneuvers of recovered memory therapists also accomplish little more than compromising the social support available to clients.

In their attempts at maintaining their savior roles, recovered memory therapists persistently persuade clients that their welfare is jeopardized by villains. Therefore, clients can find themselves trapped in a vicious cycle. The closer they gravitate to the therapist, the more convinced they become that they are victims. And the more convinced they are of their status as victims, the closer they dependently gravitate to their therapist.

STRENGTHS VERSUS DEFICITS?

The Freudian pursuit of insight predisposes legions of therapists to lead their clients into detailed analyses of their maladjustments. Treatments focusing primarily on deficits suggest that clients must understand their many supposed maladjustments in great depth and detail. In their determination to promote these kinds of insights, therapists can prime their dialogues with clients.

Therapists exercise priming effects via leading questions, persistently examining particular topics, and resorting to slanted adjectives. In turn, the responses expected of clients—inventorying their many, supposed deficits—prompt heightened therapist interest and attention. Therefore, priming effects afford therapists the opportunity to lead clients into biased searches for their deficits and shortcomings. Simultaneously, therapists overlook their clients' strengths and resources. These biased searches then leave clients more discouraged and pessimistic via mood-congruent memory effects.

Mood-Congruent Memory Effects

For more than 15 years, laboratory research has examined mood-congruent memory effects. This research demonstrates that induced mood states significantly influence how people think about themselves and their life situations.[35-37] Simply asking people to think about a sad event, for example, leads to significant increases in depression and anxiety.[38] Inducing a sad mood also increases the extent to which people anticipate negative events.[39] Conversely, inducing a happy mood prompts marked decreases in levels of depression and anxiety. Creating an upbeat mood also increases the level of expectations for positive events.

Persuading clients they must undergo detailed dissections of their problems and deficits arouses their depression and anxiety. Increasing clients' depression and anxiety, while also creating heightened expectations for negative events, decreases their self-confidence.[40] Therefore, persistently examining the supposed shortcomings and deficits of clients leads to unfortunate outcomes.

On the other hand, priming and mood-congruent memory effects can also facilitate positive treatment effects. Treatments that lead clients into detailed, comprehensive assessments of their strengths assist them more effectively. This approach encourages clients to seek solutions for the problems that motivated their undertaking therapy. In these circumstances, mood-congruent memory effects arouse more optimistic expectations. Clients inventory their existing strengths identifying how to most efficiently solve their problems.

Inventorying strengths moreover directs clients to issues of *what* needs to be done to cope more effectively.[41] Too often, inventorying client deficits deteriorates into a never-ending, circular endeavor examining *why* those supposed deficits exist. In other words, treatment questions of "What" motivate well-defined courses of action compared with questions of "Why." Therefore, psychotherapy responds more effectively to the welfare of clients when it seeks to identify their strengths, as opposed to analyzing their deficits.

DSM-IV

If carefully assessing the strengths of clients leads to better outcomes than emphasizing their deficits, then diagnostic labels can compromise the effectiveness of psychotherapy. This observation is especially applicable to the *Diagnostic and Statistical Manual of Mental Disorders* (DSM) published by the American Psychiatric Association.[42] This is the definitive reference for diagnosing the problems of clients.

From the time of its first edition published in 1952, through its most recent 1994 fourth edition, each DSM has progressively increased the number of diagnosable disorders.[43] The 1952 edition specified 60 categories of mental disorders. The second edition, published in 1968, contained 145 diagnoses. DSM-III, published in 1980, expanded to 230 disorders. DSM-III-R, published in 1987, listed more than 300 diagnostic categories. Most recently, the 1994 DSM-IV has grown to over 400 disorders. To briefly belabor the obvious, none of the various DSM editions addresses client strengths and resources.

Given the emphasis of diagnostic labeling on client deficits, therapists preoccupied with such labeling too often overlook client strengths. Without a formal system for classifying client strengths, the thinking of therapists gravitates to the more familiar categories of DSM-IV. Consequently, the effectiveness of psychotherapy would be enhanced by developing a comprehensive procedure for classifying client strengths and resources. Such a procedure could be used to develop a standardized interview procedure for identifying client strengths.

Recovered memory therapists, however, continually direct their clients' attention to their supposed problems and deficits. These therapists repeatedly suggest to clients that they exhibit evidence of sexual problems, sleep disturbances, eating disorders, and compulsive behaviors. The therapists then suggest that these many problems confirm the client's repressed memories of childhood sexual abuse. To further persuade clients regarding this conclusion, the therapist diagnoses them with labels supposedly consistent with a history of childhood abuse. Inundated by this propaganda, clients increasingly disregard their own legacy of strengths and resources.

WITHIN VERSUS BETWEEN?

Despite recent developments in marital and family therapies, individual psychotherapy remains the treatment available to most clients. Individual therapy, however, can succumb to the myth of the "self-contained individual."[44] This myth leads therapists into acting as if the psychological distress of clients is confined entirely and exclusively within themselves. In fact, however, psychological distress both influences and is influenced by the recurring interpersonal relationships between clients and the other people in their lives who are significant to them.

Role Performances

Individual therapists recognize the interpersonal contexts within which clients function:

> a patient plays parts in numerous subsystems (e.g., with a spouse, in relation to work assignments, with friends), some of which may be functioning well whereas others are problematic (in someone's opinion).[45]

Indeed, we can evaluate the severity of psychological distress by assessing how many different roles, and to what degree, the distress interferes with a client's life. For example, client A contends with problems confined to a career role. Client B struggles with problems involving roles as spouse, parent, and employee. More often than not, we can accurately assume that client B endures greater psychological distress than client A.

Given the complexities of role performance inevitably characterizing the lives of all clients, it seems reasonable to ask: *How can individual psychotherapy effectively respond to events transpiring between clients and the other important people in their lives?* Whether individual treatment pursues insight, awareness of feelings, or modification of thoughts and actions, it runs the risk of limiting itself to events that occur within clients.

When preoccupied with what transpires within clients, therapists are more inclined to commit the "fundamental attribution error."[46] This error leads therapists into overestimating the influence of internal states on a client's behavior. At the same time, they underestimate the influences of situational factors. Therapists who are excessively preoccupied with what transpires within their clients, while neglecting to effectively address what occurs between those clients and the other important people in their lives, can find their treatment efforts rapidly floundering.

Seeking Consistency

For example, depressed clients actively solicit negative feedback about themselves from other people.[47] Depressed people will put forth herculean efforts to obtain the unfavorable evaluations of themselves they consider appropriate.[48] Simultaneously, they reject favorable evaluations of themselves, assuming that the people who express them are seriously mistaken in their thinking. In other words, depressed and self-rejecting clients actively train other people to confirm their negative assessments of themselves, and once these other people are sufficiently trained, it is exceedingly difficult to alter their confirmatory behavior.

Without the necessary support from family and friends, clients find it difficult to alter their role behavior. Friends and family are used to responding to the client in predictable ways. All of us tend to prefer familiar exchanges with other people because we know what to expect. Friends and family, therefore, may resist the changes therapists encourage clients to undertake. Rather than reacting as villains, their resistance merely corresponds to not understanding the client's needs for changes. Consequently, individual therapy can deteriorate into a "tug of war" with therapists pulling clients in one direction and friends and family pulling them in another. The loyalty conflicts ensuing from these circumstances can leave clients more distressed than before they initiated treatment.[49]

Recovered memory therapists regularly lead their clients into self-centered preoccupations bordering on the narcissistic. These therapists urge clients to make their "recovery" more important than considerations of effective living on a day-to-day basis. While withdrawing *within* their self-absorbed shells, clients suffer massive losses. In neglecting the significance of the relationships *between* themselves and important others, they lose their marriages, their children, their careers, and too often, while deteriorating into self-destructive despair, they lose their sanity.

HISTORICAL VERSUS CONTEMPORARY FOCUS

Countless therapists, especially those with an affinity for Freudian thinking, assume that here-and-now psychological distress originates with traumatic events of the distant past. A particularly prominent therapist, for example, emphasized:

> My fundamental proposition is that an interpersonal relationship—or more accurately, the cumulative effects of interpersonal relationships, typically in childhood—has made the patient "ill."[50]

Despite the continuing prevalence of therapeutic thinking embracing assumptions about "the tyranny of the past"[51]—and its supposedly never-ending influence on the present—the relevant research supports neither this thinking nor its related assumptions.

Tyranny of the Past?

A 1990 review of the relevant research found only modest relationships between early childhood experience and later development.[52] This review concluded that life-span continuity does not imply developmental inevitability. Another study, for example, obtained life history interviews from 100 well-adjusted, successful, adult males.[53] Quite unexpectedly, it found numerous instances of childhood trauma, evidence of poor parental judgment, and episodes of unresolved conflicts with other people persisting over long periods of time. Nevertheless, these males had managed to function quite effectively over the course of their adult lives.

Another study examined 2600 children with histories of abuse and neglect versus a nonabused and nonneglected control group.[54] Subsequent court records accumulated over 20 years revealed that compared with controls, the abused and neglected sample were arrested more often as juveniles (26 versus 17%), arrested more often as adults (29 versus 21%), and arrested more often for violent offenses (11 versus 8%). These data make it tempting to conclude that childhood neglect and abuse leads to criminal behavior. A more detailed examination of these results, however, indicates that such a conclusion is ill-advised.

In fact, the vast majority of abused and neglected children never involved themselves in delinquent, criminal, or violent offenses. If a childhood history of abuse and neglect profoundly influences adult criminality, we would expect a majority of the abused and neglected sample to have criminal records as adults. Perhaps even more importantly, consider the abused and neglected children who committed offenses as juveniles. They continued to commit adult offenses at approximately the same rate as control subjects who committed offenses as juveniles (53 versus 50%). Similarly, those subjects who committed violent offenses as juveniles also proceeded to commit approximately the same frequency of violent offenses as adults regardless of their abuse and neglect history (34.2 versus 36.8%). In other words, the traumas of abuse and neglect moderately increase the likelihood of juvenile offenses, but these effects dissipate in adulthood.

Research regarding Holocaust survivors also demonstrates that traumatic history does not necessarily mean pathological destiny. One study, for example, obtained psychological testing and related survey data from concentration camp survivors. This study found that survivors did not demonstrate any signs of serious psychological impairment, nor did they manifest any evidence of survivor syndrome or survivor guilt.[55] Another study found the vast majority of survivors exhibiting good physical health, holding productive jobs, and enjoying an array of leisure activities.[56] Moreover, the available data do not support clinical assumptions characterizing survivor families as dysfunctional. These previously cited studies describe survivors as well-identified with their families, enjoying family stability, and benefiting from cohesive familial relationships.

Rather than respond to the previously dormant effects of some trauma from the distant past, psychological distress more often reflects the influences of contemporary life-cycle events. Change is an inevitable characteristic of the human condition, and the magnitude and timing of life-cycle changes can disrupt the functioning of families and individuals alike.[57] Clients who present well-established histories of effective functioning—before the onset of a clinical condition necessitating treatment—are most likely contending with difficult changes in the relative here and now. Leading such clients into a kind of archaeological expedition, digging for evidence of the remote origins of their problems, responds more to considerations of theory than to the client's welfare.[58]

Clients are served more effectively when treatment addresses the question of "Why now?" This question examines contemporary events in the lives of clients asking:

> why a family (or client) decides to enter treatment when it does. Why is it arriving at one's office now, rather than 2 years ago or 6 months hence? What has changed, what has made a difference? In other words, what has pressed this family to seek help at this particular time?[59]

Identifying the contemporary events related to the "Why now" question allows therapists to undertake well-defined courses of action on behalf of clients. In turn, here-and-now problem resolution aids clients more effectively than passively speculating about their remote pasts.

Retrospective Memory

Dwelling inordinately on the childhood histories of clients also assumes they can accurately recall past events. As pointed out in previous chapters, however, the recall of remote events is notoriously unreliable. Indeed, people frequently revise their memory of the past to suit their present circumstances.[60] Therapists too often ignore the limitations of retrospective memory. They instead attempt to reconstruct the subjective events of clients' life histories, trying to assess previous childhood experiences and family circumstances. Quite obviously, though, these attempts at inventorying the past invite conjecture and distortion.

Recovered memory therapists act as if their clients contend with ticking time bombs, hidden for decades deep within their psyches. Without almost any warning, these devices presumably explode, destroying the lives of people who previously appeared well-adjusted. Appealing as such narratives may be to novelists and filmmakers, their assumptions amount to science fiction. Acute psychological disturbance responds to here-and-now changes in one's life circumstances. Over the course of our lives, we assume an increasing number of roles. For example, we become more progressively independent as children and adolescents, and then assume responsibilities as adults, spouses, parents, parents-in-law, and grandparents.

It often seems that as soon as we solve the demands and challenges of living, they change. Hero-worshipping children develop into combative teenagers, and shortly after the wars of adolescence end in a shaky truce, your child falls in love—obligating you to learn how to function as a father-in-law or mother-in-law. Each of these events brings pressing demands for learning and adjustment. Sometimes, the sequence of life-cycle changes is timed in such a manner that they overwhelm the already strained resources of those contending with them. These are the kinds of contemporary circumstances that provoke psychological crises. Here-and-now psychological crises rarely, if ever, develop in response to there-and-then events of the distant past.

CLINICAL EXPERIENCE VERSUS TREATMENT MANUALS

Truth in Labeling

Therapists often describe their work by referring to the treatment procedures they use. They might say they use procedures such as structural family therapy, or narrative therapy, or cognitive-behavioral therapy. Therapist A and therapist B, for example, might identify themselves as both using cognitive-behavioral therapy. It does not necessarily follow, however, that they use these procedures in the same manner. How therapist A uses cognitive-behavioral therapy can be very different from therapist B's use of these procedures. These circumstances partially explain the limited evidence demonstrating any effectiveness of specific therapy techniques.

If there are substantial variations in how therapists use the same treatment procedure, then ascertaining the effectiveness of that procedure is very difficult. Therapist A's method of using cognitive-behavioral techniques might be effective, but therapist B's method is not. Combining the effects of therapist A and therapist B can lead to the mistaken conclusion that cognitive-behavioral procedures are ineffective. Additionally, we need to identify the kinds of client problems that respond well to therapist

A's use of cognitive-behavioral procedures. Basically, then, we are returning to the question posed earlier in this chapter: "What treatment, by
whom, is most effective for this individual with that specific problem,
under which set of circumstances?"

Effective psychotherapy, therefore, necessitates that we design well-defined treatment procedures that respond effectively to particular types of
problems. These kinds of treatment procedures are available. Clients struggling with a generalized anxiety disorder, for example, respond well to cognitive-behavioral therapy.[61] Rape victims contending with the debilitating
effects of posttraumatic stress disorder also respond quite well to cognitive-
behavioral treatments.[62] The specific cognitive-behavioral procedures for
these two groups of clients were clearly specified in well-defined treatment
manuals. All of the therapists treating the anxiety-disordered clients, and
the rape victims, responded to each group in essentially the same manner.
Rather than resort to their clinical experience, these therapists used standardized approaches in a consistent manner.

Standardized Treatments

Utilizing standardized treatment methods, specified by well-defined
manuals, is very different than therapists relying on their clinical experience. Consistent compliance with a treatment manual is the defining characteristic of standardized treatments. Clinical experience encourages
therapists to use their own intuitive impressions when selecting and applying treatment methods. Most therapists prefer to rely on their own
clinical experience when treating clients. They challenge the appropriate-
ness of standardized treatments, insisting they should be able to use their
creative thinking and professional judgment.

Examining the effects of standardized treatments versus therapies directed by clinical experience has led to interesting outcomes. One study, for
example, examined the effectiveness of standardized treatments—compared
with clinical experience—when treating phobic clients. Much to the surprise
of both the investigators and therapists participating in the study, standardized treatments emerged as clearly superior.[63] Another study contrasted the
effects of a structured, short-term therapy program—the standardized treatment—with allowing therapists to "ad lib" as they thought best. Again, the
results clearly demonstrated the greater effectiveness of the standardized approach.[64] Interestingly enough, the therapists in both studies protested what
they considered the arbitrary constraints of the standardized treatment.

Despite the accumulating evidence dramatically underscoring the benefits of standardized treatments, most therapists resist them. Rather than use well-defined treatments in standardized ways, most therapists prefer to rely on their own clinical experience. They frequently insist, for example, that psychotherapy is an "art," and their work as "therapeutic artists" deserves respect. Ultimately, however, clinical experience betrays clients more often than not. The legacy of clinical experience involves ill-conceived treatment methods premised on horribly ill-informed assumptions.

Consider, for example, a therapist who proposes to treat all kinds of problems by restoring clients' "beta elements." Though unable to clearly define the substance and significance of beta elements, this therapist uses them to "treat the ambivalent, archaic, primitive, liquid, symbiotic transference" problems of clients. Another therapist enthusiastically touts the supposed benefits of "prenatal bonding." Expectant mothers apparently need to establish special relationships with their children in utero. Still another therapist offers to assist those who have suffered the traumas of abduction by outer-space aliens. None of these therapists can be dismissed as simply ding-a-ling wackos stumbling along the fringe of some lunatic movement. Instead, they are all doctoral-level psychologists enjoying good standing as members of the APA.[65]

In contrast to the treatment approaches of numerous therapists relying on their clinical experience, consider the example of surgeons doing appendectomies. Appendectomies necessitate an incision in the lower right-hand quadrant of the abdomen; consequently, all competent surgeons proceed in this manner. As you read this, there are likely numerous surgeons throughout our nation engaged in appendectomies all of which are proceeding in the same manner. A competent surgeon would never suggest, "Depending on how I feel about the patient, sometimes I open the lower left-hand quadrant and work my way over." Ludicrous as this example is, it corresponds to how therapists frequently fly by the seat of their pants, straddling their clinical experience.

Recovered Memory Therapy and Clinical Experience

Like the "anything goes" approach of too many of their colleagues, recovered memory therapists also rely excessively on clinical experience. Rather than help clients with standardized treatments proven to be safe and effective, they respond to the biases of their own horribly mistaken assumptions. In particular, recovered memory therapists lead clients into speculating about *why* their problems exist. Simultaneously, they distract themselves and their clients from considerations of *what* should be done to solve their problems.

Chronic anxiety disorders, for example, leave the clients who suffer them feeling overwhelmed. Effective treatment for these clients persistently seeks solutions for their condition. In other words, what can be done so that clients control their anxiety, instead of their anxiety controlling them? Resorting to clinical experience, and suggesting to these clients that their anxiety originated with episodes of childhood abuse, amounts to irresponsible neglect.

The growing criticisms directed at recovered memory therapy are beginning to drive its practitioners underground. Though they persist in betraying clients and their families alike, these therapists are less than candid about what they do. Rather than overtly acknowledge they practice recovered memory therapy, they claim to use approaches such as narrative therapy, or ego analysis, or expressive bioenergetics. As previously pointed out, there are often profound differences between what therapists actually do in therapy and what they say they do. It is necessary to extend this observation to recovered memory therapists. Their determination to avoid scrutiny should not be underestimated.

SECOND- VERSUS FIRSTHAND INFORMATION

Surprising as it may seem, therapists typically proceed through their training without supervisors directly observing their treatment work. Live supervision facilitated by one-way mirrors and videotape technology is a hallmark of family therapy.[66,67] Most trainees, however, rely on verbal reports and written notes of their sessions.[68] Related research has reported low correlations between written notes and videotapes obtained from the same interviews.[69] Additionally, videotapes of trainees indicate that they overlook as many as 50% of the important issues that transpire in an interview, and another 50% of what they do report to supervisors is also distorted.[70] When relying on their notes, experienced therapists also find it difficult to accurately recall how actively they responded to their clients.[71]

Supervisory Confusion

Without the benefit of live supervision and videotape technology, supervisees find it quite difficult to recall what transpired in their therapy sessions. They frequently labor with major discrepancies between what they did in treatment and what they say they did, or think they did, or say they think they did. These circumstances make it exceedingly difficult for supervisees to even identify their errors, let alone correct them. Moreover, therapists and trainees alike commonly arrive at their diagnostic impressions within the first 2 to 3 minutes of an interview, and sometimes as rapidly as 30 seconds.[72] In turn, they cling to those impressions even when confronted with contrary evidence.[73]

The expectations of supervisees can profoundly influence their impressions of their clients.[74] Assumptions about a client's symptoms, childhood, or memories, for instance, increase the frequency of questions directed at those topics. In turn, asking enough questions allows supervisees to think they found the answers they expected.[75] Anchoring effects then leave them excessively influenced by earlier information. As a result, they are unable to appropriately adjust their opinions in response to subsequent information.[76] Supervisees then insist that symptoms consistent with their preliminary impressions were evident in an interview, when, in fact, they were not.[77] Simultaneously, they are also less likely to recall symptoms actually present but inconsistent with their impressions.

Judgmental Confidence

Therapists in general, and supervisees in particular, are prone to overestimating the amount of information they process during their interviews. They assume they weigh multiple factors in making their judgments, but the relevant evidence demonstrates that they rely on minimal data.[78,79] Without a videotape directing and maintaining attention on what actually transpired in a therapy session, dialogues between supervisor and supervisee drift into theoretical speculation.

Speculative exchanges, however, also lead to overconfidence. Conjecture addressing why some event might have occurred leaves people more confident that the event did occur. Therapists maintain their convictions in this regard despite the unavailability of any evidence to support such a conclusion.[80] Furthermore, these speculative exchanges frequently respond to the effects of leveling and sharpening.[81] Both supervisors and supervisees may sharpen their impressions related to what seems significant about a client, and simultaneously, they level what seems less than significant. Often, however, the processes of sharpening and leveling respond more to the theoretical convictions of supervisor and supervisee than reflecting an accurate assessment of a client. Nevertheless, the consensus they share can create unwarranted confidence in their conclusions.

Ethical problems related to supervision most often involve complaints regarding the failure to provide relevant and timely feedback.[82] Live supervision supported by videotape technology can respond to supervisees in a more relevant and timely manner by capitalizing on firsthand information. Supervisory relationships premised on secondhand information are inevitably more subjective than objective, and as result, they can betray supervisees and their clients alike.

Additionally, supervisees who rely predominantly on verbal reports and written notes create considerable exposure to malpractice litigation.[83] If a plaintiff contends that a supervisee's treatment violated the appropriate standard of care, supervisors can find themselves in an indefensible position. Secondhand impressions make it exceedingly difficult for a defendant-supervisor to testify regarding the treatment work of a supervisee. Consequently, the impetus for more responsible supervisory practices may eventually originate from the insurance carriers that insure therapists against malpractice litigation.

In response to lawsuits alleging they seriously damaged their clients, recovered memory therapists typically claim they never did anything to harm the client. The specifically deny using any treatment methods that might have contaminated and distorted the client's memory. When therapists in these circumstances have been under supervision, it is virtually impossible for their supervisors to support their claims. Any and all professionals, therefore, who supervise the work of other therapists must realize how vulnerable they are to legal action. Without firsthand familiarity with what supervisees do in therapy, supervisors cannot support their claims.

Overview

The chaos inundating psychotherapy demands wholesale revisions in its methods and approach. This chapter has defined a very different direction for psychotherapy compared with the status quo of prevailing treatment practices. Psychotherapy will respond most effectively to the needs and welfare of clients when:

- Therapists assume a more peripheral role while mobilizing the family and friends of clients into positions of central significance.

- Treatment focuses on identifying clients' strengths and resources rather than their supposed deficits and shortcomings.
- Treatment no longer leads clients into self-absorbed excesses dissecting what transpires *within* their psyches. Instead, it focuses on events occurring *between* clients and the other important people in their lives.
- Treatment focuses more on here-and-now issues than speculating about the distant past.
- Therapists reject the biases of their clinical experience, and use standardized treatments specified by well-defined manuals.
- Training and supervision in psychotherapy rely on firsthand information supported by videotape technology.

Without undertaking these profoundly necessary changes, psychotherapy will continue offering clients merely the chance of effective treatment. Fortunate clients stumble on well-trained and well-informed therapists who practice effectively as a result. Unfortunate clients suffer the damages inflicted by ill-trained and ill-informed therapists who typically harm more than help. The majority of clients benefit moderately from the social support of a therapist—the same kind of support otherwise available to them from a close, trusted friend.

Clients who need effective treatment deserve more than the equivalent of a therapeutic lottery. Blindly relying on Dame Fortune merely heightens the fear and anxiety of clients who need psychotherapy. The likelihood of the relevant professional organizations dealing responsibly with the chaotic crises of psychotherapy is remote—probably exceeded only by the chances of my golfing prowess winning the U.S. Open. The continuing irresponsibility of these professional organizations necessitates the public demand action from governmental agencies. The time has come for regulatory bodies such as licensing boards to clean house. The damage done by too many charlatans calling themselves psychotherapists prohibits continuing with business as usual. The incompetence of legions of psychotherapists amounts to a public health hazard, and decisive action is warranted as a result.

Notes

CHAPTER 1

1. *New York Times* (1990 January 24). McMartin case: Swept away by panic about molestation, pp. A1, A18.
2. Spiegel, L. D. (1990). The phenomenon of child abuse hysteria as a social syndrome: The case for a new kind of expert testimony. *Issues in Child Abuse Accusations,* 2, 17–26 (p. 21).
3. *New York Times* (1990 July 28). 7 years later, McMartin case ends in a mistrial, pp. A1, A7.
4. Buckey, P., Buckey, R., & Buckey, P. A. (1990). After the McMartin trials: Some reflections from the Buckeys. *Issues in Child Abuse Accusations,* 2, 220–225.
5. Carlson, A. (1986 August). The child savers ride again. *Persuasion at Work,* 8 (8), 1–8.
6. Victor, J. S. (1991). The satanic cult scare and allegations of ritual child abuse. *Issues in Child Abuse Accusations,* 3, 135–143.
7. Hobbs, C. J., & Wynne, J. M. (1986 October 4). Buggery in childhood— A common syndrome of child sexual abuse. *Lancet,* p. 792.
8. Coleman, L. (1989). Medical examination for sexual abuse: Have we been misled? *Issues in Child Abuse Accusations,* 1 (3), 1–9.

9. Butler-Sloss, E. (1988). *Report of the inquiry into child abuse in Cleveland, 1987.* London: Her Majesty's Stationery Office.
10. Ceci, S. J., & Bruck, M. (1995). *Jeopardy in the courtroom.* Washington, DC: American Psychological Association. (See "Old Culter case.")
11. Armbrister, T. (1994 January). Justice gone crazy. *Reader's Digest, 73* (1), 33–40 (p. 35).
12. Ibid., p. 35.
13. Ibid.
14. Ibid.
15. Ibid., p. 38
16. Ibid.
17. Ibid., p. 39.
18. Superior Court of New Jersey–Appellate Division. (1993 March 26.) *State of New Jersey v. Margaret Kelly Michaels.* Argued February 1, 1993.
19. Supreme Court of New Jersey. (1994 June 23). *State of New Jersey v. Margaret Kelly Michaels.* Argued January 31, 1994.
20. Ibid., p. 17.
21. Rosenthal, R. (1995). State of New Jersey v. Margaret Kelly Michaels: An overview. *Psychology, Public Policy, and Law,* 1, 246–271 (p. 251).
22. Myers, J. E., Bays, J., Becker, J., Berliner, L., Corwin, D. L., & Saywitz, K. J. (1989). Expert testimony in child sexual abuse litigation. *Nebraska Law Review,* 68, 1–145 (p. 68).
23. Sgroi, S. M. (1982). *Handbook of clinical intervention in child sexual abuse.* (p. 78).
24. Superior Court of New Jersey, p. 28.
25. Ibid., p. 46.
26. Supreme Court of New Jersey, p. 10.
27. Ibid., p. 18.
28. Eckenrode, J., Powers, J., Doris, J., Munsch, J., & Bolger, N. (1988). Substantiation of child abuse and neglect reports. *Journal of Consulting and Clinical Psychology,* 56, 9–16.
29. Lewis, E. (1996 Summer). Reliability rather than zealotry. *Kentucky Bench & Bar,* 60, 23–30.
30. Ibid.

Chapter 2

1. Milgram, S., Bickman, L., & Berkowitz, L. (1969). Note on the drawing power of crowds of different size. *Journal of Personality and Social Psychology,* 13, 79–82.

2. Sherif, M. (1935). A study of some social factors in perception. *Archives of Psychology, 27*, No. 187.
3. Ross, L., Lepper, M.R., Strack, F., & Steinmetz, J. L. (1977). Social explanation and social expectation: Effects of real and hypothetical explanations on subjective likelihood. *Journal of Personality and Social Psychology, 35*, 817–829.
4. Newcomb, T. M. (1961). *The acquaintance process.* New York: Holt, Rinehart & Winston.
5. Heider, F. (1958). *The psychology of interpersonal relations.* New York: Wiley.
6. Allport, G. W., & Postman, L. (1947). *The psychology of rumor.* New York: Holt, Rinehart & Winston.
7. Blush, G. J., & Ross, K. L. (1990). Investigation and case management issues and strategies. *Issues in Child Abuse Accusations, 2*, 152–160.
8. Rosnow, R. L. (1991). Inside rumor: A personal journey. *American Psychologist, 46*, 484–496.
9. Bordia, P. (1994). Rumor talk: Content analysis of an electronic network rumor. *Paper presented at the Sixth Annual Convention of the American Psychological Society, Washington, DC, July 1994.*
10. Eysenck, M. W., Mogg, K., May, J., Richards, A., & Mathews, A. (1991). Bias in interpretation of ambiguous sentences related to threat in anxiety. *Journal of Abnormal Psychology, 100*, 144–150.
11. Halberstadt, J. B., Niedenthal, P. M., & Kushner, J. (1995). Resolution of lexical ambiguity by emotional state. *Psychological Science, 6*, 278–282.
12. Rossen, B. (1989). Mass hysteria in Oude Pekela. *Issues in Child Abuse Accusations, 1* (1), 49–51.
13. Gilovich, T. (1987). Secondhand information and social judgment. *Journal of Experimental Social Psychology, 23*, 59–74.
14. DiFonzo, N. (1994). The fundamental attribution error in persistence studies. *Paper presented at the Sixth Annual Convention of the American Psychological Society, Washington, DC, July 1994.*
15. Siegel, M., Waters, L. J., & Dinwiddy, L. S. (1988). Misleading children: Causal attributions for inconsistency under repeated questioning. *Journal of Experimental Child Psychology, 45*, 438–456.
16. Loftus, E. (1979). *Eyewitness testimony.* Cambridge, MA: Harvard University Press.
17. Goodman, G. S., & Clarke-Stewart, A. (1991). Suggestibility in children's testimony: Implications for sexual abuse investigations. In J. Doris (Ed.)., *The suggestibility of children's recollections.* Washington, DC: American Psychological Association.

18. Bradburn, N. M., Rips, L. J., & Shevell, S. K. (1987). Answering autobiographical questions: The impact of memory and inference on surveys. *Science*, 236, 157–161.
19. Friedman, W. J. (1993). Memory for the time of past events. *Psychological Bulletin*, 113, 44–66.
20. Ross, M. (1989). Relation of implicit theories to the construction of personal histories. *Psychological Review*, 96, 341–357.
21. Gilovich.

Chapter 3

1. Kempe, C. H., Silverman, F. N., Steele, B. F., Droegmuller, W., & Silver, H. K. (1962). The battered-child syndrome. *Journal of the American Medical Association*, 181, 17–24.
2. Summitt, R. (1983). The child sexual abuse accommodation syndrome. *Child Abuse and Neglect*, 7, 177–193.
3. Myers, J. E., Bays, J., Becker, J., Berliner, L., Corwin, D. L. & Saywitz, K. (1989). Expert testimony in child sexual abuse litigation. *Nebraska Law Review*, 68, 1–145.
4. American Medical Association (1985). Diagnostic and treatment guidelines concerning child abuse and neglect. *Journal of the American Medical Association*, 254, 796–800.
5. Sgroi, S. M. (1982). *Handbook of clinical intervention in child sexual abuse.* Lexington, MA: Lexington Books.
6. Campbell, T. W. (1997). Indicators of child sexual abuse and their unreliability. *American Journal of Forensic Psychology*, 15 (1), 1–13.
7. Koocher, G. P., Goodman, G. S., White, C. S., Friedrich, W. N., Sivan, A. B., & Reynolds, C. R. (1995). Psychological science and the use of anatomically detailed dolls in child sexual-abuse assessments. *Psychological Bulletin*, 118, 199–222.
8. Lamb, S., & Coakely, M. (1993). "Normal" childhood sex play and games: Differentiating play from abuse. *Child Abuse and Neglect*, 17, 515–526.
9. American Psychological Association (1992). Ethical principles of psychologists and code of conduct. *American Psychologist*, 47, 1597–1611 (p. 1600).
10. Ibid., p. 1610.
11. Gardner, R. A. (1991). The "validators" and other examiners. *Issues in Child Abuse Accusations*, 3, 38–53.

12. Campbell, T. W. (1993). The reliability and validity of Gardner's indicators of pedophilia. *Issues in Child Abuse Accusations*, 5, 170–182.
13. Anastasi, A. (1982). *Psychological testing* (5th ed.). New York: Macmillan Co. (p. 582).
14. Swenson, C. H. (1957). Empirical evaluations of human figure drawings. *Psychological Bulletin*, 4, 431–468.
15. Wanderer, Z. W. (1969). Validity of clinical judgments based on human figure drawings. *Journal of Consulting and Clinical Psychology*, 33, 143–150.
16. Smith, D., & Dumont, F. (1995). A cautionary study: Unwarranted interpretations of the Draw-a-Person test. *Professional Psychology: Research and Practice*, 26, 298–303 (p. 301).
17. Ibid., p. 302.
18. Bricklin, B. (1995). *The custody evaluation handbook: Research-based solutions and applications*. New York: Brunner/Mazel (p. 83).
19. Ibid., pp. 84–85.
20. American Psychological Association, p. 1603.
21. Ibid., p. 1603.
22. White, S. (1988). Should investigatory use of anatomical dolls be defined by the courts? *Journal of Interpersonal Violence*, 3, 471–475 (p. 472).
23. Edwards, C. A., & Forman, B. D. (1989). Effects of child interview method on accuracy and completeness of sexual abuse information recall. *Social Behavior and Personality*, 17, 237–247 (p. 238).
24. Everson, M.D., & Boat, B.W. (1994). Putting the anatomical doll controversy in perspective: An examination of the major uses and criticisms of the dolls in child sexual abuse evaluations. *Child Abuse & Neglect*, 18, 113–129 (p. 113).
25. Boat, B. W., & Everson, M. D. (1988). Use of anatomical dolls among professionals in sexual abuse evaluations. *Child Abuse & Neglect*, 12, 171–179.
26. Glaser, D., & Collins, C. (1989). The response of young, non-sexually abused children to anatomically correct dolls. *Journal of Child Psychology and Psychiatry and Applied Disciplines*, 30, 547–560.
27. Cohn, D. S. (1991). Anatomical doll play of preschoolers referred for sexual abuse and those not referred. *Child Abuse & Neglect*, 15, 455–466.
28. Maan, C. (1991). Assessment of sexually abused children with anatomically detailed dolls: A critical review. *Behavioral Sciences and the Law*, 9, 43–51 (p. 49).

29. Wolfner, G., Faust, D., & Dawes, R. M. (1993). The use of anatomically detailed dolls in sexual abuse evaluations: The state of science. *Applied and Preventive Psychology, 2*, 1–11 (p. 9).

CHAPTER 4

1. Ceci, S. J., & Bruck, M. (1995). *Jeopardy in the courtroom: A scientific analysis of children's testimony.* Washington, DC: American Psychological Association.
2. Livermore, J. M., Malmquist, C. P., & Meehl, P. E. (1968). On the justifications for civil commitment. *University of Pennsylvania Law Review, 117.*
3. Sattin, D. B. (1980). Possible sources of error in the evaluation of psychopathology. *Journal of Clinical Psychology, 36*, 99–105.
4. Bruck, M., & Ceci, S. J. (1995). Amicus brief for the case of *State of New Jersey v. Michaels* presented by Committee of Concerned Social Scientists. *Psychology, Public Policy, and Law, 1*, 272–322 (pp. 304–305).
5. Ibid., pp. 298–299.
6. Ibid., pp. 283–284.
7. Binet, A. (1900). *La suggestibilite.* Paris: Schleicher Freres.
8. Pynoos, R. S., & Nader, K. (1989). Children's memory and proximity to violence. *Journal of the American Academy of Child and Adolescent Psychiatry, 28*, 236–241 (p. 238).
9. Bruck & Ceci, pp. 297–298.
10. Lyon, T. D. (1995). False allegations and false denials in child sexual abuse. *Psychology, Public Policy, and Law, 1*, 429–437.
11. Myers, J. E. B. (1995). New era of skepticism regarding children's credibility. *Psychology, Public Policy, and Law, 1*, 387–398.
12. Lepore, S. J., & Sesco, B. (1994). Distorting children's reports and interpretations of events through suggestion. *Applied Psychology, 79*, 108–120.
13. Clarke-Stewart, A., Thompson, W., & Lepore, S. (1989). Manipulating children's interpretations through interrogation. *Paper presented at the Biennial Meeting of the Society for Research in Child Development, Kansas City, MO.*
14. Siegel, M., Waters, L. J., & Dinwiddy, L. S. (1988). Misleading children: Causal attributions for inconsistency under repeated questioning. *Journal of Experimental Child Psychology, 45*, 438–456.
15. Johnson, M. K., Hashtroudi, S., & Lindsay, D. S. (1993). Source monitoring. *Psychological Bulletin, 114*, 3–28.
16. Ceci & Bruck.

17. Loftus, E. F., & Hoffman, H.G. (1989). Misinformation and memory: The creation of new memories. *Journal of Experimental Psychology: General*, 118, 100–104.
18. Loftus, E.F. (1992). When a lie becomes memory's truth: Memory distortion after exposure to misinformation. *Current Directions in Psychological Science*, 1, 121–123.
19. Piaget, J. P. (1962). *Play, dreams, and imitation*. New York: Norton.
20. Ceci & Bruck.
21. Ibid., p. 219.
22. Johnson et al.
23. Foley, M. A., & Johnson, M. K. (1985). Confusion between memories for performed and imagined actions. *Child Development*, 56, 1145–1155.
24. Lindsay, D. S., Johnson, M. K., & Kwon, P. (1991). Developmental changes in memory source monitoring. *Journal of Experimental Child Psychology*, 52, 297–318.
25. Pezdek, K., & Roe, C. (1997). The suggestibility of children's memory for being touched: Planting, erasing, and changing memories. *Law and Human Behavior*, 21, 95–106.
26. Bruck & Ceci.
27. Ibid., p. 301.

Chapter 5

1. State v. Johnson (1996), 83 Ohio Misc. 2d 26. Court of Common Pleas of Ohio, Washington County. No. 96CR86. Decided November 15, 1996. Cited in: Ohio State Bar Association (1997 May 5). *Bar Report Index*, 70 (18), 26–44.
2. American Academy of Child and Adolescent Psychiatry. (Modified 12-14-90). Guidelines for the clinical evaluation of child and adolescent sexual abuse.
3. Attorney General's Task Force on Family Violence. (1984). *Final report*. Washington, DC: U.S. Department of Justice.
4. Ceci, S. J., Ross, D. F., & Toglia, M. P. (Eds.). (1989). *Perspectives on children's testimony*. Berlin: Springer-Verlag.
5. McGough, L. S. (1991). Commentary: Sexual abuse and suggestibility. In J. Doris (Ed.), *The suggestibility of children's recollections: Implications for eyewitness testimony*. Washington, DC: American Psychological Association.
6. Yuille, J. C., Hunter, R., Joffe, R., & Zaparniuk, J. (1993). Interviewing children in sexual abuse cases. In G. S. Goodman & B. L. Bottoms

(Eds.), *Child victims, child witnesses: Understanding and improving testimony.* New York: Guilford (pp. 100–101).

7. Friedlander, M. L., & Stockman, S. J. (1983). Anchoring and publicity errors in clinical judgment. *Journal of Clinical Psychology, 39*, 637–643.

8. Friedlander, M. L., & Phillips, S. D. (1984). Preventing anchoring errors in clinical judgment. *Journal of Consulting and Clinical Psychology, 52*, 366–371.

9. Fisch, H. U., Hammond, K. R., & Joyce, C. R. (1982). On evaluating the severity of depression: An experimental study of psychiatrists. *British Journal of Psychiatry, 140*, 378–383.

10. Yager, J. (1977). Psychiatric eclecticism: A cognitive view. *American Journal of Psychiatry, 134*, 736–741.

11. Dawes, R. M. (1986). Representative thinking in clinical judgment. *Clinical Psychology Review, 6*, 425–441.

12. Dallas, M. E., & Baron, R. S. (1985). Do psychotherapists use a confirmatory strategy during interviewing? *Journal of Social and Clinical Psychology, 3*, 106–122.

13. Snyder, M., & Thomsen, C. J. (1988). Interactions between therapists and clients: Hypothesis testing and behavioral confirmation. In D. C. Turk & P. Salovey (Eds.), *Reasoning, influence, and judgment in clinical psychology.* New York: Free Press.

14. Arkes, H. R. (1981). Impediments to accurate clinical judgment and possible ways to minimize their impact. *Journal of Consulting and Clinical Psychology, 49*, 323–330.

15. Arkes, H. R., & Harkness, A. R. (1980). Effect of making a diagnosis on the subsequent recognition of symptoms. *Journal of Experimental Psychology, 6*, 99–105.

16. Faust, D. (1989). Data integration in legal evaluations: Can clinicians deliver on their premises? *Behavioral Sciences & the Law, 7*, 469–484.

17. Ceci, S. J., & Bruck, M. (1995). *Jeopardy in the courtroom.* Washington, DC: American Psychological Association (p. 80).

18. Muslin, H. L., Thurnblad, R. J., & Meschel, G. (1981). The fate of the clinical interview: An observational study. *American Journal of Psychiatry, 138*, 823–825.

19. Truax, C. B. (1966). Reinforcement and non-reinforcement in Rogerian psychotherapy. *Journal of Abnormal Psychology, 71*, 1–9.

20. Xenakis, S. N., Hoyt, M. F., Marmar, C. R., & Horowitz, M. J. (1983). Reliability of self–reports by therapists using the therapist's action scale. *Psychotherapy, 20*, 314–319.

21. Goodman, G. S., & Clarke–Stewart, A. (1991). Suggestibility in children's testimony: Implications for child sexual abuse investigations. In J. L. Doris (Ed.), *The suggestibility of children's recollections*. Washington, DC: American Psychological Association.
22. Pettit, F., Fegan, M., & Howie, P. (1990 September). Interviewer effects on children's testimony. Paper presented at the International Congress on Child Abuse and Neglect, Hamburg, Germany. Cited by: Ceci, S. J., & Bruck, M. (1993). Suggestibility of the child witness: A historical review and synthesis. *Psychological Bulletin, 113*, 403–439.
23. McGough, L. S., & Warren, A. R. (1994). The all-important investigative interview. *Juvenile and Family Court Journal, 45*, 13–29.
24. Quas, J. A., DeCicco, V., Bulkley, J., & Goodman, G. (1996). Research brief: District attorneys views of legal innovations for child witnesses. *American Psychology–Law Society News, 16* (2), 5–8.
25. Lungren, D. E. (1994 June). Child victim witness investigative pilot project: Research and evaluation. Sacramento: California Attorney General's Office. Cited by McGough, L. S. (1995). For the record: Videotaping investigative interviews. *Psychology, Public Policy, and Law, 1*, 370–386.
26. Stevenson, K. M., Leung, P., & Cheung, K. M. (1992). Competency-based evaluation of interviewing skills in child sexual abuse cases. *Social Work Research and Abstracts, 28* (3), 11–16.
27. Saywitz, K. J., & Snyder, L. (1996). Narrative elaboration: Test of a new procedure for interviewing children. *Journal of Consulting and Clinical Psychology, 64*, 1347–1357.

CHAPTER 6

1. Brewer, M. B. (1979). In-group bias in the minimal intergroup situation: A cognitive-motivational analysis. *Psychological Bulletin, 86*, 307–324.
2. Hewstone, M. (1990). The "ultimate attribution error?" A review of the literature on intergroup causal attribution. *European Journal of Social Psychology, 20*, 311–335.
3. Schopler, J., & Insko, C. A. (1992). The discontinuity effect in interpersonal and intergroup relations: Generality and mediation. In W. Stroebe & M. Hewstone (Eds.), *European review of social psychology* Vol. 3. New York: Wiley.
4. Tajfel, H., & Forgas, J. P. (1981). Social categorization: Cognitions, values, and groups. In J. P. Forgas (Ed.), *Social cognition: Persepctives on everyday understanding*. New York: Academic Press.

5. Baron, R. A. (1976). The reduction of human aggression: A field study of the influence of incompatible reactions. *Journal of Applied Social Psychology, 6,* 260–274.
6. Ausubel, D. F. (1958). *Theory and problems of child development.* New York: Grune & Stratton.
7. Gardner, R. A. (1987). *The parental alienation syndrome and the differentiation between fabricated and genuine child sex abuse.* Cresskill, NJ: Creative Therapeutics.
8. Campbell, T. W. (1993). Parental conflicts between divorced spouses: Strategies for intervention. *Journal of Systemic Therapies, 12* (4), 27–39.

CHAPTER 7

1. Kendall-Tackett, K. A., Williams, L. M., & Finkelhor, D. (1993). Impact of sexual abuse on children: A review and synthesis of recent empirical studies. *Psychological Bulletin, 113,* 164–178.
2. Wolf, T. L., & Campbell, T. W. (1994). Effective treatment for children in cases of extrafamilial sexual abuse. *Issues in Child Abuse Accusations, 6,* 207–213.
3. Johnson, M. K., Hashtroudi, S., & Lindsay, D. S. (1993). Source monitoring. *Psychological Bulletin, 114,* 3–38.
4. Campbell, T. W. (1992). False allegations of sexual abuse and the persuasiveness of play therapy. *Issues in Child Abuse Accusations, 4,* 118–124.
5. Channing L. Bete Co. Inc. (1995 edition). *What every kid should know about sexual abuse.* South Deerfield, MA: Author.
6. Ewing, C. P. (1994 January). Child's disclosure of sexual abuse held tainted by repeated exposure to suggestive book. *APA Monitor, 25,* 14.
7. Axline, V. M. (1969). *Play therapy.* New York: Ballantine (p. 9).
8. Campbell, T. W. (1992). Promoting play therapy: Marketing dream or empirical nightmare? *Issues in Child Abuse Accusations, 4,* 111–117.
9. Clement, P. W., & Milne, D. C. (1967). Group play therapy and tangible reinforcers used to modify the behavior of eight-year-old boys. *Behavior Research and Therapy, 5,* 301–312.
10. Clement, P. W., Fazzone, R. A., & Goldstein, B. (1970). Tangible reinforcers and child group therapy. *Journal of the American Academy of Child and Adolescent Psychiatry, 9,* 409–427.
11. Kelly, C. (1976). Play desensitization of fear of darkness in preschool children. *Behavior Research and Therapy, 14,* 79–81.

12. Milos, M. E., & Reiss, S. (1982). Effects of three play conditions on separation anxiety in young children. *Journal of Consulting and Clinical Psychology, 50,* 389–395.

13. McBrien, R. J., & Nelson, R. J. (1972). Experimental group strategies with primary grade children. *Elementary School Guidance and Counseling, 6,* 170–174.

14. Yates, L. E. (1976). The use of sociometry as an identifier of a research sample for psychological treatment and quantifier of change among second grade students. *Group Psychotherapy, Psychodrama, and Sociometry, 29,* 102–110.

15. Friedberg, R. D. (1995). Book review of: Handbook of play therapy, Volume 2: Advances and innovations. *Psychotherapy, 32,* 710–711.

16. Davids, A. (1975). Therapeutic approaches to children in residential treatment: Changes from the mid-1950s to the mid-1970s. *American Psychologist, 30,* 809–814.

17. Reams, R., & Friedrich, W. (1994). The efficacy of time-limited play therapy with maltreated preschoolers. *Journal of Clinical Psychology, 50,* 889–899 (p. 897).

18. Phillips, R. D. (1985). Whistling in the dark? A review of play therapy research. *Psychotherapy, 22,* 752–760 (p. 757).

19. King, B. T., & Janis, I. L. (1956). Comparison of the effectiveness of improvised versus non-improvised role playing in producing opinion changes. *Human Relations, 9,* 177–186.

20. Bem, D. J. (1972). Self-perception theory. In L. Berkowitz (Ed.), *Advances in experimental social psychology,* Vol. 6. New York: Academic Press.

21. Festinger, L. (1957). *A theory of cognitive dissonance.* Evanston, IL: Row, Peterson.

22. Bonnano, G. A. (1990). Remembering and psychotherapy. *Psychotherapy, 27,* 175–186.

23. Spence, D. P. (1982). *Narrative truth and historical truth: Memory and interpretation in psychoanalysis.* New York: Norton.

24. Campbell, T. W. (1992). Psychotherapy with children of divorce: The pitfalls of triangulated relationships. *Psychotherapy, 29,* 646–652.

25. Sartre, J. P. (1964). *St. Genet.* London: W.H. Allen.

26. Weithorn, L. A. (1987). Psychological consultation in divorce custody litigation: Ethical considerations. In L. A. Weithorn (Ed.), *Psychology and child custody determinations: Knowledge, roles, and expertise.* Lincoln: University of Nebraska Press (p. 195).

27. Campbell, T. W. (1992). Therapeutic relationships and iatrogenic outcomes: The blame-and-change maneuver in psychotherapy. *Psychotherapy, 29,* 474–480.
28. Emery, R. E., Hetherington, E. M., & DiLalla, L. F. (1985). Divorce, children, and social policy. In H. Stevenson & A. Siegel (Eds.), *Child development research and social policy.* Chicago: University of Chicago Press.
29. Isaacs, M.B., Montalvo, B., & Abelsohn, D. (1986). *The difficult divorce: Therapy for children and families.* New York: Basic Books.
30. Wallerstein, J., & Kelly, J. (1980). *Surviving the breakup: How children and parents cope with divorce.* New York: Basic Books.
31. Schein, E. H., Schneier, I., & Barker, C. H. (1961). *Coercive persuasion.* New York: Norton.
32. Ibid., p. 285.
33. Nemiroff, M. A., & Annunziata, J. (1990). *A child's first book about play therapy.* Washington, DC: American Psychological Association.
34. Haley, J. (1981). *Reflections on therapy.* Chevy Chase, MD: The Family Therapy Institute of Washington, DC.
35. Montalvo, B., & Haley, J. (1973). In defense of child therapy. *Family Process, 12,* 227–244.
36. Gorin, S. S. (1993). The prediction of child psychotherapy outcome: Factors specific to treatment. *Psychotherapy, 30,* 152–158.
37. Bennett, B. E., Bryant, B. K., VandenBos, G. R., & Greenwood, A. (1990). *Professional liability and risk management.* Washington, DC: American Psychological Association.
38. Ibid.

Chapter 8

1. FMS Foundation Newsletter. (1995 October). Philadelphia, PA (p. 3).
2. Masson, J.M. (1984). *The assault on truth: Freud's suppression of the seduction theory.* New York: Farrar, Straus & Giroux.
3. Courtois, C. A. (1988). *Healing the incest wound.* New York: Norton (p. 298).
4. van der Kolk, B. A. (1987). The psychological consequences of overwhelming life experiences. In B.A. van der Kolk (Ed.), *Psychological trauma.* Washington, DC: American Psychiatric Press (p. 7).
5. Claridge, K. (1992). Reconstructing memories of abuse: A theory-based approach. *Psychotherapy, 29,* 243–252 (p. 245).
6. FMS Foundation Newsletter. (1996 November/December). Philadelphia, PA (p. 17).

7. Survivors of Incest Anonymous. (Undated). The experience of ritual abuse. Unpublished flier.
8. FMS Foundation Newsletter. (1993 October). Philadelphia, PA (p. 11).
9. Ibid., p. 12.
10. FMS Foundation Newsletter. (1995 January). Philadelphia, PA (p. 10).
11. FMS Foundation Newsletter. (1993 October). Philadelphia, PA (p. 11).
12. FMS Foundation Newsletter. (1995 June). Philadelphia, PA (pp. 3–4).
13. FMS Foundation Newsletter. (1996 March). Philadelphia, PA (p. 5).
14. Fredrickson, R. (1992). *Repressed memories: A journey to recovery from sexual abuse.* New York: Simon & Schuster.
15. Lees-Haley, P. R., Williams, C. W., & Brown, R. S. (1993). The "Barnum effect" and personal injury litigation. *American Journal of Forensic Psychology,* 11 (2), 21–28.
16. Snyder, C. R., Shenkel, R. J., & Lowery, C. R. (1977). Acceptance of personality interpretations: The "Barnum effect" and beyond. *Journal of Consulting and Clinical Psychology,* 38, 384–388.
17. Logue, M. R., Sher, K. J., & Frensch, P. A. (1992). Purported characteristics of adult children of alcoholics: A possible "Barnum effect." *Professional Psychology: Research and Practice,* 23, 226–232.
18. Faust, D. (1989). Data integration in legal evaluations: Can clinicians deliver on their premises? *Behavioral Sciences & the Law,* 7, 469–483.
19. Arkes, H. R. (1981). Impediments to accurate clinical judgment and possible ways to minimize their impact. *Journal of Consulting and Clinical Psychology,* 49, 323–330.
20. Snyder, M., & Swann, W. B. (1978). Hypothesis testing processes in social interaction. *Journal of Personality and Social Psychology,* 36, 1202–1212.
21. FMS Foundation Newsletter. (1993 March). Philadelphia, PA (p. 9).
22. FMS Foundation Newsletter. (1993 July). Philadelphia, PA (p. 7).
23. FMS Foundation Newsletter. (1993 March). Philadelphia, PA (p. 9).
24. FMS Foundation Newsletter. (1993 May). Philadelphia, PA (p. 5).
25. FMS Foundation Newsletter. (1995 June). Philadelphia, PA (p. 2).
26. FMS Foundation Newsletter. (1994 February). Philadelphia, PA (p. 9).
27. FMS Foundation Newsletter. (1996 September). Philadelphia, PA (p. 15).
28. FMS Foundation Newsletter. (1993 May). Philadelphia, PA (p. 11).
29. FMS Foundation Newsletter. (1993 June). Philadelphia, PA (p. 6).
30. FMS Foundation Newsletter. (1993 February). Philadelphia, PA (p. 1).
31. FMS Foundation Newsletter. (1993 October). Philadelphia, PA (p. 9).
32. Ibid.
33. Ibid.
34. FMS Foundation Newsletter. (1995 September). Philadelphia, PA (p. 15).

35. FMS Foundation Newsletter. (1993 May). Philadelphia, PA (p. 11).
36. FMS Foundation Newsletter. (1994 March) Philadelphia, PA (p. 10).
37. FMS Foundation Newsletter. (1993 March). Philadelphia, PA (p. 8).
38. FMS Foundation Newsletter. (1995 June). Philadelphia, PA (p. 12).
39. Ibid., p. 11.
40. FMS Foundation Newsletter. (1996 March). Philadelphia, PA (p. 6).
41. FMS Foundation Newsletter. (1995 September). Philadelphia, PA (p. 7).
42. Eagle, M. N., & Wolitzky, D. L. (1985). The current status of psychoanalysis. *Clinical Psychology Review*, 5, 259–269.
43. Marmor, J. (1966). Psychoanalysis at the crossroads. In J. Masserman (Ed.), *Science and psychoanalysis*, Vol. 10. New York: Grune & Stratton.
44. Spence, D. P. (1982). *Narrative truth and historical truth: Meaning and interpretation in psychoanalysis*. New York: Norton.
45. Hall, C. S., & Lindzey, G. (1970). *Theories of personality* (2nd ed.) New York: Wiley (p. 71).
46. Sarason, I.G. (1972). *Personality: An objective approach.* (2nd ed.) New York: Wiley.
47. Slater, E. (1975). The psychiatrist in search of science: The depth psychologies. *British Journal of Psychiatry*, 126, 205–244.

CHAPTER 9

1. Holmes, D. S. (1974). Investigations of repression: Differential recall of material experimentally or naturally associated with ego threat. *Psychological Bulletin*, 81, 632–653.
2. Holmes, D. S. (1990). The evidence for repression: An examination of sixty years of research. In J.L. Singer (Ed.), *Repression and dissociation*. Chicago: University of Chicago Press (p. 96).
3. Malmquist, C. P. (1986). Children who witness parental murder: Posttraumatic aspects. *Journal of the American Academy of Child and Adolescent Psychiatry*, 25, 320–325.
4. Pynoos, R. S., & Eth, S. (1984). The child as witness to homicide. *Journal of Social Issues*, 2, 87–108.
5. Dollinger, S. J. (1985). Lightning-strike disaster among children. *British Journal of Medical Psychology*, 58, 375–383.
6. Jones, D. P., & Krugman, R. D. (1986). Can a three-year-old child bear witness to her sexual assault and attempted murder? In J. Krivacsksa & J. Money (Eds.), *Handbook of sexology*, Vol. 8. Amsterdam: Elsevier Science Publishers.

7. Wagenaar, W. A., & Groeneweg, J. (1990). The memory of concentration camp survivors. *Applied Cognitive Psychology, 4*, 77–87.
8. Terr, L. C. (1990). *Too scared to cry.* New York: Harper & Row.
9. Terr, L. C. (1994). *Unchained memories.* New York: Basic Books.
10. Herman, J.L. (1981). *Father–daughter incest.* Cambridge, MA: Harvard University Press.
11. Herman, J.L. (1992). *Trauma and recovery.* New York: Basic Books.
12. Herman, J. C., & Schatzow, E. (1987). Recovery and verification of memories of childhood sexual abuse. *Psychoanalytic Psychology, 4,* 1–14.
13. Ibid., p. 8.
14. Ibid., p. 9.
15. Briere, J., & Conte, J. (1993). Self reported amnesia for abuse in adults molested as children. *Journal of Traumatic Stress, 6*, 21–31.
16. Summit, R. (1992). Misplaced attention to delayed memory. *The Advisor, 5*, 21–25.
17. Williams, L. M. (1994). Recall of childhood trauma: A prospective study of women's memories of child sexual abuse. *Journal of Consulting and Clinical Psychology, 62*, 1167–1176.
18. Murdock, B. B. (1995). Human memory in the twenty-first century. In R. L. Solso & D. W. Massaro (Eds.), *The science of the mind.* New York: Oxford University Press.
19. Stigler, S. M. (1978). Some forgotten work on memory. *Journal of Experimental Psychology: Human Learning and Memory, 4*, 1–4.
20. Ceci, S. J., & Bruck, M. (1995). *Jeopardy in the courtroom.* Washington, DC: American Psychological Association (p. 198).
21. Williams, p. 1170.
22. Nelson, K. (1993). The psychological and social origins of autobiographical memory. *Psychological Science, 4*, 7–14.
23. Loftus, E. F., Polonsky, S., & Fullilove, M. T. (1994). Memories of childhood sexual abuse: Remembering and repressing. *Psychology of Women Quarterly, 18*, 67–84.
24. Farr, S. P., Greene, R. L., & Fisher-White, S. P. (1986). Disease process, onset, and course and their relationship to neuropsychological performance. In S. B. Filskov & T. J. Boll (Eds.), *Handbook of clinical neuropsychology* (Vol 2, pp. 213–253). New York: Wiley.
25. Brandt, J., Butters, N., Ryan, C., & Bayog, R. (1983). Cognitive loss and recovery in long-term alcohol abusers. *Archives of General Psychiatry, 40*, 435–442.

26. Niaura, R. S., Nathan, P.E., Frankenstein, W., Shapiro, A. P., & Brick, J. (1987). Gender differences in acute psychomotor, cognitive, and pharmacokinetic response to alcohol. *Addictive Behaviors,* 12, 345–356.

27. Acker, C. (1986). Neuropsychological deficits in alcoholics: The relative contributions of gender and drinking history. *British Journal of Addiction,* 81, 395–403.

28. Feldman-Summers, S. & Pope, K. S. (1994). The experience of "forgetting" childhood abuse: A national survey of psychologists. *Journal of Consulting and Clinical Psychology,* 62, 636–639.

29. Norcross, J. C., Prochaska, J. O., & Farber, J. A. (1993). Psychologists conducting psychotherapy: New findings and historical comparisons on the Psychotherapy Division membership. *Psychotherapy,* 30, 692–697.

30. Kihlstrom, J. F., & Harackwicz, A. (1982). The earliest recollection: A new survey. *Journal of Personality,* 50, 134–148.

31. Pillemer, D. B., & White, S. H. (1989). Childhood events recalled by children and adults. *Advances in child development and behavior,* Vol. 21. New York: Academic Press.

32. Winograd, E., & Killinger, W. A. (1983). Relating age at encoding in early childhood to adult recall: Development of flashbulb memories. *Journal of Experimental Psychology: General,* 112, 413–422.

33. Henry, B., Moffitt, T. E., Caspi, A., Langley, J., & Silva, P. A. (1994). On the "remembrance of things past": A longitudinal evaluation of the retrospective method. *Psychological Assessment,* 6, 92–101.

34. Johnson, M. K., Nolde, S. F., Mather, M., Kounios, J., Schacter, D. L., & Curran, T. (1997). The similarity of brain activity associated with true and false recognition memory depends on test format. *Psychological Science,* 8, 250–257.

35. Ross, M. (1989). Relation of implicit theories to the construction of personal histories. *Psychological Review,* 96, 341–357.

36. Markus, G. B. (1986). Stability and change in political attitudes: Observe, recall, and "explain." *Political Behavior,* 8, 21–44.

37. Smelser, N. J., & Gerstein, D. R. (1986). *Behavioral and social sciences: Fifty years of discovery.* Washington, DC: National Academy Press.

38. Gerstein, D. R., Smelser, N. J., Luce, R. D., & Sperlich, S. (1988). *The behavioral and social sciences: Achievements and opportunities.* Washington, DC: National Academy Press.

39. Campbell, T. W. (1992). Diagnosing incest: The problems of false positives and their consequences. *Issues in Child Abuse Accusations,* 4, 161–168.

40. Yapko, M. D. (1994). *Suggestions of abuse.* New York: Simon & Schuster (pp. 229–233).
41. Loftus, E. F., & Ketcham, K. (1991). *Witness for the defense.* New York: St. Martin's Press.
42. Nelson.
43. Ceci, S. J., & Bruck, M. (1995). *Jeopardy in the courtroom.* Washington, DC: American Psychological Association.
44. Campbell, T. W. (1994). *Beware the talking cure: Psychotherapy may be hazardous to your mental health.* Boca Raton, FL: Upton Books (Division of Social Issues Resources Press).
45. Campbell, T. W. (1992). Therapeutic relationships and iatrogenic outcomes: The blame-and-change maneuver in psychotherapy. *Psychotherapy, 29,* 474–480.
46. Arkes, H. R., & Harkness, A. R. (1980). Effect of making a diagnosis on subsequent recognition of symptoms. *Journal of Experimental Psychology: Human Learning and Memory, 6,* 568–575.
47. Miller, T. (1991 November). Opinion–letters: Child abuse assumptions. *The APA Monitor, 22* (11), 4.
48. Barclay, C. R., & Wellman, H. M. (1986). Accuracies and inaccuracies in autobiographical memories. *Journal of Memory and Language, 25,* 93–103.
49. Roediger, H. L., III, & McDermott, K. B. (1995). Creating false memories: Remembering words not presented in lists. *Journal of Experimental Psychology: Learning, Memory and Cognition, 21,* 803–814.
50. Loftus, E. F. (1993). The reality of repressed memories. *American Psychologist, 48,* 518–537.
51. Bonanno, G. A. (1990). Remembering and psychotherapy. *Psychotherapy, 27,* 619–627.
52. Spence, D. P. (1982). *Narrative truth and historical truth: Meaning and interpretation in psychoanalysis.* New York: Norton.
53. Johnson, M. K., Hashtroudi, S., & Lindsay, D. S. (1993). Source monitoring. *Psychological Bulletin, 114,* 3–28.
54. Foley, M. A., & Johnson, M. K. (1985). Confusion between memories for performed and imagined actions. *Child Development, 56,* 1145–1155.
55. Johnson, M. K., Foley, M. A., & Leach, K. (1988). The consequences for memory of imagining in another person's voice. *Memory & Cognition, 16,* 337–342.
56. Baker, R. C., & Guttfreund, D. G. (1993). The effects of written autobiographical recollection induction procedures on mood. *Journal of Clinical Psychology, 49,* 563–567.

57. Singer, J. A., & Salovey, P. (1988). Mood and memory: Evaluating the network theory of affect. *Clinical Psychology Review*, 8, 211–251.
58. Lewinsohn, P. M., & Rosenbaum, M. (1987). Recall of parental behavior by acute depressives, remitted depressives, and nondepressives. *Journal of Personality and Social Psychology*, 52, 611–620.
59. Dawes, R. M. (1988). *Rational choice in an uncertain world.* San Diego, CA: Harcourt, Brace, Jovanovich.

CHAPTER 10

1. Campbell, T. W. (1994). *Beware the talking cure: Psychotherapy may be hazardous to your mental health.* Boca Raton, FL: Upton Books (Division of Social Issues Resources Press).
2. Williams, M. H. (1985). The bait-and-switch tactic in psychotherapy. *Psychotherapy*, 22, 110–113.
3. Tarragona, M., & Orlinsky, D. E. (1988 June). During and beyond the therapeutic hour: An exploration of the relationship between patients' experiences of therapy within and between sessions. *Paper presented at the 19th Annual Meeting of the Society for Psychotherapy Research, Santa Fe, NM.*
4. Dashovsky, D. (1988). The patient's assets for psychotherapy. PhD dissertation, Northwestern University, Evanston, IL.
5. David, J. P., & Baron, R. S. (1994 July). Cognitive load heightens the extremity of interpersonal judgments based on secondhand information. *Paper presented at the Sixth Annual Convention of the American Psychological Society, Washington, DC.*
6. Prager, I. G., & Cutler, B. L. (1990). Attributing traits to oneself and to others: The role of acquaintance level. *Personality and Social Psychology Bulletin*, 16, 309–319.
7. Gilovich, T. (1987). Secondhand information and social judgment. *Journal of Experimental Social Psychology*, 23, 59–74.
8. Gilovich, T. (1991). *How we know what isn't so: The fallibility of human reason in everyday life.* New York: Free Press.
9. Stangor, C., & Lange, J. (1993). Mental representations of social groups: Advances in understanding stereotypes and stereotyping. *Advances in Experimental Social Psychology*, 26, 357–416.
10. Bodenhausen, G. V. (1988). Stereotypic biases in social decision making and memory: Testing process models of stereotype use. *Journal of Personality and Social Psychology*, 55, 726–737.

11. Myers, D. G. (1993). *Social psychology* (4th ed.). New York: McGraw–Hill.
12. Rothbart, M., Evans, M., & Gulero, S. (1979). Recall for confirming events: Memory processes and the maintenance of social stereotypes. *Journal of Experimental Social Psychology, 15,* 343–355.
13. Allport, G. W. (1954). *The nature of prejudice.* Reading, MA: Addison–Wesley.
14. Jackman, M. R., & Crane, M. (1986). "Some of my best friends are black . . .": Interracial friendship and whites' racial attitudes. *Public Opinion Quarterly, 50,* 459–486.
15. Cook, S. W. (1990). Toward a psychology of improving justice: Research on extending the equality principle to victims of social injustice. *Journal of Social Issues, 46,* 147–161.
16. Maass, A., & Arcuri, L. (1996). Language and stereotyping. In C. N. Macrae, C. Stangor, & M. Hewstone (Eds.), *Stereotypes and stereotyping.* New York: Guilford.
17. Strupp, H. H. (1989). Psychotherapy: Can practitioners learn from the researcher? *American Psychologist, 44,* 717–724 (p. 718).
18. Cushman, P. (1990). Why the self is empty: Toward a historically situated psychology. *American Psychologist, 45,* 599–611 (p. 607).
19. Silberschatz, G., Curtis, J. T., Sampson, H., & Weiss, J. (1991). Mount Zion Medical Center: Research on the process of change in psychotherapy. In L. E. Beutler & M. Crago (Eds.), *Psychotherapy research.* Washington, DC: American Psychological Association (p. 56).
20. Bradford, D. T. (1990). Early Christian martyrdom and the psychology of depression, suicide, and bodily mutilation. *Psychotherapy, 27,* 30–41 (p. 36).
21. Lundberg, S. G. (1990). Domestic violence: A psychodynamic approach and implications for treatment. *Psychotherapy, 27,* 243–248 (p. 246).
22. Scher, M. (1990). Effect of gender role incongruities on men's experience as clients in psychotherapy. *Psychotherapy, 27,* 322–326 (p. 326).
23. Bienen, M. (1990). The pregnant therapist: Countertransference dilemmas and willingness to explore transference material. *Psychotherapy, 27,* 607–612 (p. 611).
24. Loftus, E. F. (1996). Memory distortion and false memory creation. *Bulletin of the American Academy of Psychiatry and Law, 24,* 281–295 (p. 288).
25. Bass, E., & Davis, L. (1988). *The courage to heal.* New York: Harper & Row.
26. Brems, C., Tryck, S., Garlock, D., Freemon, M., & Bernzott, J. (1995). Differences in the family of origin functioning among graduate students in different disciplines. *Journal of Clinical Psychology, 51,* 434–441.

27. Elliot, D. M., & Guy, J. D. (1993). Mental health professionals versus non–mental health professionals: Childhood trauma and adult functioning. *Professional Psychology: Research and Practice, 24,* 83–90.
28. Murphy, R. A., & Halgin, R. P. (1995). Influences on the career choices of psychotherapists. *Professional Psychology: Research and Practice, 26,* 422–426.
29. Franks, P., Shields, C., Campbell, T., McDaniel, S., Harp, J., & Botelho, R.J. (1992). Association of social relationships with depressive symptoms: Testing an alternative to social support. *Journal of Family Psychology, 6,* 49–59.
30. Durkheim, E. (1897/1958). *Suicide.* Translated by J. Spaulding & G. Simpson. New York: Free Press.
31. Anderson, C. A., Lepper, M. R., & Ross, L. (1980). Perseverance of social theories: The role of explanation in the persistence of discredited information. *Journal of Personality and Social Psychology, 45,* 127–136.
32. Gilovich, T. (1987). Secondhand information and social judgment. *Journal of Experimental Social Psychology, 23,* 59–74.
33. Chevron, E. S., & Rounsaville, B. (1983). Evaluating the clinical skills of psychotherapists: A comparison of techniques. *Archives of General Psychiatry, 40,* 1129–1132.
34. Muslin, H. L., Thurnblad, R. J., & Meschel, G. (1981). The fate of the clinical interview: An observational study. *American Journal of Psychiatry, 138,* 823–825.
35. Xenakis, S. N., Hoyt, M. F., Marmar, C. R., & Horowitz, M. J. (1983). Reliability of self-reports by therapists using the therapist's action scale. *Psychotherapy, 20,* 314–319.
36. American Psychological Association. (1992). Ethical principles of psychologists and code of conduct. *American Psychologist, 47,* 1597–1611.

CHAPTER 11

1. Dineen, T. (1996). *Manufacturing victims: What the psychology industry is doing to people.* Montreal: Robert Davies Publishing (p. 161).
2. Faust, D. (1989). Data integration in legal evaluations: Can clinicians deliver on their premises? *Behavioral Sciences & the Law, 7,* 469–485 (p. 475).
3. Aldridge-Morris, R. (1989). *Multiple personality: An exercise in deception.* Hillsdale, NJ: Erlbaum.
4. North, C. S., Ryall, J. M., Ricci, D. A., & Wetzel, R. D. (1993). *Multiple personalities, multiple disorders: Psychiatric classification and media influence.* New York: Oxford University Press.

5. Spanos, N. P. (1994). Multiple identity enactments and multiple personality disorder: A sociocognitive perspective. *Psychological Bulletin*, 116, 143–165.

6. Ibid.

7. Fahy, T. A. (1988). The diagnosis of multiple personality disorder: A critical review. *British Journal of Psychiatry*, 153, 597–606.

8. Allison, R. M. (1991). Travel log: In search of multiples in Moscow. *American Journal of Forensic Psychiatry*, 12, 51–56.

9. Adityhanjee, R., & Khandelwal, S. (1989). Current status of multiple personality disorder in India. *American Journal of Psychiatry*, 146, 1607–1610.

10. Takahashi, Y. (1990). Is multiple personality disorder really rare in Japan? *Dissociation*, 3, 57–59.

11. American Psychiatric Association. (1994). *Diagnostic and statistical manual of mental disorders* (4th ed.). Washington, DC: Author (p. 484).

12. Spanos, N. P., Menary, E., Gabora, N. J., DuBreuil, S. C., & Dewhirst, B. (1991). Secondary identity enactments during hypnotic past-life regression: A sociocognitive perspective. *Journal of Personality and Social Psychology*, 61, 308–320.

13. Ibid.

14. Lanning, K. V. (1989 October). Satanic, occult, ritualistic crime: A law enforcement perspective. National Center for the Analysis of Violent Crime, FBI Academy, Quantico, VA. Unpublished paper (p. 11).

15. Lanning, K. V. (1991). Ritual abuse: A law enforcement view or perspective. *Child Abuse & Neglect*, 15, 171–173.

16. Victor, J. S. (1991). The satanic cult scare and allegations of ritual child abuse. *Issues in Child Abuse Accusations*, 3, 135–143.

17. Cohen, S., & Syme, S. L. (Eds.). (1985). *Social support and health*. New York: Academic Press.

18. Peterson, R. A. (1991). Psychosocial determinants of disorder: Social support, coping and social skills in interactions. In P.R. Martin (Ed.), *Handbook of behavior therapy and psychological science*. New York: Pergamon Press.

19. Sarason, B. R., Sarason, I. G., & Pierce, G. R. (Eds.). (1990). *Social support: An interactional view*. New York: Wiley.

20. Cohen, S., & Hoberman, H. (1983). Positive events and social supports as buffers of life change stress. *Journal of Applied Social Psychology*, 13, 99–125.

21. Barrera, M., Jr. (1986). Distinctions between social support concepts, measures, and models. *American Journal of Community Psychology*, 14, 413–445.

22. Heller, K., Swindle, R. W., & Dusenbery, L. (1986). Component social support processes: Comments and integration. *Journal of Consulting and Clinical Psychology*, 54, 466–470.
23. Lakey, B., & Cassady, P. B. (1990). Cognitive processes in perceived social support. *Journal of Personality and Social Psychology*, 59, 337–343.
24. Erdley, C. A., & D'Agostino, P. R. (1988). Cognitive and affective components of automatic priming effects. *Journal of Personality and Social Psychology*, 54, 741–747.
25. Lees-Haley, P. R., Williams, C. W., & Brown, R. S. (1993). The Barnum effect and personal injury litigation. *American Journal of Forensic Psychology*, 11 (2), 21–28.
26. Rosen, A., & Proctor, E. K. (1981). Distinctions between treatment outcomes and their implications for treatment evaluations. *Journal of Consulting and Clinical Psychology*, 49, 418–425.

CHAPTER 12

1. American Psychological Association. (1990). Ethical principles of psychologists (Amended June 2, 1989). *American Psychologist*, 45, 390–395.
2. Ibid, pp. 390–391.
3. Ibid, p. 393.
4. Piper, A., Jr. (1993). "Truth serum" and "recovered memories" of sexual abuse: A review of the evidence. *The Journal of Psychiatry & Law*, Winter, 447–471.
5. American Psychological Association, p. 393.
6. Kihlstrom, J., & Harackiewicz, J. (1982). The earliest recollection: A new survey. *Journal of Personality*, 50, 134–148.
7. Winograd, E., & Killinger, W.A. (1983). Relating age at encoding in early childhood to adult recall: Development of flashbulb memories. *Journal of Experimental Psychology: General*, 112, 413–422.
8. Morton, J. (1990). The development of event memory. *The Psychologist*, 1, 3–10 (p. 3).

CHAPTER 13

1. Poole, D. A., Lindsay, D. S., Memon, A., & Bull, R. (1995). Psychotherapy and the recovery of memories of childhood sexual abuse: U.S. and British practitioners' opinions, practices, and experiences. *Journal of Consulting and Clinical Psychology*, 63, 426–437.

2. Ibid., p. 430.

3. FMS Foundation Newsletter. (1995 January). Philadelphia, PA (p. 12).

4. FMS Foundation Newsletter. (1995 July/August). Philadelphia, PA (p. 1).

5. Cohen, L. (1979). The research readership and information source reliance of clinical psychologists. *Professional Psychology*, 10, 780–785.

6. Norris, E. L., & Larsen, J. K. (1976). Critical issues in mental health service delivery: What are the priorities? *Hospital and Community Psychiatry*, 27, 561–566.

7. Cohen, L. H., Sargent, M. M., & Sechrest, L. B. (1986). Use of psychotherapy research by professional psychologists. *American Psychologist*, 41, 198–206.

8. O'Donohue, W. T., Curtis, S. D., & Fisher, J. E. (1990). Use of research in the practice of community mental health: A case study. *Professional Psychology*, 16, 710–718.

9. O'Donohue, W. T., Fisher, J. E., Plaud, J. J., & Curtis, S. D. (1990). Treatment decisions: Their nature and their justification. *Psychotherapy*, 27, 321–327.

10. Santrock, J. W., & Minnett, A. M. (1994). *The authoritative guide to self-help books.* New York: Guilford.

11. Miller, C. (1994). APA Council report. *Dialogue* (Newsletter for the Society for Personality and Social Psychology), 9 (1), 11.

12. Rice, S. A. (1929). Interviewer bias as a contagion. *American Journal of Sociology*, 35, 421–423.

13. Rothbart, M., Evans, M., & Fluero, S. (1979). Recall for confirming events: Memory processes and the maintenance of social stereotypes. *Journal of Personality and Social Psychology*, 15, 343–355.

14. Chapman, L. J., & Chapman, J. P. (1967). Genesis of popular but erroneous psychodiagnostic observations. *Journal of Abnormal Psychology*, 72, 193–204.

15. Chapman, L. J. & Chapman, J. P. (1969). Illusory correlation as an obstacle to the use of valid psychodiagnostic signs. *Journal of Abnormal Psychology*, 74, 271–280.

16. Dawes, R. M. (1986). Representative thinking in clinical judgment. *Clinical Psychology Review*, 6, 425–441.

17. California v. Akiki. (1993 June 14). Computerized transcription, pp. 5113–5114.

18. Alpert, J. L., Brown, L. S., & Courtois, C. A. (1996). The politics of memory: A response to Ornstein, Ceci and Loftus. *Working group on in-*

vestigation of memories of childhood abuse. Washington, DC: American Psychological Association (p. 141).

19. Ibid., p. 136.
20. Ibid.
21. Poole *et al.,* p. 430.
22. Ibid.
23. Alpert, J. L., Brown, L. S., & Courtois, C. A. (1996). Symptomatic clients and memories of childhood abuse: What the trauma and child sexual abuse literature tells us. *Working group on investigation of memories of childhood abuse.* Washington, DC: American Psychological Association (p. 16).
24. Courtois, C. A. (1988). *Healing the incest wound: Adult survivors in therapy.* New York: Norton (p. 130).
25. Alpert *et al.,* p. 135.
26. Courtois, p. 140.
27. Ibid., p. 199.
28. Ibid., p. 297.
29. Alpert, J. L., Brown, L. S., & Courtois, C. A. (1996). Response to adult recollections of childhood abuse: Cognitive and developmental perspectives. *Working group on investigation of memories of childhood abuse.* Washington, DC: American Psychological Association (p. 204).
30. Courtois, p. 299.
31. Alpert *et al.,* p. 205.
32. Ibid., pp. 132–149.
33. Eldridge, N. S., & Scrivner, R. (1994). Report of Division 43 consultant to APA Ethics Committee. *The Family Psychologist* 10 (3), 5.
34. Ibid.
35. Martin, S. (1995 April). Council condemns obstacle to practice. *APA Monitor,* 25, 10.
36. Follette, V. (1993). An ecological approach to treatment: An interview with Scott Henggeler. *The Scientist Practitioner,* 3 (1), 10–17 (p. 13).
37. Maher, B. A. (1991). A personal history of clinical psychology. In M. Hersen, A. Kazdin, & A. S. Bellack (Eds.), *The clinical psychology handbook,* (2nd ed.). New York: Pergamon (p. 24).
38. Peterson, D. R. (1995). The reflective educator. *American Psychologist,* 50, 975–983 (p. 978).
39. Christensen, A., & Jacobson, N. S. (1994). Who (or what) can do psychotherapy: The status and challenge of nonprofessional therapies. *Psychological Science,* 5, 8–14.

40. Cullen, E. A., & Newman, R. (1997). In pursuit of prescription privileges. *Professional Psychology: Research and Practice, 28*, 101–106.
41. The National Psychologist. (1997 July/August). Parliamentary tactic ends Louisiana prescription bill. *The National Psychologist, 6* (4), 24.
42. Watson, J. B., & Raynor, R. (1920). Conditioned emotional reactions. *Journal of Experimental Psychology, 3*, 1–14.
43. Harris, B. (1979). Whatever happened to Little Albert? *American Psychologist, 34*, 151–160.
44. Eysenck, H. J. (1960). Learning theory and behaviour therapy. In H.J. Eysenck (Ed.), *Behaviour therapy and the neurosis: Readings in modern methods of treatment derived from learning theory.* New York: Pergamon Press.
45. Telford, C. W., & Sawrey, J. M. (1968). *Psychology.* Belmont, CA: Brooks/Cole.
46. Boring, E. G., Langfeld, H. S., & Weld, H. P. (Eds.). (1948). *Foundations of psychology.* New York: Wiley.
47. American Psychiatric Association. (1993 December 12). *Statement on memories of sexual abuse.* Approved by the Board of Trustees of the American Psychiatric Association. Unpublished paper.
48. Horn, M. (1993 November 29). Memories lost and found. *U.S. News & World Report*, p. 52.
49. Ibid.
50. Ibid., p. 55.
51. Houghton Mifflin. (1982). *The American heritage dictionary–2nd college edition.* Boston: Author (p. 460).
52. Prendergrast, M. (1996). *Victims of memory: Sex abuse accusations and shattered lives* (2nd ed.). Hinesburg, VT: Upper Access, Inc. (p. 91).
53. Alpert *et al.*, p. 141.
54. FMS Foundation Newsletter. (1994 April). Philadelphia, PA (p. 5).
55. Ibid.
56. Ibid.
57. Karon, B. P., & Widener, A. J. (1997). Repressed memories and World War II: Lest we forget! *Professional Psychology: Research and Practice, 28*, 338–340.
58. Ibid., p. 339.
59. Ibid.
60. Ibid., p. 338.

CHAPTER 14

1. Colby, K. M. (1964). Psychotherapeutic processes. *Annual Review of Psychology,* 15, 347–360.
2. Eysenck, H. J. (1952). The effects of psychotherapy: An evaluation. *Journal of Consulting Psychology,* 16, 319–324.
3. DeLeon, P. H., VandenBos, G. R., & Cummings, N. A. (1983). Psychotherapy: Is it safe, effective and appropriate? *American Psychologist,* 38, 907–971.
4. VandenBos, G. R., & Pino, C. D. (1980). Research on the outcome of psychotherapy. In G.R. VandenBos (Ed.), *Psychotherapy: Practice, research, policy.* Beverly Hills: Sage.
5. Smith, M. L., Glass, G. V., & Miller, T. I. (1980). *The benefits of psychotherapy.* Baltimore: Johns Hopkins University Press.
6. Shapiro, D. A., & Shapiro, D. (1982). Meta-analysis of comparative therapy outcome studies: A replication and refinement. *Psychological Bulletin,* 92, 581–604.
7. Shadish, W. R., Jr., & Sweeney, R. B. (1991). Mediators and moderators in meta-analysis: There's a reason we don't let dodo birds tell us which psychotherapies should have prizes. *Journal of Consulting and Clinical Psychology,* 59, 883–893.
8. Paul, G. L. (1967). Strategy of outcome research in psychotherapy. *Journal of Consulting Psychology,* 31, 109–118 (p. 111).
9. Kazdin, A. E. (1986). Comparative outcome studies of psychotherapy: Methodological issues and strategies. *Journal of Consulting and Clinical Psychology,* 54, 95–105.
10. Stiles, W. B., Shapiro, D. A., & Elliott, R. (1986). Are all psychotherapies equivalent? *American Psychologist,* 41, 165–180.
11. Luborsky, L., Singer, B., & Luborsky, L. (1975). Comparative studies of psychotherapies: Is it true that "everyone has won and all must have prizes?" *Archives of General Psychiatry,* 32, 995–1008.
12. Lambert, M. J. (1991). Introduction to psychotherapy research. In L.E. Beutler & M. Crago (Eds.), *Psychotherapy research.* Washington, DC: American Psychological Association.
13. Stiles *et al.*
14. Strupp, H. H. (1989). Psychotherapy: Can practitioners learn from the researcher? *American Psychologist,* 44, 717–724.
15. Luborsky, L., Crits-Christoph, P., Mintz, J., & Auerbach, A. (1988). *Who will benefit from psychotherapy? Predicting therapeutic outcomes.* New York: Basic Books.

16. Stubbs, J. P., & Bozarth, J. D. (1994). The dodo bird revisited: A qualitative study of psychotherapy efficacy research. *Applied & Preventive Psychology, 3,* 109–120.

17. Whiston, S. C., & Sexton, T. L. (1993). An overview of psychotherapy outcome research: Implications for practice. *Professional Psychology: Research and Practice, 24,* 43–51.

18. Christensen, A., & Jacobson, N. S. (1994). Who (or what) can do psychotherapy: The status and challenge of nonprofessional therapies. *Psychological Science, 5,* 8–14.

19. Hattie, J. A., Sharpley, C. F., & Rogers, H. J. (1984). Comparative effectiveness of professional and paraprofessional helpers. *Psychological Bulletin, 95,* 534–541.

20. Durlak, J. (1979). Comparative effectiveness of paraprofessional and professional helpers. *Psychological Bulletin, 86,* 80–92.

21. Strupp, H. H., & Hadley, S. W. (1979). Specific vs. nonspecific factors in psychotherapy: A controlled study of outcome. *Archives of General Psychiatry, 36,* 1125–12136.

22. Cohen, S., & Syme, S. L. (Eds.). (1985). *Social support and health.* New York: Academic Press.

23. Peterson, R. A. (1991). Psychosocial determinants of disorder: Social support, coping and social skills in interactions. In P. R. Martin (Ed.), *Handbook of behavior therapy and psychological science.* New York: Pergamon Press.

24. Sarason, B. R., Sarason, I. G., & Pierce, G. R. (Eds.). (1990). *Social support: An interactional view.* New York: Wiley.

25. Evans, I. M. (1993). Constructional perspectives in clinical assessment. *Psychological Assessment, 5,* 264–272.

26. Cohen, S., & Hoberman, H. (1983). Positive events and social supports as buffers of life change stress. *Journal of Applied Social Psychology, 13,* 99–125.

27. Cusmille, P. E., & Epstein, N. (1994). Family cohesion, family adaptability, social support, and adolescent depressive symptoms in outpatient clinic families. *Journal of Family Psychology, 8,* 202–214.

28. Holahan, C. J., Valentiner, D. P., & Moos, R. H. (1994). Parental support and psychological adjustment during the transition to young adulthood in a college sample. *Journal of Family Psychology, 8,* 215–223.

29. Phillips, M. A., & Murrell, S. A. (1994). Impact of psychological and physical health, stressful events, and social support on subsequent mental health seeking among older adults. *Journal of Consulting and Clinical Psychology, 62,* 270–275.

30. Hays, R. B., Turner, H., & Coates, T. J. (1992). Social support, AIDS-related symptoms, and depression among gay men. *Journal of Consulting and Clinical Psychology, 60,* 463–469.

31. Kimerling, R., & Calhoun, K. S. (1994). Somatic symptoms, social support, and treatment seeking among sexual assault victims. *Journal of Consulting and Clinical Psychology, 62,* 333–340.

32. Newcomb, T. M. (1956). The prediction of interpersonal attraction. *American Psychologist, 11,* 575–586.

33. Bowen, M. (1978). *Family therapy in clinical practice.* New York: Jason Aronson.

34. Abelson, R. P., & Rosenberg, M. J. (1958). Symbolic psychologic: A model of attitudinal cognition. *Behavioral Science, 3,* 1–13.

35. Bower, G. J. (1981). Mood and memory. *American Psychologist, 36,* 129–148.

36. Clark, D. M., & Teasdale, J. D. (1982). Diurnal variation in clinical depression and accessibility of memories of positive and negative experiences. *Journal of Abnormal Psychology, 91,* 87–95.

37. Snyder, M. & White, P. (1982). Moods and memories: Elation, depression, and the remembering of the events of one's life. *Journal of Personality, 50,* 149–167.

38. Baker, R. C., & Guttfreund, D. G. (1993). The effects of written autobiographical recollection induction procedures on mood. *Journal of Clinical Psychology, 49,* 563–567.

39. Hendrickx, L., Vlex, C., & Calje, H. (1992). Mood effects of subjective probability assessment. *Organizational Behavior & Human Decision Processes, 52,* 256–275.

40. Bandura, A. (1986). *Social foundations of thought and action: A social cognitive theory.* Englewood Cliffs, NJ: Prentice–Hall.

41. Campbell, T. W. (1994). *Beware the talking cure: Psychotherapy may be hazardous to your mental health.* Boca Raton, FL: Upton Books (Division of Social Issues Resources Press).

42. American Psychiatric Association. (1994). *Diagnostic and statistical manual of mental disorders* (4th ed.). Washington, DC: Author.

43. Tavris, C. (1994). The illusion of science in psychiatry. *Skeptic, 2* (3), 77–85.

44. Sarason, S. B. (1981). An asocial psychology and a misdirected clinical psychology. *American Psychologist, 36,* 827–836.

45. Strupp, H. H. (1986). Psychotherapy: Research, practice, and public policy (how to avoid dead ends). *American Psychologist, 41,* 120–130 (p. 124).

46. Ross, L. D. (1977). The intuitive psychologist and his shortcomings: Distortions in the attribution process. In L. Berkowitz (Ed.), *Advances in experimental social psychology*, Vol. 10. New York: Academic Press.

47. Swann, W. B. (1987). Identity negotiation: Where two roads meet. *Journal of Personality and Social Psychology*, 53, 1038–1051.

48. Swann, W. B. (1992). Seeking "truth," finding despair: Some unhappy consequences of a negative self-concept. *Current Directions in Psychological Science*, 1, 15–17.

49. Boszormenyi-Nagy, I. (1972). Loyalty implications of the transference model in psychotherapy. *Archives of General Psychiatry*, 27, 374–380.

50. Strupp, H. H. (1989). Psychotherapy: Can practitioners learn from the researcher? *American Psychologist*, 44, 717–724 (p. 717).

51. Dawes, R. M. (1994). *A house of cards: Psychology and psychotherapy built on myth.* New York: Free Press.

52. Scarr, S., Phillips, D., & McCartney, K. (1990). Facts, fantasies, and the future of child care in the United States. *Psychological Science* 1, 26–33.

53. Renaud, H., & Estess, F. (1961). Life history interviews with 100 normal American males: "Pathogenicity" of childhood. *American Journal of Orthopsychiatry*, 31, 786–802.

54. Widom, C. S. (1989). Does violence beget violence? A critical examination of the literature. *Psychological Bulletin*, 106, 3–28.

55. Almagor, M., & Leon, G. R. (1989). Transgenerational effects of the concentration camp experience. In P. Marcus & A. Rosenberg (Eds.), *Healing their wounds.* New York: Praeger.

56. Helmreich, W. B. (1992). *Against all odds—Holocaust survivors and the successful lives they made in America.* New York: Simon & Schuster.

57. Bronfenbrenner, U. (1977). Toward an experimental ecology of human development. *American Psychologist*, 32, 513–531.

58. Williams, M. H. (1985). The bait-and-switch tactic in psychotherapy. *Psychotherapy*, 22, 110–113.

59. Stanton, M. D. (1992). The time line and the "why now?" question: A technique and rationale for therapy, training, organizational consultation and research. *Journal of Marital and Family Therapy*, 18, 331–343 (p. 338).

60. Ross, M. W. (1989). Relation of implicit theories to the construction of personal histories. *Psychological Review*, 96, 341–357.

61. Borkovec, T. D., & Costello, E. (1993). Efficacy of applied relaxation and cognitive-behavioral therapy in the treatment of generalized anxiety disorder. *Journal of Consulting and Clinical Psychology*, 59, 333–340.

62. Foa, E. B., Rothbaum, B. O., Riggs, D. S., & Murdock, T. B. (1991). Treatment of posttraumatic stress disorder in rape victims: A comparison between cognitive-behavioral procedures and counseling. *Journal of Consulting and Clinical Psychology, 59*, 715–723.

63. Schulte, D., Kunzel, R., Pepping, G., & Schulte-Bahrenberg, T. (1992). Tailor-made versus standardized therapy of phobic patients. *Advances in Behaviour Research and Therapy, 14*, 67–92.

64. Chambless, D. L. (1996). In defense of dissemination of empirically supported psychological interventions. *Clinical Psychology: Science and Practice, 3*, 230–235.

65. Sechrest, L. (1992). The past future of clinical psychology: A reflection on Woodworth (1937). *Journal of Consulting and Clinical Psychology, 60*, 18–23 (pp. 21–22).

66. Berger, M., & Damman, C. (1982). Live supervision as context, treatment and training. *Family Process, 21*, 337–344.

67. Lewis, W., & Rohrbaugh, M. (1989). Live supervision by family therapists: A Virginia survey. *Journal of Marital and Family Therapy, 15*, 323–326.

68. McCarthy, P., Kulakowski, D., & Kenfield, J. A. (1994). Clinical supervision practices of licensed psychologists. *Professional Psychology: Research and Practice, 25*, 177–181.

69. Chevron, E. S., & Rounsaville, B. (1983). Evaluating the clinical skills of psychotherapists: A comparison of techniques. *Archives of General Psychiatry, 40*, 1129–1132.

70. Muslin, H. L., Thurnblad, R. J., & Meschel, G. (1981). The fate of the clinical interview: An observational study. *American Journal of Psychiatry, 138*, 823–825.

71. Xenakis, S. N., Hoyt, M. F., Marmar, C. R., & Horowitz, M. J. (1983). Reliability of self-reports by therapists using the therapist's action scale. *Psychotherapy, 20*, 314–319.

72. Yager, J. (1977). Psychiatric eclecticism: A cognitive view. *American Journal of Psychiatry, 134*, 736–741.

73. Robins, L. N., & Helzer, J. E. (1986). Diagnosis and clinical assessment: The current state of psychiatric diagnosis. *Annual Review of Psychology, 37*, 409–432.

74. Sattin, D. B. (1980). Possible sources of error in the evaluation of psychopathology. *Journal of Clinical Psychology, 36*, 99–105.

75. Arkes, H. R. (1981). Impediments to accurate clinical judgment and possible ways to minimize their impact. *Journal of Consulting and Clinical Psychology, 49*, 323–330.

76. Friedlander, M. L., & Stockman, S. J. (1983). Anchoring and publicity effects in clinical judgment. *Journal of Clinical Psychology, 39*, 637–643.
77. Arkes, H. R., & Harkness, A. R. (1980). Effect of making a diagnosis on subsequent recognition of symptoms. *Journal of Experimental Psychology: Human Learning and Memory, 6*, 568–575.
78. Fisch, H. U., Hammond, K. R., & Joyce, C. R. (1982). On evaluating the severity of depression: An experimental study of psychiatrists. *British Journal of Psychiatry, 140*, 378–383.
79. Gillis, J. S., & Moran, T. J. (1981). An analysis of drug decisions in a state psychiatric hospital. *Journal of Clinical Psychology, 37*, 32–42.
80. Anderson, C. A., Lepper, M. R., & Ross, L. (1980). Perseverance of social theories: The role of explanation in the persistence of discredited information. *Journal of Personality and Social Psychology, 45*, 127–136.
81. Gilovich, T. (1987). Secondhand information and social judgment. *Journal of Experimental Social Psychology, 23*, 59–74.
82. Keith-Spiegel, P., & Koocher, G. P. (1985). *Ethics in psychology: Professional standards and cases.* New York: Random House.
83. Campbell, T. W. (1994). Psychotherapy and malpractice exposure. *American Journal of Forensic Psychology, 12* (1), 5–41.

Index

About the Author

Terence W. Campbell, Ph.D., earned a doctoral degree in Human Development and Clinical Psychology at the University of Maryland and completed postdoctoral training in family therapy at the University of Rochester School of Medicine. He specializes in family psychology and forensic psychology in his private practice in Sterling Heights, Michigan (a suburb of Detroit). Dr. Campbell's work has appeared in many scientific and professional journals, including the *American Journal of Forensic Psychology, American Journal of Forensic Psychiatry, Issues in Child Abuse Accusations, Journal of Systemic Therapies, Michigan Bar Journal, Michigan Lawyers Weekly,* and *Psychotherapy.* Dr. Campbell serves on the editorial board of the *Journal of Systemic Therapies,* and acts as an editorial consultant for *Issues in Child Abuse Accusations.* He is a member of the Scientific and Professional Advisory Board of the False Memory Syndrome Foundation of Philadelphia, and serves on the Scientific Advisory Board of the National Association for Consumer Protection in Mental Health Practices. He has been designated a Fellow of the American Psychological Society in recognition of a distinguished contribution to psychological science. Dr. Campbell resides in Troy, Michigan.